North Carolina Wesleyan College Library

Scurry - Drum Collection
Given by:
Dr. Frank Scurry and
Carolina Evangelical
Divinity School

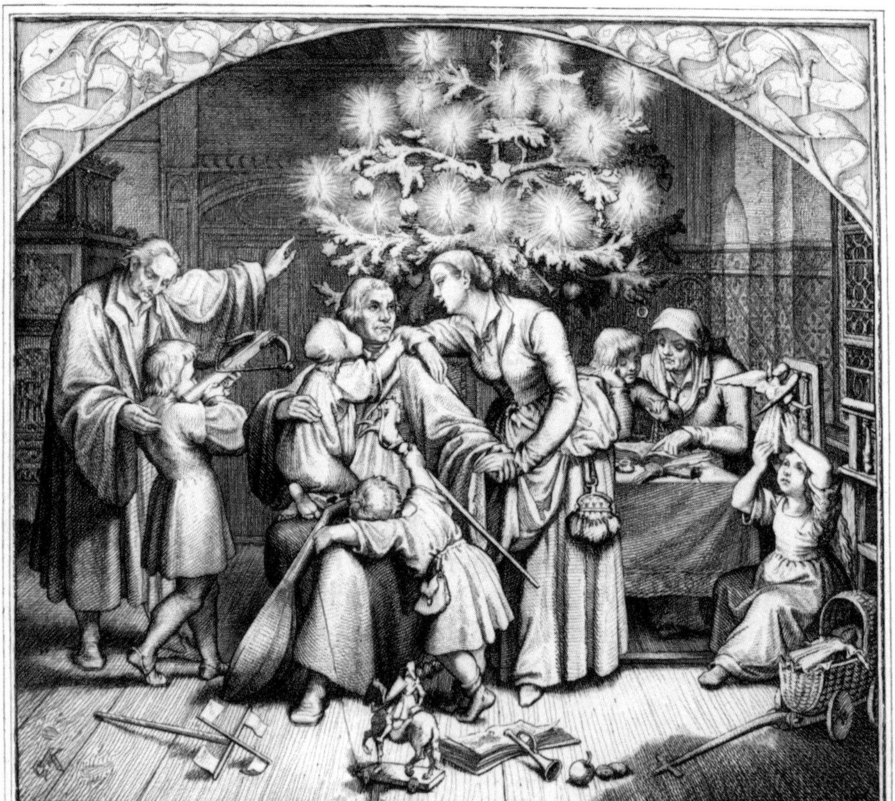

Sermons of Martin Luther

Volume 3

Sermons on Gospel Texts for the Fifteenth through Twenty-Sixth Sundays after Trinity, the Festival of Christ's Nativity, and Other Occasions

© 1996 by Eugene Klug

Published by Baker Books
a division of Baker Book House Company
PO Box 6287, Grand Rapids, Michigan 49516-6287

Printed in the United States of America

All rights reserved. No part of this publication may be reproduced, stored in a retrieval system, or transmitted in any form or by any means—electronic, mechanical, photocopy, recording, or any other—without the prior written permission of the publisher. They only exception is brief quotations in printed reviews.

Library of Congress Cataloging-in-Publication Data

Luther, Martin, 1483–1546.
 [Hauspostille. English]
 Sermons of Martin Luther : the house postils / edited by Eugene F.A. Klug; translated by Eugene F.A. Klug . . . [et al.].
  p. cm.
 Includes bibliographical references.
 ISBN 0-8010-2071-9 (cloth)
  1. Bible. N.T. Gospels—Sermons—Early works to 1800. 2. Church year sermons—Early works to 1800. 3. Lutheran Church—Sermons—Early works to 1800. I. Klug, Eugene F.A., 1917– . II. Title.
BR332.H4   1996
252'.041—dc20   96-12327

Frontispiece from Gustav Koenig, *The Life of Luther in Forty-Eight Historical Engravings*. New York: Charles Scribner, 1857.

Contents

Fifteenth Sunday after Trinity. First Sermon. 1532.   7
Fifteenth Sunday after Trinity. Second Sermon. 1534.   16
Sixteenth Sunday after Trinity. First Sermon. 1532.   24
Sixteenth Sunday after Trinity. Second Sermon. 1533.   30
Seventeenth Sunday after Trinity. First Sermon. 1532.   36
Seventeenth Sunday after Trinity. Second Sermon. 1533.   44
Eighteenth Sunday after Trinity. First Sermon. 1532.   51
Eighteenth Sunday after Trinity. Second Sermon.   61
Eighteenth Sunday after Trinity. Third Sermon.   70
Nineteenth Sunday after Trinity. 1533.   79
Twentieth Sunday after Trinity. First Sermon. 1532.   91
Twentieth Sunday after Trinity. Second Sermon. 1533.   100
Twentieth Sunday after Trinity. Third Sermon. 1534.   107
Twenty-First Sunday after Trinity. First Sermon. 1533.   117
Twenty-First Sunday after Trinity. Second Sermon. 1534.   122
Twenty-Second Sunday after Trinity.   130
Twenty-Third Sunday after Trinity. First Sermon.   146
Twenty-Third Sunday after Trinity. Second Sermon.   157
Twenty-Third Sunday after Trinity. Third Sermon. 1533.   169
Twenty-Fourth Sunday after Trinity. First Sermon. 1532.   176
Twenty-Fourth Sunday after Trinity. Second Sermon. 1533.   184
Twenty-Fifth Sunday after Trinity.   192
Twenty-Sixth Sunday after Trinity.   207
Festival of Christ's Nativity. First Sermon.   209
Festival of Christ's Nativity. Second Sermon.   221
Festival of Christ's Nativity. Third Sermon.   229
Festival of Christ's Nativity. Fourth Sermon.   237
Festival of Christ's Nativity. Fifth Sermon.   246
The Day of the Holy Innocents.   255
The Conversion of St. Paul.   265
The Day of Mary's Purification.   274
The Day of Annunciation to Mary. First Sermon.   284
The Day of Annunciation to Mary. Second Sermon. 1534.   294
Holy Trinity Sunday.   299
The Day of St. John the Baptist. First Sermon. 1532.   310
The Day of St. John the Baptist. Second Sermon. 1533.   324
The Day of St. John the Baptist. Third Sermon.   327

The Day of Mary's Visitation. First Sermon. 1532.   341
The Day of Mary's Visitation. Second Sermon. 1533.   357
The Day of St. Mary Magdalene.   365
The Day of St. Michael and All Angels. First Sermon. 1532.   374
The Day of St. Michael and All Angels. Second Sermon. 1534.   386
Conclusion to the Hauspostille.   390
Index of Sermon Texts.   393

FIFTEENTH SUNDAY AFTER TRINITY

First Sermon—1532

So that we may thank our Lord God and on this day follow his commandment, let us hear and learn from his Word. For this is his will for us, and the first and foremost thing on the day of rest is to listen to his Word, for God is speaking to us today through this Gospel lesson:

Matthew 6:24–34

No man can serve two masters: for either he will hate the one, and love the other; or else he will hold to the one, and despise the other. Ye cannot serve God and mammon. Therefore I say unto you, Take no thought for your life, what ye shall eat, or what ye shall drink; nor yet for your body, what ye shall put on. Is not the life more than meat, and the body than raiment? Behold the fowls of the air: for they sow not, neither do they reap, nor gather into barns; yet your heavenly Father feedeth them. Are ye not much better than they? Which of you by taking thought can add one cubit unto his stature? And why take ye thought for raiment? Consider the lilies of the field, how they grow; they toil not, neither do they spin. And yet I say unto you, That even Solomon in all his glory was not arrayed like one of these. Wherefore, if God so clothe the grass of the field, which today is, and to morrow is cast into the oven, shall he not much more clothe you, O ye of little faith? Therefore take no thought, saying, What shall we eat? or, What shall we drink? or, Wherewithal shall we be clothed? (For all these things do the Gentiles seek:) for your heavenly Father knoweth that ye have need of all these things. But seek ye first the kingdom of God, and his righteousness; and all these things shall be added unto you. Take therefore no thought for the morrow: for the morrow shall take thought for the things of itself. Sufficient unto the day is the evil thereof.

1. Our dear Lord spoke the words of this Gospel in order to ward off the serving of Mammon. For his concern is that Mammon and

worldliness would hinder our service to him. He wants serving him to be pure, to be rendered solely to him and not to Mammon.

2. This Gospel, therefore, is not particularly addressed to young people; for their taste—God be praised!—inclines more towards eating plums and cherries than for possessing money; they are more interested in a good apple than in shiny gold pieces; they are not concerned about the market price for grain, nor do they give much thought to what they are going to eat, but let father and mother worry about that.

3. So, this sermon concerns especially father and mother, and those who hold positions of authority and govern, and most of all preachers for whom things go badly in this world; some of them, due to want, are forced to be concerned about how to support themselves and their wives and children. For because they speak the truth, they run the risk of being harassed and persecuted, left to die of hunger. These the Lord comforts here and wants to dispel such worries, saying, Look at the beautiful lilies and roses and the birds, but particularly at the ravens, as St. Luke states (12:24). Since God so richly feeds them without their fretting or efforts, and decks out the flowers so beautifully, so will he also clothe them and provide crumbs of bread for them, so that they do not die of hunger.

4. This sermon, therefore, does not particularly concern the youth, since, when it comes to being dependent, youth are disposed like birds, confident that kitchen and cellar are fully stocked, depending upon others to do the providing. But they have other thoughts, about how they can pull off this or that naughtiness. We old fools are the ones burdened with the tough luck of having to feed ourselves, always fearful of dying of hunger. However, with the children of Mammon the story is quite otherwise, for they put on a show with clothes and deck themselves out—their boys with beautiful jackets; girls with beautiful purses, laces, and other baubles.

5. That is why there is little for young people to learn from this lesson, except this statement of Christ: "No man can serve two masters: for either he will hate the one, and love the other; or else he will hold to the one, and despise the other." This much, at least, a young man ought to learn, that, while as yet he is not troubled by concerns about food, he must serve God and know what this means. If he learns and

understands this well, he has then learned what is fundamental. And a child, servant, maid, and everyone in the house can do this. For no one is of such lowly station that he cannot perform this beautiful work of serving God.

6. But what does it mean to serve God? The answer is, doing what he has commanded; for just as in the world, "to serve" commonly means nothing else than to do what someone has commanded. In other words, if I am serving my master, I am doing what my master requires. A domestic serves his master when he does what his master commands and wants. A maid serves her mistress simply and well by doing what she is supposed to do. We all understand this. For servants and maids receive their wages because they readily serve their masters and mistresses, that is, perform their duties and do what they command. Service, therefore, impacts not merely the person, but the word and command. For masters and mistresses do not require domestics for their person, since they are well able, without servants and maids, to take care of their own personal needs, eat and drink, dress and undress, and mature enough to do these things on their own because they are healthy and strong. But tending the house and carrying out every command of their master and mistress is a servant's responsibility and for this they were engaged. If, however, the servant is a scoundrel and puts off doing his master's word and command, listening rather to what others tell him to do and serving them, he is serving two masters.

7. This is the way we must express the matter, also, about serving God, that nothing else is meant than hearing what he says and gladly and diligently doing it. But what does God enjoin? Above all things, that a person should listen to Christ and accept the gospel. This is the only, true, well-pleasing service we can render God. For right before our eyes stands the injunction: "This is my beloved Son, in whom I am well pleased; hear ye him."

8. In similar manner, God commands children to honor father and mother, parents to nourish, rear, and teach their children, a wife to love her husband and attend to housekeeping, and, on the other hand, the husband to nourish and protect her, and so forth. All these things God has said and commanded. Where children now honor their father and mother, they not only honor their parents but honor

and serve God, who has commanded this. Where a husband loves his wife, and a wife is subject to her husband, and each is faithful to the other, rule their household and treat children and servants with due propriety, they are thereby serving God. For God's Word and command stand there, requiring it of us. Therefore, when servants and maids serve faithfully and diligently do what is commanded them, they serve not only their masters and mistresses, but God in heaven who requires this of them in his Word.

9. The same applies to other stations as well. When a citizen does what the magistrate requires, and subjects do what their ruler legislates (as long as it is not contrary to God), they are then involved in serving God. And there is no one in the world who thus could not serve God, if we would only learn what it means to serve God. For serving God does not rest on the thing done, but on God's Word and command. The whole world would be replete with service to God were each individual to live and do what was commanded him. In the world's eyes it's a big deal when a monk denies himself everything, enters a cloister, leads a disciplined, austere life, fasts, prays, and so on. No lack of activity exists there, except only that God's command is lacking to do these things. Therefore, this cannot be extolled as serving God. On the other hand, when a maid cooks, washes, sweeps, and does other housework, it is looked down upon as trivial. But since there is a command from God for this, such trivial work cannot but be extolled as a service to God, surpassing by far all the holiness and austere life of all monks and nuns. For there is no command from God for this; but here is God's command to honor father and mother, and help in keeping the household.

10. In every way, therefore, it is serving God when one does what God has commanded, and does not do what God has forbidden. When a preacher preaches God's Word, baptizes, administers the Sacrament, exhorts, rebukes, warns the secure, comforts the timid and distressed, he in this way is serving not only men but God, who has ordained and commanded these things; and there is joy in doing them, knowing of a certainty that it is God's will and command.

11. In the same way a poor servant girl has joy in her heart and can say, My job is to cook, make the bed, and clean the house; who has commanded me to do these things? My master and mistress have commanded me to do them. Who has given them such authority over

me? God has ordained this. Ah, then it must be true that I am serving not only them but also God in heaven and that God has pleasure in this. How, indeed, could I be more blest? It is tantamount to cooking for God in heaven.

12. Therefore, with all his effort and labor a person can have all that is good, joy in the heart and a good conscience, because he knows that his work and labor are a service pleasing to God; also, things need not become a grind for him if he thus resigns himself to his service and calling. For there can be no greater joy than knowing that our life and deeds are a service to God, and that God says to us, What you do for master, mistress, or neighbor, in accord with my command, you have done unto me, just as if I in heaven above were to have commanded you to do these things; for by my Word I have so ordained. But at that point the devil resists with might and main, so that man does not achieve this joy; for every man resents doing what he should and is commanded to do, which results in no love being bestowed on people and no service rendered to God.

13. A person ought to be willing to buy, in exchange for all earth's wealth, the treasure and joy in the heart of reaching the point where he knew for sure that he was serving God and that God had pleasure in his deeds and life. Now, an individual can reach that point free of charge and without money, if he remains in his calling and does all that his calling requires. In times past the rule was: If you wish to serve God, enter a cloister, put on a hood, and so on. But if you asked who commanded this, you would not have found God there or God's Word. But you say, Yes, I personally have a right spirit, and intention for this. For this you can thank the accursed devil! Who has commanded you, says God, to want to give special service to me in heaven above, and, in the meantime, exempt yourself from doing on earth what I have commanded you? It is as if I told my servant to go for wine, and on his own he put off doing that and instead went and brought me a bowl of apples. With such service he, of course, would not be pleasing me; I ought to bring the bowl down on his head and say, Don't you know what I told you to do? Yes, master, he probably will say, my intentions were good; I know that you like to eat apples. But then I would say, Indeed, to the devil with you! Did I not tell you to go for wine? Why don't you do what I tell you to do?

14. God's pleasure is somewhat equivalent if a person negates what he has commanded and does something he has not commanded. It was the common perception of all monks and nuns that they left undone what God commanded and, instead, undertook extra things not commanded by God.

15. For this reason we must learn what it means to serve God, namely, to serve him in accordance with his Word and command, doing what he has commanded and leaving undone what God has forbidden. When you do that, your heart can rest securely before God, you can do everything with joy, and your work or service will not be burdensome and difficult for you. Instead your heart will be filled with joy, for it knows that it is a true service to God and pleases God in heaven. Whatever you do in your home is just as if you were to have done it for our Lord God above in heaven. For he has so ordained: The things we do in our calling here on earth in accordance with his Word and command are tantamount to having done them unto him in heaven.

16. It is even true for all other creatures: they simply go in service and obedience to God. God has commanded the sun to light up the day for the entire world. This the sun faithfully does, not lighting up the night but the day, just as its creator has commanded. God has commanded the moon to preside over the night; this the moon obediently does. In fact, all other creatures strive faithfully to do what God has commanded them and nothing else; and for that reason all are dressed in the beautiful garments of service and obedience to God. This includes water also. What kind of a command does it have? What is it supposed to do? It is to teem with fish, says God in Genesis. This it does everywhere, even where people by their sin do nothing but impede God's blessings and thwart his command. Just as creatures now are equipped to walk according to divine ordinance and in obedience, so the human being, who in his calling acts according to the divine word and command, is equipped more wonderfully than all other creatures on earth. Here Christ says that even Solomon in all his splendor was not as beautifully adorned as is a flower in the field. Just what does a flower do? What is its command? Nothing other than to stand there as clothed, look lovely, smell good, and allow itself to be looked at and picked. If God so highly praises a flower, what kind of

adornment, do you think, is man's, when he walks in God's Word and command? He is much more beautifully adorned when he does these things than sun and moon and all flowers on earth.

17. When a young woman decks herself out for dancing, hers, too, is an adornment, one that pays court to the world. But it is as dirt when compared with the adornment of her duties and calling—tending to the children, the kitchen, the house, and doing what she is commanded to do; so also when a servant takes manure to the field and discharges his duty. Psalm. 45:9 commends Christian believers in like manner: "Kings' daughters were among thy honourable women: upon thy right hand did stand the queen in gold of Ophir." What kind of adornment might this be, since on earth things go so poorly for Christians? They are poor, miserable, and despised; what they do is not highly thought of in the world; this one cleans out the stable, another takes care of the cows; yes, what is more, he is thrown into prison, tortured, and slain. That is the way it goes on earth for this bride, the Christian church. How then is she adorned? She is adorned with a spiritual adornment, not with silver, pearls, velvet, or things of gold, but with the Word and command of our Lord God. There is no greater glory on earth than where a person takes up God's Word and command. Such adornment is a jewel to which sun and moon are not to be compared. For it is God's adornment. All adornment of God is his Holy Word. The one who does what God's Word commands walks in God's own adornment; yes, he is adorned with God himself.

18. Now imagine for yourself how exquisite and glorious it is when one adorns himself in our Lord God's own adornment. How lovely must a maiden imagine herself to be, were she able to go about in the adornment of the queen of France? or a servant, were he to go about in the adornment and crown of the emperor? And yet all this is but a worldly adornment and as nothing compared with this spiritual, divine adornment of a Christian, when a servant and maid are faithful and obedient to masters and mistresses; or when a wife goes about serving and obeying God, loves and esteems her husband, rears her children properly and well, and conducts herself in her vocation according to God's Word and command. Defined in such adornment, pearls, velvet, and gold are merely dirt. What is all worldly adorn-

ment but mere shadowy symbols through which God shows what sort of adornment it is in heaven before him, when one lives and acts according to his Word and command?

19. This is the real crown, a beautiful gold necklace, shining more beautifully than the sun. About it Solomon says (Prov. 1:8–9): "My son, hear the instruction of thy father, and forsake not the law of thy mother: For they shall be an ornament of grace unto thy head, and chains about thy neck." When you hear what God has commanded you in his Word, through preachers, through father and mother, through master and mistress, and act accordingly, then you possess the most beautiful pearls and most precious stones that a person can have on earth.

20. This adornment does not glitter here on earth; however, in yonder life it will radiate as God unveils it and says, Come, you blessed of my Father! You are a pious, obedient child, a diligent, faithful servant, a pious, faithful maid, a pious, obedient citizen, a pious husband, a pious wife, a pious, faithful preacher. When God then brings to light what has been hidden, for us to see with our eyes, then we will understand that obedience to God and his Word, also in such lowly circumstances, is more resplendent than all the adornment of the world.

21. That is why we should get young hearts accustomed to esteeming God's Word and command highly in their station and calling, learning to fear God in his Word, to know what it means to serve God; in other words, to be obedient to God's Word and command, each performing faithfully and diligently the duties of his calling, and loving his neighbor. The one who does this has put on God's own adornment, yes, is adorned with God himself, and already here on earth shines as beautiful as the angels in heaven. Even though he does not glisten like this before men, still, before God he radiates.

22. So, let us learn from this Gospel that we must serve God in heaven, and not Mammon. Second, that serving God means to do what God has commanded in his Word, each person in his station and calling. And third, that the good, the blessing, and the beautiful adornment one receives when he serves God, as for example a maid who serves her master and mistress according to God's command, a child who is obedient to its parents, and so on, this is more beautiful adornment before God in heaven than all adornment on earth.

23. Accordingly, we have both, *dialecticam* and *rhetoricam*, "definition" and "exhortation." *Dialectica* is that one recognizes what it means to serve God, namely, to do according to God's command. *Rhetorica* is that one shows what a glorious thing and beautiful adornment such obedience and service to God are. *Dialectica* is the body; *rhetorica* is the adornment with which the body is adorned. The adornment is God himself or really his Holy Word. Whoever adheres to God's Word and does what God has commanded him in his calling is adorned with divine adornment, yes, is adorned with God himself. For this reason there is nothing more beautiful than serving God, that is, doing according to God's Word and command. In short, it is wisdom and power at its highest, to know how one ought to serve God, and with faith in Christ to do according to God's Word and will, and ever to be found in such precious adornment. May our dear God and Father help us to achieve this through Christ our Lord. Amen.

FIFTEENTH SUNDAY AFTER TRINITY

Second Sermon—1534

Matthew 6:24–34

1. This is a rich Gospel and a lengthy sermon against greed. Our Lord especially loathes greed, for there is no other vice that contravenes the gospel more and does more harm to the Christian than greed. And yet it is so common that the whole world is literally engulfed by it. Day and night everybody's greatest concern is how to make a living. And this stimulates greed to the point where no one is content with what God provides and bestows. Everybody wants more and craves moving up the ladder. Whomever God has blessed with a beautiful house covets owning a mansion. And if he has a mansion, he then wants a villa with expansive grounds, and so is never satisfied. Everyone wants to get on better and have more. If it were not for greed and pride, everybody would have enough, and people would not be so concerned about things, scraping and scratching.

2. With this sermon the Lord endeavored to put a brake on such attitude and conduct. He gets right to the point, saying, "No man can serve two masters: for either he will hate the one, and love the other," and so on. He calls the two masters by name. The one is called God, who is the true Lord, and whom we are obliged to serve. The other is called Mammon; it is not the true Lord, and, therefore, he does not want us to serve it.

3. He also tells us just what it means to serve Mammon. It is to be anxious about your livelihood, about what to eat and drink, about taking care of the body, and having clothes to wear. The tenor of the entire sermon is that we are to dismiss such fretting. Not only is such anxiety needless and useless; it is an obstacle to true worship of God. For this reason we are to guard against it and train ourselves to serve God and wait for his provision. He knows what we need and earnestly desires to give us what we need. All we have to do is ask him.

4. Such trust benefits us greatly, for we discern that God, without any care on our part, has given us body and life. Let the whole world evaluate and judge this. Isn't it true that if you had all the food there was to eat right in front of you, it would not mean as much to you as does your life? By the same token, your body means more to you than clothing. Aren't we ungrateful people, with whom God should justly be angry? We must confess that he has already given us the best and greatest, and should we not trust that he will also give us lesser things? If a rich man were to give you a thousand pieces of gold—something that would be painful for him to do—wouldn't you trust him to give you a pair of old shoes? This is precisely how we treat our Lord God in heaven when we are anxious about food and drink, since he has already given us the greatest and best. Just think how such anxiety must displease him.

5. For this reason Christ says, If you want to be Christians, then have God in your heart. Let him take care of food, drink, and clothing; he wants to be your Father. If he has given you body and life, he will also give you food and clothing. Just don't become anxious, don't fret, don't despair of him. Hasn't he already provided you with enough? He has given you body and life; everything you have you have received from him. Over and above that, he daily gives you meat, fish, fowl, bread, wine, gold, silver, and so on. It all is yours. What more could he do? Hasn't he provided enough to merit your trust? He doesn't want you to be in need of anything; simply believe that it is true and that he wants to be your God and Father.

6. All of this teaches us to trust God, that, having received the little things which serve to nourish this life and clothe the body, we begin to entrust the greater things to our Lord God as well. For if we do not believe that God will fill the stomach and clothe the body, how can we commend our souls to his keeping when we die? It may be that we have neither house nor shelter, neither food nor raiment; nevertheless, we must simply believe and surrender to the simple Word and so go on living in faith. How is it possible for us to rely on God for these great things, if we cannot rely on him to fulfill the needs of the body?

7. Just as regards our body and life—eyes, ears, hands, feet, and all our members—we must learn and confess that God has given us

much and been gracious to us. The examples cited by our Lord in support of other creatures should teach us to trust in God and not be anxious. "Behold the fowls of the air," he says, and learn from them. No raven is concerned about food, about what it will eat on the morrow. At night it settles down in its nest and in the morning arises to find the food the Lord has set out for it. So with all the birds: They find enough to eat without having the least concern. Now if your heavenly Father feeds the birds, will he not also feed you? Are you not much better than they?

8. By this, however, Christ does not command that people should not work. For even birds, though they neither sow nor reap, nor gather into granaries, nor do the kind of work that man does, nevertheless, have their work cut out for them; they have to spread their wings and fly about to get their food. Similarly we, too, must work. For God has mandated that we are to work, as it is written in Genesis 3:19: "In the sweat of thy face shalt thou eat bread"; again, 2 Thessalonians 3:10: "If any would not work, neither should he eat." Worry is forbidden, that people think God has deserted them and believe they must occupy their minds with anxiety. Even though they have enough of everything, some still do not want to trust in God. This is forbidden; for when we fret, we are fools. If grain is to thrive in the ground, God alone must grant it; our worrying will not accomplish it. For what can we do about it if this year everything in the field wilts and dies off? Clearly, right before our eyes, everything is in God's hands; he is the one who must bring it to pass. However, we are doubting people; we have not learned to believe, but instead we worry.

9. Thus the birds that fly before us put us to shame, and we might well take off our hats to them and say, My dear teacher, I have to admit that I don't have the art you have. You sleep all night long in your little nest without a care in the world. In the morning you leave the nest; you are happy and bright; you sit on the limb of a tree and sing, praise, and give thanks to God. Then you go looking for your little kernel of grain and find it. For shame! Why haven't I, old fool that I am, learned to do the same? I, who have so much reason to do so? If a bird can live without a care in the world and look after itself, deporting itself like a saint—it sings, praises God, is happy and in good spirits, for it knows that its granary is already built, even as promised:

"Your heavenly Father feeds them"—why don't we do the same thing, we who have the advantage and can cultivate the field, gather in fruits, and lay in store for a time of want?

10. Thus our dear Lord holds before us the example of the birds, as if to say, Birds have not a care in the world; for they know they have an excellent kitchen chef and generous butler whose name is the heavenly Father. That is the reason they say, Not to worry! Haven't you heard what kind of cuisine and cellar we have, namely, as wide as the world is wide? That's the reason we fly wherever we wish, we find our food, and the table is well prepared. The same heavenly Father wants gladly to be your kitchen chef and butler, if you would only believe it or want to have him. He proves it by what he does; he gives you land, granary, cellar, and barns; he gives you in abundance much more than he gives the birds. Why then won't you trust in him? Do like the birds—learn to believe, sing, be happy, and let your heavenly Father do the caring for you. You surely are the unhappiest people when you worry and do not choose to trust in God. These are, indeed, comforting words and beautiful examples which ought to move us deep within.

11. But our experience, alas, is that the whole world is filled with despairing skinflints, who do not trust in God, who do not serve God but the devil. For Mammon is the world's god. To have Mammon is to have something good. The world is not looking for what is good to eat and drink; its only concern is simply to pile up a lot of money, have Mammon in its coffers and worship it. This is the reason the world overflows with Mammon worshipers. Now tell me, isn't this true? If your house were filled with money and built of gold, and the waters of the Elbe or the Rhine were flowing with gold, of what good would this be to you if you had no corn, no beer, no wine, no water? Ah! how splendidly you then have served Mammon! There's no way you can eat your gold!

12. This is a despicable adoration of Mammon, which even the Gentiles mocked by inventing a fable of a rich king in Phrygia by the name of Midas. He was so greedy that he wished everything he touched would turn to gold. His wish was granted. When he touched his coat, table, bench, bed, door, pillars, everything immediately turned to gold. The knife with which he ate, the bread, and the wine,

all turned to gold. As a result the miser had no bread or drink and starved himself to death. He had wished well! For this reason abhor greed, and flee from it if you can. Even though you had all the gold in the world, you still need food. You cannot live on silver and gold. Yet, the world is so blind and mad that it is not satisfied with food and drink but craves gold and money as well. Just as if it did not need what God supplies richly and running over, and it stood in need only of what he does not hand out so bountifully. Christ continues: What are you accomplishing if already you are worrying yourselves to death? It would be a very foolish stunt were a man who is small in stature to seat himself in a corner and there all his life worry and plan how to become taller. Wouldn't the whole world mock him and regard him a fool? It's the same with the world, says Christ, when it craves money and goods. No one can become rich by craving for wealth. It all depends on whether God blesses you, not on your caring. If God's blessing is there, then you have all you need. If not, even though you already have it, you will not be able to enjoy or retain it, as the examples before us indicate.

13. A Christian must not be overcome with greed and worry, but must learn to trust in God. . . . work, and let God do the caring. Indeed, our job is to toil till it hurts; yet, we are to know that it is not our labors that produce the fruits. We plow and sow seed, and, when things ripen, harvest. Yet we must confess that unless God grants it, all our labor will be in vain, because, dear Lord God, it is a gift from you. Thus we should give God the glory, acknowledge his blessing, and thank him for it.

14. This is what our dear Lord wants to discuss with us. He is telling us: Put away your confounded caring and doubting; learn to believe and trust in God; then see whether God lets you go hungry. If you trust in him, he will bless your labor; but if you do not, and refuse to commend your growling stomach to him, he will not allow corn to grow. If it is already growing, he can let it dry up, so that you realize your worrying does not accomplish anything, your unbelief and despair even less. Faith, however, avails; faith that works and trusts in God, commending to him the caring and accepting of what he bestows.

15. Christ, next, sets in front of us the example of the flowers of the field, stating, The flowers of the field do not toil, do not spin and

do not sew; yet they are endowed with such beautiful colors, they put silk embroidery with all its loveliness to shame. Let this serve as an example for you. Since God thus adorns the flowers, which barely last one day in the field, how can you be so godless as not to believe that God will also feed and clothe you, and instead think he has entirely deserted you?

16. The flowers of the meadow are like a master teacher for us, to teach us the supreme art of trusting God and confiding in him for all good things. Now, we have an advantage over the flowers, just as we had over the birds. We till the ground, we harvest, we fill granaries and cellars, and are able at least to build up a reserve for a time of want, something that birds cannot do, and still they are fed. We also have an advantage when it comes to clothing. We produce so much linen, flax, and hemp, we raise so many sheep, and all over the world, in every home, there are women spinning and weaving. How, then, can anyone be so absolutely destitute of faith that he should have no hope of sharing in the results, especially if he is faithful in his work and trusts in God?

17. Finally Christ says, "After all these things do the Gentiles seek." However, you are not to be Gentiles, but Christians. "Therefore take no thought, saying, What shall we eat? or, What shall we drink? or, Wherewithal shall we be clothed?" The Gentiles despair of God, are loaded down with cares, and do not believe that God will give them something. But you have a Father in heaven; he knows what you need. So, you are not to fret, but let your Father in heaven care for you.

18. And he concludes this sermon by saying, "Seek ye first the kingdom of God, and his righteousness; and all these things shall be added unto you." Mammon, you see, permits no trust in God. For whoever is a servant of Mammon must despair of God and put his trust in money and goods. Your heavenly Father understands very well that you have to eat, drink, and clothe yourselves; thus he finds it within his heart to give you what you need. For this reason you must put away care for the morrow (it is not to be your concern, since your heavenly Father is taking care of you) and seek first the kingdom of God and his righteousness, so that God may rule within you.

19. However, what the kingdom of God is and wherein it consists Christ teaches elsewhere (Luke 17:20–21): "The kingdom of God

cometh not with observation: Neither shall they say, Lo here! or, Lo there! for, behold, the kingdom of God is within you." The kingdom of God, therefore, is nothing else but hearing and believing God's Word. God rules within us when we do not despair of him, but trust him wholeheartedly and esteem him as our God and Father. Where such faith exists, there God dwells, and righteousness immediately follows, that is, forgiveness of sins. A believing heart thinks of God, speaks of him, prays to him, and, in turn, God dwells there. The word that we read and hear is the Word of God; the tongue is the tongue of God; the ears are the ears of God. Thus faith constitutes the kingdom of God. For where there is a believing heart, there you will find the kingdom of God. Works, then, will follow, as the believer pursues his calling—works, eats and drinks, in a good and happy spirit, like a bird. Such is the kingdom of God and his righteousness.

20. Let this be your concern, says Christ, that you seek the kingdom of God and his righteousness. Be concerned, first of all, that you come to faith and that God rules within you. When you have that, God will not suffer your stomach to be empty. He has made you lords over everything that grows on earth. The earth will supply you with your needs, with corn, wheat, barley, oats, wine, and whatever you require. The air is to furnish you with fowl, the water, with fish. Simply believe that your heavenly Father will provide for you. But if you are unbelieving, you will get nothing.

21. The world can do nothing but be greedy and despair of God. It toils and moils, and accumulates a lot of money. And once it has done so, it is not happy with the results. Many accumulate money and all kinds of reserve goods and yet do not have their fill. When they die, some evil scoundrel, perhaps, gets hold of what they have. They did not trust in God when they were alive; hence, they die with nothing and will be damned in the process. That is how the world serves Mammon. But if you want to be a Christian, do not conform to this, but seek first the kingdom of God, listen to the preaching of God's Word, trust in God, and work joyfully. God will not desert you; you will not starve to death. And though all the grain on earth should go to rot, he will, notwithstanding, provide you with something to eat. For he created heaven and earth out of nothing, and so he can also make soil produce food to eat. Only see to it that you trust in him and stay away from greed, from scraping and scratching.

22. So, in this Gospel our dear Lord Jesus Christ entices us with beautiful pictures and examples, in order that we learn to trust in God; and he promises that God will give us all we need if we but trust him and do our work. In fact, God has already demonstrated, and demonstrates every day, that he wants to provide for our needs. Through the earth, the air, and water, he daily bestows his gifts to us human beings, for angels need nothing of this. Yet, as a people, we are so wicked that we fail to trust in God.

23. We ought surely remember, therefore, that he says, "Ye cannot serve God and Mammon; no man can serve two masters." Either you will hate Mammon and love God, or you will hate God and love Mammon. The two stand juxtaposed as opposites. Indeed, the bed is narrow, so that there is room for one only; the blanket is short, so that only one can wrap himself up in it, as is written in Isaiah 28:20. God and Mammon cannot exist side by side in the heart. One must drop out, either God or Mammon.

24. Today's Gospel warns us, therefore, that we must learn to believe and guard against greed and serving Mammon. May our dear Lord God through Christ grant us his Holy Spirit so that we mend our ways and grow in sanctification. Amen.

SIXTEENTH SUNDAY AFTER TRINITY

First Sermon—1532

Luke 7:11–17

And it came to pass the day after, that he went into a city called Nain; and many of his disciples went with him, and much people. Now when he came nigh to the gate of the city, behold, there was a dead man carried out, the only son of his mother, and she was a widow: and much people of the city was with her. And when the Lord saw her, he had compassion on her, and said unto her, Weep not. And he came and touched the bier: and they that bare him stood still. And he said, Young man, I say unto thee, Arise. And he that was dead sat up, and began to speak. And he delivered him to his mother. And there came a fear on all: and they glorified God, saying, That a great prophet is risen up among us; and, That God hath visited his people. And this rumour of him went forth throughout all Judaea, and throughout all the region round about.

1. There are two things we ought to learn from this Gospel lesson: first, as regards faith, that we recognize our Lord Christ from his works and believe in him; and, second, that we should practice Christian charity and compassion towards one another.

2. Let us consider the first thought. At the end of this lesson the Evangelist Luke points out how the people reacted to this happening as Christ raised the youth from the dead. Filled with fear, they praised God, and the report concerning what Christ had done spread throughout Judaea and all the surrounding regions. It is an example that reminds us to esteem God's Word and wondrous works highly and praise him for them. We must regard the works of our Lord Jesus Christ much more highly than those of men. His works, after all, are recorded for us, in order that we might perceive from them how great a Lord he is, our God, who is able to help where no one else can. There is no dilemma so great, no matter what the difficulty, that he cannot help.

3. He manifested this very plainly in the case of this poor widow, whose burden could hardly have been heavier. First of all, there was the fact that she was a widow, which was bad enough; for, as the Scripture points out, a widow's life in this world is difficult in itself, without additional grief. But then another cross is added to her misery in that her only son is taken from her through death, and even now is being carried out for burial. All hope of life is gone, and not even all the world's resources could come to her aid. To take her son out and bury him in the ground is the only advice the world can give her. No doctor, king, or emperor could help now. In that predicament Christ lets himself be seen for the kind of Lord he is. He comes to this poor widow's aid by restoring to life her only son, lying here dead in the coffin and on the way out of the gate to be buried, and she could thereupon take him back with her to her house.

4. This and similar works of Christ should remind us that we must be very courageous and unafraid in times of sickness, pestilence, and life-threatening danger. At moments when the world says, All is lost, the Christian always responds, Not so, God still lives, and Christ rules at the right hand of God. Psalm 112:7–8 praises the godly and pious who maintain unwavering and fearless trust in God's grace and help: "He shall not be afraid of evil tidings: his heart is fixed, trusting in the LORD. His heart is established, he shall not be afraid, until he see his desire upon his enemies."

5. Is anything impossible for our Lord God that should cause us not to rely on him with absolute trust? After all, he created heaven and earth out of nothing, and still causes the trees to bear cherries, plums, apples, and pears by his mighty power. When in winter the snow lies on the ground, there isn't a man who could bring forth a cherry out of the snow. But God is the one who can do absolutely everything. Our Lord Christ can restore life to the dead, call into being that which is not; in short, no matter how deep the problem, he can mend and straighten things out no matter how profound and perplexing it is. We must recognize God's power and be convinced that nothing is impossible for him, so that when things go bad we remember to be unafraid and trust that he is omnipotent. Whether the Turk or some other evil threatens, we must remember that we have a helper and Saviour who is almighty and who is able to help. That is true, genuine faith.

6. Now, that is the first lesson we ought to learn out of today's Gospel, namely, to reverence and praise our Lord God who is able to succor us no matter how great the trouble, never wavering in our trust in him. Were it up to us or other people, we could only despair, for the difficulty is often so great that it lies beyond human help, specifically, for example, with death, where no man, be he king or emperor, rich or powerful, could be of any help. Only with God can we confidently rest our case. Where I and other people are powerless, there he can and is able. If neither I, myself, nor other people can avail in my time of need, he can, even as regards death, as Psalm 68:20 has it: "He that is our God is the God of salvation; and unto God the Lord belong the issues from death." So our heart must always boldly trust in God. Such unwavering, unafraid hearts are the ones that truly love and serve him. Those who waver and doubt do not really love God, but are at enmity with him, indeed, judge him not to be God, throwing his word and his works to the wind.

7. Now, the second thing to learn here from Christ, our Lord, is how to be merciful. Many times, over and over again, we have been reminded that we ought to love and serve one another. But to be merciful means more than merely to empathize with people's grief and suffering. When my poor neighbor is sick it doesn't only mean that I should gladly help him, but his suffering must become mine in such a way that I feel it as my own, as we see here with our Lord. He is a stranger, an unknown visitor, but when he sees the widow's suffering, he identifies with it in himself, as though it were his own, sheds tears with the widow, comforts and helps her.

8. It is a paradigm that illustrates the love that follows upon faith; it cannot remain uninvolved because it is genuine faith! We cannot act like wicked, notoriously evil people—we have plenty of them today among our peasants and townsfolk—who have hearts of stone and iron, who rejoice and snicker with glee over their neighbor's misfortune, but are grieved if he has one penny more than they. Christians cannot be like this. Instead, they are to be compassionate wherever they see grief, rejoicing when others have food, drink, clothes, and shoes, or when they prosper, as St. Paul says, We weep with those who weep, rejoice with those who rejoice. A Christian cannot be a devil's henchman or such a stony-hearted clod who re-

joices in other people's misfortune and counts it good when his neighbor is in want and trouble, and then is grieved when things go well for him.

9. Now mercifulness, however, is of two kinds, even as trouble is of twofold nature, spiritual and physical. Where there are physical needs we should be quick to help and give counsel as we are able, if we see that our neighbor is in need of clothing and care, is naked and sick, his child covered with filth and likely to perish. Poor people are unable to make provision and care for themselves.

10. Spiritual trouble has to do with soul needs, as, for example, when I see a young person growing up without any knowledge of the gospel, who doesn't know how to pray, is unchaste, unruly, and full of evil habits. To admonish such a one and—if that doesn't help—to discipline very severely, even lay on the switch or stick, so that they put off their sin and ill behavior, that is what it means to be merciful, for that is a grave condition. When the soul is afflicted with such evil it is a more serious, indeed, dangerous situation than when the body is sick. Neither disease, nor thunder and lightning that may affect the body, is as terrible as the evil that affects the soul. We owe such a person mercy—by means of the word, switch, or cane—for his sake, as the situation requires.

11. Yes, you say, but that is a terrible sort of mercy, to apply a switch to his hide! Indeed! but how else shall he be dealt with? If that's what is needed, how can it be avoided? Doctors must often amputate a leg or an arm in order to save a life. The same is true here. Such chastisement is called for in order that the person may be saved, rescued from the devil and his dominion. Isn't it true that you will be glad and thank me if, when you have fallen into the water, I pull you out by the hair or have poked you in the eye? or do you complain because I roughed up your head? Surely it is better to be pulled by the hair or poked in the eye than to drown. So, you endure it gladly even though it hurts, when the physical necessity requires it. Why, then, in spiritual needs should you not be willing to suffer admonition when you sin or act wickedly? Here the concern is not for this temporal life but for the eternal, not for the body but for the soul.

12. It is, therefore, an act of mercifulness, chastisement from God, when, in the case of wicked children or household servants, an oaken

butter switch is taken in hand and a little bit of pastry is applied to their hide, in order to soften it up a little. This is spiritual ointment for soul sickness, for their disobedience towards father and mother, masters and mistresses of the house. It is a work of mercy, you see, when we help an individual in his trouble and spiritual dilemma.

13. Such charity, parish pastors and curates of souls in the church must provide their parishioners; fathers and mothers, their children and household servants; those in authority, their subjects, and every man, his neighbor. Each one in his station must be willing to show such love and not be unconcerned, as is so commonly the case. Whoever thinks that the way to be merciful is not to castigate sin and unrighteousness is doubly unmerciful to his neighbor and invites God's wrath upon himself. Physical trouble can also be great, as, for example, when a person falls into the water or fire and, without concern for hurting him or handling him gently, we grab him in order to save him. Why should we not view spiritual trouble and need the same way? Hard words and stinging switches must be employed with all earnestness to rescue the poor individuals out of the devil's net and lead them back to obedience. When a father whips and spanks a disobedient son, he does it not to knock the life out of him, but as an act of mercy, so that he does not perish in sin and disobedience, and be damaged in soul.

14. Let us, therefore, consider seriously the example of our dear Lord Christ here and learn what compassion is, namely, the kind of virtue that identifies itself with the neighbor's grief. Trouble really is of two kinds, as stated. There is physical distress, as in sickness, poverty, or the like. When you take such misery of your neighbor to heart and help him, that is right and good, and you have served not only your neighbor, but also your God who will also reward you. The nature of spiritual distress—which is sin—is when there is disobedience, laziness, wrathful words and actions in the house. It is compassionate then to rebuke with sharp words all such individuals in your household. If that does not help, they will be handed over to the hangman, for they need to be punished. The executioner is also a compassionate preacher, inasmuch as wicked rogues have gone beyond admonition or being helped. They corrupt themselves, and others with them, if compassion is not exercised and they are not

resisted with force, with the sword. God has ordained the sword to be used for that purpose in the world.

15. Thus capital punishment, too, is a work of compassion, terrible though it is to behold the hurt that it inflicts. Where it has ceased, people can no longer eat a morsel of bread in peace or keep a garment safely on their backs. In order for that not to happen, our Lord God has given the executioner the sword, father and mother the switch into their hands, to punish and restrain, keeping wickedness under control. Let us, therefore, learn to exercise compassion, each of us in his station, giving aid not only where bodily distress is present, but also spiritual.

16. These are the two lessons of today's Gospel. First, the great lesson that comes with faith, not to be overwhelmed when things go evilly, especially when we must die, but to remember that in the Lord Christ we have a helper whose hand is almighty. Of him we must not despair; of ourselves and of other people we may indeed despair, in fact we must; none of these can put a stop to death, for it is too mighty for them. But we can be bold in God and his Son, Jesus Christ. For he can do what we cannot; what we don't possess, he does. If we cannot help ourselves, he is able, and he does so gladly and willingly, as we see here. Such a heart that persists in trust on the Lord Christ serves God truly, even as the Lord desires. Those who despair and doubt are God's enemies and really do not esteem him to be God; otherwise, they would allow themselves to be comforted. The second lesson is that we, like Christ, must take our neighbor's misery upon ourselves and identify with his grief, whether physical or spiritual. May our dear Lord grant us his grace so that we might learn both things, joining together with the godly people here in this Gospel to praise the Lord Christ eternally for his goodness, and also learn to be compassionate toward our neighbor. Amen.

SIXTEENTH SUNDAY AFTER TRINITY

Second Sermon—1533

Luke 7:11–17

1. There is very much one could say in connection with today's Gospel. However, for the present moment we will limit ourselves to one point, undoubtedly the most important one, namely, how we should find comfort in the face of death. Certainly there is great need for such comfort and teaching.

2. Dearly beloved, we are considering here the account of a poor widow, whose husband is already dead, and whose only son now also dies, leaving her in every way very dejected and destitute. For in Judaism it was reckoned especially a great misfortune if there was no son in the family, because under Jewish law that would leave a person without an heir. That explains why this widow is distressed and troubled, for it appeared as though God were against her and had completely abandoned her, first by taking away her husband and now also her son. Her heart was very weighed down; she might well have despaired of God and concluded that he had forsaken her, allowing both her husband and son to die, thus taking away all earthly solace.

3. Christ, our dear Lord, feels deeply for her, and with sincere compassion gladdens her heart by raising her son from the dead and giving him back to his mother, so that her joy now becomes ten times greater than was her grief before. And it is a wonder that she did not immediately keel over and succumb because of her happiness.

4. It is a story we ought to remember, so that by it we might learn to exercise, strengthen, and confirm our faith. For the Lord is not interested only in this woman; he wants to teach all of us how powerless and insignificant death is. He pictures death that way so that we are not frightened by it but live confidently and patiently from day to day, untroubled by death, since in him we have a Lord who can readily deliver from death. Naturally, those who will learn most from

this are people who are in distress and in peril of death, like this widow; others, who know nothing of anguish and are not in peril of death, will take nothing from this lesson. But see how quickly and readily this woman is helped, considering she had given up all hope of help. Her son has died and is even now being carried to the grave. She has no expectation at all that he might be restored to life.

5. With all hope gone, and everyone disheartened by the death of the son, our dear Lord comes, without healing medicines, and speaks merely a word, "Young man, I say unto thee, Arise!" At once the dead man arises and is alive. By this Christ powerfully proves that in his sight there is no barrier between death and life; they are neither more nor less, one is like the other to him. So, to him it is all the same, whether we live or die. Though we die, with him we are not dead. The fact is that as far as he is concerned, death is merely a word; thus death is gone, and life has returned. It is just as Christ states in the Gospel: "God is not the God of the dead but of the living." Scripture, moreover, affirms God's position; "I am the God of Abraham, and the God of Isaac, and the God of Jacob." Therefore, although Abraham, Isaac, and Jacob are dead, with God they are still alive.

6. That is what we should learn from today's Gospel lesson, namely, the great power God will exert upon us through Christ on Judgment Day, when with one word he will call forth from the dead all people and bless the believers eternally. He will say, Martin Luther, Arise! and it will be so, and immediately I shall stand there. Therefore, we must not doubt that Christ possesses both the power to do it, as he demonstrates here, and the will, earnestly desiring to do it. For here we have a prototype: The widow's son is dead, with all senses and hearing stopped; but as soon as Christ speaks to him, he hears. This is certainly an unusual, astonishing story. The one who does not hear, hears; the one who does not live, lives. And yet Christ does nothing more than open his mouth and tell him to arise. That one word is so powerful that death must yield, and life again returns.

7. So, because we see how Christ can very easily snatch us from death and restore us to life, and so earnestly wants to do so as we see here (for no one there is asking him to do it; he is moved to pity by the poor widow's distress, and without being asked raises her son from the dead); therefore, we should accept this example as sure ev-

idence of how Christ demonstrates his power over death, in order that we might take comfort in him and not fear death. For it is for our sake that this wonder occurred. We are to understand that Christ is saying to us, I well know that you are afraid of death; but you must not be afraid, do not let your heart be troubled; for even though it has terrors for you, what can it do to you? Terrify you, it may. But, on the other hand, learn not merely to look at how it affects you and causes you terror, but also look to me and see what I am able to do and earnestly want to do, namely, I can very readily raise you from the dead—as easily as you rouse someone from sleep—and desire very much to do so, having both the necessary power and intention.

8. It follows from this, therefore, that those who lie dead and buried in the churchyard and under the ground sleep more lightly than we do in our beds. We know it can easily happen that a person sleeps so soundly that he is called ten times before he ever hears. But the dead hear that lone word of Christ and wake up. The moment he speaks that one word, "Young man, I say unto thee, Arise!"; "Lazarus, come forth!"; "Talitha cumi, Damsel, I say unto thee, Arise!" they hear in that very instant. And on Judgment Day, when he speaks that one word, the dead will hear in that very same moment and come forth from the graves. It is true, we sleep much more soundly in bed than we do in the churchyard!

9. Thus before our Lord God, death is not death but a sleep. For us, when we die it is and is termed death, but before God it is but a sleep and a very light sleep at that.

10. Of this our dear Lord wants to convince us, so that we do not become frightened if pestilence, or death itself, approach, but learn to say, Death, what is the worst you can do to us? You have frightening teeth, you bare them and you terrify me, and I do not die gladly. But I don't want to consider only what you can do, and how, as you, like the executioner, draw the sword; but I want to ponder and perceive how our Lord God will intervene, even though you strangle me. He does not fear you, nor is he awed by your raging and ravaging, but says, "Death, I shall be the death of you; grave, I shall be your destruction." If you can kill my Christians, I can in turn throttle you and recall them to life.

11. That is the comfort which the Lord holds before us in today's Gospel as he defiantly confronts death, Death, you are terrifying my

Christians to keep them from dying cheerfully; but beware, I shall terrify you in turn. You strangle them, but when you have done so, I shall in return destroy you. You say: Paul I have devoured, Luther I have cut down. But, death, boast all you want; those whom you have put to death are not dead to me; instead, they sleep, and they sleep so lightly that I am able to awaken them with my little finger. It will infuriate death that it is capable of doing and accomplishing nothing more than putting a person to sleep, and that when Christ will say, Arise, you dead! they will at once awaken from sleep and come forth, as he says (John 5:28–29): "The hour is coming, in the which all that are in the graves shall hear his voice, And shall come forth; they that have done good, unto the resurrection of life; and they that have done evil, unto the resurrection of damnation."

12. This comfort Christians enjoy. Turks and Jews do not have it, nor do monks and papists around us enjoy it, for they do not set their hearts and their hope on Christ, but scurry after their own works and make of Christ a stern judge. They know that they must die and that they must face judgment and hell. For this reason they try to entreat Christ through their praying, having Masses said, buying indulgences, fasting, and who knows what. They regard him as nothing else but a judge whose answer is, You have prayed, fasted so much, had Masses celebrated, therefore, come and be saved; or contrariwise, You are nothing but sinners, and, therefore, be damned. In this way they make Christ a judge over Christians and over their lives, believing that he lets them reconcile themselves before God by their deeds, and condemns those sinners who do not do these works. This is the accursed devil's doing, that they make Christ worse than death itself, and that is why they are so afraid of Judgment Day, for they do not know Christ, and they have evil consciences and despondent hearts.

13. Christians are not like this. They well know that Christ is a judge, who on Judgment Day will judge the unbelievers who refuse to accept or believe his Word. Believers, on the other hand, are perceived differently because they say, I am baptized and believe in my Lord Jesus Christ; I believe that he has died for my sins and by his resurrection has won for me righteousness and eternal life; why then should I fear the judgment? He is not my enemy but my friend, not my judge who wants to damn me but my helper and advocate with

the Father. Therefore, even though Judgment Day should dawn or I should die, I am not concerned. For a little while my Lord Jesus Christ delays while death throttles me. Yet, though death thinks that I am done for and that I have died, I am merely sleeping, and my repose is so sweet and light that the Lord scarcely need open his mouth before I hear him and rise to eternal life.

14. Let us learn and mark this well so that we do not fear death or Judgment Day. For Christ is coming not to judge and damn us; he is coming just as he comes here to the distressed widow and to her son, to console her and deliver her son from death, and to cause the son to sit up in his coffin, again to see, hear, and speak. . . . the selfsame one who before neither saw, nor heard, nor spoke, but was blind, deaf, dumb, and dead to everything. In the same way he wants to set things right again for all, that we, awakened from death, can once again hear, see, speak, and the like. In short, he wants to come to us who trust in him for our salvation's sake; however, those who do not believe he will judge.

15. We should learn to yearn for this Saviour, ever becoming more and more certain in confident expectation of his help and grace. We should rejoice when we hear that pestilence, death, and Judgment Day are coming. If, however, we become terrified and afraid, we then are letting the "old Adam" and the flesh govern us, not the Lord Christ and his Word. For it is very sure that Christ is coming on Judgment Day and will awaken us from death. In the meantime, our bodies are to rest in the grave and sleep until Christ comes and knocks on the grave and says, Arise, arise, Martin Luther, come forth! Then in a moment we shall rise, as if from a light, pleasant sleep, and live forever with the Lord, rejoicing.

16. Accordingly, a Christian must have a different heart from that of Turks, Jews, papists, and monks. They become fainthearted, terrified, and despairing because they do not know which way to turn. And it serves them right. Why don't they learn and believe that Christ is a Saviour and helper of those who believe, but the judge of all unbelievers? To me he is a physician, helper, and deliverer from death and the devil; but for the pope, for H.G.,° for the wicked, and for the devil and his emissaries he is a judge. Because the pope and

---

° Luther's acronym and nickname for Duke George (Herzog Georg) of Saxony, feisty opponent of the Reformation.

the wicked are lackeys of the devil and of death, their preference and dealings correspond to what death and devil effect. They are opposed to Christ and do not want to espouse his kingdom. Christ is their judge, while for the pious who trust in him, he provides peace and rest in eternity.

17. So much in brief about the poor widow and her dead son! May our dear Lord God help us come to perceive the man, Christ, as this Gospel presents him to us, so that we may take comfort in him when our time comes to die. Amen.

SEVENTEENTH SUNDAY AFTER TRINITY

First Sermon—1532

Luke 14:1–11

And it came to pass, as he went into the house of one of the chief Pharisees to eat bread on the sabbath day, that they watched him. And, behold, there was a certain man before him which had the dropsy. And Jesus answering spake unto the lawyers and Pharisees, saying, Is it lawful to heal on the sabbath day? And they held their peace. And he took him and healed him, and let him go; And answered them, saying, Which of you shall have an ass or an ox fallen into a pit, and will not straightway pull him out on the sabbath day? And they could not answer him again to these things. And he put forth a parable to those which were bidden, when he marked how they chose out the chief rooms; saying unto them, When thou art bidden of any man to a wedding, sit not down in the highest room; lest a more honourable man than thou be bidden of him; And he that bade thee and him come and say to thee, Give this man place; and thou begin with shame to take the lowest room. But when thou art bidden, go and sit down in the lowest room; that when he that bade thee cometh, he may say unto thee, Friend, go up higher: then shalt thou have worship in the presence of them that sit at meat with thee. For whosoever exalteth himself shall be abased; and he that humbleth himself shall be exalted.

1. There are two points in today's Gospel. The first concerns divine worship, how we should conduct ourselves before God; the second concerns how we are to deal with people.

2. Relative to the first point, the question arises as to whether it is better in God's sight to keep the Sabbath or to help and do good to our fellowmen. For the object of the Pharisees here is to watch closely what Christ will do with the man suffering from dropsy. They think that if he does not help him, then he could be charged with being unmerciful and neglecting to help others. But if he does help him, then he is irreverent and in violation of the Sabbath, and can, therefore, be charged with disobeying God and his Word. Thus, whichever way the Lord goes, he is caught. For they want to

box him in on both sides, and they considered it particularly offensive to break the Sabbath; for with the Jews the matter involving the Sabbath was so sacred that they guarded their observance of it scrupulously. But what does the Lord do, entrapped as he appears to be in the assessment of the Pharisees, with absolutely no chance of escape? He parries both thrusts, goes to the heart of the matter, and does what is right, putting the Pharisees to shame and driving home his point in such a way that everybody regards them as utter fools, even though they have the reputation of being spiritual leaders who are to teach and guide the people, and, therefore, were esteemed as great theological experts.

3. Now, therefore, the sum and substance of this is that he confronts them straight to their faces, showing them that they don't know what it means to keep or sanctify the Sabbath. Your thinking, he says, is that sanctifying the Sabbath means to do no work whatever and to be idle. No, you must not construe the Sabbath in this manner. Sanctifying the Sabbath means to hear God's Word and to assist your neighbor however you can. For God does not want the Sabbath to be kept holy in such a way that you allow your neighbor to languish and be in need. Therefore, if I serve and help my neighbor, even though it requires physical labor, I still have kept the Sabbath very properly, because in so doing I have done a God-pleasing work. This doctrine of the Sabbath, therefore, shows us how to understand what the third commandment is all about and what it demands of us, namely, not that we observe it in idleness, but that we hearken to God's Word, and act and live in harmony with it. So, what is its lesson? It teaches us that, in accord with the second table, we are to love one another and do all manner of good works. On the Sabbath, if I listen to and obey God's Word, it surely then follows that I also should act in accord with it, for by doing good I am not breaking or desecrating the Sabbath, but acting in accord with his Word.

4. Therefore, says Christ, you Pharisees are not competent teachers when you call doing good works a breaking of the Sabbath. The burden of what is preached on the Sabbath is that we should love one another. But what does it mean to love? It does not mean to have the thought in mind, or to give off the appearance, but from the heart to be kindly disposed toward our neighbor, to comfort or to rebuke him

with the Word, as necessary, and by word and deed assist him, and thus be of service to him in body and soul. As St. John says (1 John 3:18): "My little children, let us not love in word, neither in tongue; but in deed and in truth." To love, then, means to deal kindly with one's neighbor. And God commands you to do this, also on the Sabbath, as well as during the week. Yes, and what is more, God instituted the Sabbath for this purpose, that on this day you should hear and learn from his Word, love your neighbor, and help him, being kind in word, helpful in deed, whatever the neighbor requires.

5. Thus the Lord rebukes those false saints who perverted God's commandment and boasted that they were keeping the Sabbath, saying, I observe the Sabbath so perfectly that I refrain from giving a garment to a naked person on the Sabbath or offering a helping hand to the feeble or sick person. They are scoundrels who pervert God's Word. For where God's Word enjoins, Love your neighbor and do good to him, they say: Oh no, by doing that I would be breaking the Sabbath. This is to teach falsely, completely subverting God's command. For God commands that also on the Sabbath you are to love your neighbor and befriend him graciously in all his needs of body and soul, just as our Lord directs in the example here. Is it not a shame, says he, to think that, if on the Sabbath your ox or ass falls into a pit and you pull the animal out, you are breaking the Sabbath? You care for the animal just as much on the Sabbath as on an ordinary workday. So if you now demonstrate loving concern for an animal on the Sabbath, why should one not do so also for a human being? Are you not unfeeling saints? You care for oxen and asses on the Sabbath, get hold of them with halter and harness, and help rescue them out of a pit, and can you not love or help a needy man on the Sabbath? Oh, what unfeeling saints!

6. This is always the case with those who try to be our Lord's teachers, that they entrap themselves and must admit publicly that they are great fools. It was so here with the Pharisees who impudently thought they had trapped our Lord whichever way he answered; for if he helps the poor man with the dropsy, he sins against the Sabbath and third commandment; if he does not help him, he then is acting contrary to love of thy neighbor and is unmerciful. So, they think, whichever way he goes he butts his head against a brick wall.

But his reply is of such a nature that it makes them blush with shame and they are unable to rebuke him further, for he says, You scoundrels, you are the ones who are desecrating and breaking the Sabbath. What you insinuate in me, you yourselves are doing. To sanctify the Sabbath means to hearken to God's Word and do good works, love your neighbor and answer his needs, be obedient, be merciful, be helpful, attentive, comforting, provide food and drink, and so forth. These things we are to do also on the Sabbath, for God has commanded us to keep the Sabbath by doing good works, and this belongs to true worship, pleasing to God. For he does not require all kinds of foolish services, nor does he want anyone to babble all day long in church, something the papists cultivate. He wants us to hearken to his Word, and to live and act in accord therewith.

7. The beautiful passage in Hosea (6:6) makes reference to this: "I desired mercy, and not sacrifice; and the knowledge of God more than burnt offerings." What does it mean to know God? Nothing other than to abide by God's Word. The reason is that without the Word no one can know God. But with the Word we are told, I am your God, I have sent my Son and given him into death for you, and received you in baptism, and so on; for through his Word we come to know that God is gracious and merciful. Otherwise, were God not to have revealed himself to us through the Word, human reason could not have known and perceived that we have a gracious God who has given us his Son and through the Son wants to save us. Accordingly, the third commandment says: "Thou shalt sanctify the sabbath day"; that is, on the Sabbath you are to hearken to God's Word and learn to know God. That is worshiping God and truly sanctifying the Sabbath. And when works follow, when one lives and acts in accord with God's Word, that also is to worship him. Thus the wicked simpletons and hypocrites, the Pharisees, attack him but neglect to do such things; they do not obey God's Word or act in accord with it, yet want to be known as people who do not break the Sabbath.

8. This is also the case with the papists, kings, and princes who have daily Masses conducted but oppose the Word, thinking their orders of worship are the highest, and indispensable for every day. On the other hand, however, not in a month, not in half a year, often not in an entire year do they hear preaching; and though they might, they

hear nothing from Scripture or God's true Word, only frivolous human prattle and falsehoods. This is their divine worship whereby they sanctify the Sabbath or festivals, even though this can occur in no other way than by hearing God's Word and keeping it. This is true worship of God and the true Mass.

9. Now, of course, with us Christians every day is to be a Sabbath; for we are to hear God's Word every day and live our lives in accord with it, just as Sunday has been appointed for God's people to listen to and learn from God's Word, and to live in accord with it. For on the other six days people must attend to their work in order to earn their daily bread. This God is pleased with, for he has ordained work. But the seventh day he wants to be sanctified. On this day he asks that we refrain from work, so that no one is kept from exercising himself in God's Word and works, focusing not on temporal things but on what God in his Word requires and urges.

10. Now, then, the first point of today's Gospel is that everyone should learn that worshiping God and sanctifying the Sabbath properly is to hear and keep God's Word. Accordingly, when you have heard the Word preached, and afterwards, when you return home and take the Bible in hand and read a Gospel, that is to worship God, and it is a much more acceptable worship to him than sacrifices and so-called holiness, as Hosea says. For the one who is attentive to God's Word and believes it learns to know God and what he desires of us.

11. The second point teaches humility. For that is how the Lord explains the parable at the end: "Whosoever exalteth himself shall be abased; and he that humbleth himself shall be exalted." We are to learn that this is so not only before God, but also before men. For all people are by nature opposed to the proud. On the other hand, it would have to be an especially wicked person who is opposed to a humble, pious heart. It is natural for everybody to love such a soul. We see this in a maid who willingly, obediently and with singleness of heart does what she is told to do; she soon has won over the mistress's heart so that she cannot be against her. The fact is, people by nature cannot be at enmity with humble people.

12. On the other hand, no one can be well disposed toward proud persons. As soon as a father and mother notice disobedience and conceit (for these two incivilities always go hand in hand) in a child,

or in a servant, to the point where they say, I do not have to do what I'm told; that heart is gone away, so that father and mother, masters and mistresses, have to figure out how to break such pride and humble them, or throw them out of the house. Secular government, also, acts like this: Whoever chooses to be proud and disobedient needs to be taught with the rod, or sword, by Master Jack [the executioner].

13. Why is it that no one can tolerate pride? Simply because God so wants it, and his Word confirms that he will unfailingly see to it that the proud are made humble. It is what we see happening in all stations, that the rich, learned, wise, beautiful, strong, and powerful are abased by God as soon as they become proud and do not of themselves become humble. For so it is written: *Deus resistit superbis*, "God resists the proud." The proud, thus, find themselves in tension with the one who stands opposed to them, namely, God in heaven, who squeezes them to death along with the whole world.

14. On the other hand, however, the one who is humble captures the hearts of God and men, and God, along with all his angels and people everywhere, smiles upon him with pleasure, for such a heart is an especially precious jewel to all in heaven and earth. Good fortune and blessing follow as well. How often we see that a poor man's son, whom his father cannot afford to give three pennies, becomes a chancellor, counselor, and so forth, and gains such esteem that princes and lords are greatly impressed because of his talents and skill.° Whence comes such good fortune? From this, that our Lord God cannot hold himself back. What is humble he alloys with his grace and mercy and all that he has. As Psalm 113:5–8 says: "Who is like unto the Lord our God, who dwelleth on high, Who humbleth himself to behold the things that are in heaven, and in the earth! He raiseth up the poor out of the dust, and lifteth the needy out of the dunghill; That he may set him with princes, even with the princes of his people." That's what God does for the humble. But they who are prideful and continually exalt themselves, and willfully refuse to obey, these God weighs down with every disgrace and does not relent until they lie totally abased. Examples of this abound everywhere.

° Here Luther referred to Dr. Gregor Brück who was chancellor of Electoral Saxony, according to the editor.

15. This should induce us all to be humble, children and servants to be obedient, and to bear in mind that God wants me to do what I'm told; I am not to be proud, but humble. Therefore, where others are unwilling, I will obey, and it will not distress me in the least that I am lowly, despised, and a menial servant; for I know that if I comport myself this way, in his good time God will have me step up and exalt me.

16. That's the way it went with Saul. He was obedient to his father, cared for the asses, and regarded himself as least in the tribe of Benjamin. To this donkey-herder, poor and lowly, God sends the prophet Samuel to anoint him king. Because he was humble and not proud, God shows him abundant grace and mercy. But what happened? When Saul became king, his ego became so inflated that he became proud, no longer caring about our Lord God and his Word. As a result, just as God had exalted him before when he was humble, so afterward, when he became proud, God cast him down again; and in despair Saul committed suicide, and his family was wiped out.

17. David, too, was a humble man who tended his father's sheep obediently. Had he been proud, he would have said: Should I really tend sheep? That is highly distasteful to me; I deserve a higher station. But this he did not do; he remained obedient and humble and cared for the sheep. Indeed, he was a fine, strong, intelligent young man, who might have said, What am I doing here tending sheep? I would like to advance and rise higher in the world. But he dutifully remained a shepherd doing what his father commanded him. On this shepherd God poured out his love, sending the prophet Samuel to anoint him king. And the account makes special mention of the fact that David had seven brothers who were all proud and arrogant, and had a low opinion of their young brother. But God said to Samuel, You are to take no account of the person nor be inquisitive about those who have their heads in the air; but you are to anoint him king whom I shall show you, namely, the shepherd; the others I do not want. Moreover, David was able to remain humble after God exalted him. Otherwise, had he become proud, God would have cast him aside just as he did Saul. But since he remains humble—even though he was dethroned—he is also eventually reinstated; and God holds

him in such high esteem that he promises him that Christ would be born from his line.

18. All this is written and preached in order that we might remain humble and guard against pride. We must not vaunt ourselves like some brash kitchen maid who defiantly complains, Who can work in the kitchen all the time, scour pans, clean, and sweep? Instead, I would like to go dancing. Do I always have to do what I am told to do? and so forth. Beware! If you exalt yourself, God will surely oppose you. For he does not lie; he cannot tolerate arrogance and pride, as we see every day. For where do you think it comes from that there's so much wickedness all over the world, with so many low-minded, inept, hapless men and women everywhere? There's no other answer but this, that from youth on everyone tends to strut about arrogantly; no one wants to do what he is told to do and should do. God, therefore, lets them rove about like swine, never learning to do anything useful. For this is his decree: Everyone who exalts himself will be abased; on the other hand, whoever humbles himself—be sure, God does not overlook it!—him will God exalt. We must never forget this!

19. So much for today in our divine service and let us learn this lesson well and act accordingly. Praise and thank God today for his instruction, and may he give us the grace to learn, remember, and do accordingly, for the sake of his Son, Jesus Christ. Amen.

SEVENTEENTH SUNDAY AFTER TRINITY

Second Sermon—1533

Luke 14:1–11

1. This Gospel develops two themes: the first, the dispute over the Sabbath; the second, the self-glorification of the Pharisees, which Christ denounced.

2. First, therefore, about the Sabbath. The Sabbath was highly esteemed by the Jews, as required by God in the first table of the Law. Their observance of the day was so rigorous that they did no work on the Sabbath, not even cooking; just as the Jews today will touch no money, as though it would desecrate the Sabbath if they reached into their purse to give a needy person a coin. This was the attitude of the scribes and Pharisees described in today's Gospel. Such great fools, that they decried Christ's healing of a sick person on the Sabbath!

3. Christ countered with the words, If one of you has an ass or an ox that falls into a well on the Sabbath day, will you not immediately pull him out? As much as to say, O you foolish and stupid scribes and Pharisees, aren't you gross, unreconstructed blockheads? You are willing to help your ox or donkey on the Sabbath without violating the sabbath law; but how much more valuable is a human being than an ox or an ass! The loss of an ox or donkey is not nearly as great as leaving a human being in distress. If you are not breaking the Sabbath law when you are helping an ox or ass, why do you denounce me when I help a human being? Is not a human person worth more than an ox or a donkey? What fools you are! You think that what you do is right and holy, but what I do, even if it is the same or something of higher value than what you do, that is wrong and unjustifiable.

4. That is the way the works-righteous hypocrites think, who know nothing else than to denigrate and find fault with other people. They are most adept at pulling slivers from someone's eye without ever being aware of the beam in their own eye. The Lord despises such

splinter—judges and beam carriers. People who prize only their own deeds as meritorious, while despising as dirt what others do, are arbitrary and disgusting. In short, they are insufferable clowns, as we say in German, *Hanswursts,* whom nothing pleases except what they themselves have done. So much for the dispute about the Sabbath and the judgment with which the Lord Christ squelches these foolish Jewish leaders, the scribes and Pharisees.

5. The point is that whoever wishes to honor and keep the Sabbath must do so by heeding God's Word and doing good works—attending church, hearing and studying God's Word, thanking, praising, and praying to God, and doing good works. In this way the Sabbath is sanctified, for God's Word is the true sanctuary which sanctifies everything that it touches, as St. Paul teaches in 1 Timothy 4:5, "For it is sanctified by the word of God and prayer." Therefore, the Sabbath is sanctified through God's Word, prayer, and faith. That is God's ordering of things. He has designated six days for work, six days for people to earn their livelihood. But on the seventh day God decreed that people should worship him, designating it as the Sabbath, that is, a holy day or day of rest, so that both men and beasts of burden might rest from their labor. Overarching the observance of this day of rest should be God's Word, that people might come to know God and obey his commandments.

6. From this we see how foolish and inconsistent the scribes and Pharisees were in their observance of the Sabbath rest by foregoing all routine tasks and considering it "breaking the Sabbath" if one nurtured the sick, gave help to the poor, or gave money to the needy. They were more disgusting, sanctimonious hypocrites than the barefoot monks who refuse to handle money. Our Lord God states very definitely that we should sanctify the Sabbath. There should be preaching on the Sabbath, listening to the sermon, praising God, giving thanks, praying, and doing good works. When an unanticipated but necessary task needs to be done on the Sabbath, that does not desecrate it. Christ was not gathering provender, nor did the unscheduled healing desecrate the Sabbath. But these scribes and Pharisees were so thickheaded that they charged him with desecrating the Sabbath by helping the poor man in his need on the Sabbath day. We ought to honor the Sabbath as a day of rest and, in addition,

be of help to suffering individuals when they need it. But these foolish Jews would permit a poor individual to die of hunger rather than help him on the Sabbath, even though they would help their ox or donkey on the Sabbath if the need arose. This is an indication of what happens when intelligent, educated, clever people do not pay attention to God's Word.

7. Let us, therefore, learn what it really means to observe the Sabbath—to hear and learn God's Word, and to help our neighbor when he is in need. The Jews would leave the neighbor in his need on the Sabbath; they would, however, not deprive themselves, but eat and drink and attend to their physical needs. Similarly, therefore, they should not have permitted a brother to suffer want on the Sabbath. Thus to sanctify the Sabbath includes doing good works on that day, hearkening to God's Word, and serving one's neighbor. If one does that, then the sabbath will be sanctified by word and by deed. That is the first lesson in today's Gospel.

8. The second thing this Gospel teaches is that we are not to be presumptuous and exalt ourselves. Christ is not condemning the various stations in life, that one individual has greater status than another, since such differences must necessarily obtain here on earth. Fathers and mothers have authority over their children; a sovereign, over his subjects; a pastor, over his parishioners in matters pertaining to his office and God's Word. One cannot dispense with such differences in this world because rank and position vary.

9. What does it mean, then, to exalt oneself? Christ, as we have said, does not forbid rank and position. Of necessity, some must be in an executive position. Not everyone is to be subservient, for there will be higher ranks and stations in the world. Christ does not forbid that some rise higher, one a sovereign, another a pastor; this we readily acknowledge. What corrupts the situation is to elevate oneself and discredit others in their rightful place and calling. To be in a position of authority is not wrong if it is either by God's ordaining or the orderly election of one's fellowmen. But to elevate oneself is wrong. If one usurps authority, that is wrong. We see it every day; the common citizen preens himself like a nobleman; the nobleman like an emperor; everyone reaches higher up, until the emperor becomes like a peasant. Pomp and pride brim over, until even the emperor cannot attain it.

10. What it means to exalt self is to scramble higher than what God ordains, or is given by the vote of the people. Some individuals have a restless disposition which is never satisfied until they are "on top." Others give the appearance of wanting to be helpful and accomplish something useful. But when they reach the top, they are only concerned with furthering their own ends, having a good time, receiving honor, and a life of ease. However, no one is given an office to enhance life for himself and for his glory, but rather that he might work faithfully in service to his fellowmen. The mayor of Wittenberg was not elected that he might become a titled landowner but rather to serve the prince, the city, and the townspeople. He should not use his position to advance his own ends, but to ascertain how he can better serve his prince, the city, and the people.

11. But what happens is another story, as we see. Before they get to the top rung, everyone is eager for the top job. But once these individuals come into an office and are expected to carry out its duties, they end up "sitting on the job." Anyone who took the office with the intent of doing what is right and serving his constituents faithfully will soon find the work too much. He very soon becomes disillusioned and weary, and, at the very least, he will think, even if he doesn't say it aloud, What the devil, who gave me this job? I myself must confess, if I were to bare my heart, that the same thought has come to me, Oh, why did not the Lord God raise up someone else to be preacher to the German people? because the lukewarm spirit is so great, the work too much, the maliciousness and thanklessness of the people so overwhelming, that flesh and blood can scarcely tolerate it but becomes morose and impatient, ready to chuck it and be free of it once and for all.

12. A young woman, unaware of the problems connected with wedlock, is not satisfied until she is married and has her man. Likewise, a young fellow is not satisfied until he has a wife. But once they are married, and she has her man and he has his woman, they would like to be out of it and free again. Similarly, the average citizen isn't satisfied with his calling, but thinks: My, I would like to be mayor. But if that happens and he becomes mayor, inheriting the stress, the work, and the trouble, then he says, To the devil with this position! I'm ready to chuck it. That's what it means to have an office. To be

on top is no frolic or bunny dance. It entails work and stress, so that no one in his right mind would actively seek it.

13. St. Paul states (1 Tim. 3:1): "If a man desire the office of a bishop, he desireth a good work." He doesn't say that he desires good days or an extravagant lifestyle, but a good and noble work. It is praiseworthy if one wishes to serve mankind as bishop, pastor, or schoolteacher, provided he has the discipline and capacity for the task. It is commendable, Paul is saying, if someone desires to be of service to people. But if you want the position only for self-glorification, you are a lazy lout, of service to no one, seeking only your own gain, glory, and self-indulgence. However, if you aspire to a given vocation, then say, Very well, if I am to have this position, may God's will be done; I will pursue my tasks with all diligence; I will not shirk my duties, but pursue the calling with all diligence. And if he does so, good! That is right and proper.

14. But the world thinks differently; everyone is on the make and take, in order to become a squire with its attending honor. But to actually work and carry out the demands of the position, no one wants that. This is the way it is in the courts of the lords and princes—attendants sitting about, but only three or four working, the rest doing nothing but eating, drinking, and engaging in debauchery. They are the worms in the cabbage, the fly in the soup—really "useful" sycophants. The same happens in other stations as well.

15. That is why each should be content with his station in life, carry out his duties with diligence, being useful to his fellowmen. For God is pleased with those who are content with their calling in life and faithfully carry out their duties. Let a young lad study diligently until our Lord God elevates him and directs him: You have studied long enough now to become a schoolteacher, perhaps even a preacher! If this were our attitude, each would say, I desire no honor, but I wish to be useful to God; I will follow his direction to do what I can to glorify him and to be of service to my neighbor.

16. The Pharisees in this account did not act in that manner, but simply wanted a place of esteem and honor. The Lord was aware of this, and that is why he could not remain silent, but chastised them by saying, What high society fellows you are, always desirous of honor. But I tell you to humble yourselves as I do and be a servant to

your fellowman. Christ is not decrying that a person should have a position of honor, but rather the motive of self-glorification. To have a position of honor is not wrong, but what is wrong is to place oneself in the position of honor. Christ contrasts the two who have positions of honor: the first usurped the position, but has no right to the position; the second abased himself and was asked to take the position of honor; he has the right. The bottom line is whether an individual has usurped the position in order to be on top. It is one situation if I desire the honor which belongs to someone else, and quite another situation when the honor is conferred upon me.

17. The Lord passes judgment upon those who exalt themselves and reassures those who humble themselves, saying, "For everyone who exalts himself will be humbled, and who humbles himself will be exalted." This doesn't need much proof; everyday circumstances prove the same. I have seen it myself that some who had climbed to the top have been shamefully knocked down. This Gospel doesn't deceive. The person who strives to gain recognition for his own glorification will not prosper. However, the man who is chosen for a calling and who is willing to serve will succeed. If a prince asks someone to be his counsel and the individual has the expertise, he should do it. But to force oneself into a position, that God will not have.

18. In temporal affairs there will be those who hold stations of honor and power. We cannot all be the same. It often happens that given individuals climb the leadership ladder of life from bottom to top. To be on top, to have honor and power, to be a doctor or a prince is not wrong. What is bad is to seek one's own glory and well-being rather than to honor God and do one's duty. Then one's activity serves only one's own depraved heart. A preacher should not merely have honor but he should work to deserve the honor, otherwise there is no worth to it. A ruler should not merely sit on his throne, but should protect his subjects, maintain peace in his country, and do away with dissension. He does not rule well if he only wants to banquet and whitewash his deeds. Such a ruler is a bad administrator in a noble calling.

19. To summarize, one should not refuse an office, but he ought not seek his own glory in the office. Our Lord God will knock down those who seek only their own glory, as he has many kings and princes. So God humbled the Jews, disgracing them by stripping them of

their own government. They were the noblest people on earth, sat at God's head table, had God's Word, were God's chosen people, but now they are of lowest rank. God cannot abide arrogance. From the very beginning he has knocked down pride. He wouldn't abide arrogance in heaven, as Lucifer's example proves.

20. To have a position of importance is not wrong, but to strive to have it for the sake of being on top, that is wrong. That is true, for example, of an individual who is not qualified to be either a teacher or a preacher, and yet aspires to be a doctor of philosophy and a professor. Such a scoundrel amounts to nothing, but wants recognition, aspires to an office not to carry out the duties of the office, but for his own glorification and gratification. He needs to be humbled. We must be careful to differentiate. To receive recognition is not bad, but to covet recognition for personal honor and gain is wrong. May the Lord God give us his grace, and help us remember to do what is right. Amen.

EIGHTEENTH SUNDAY AFTER TRINITY

First Sermon—1532

In order that we might give glory to our Lord God, let us listen to what he has to say to us in his Word; and by his grace may we believe and cling to what he tells us.

Matthew 22:34–46

> *But when the Pharisees had heard that he had put the Sadducees to silence, they were gathered together. Then one of them, which was a lawyer, asked him a question, tempting him, and saying, Master, which is the great commandment in the law? Jesus said unto him, Thou shalt love the Lord thy God with all thy heart, and with all thy soul, and with all thy mind. This is the first and great commandment. And the second is like unto it, Thou shalt love thy neighbour as thyself. On these two commandments hang all the law and the prophets. While the Pharisees were gathered together, Jesus asked them, Saying, What think ye of Christ? whose son is he? They say unto him, The son of David. He saith unto them, How then doth David in spirit call him Lord, saying, The LORD said unto my Lord, Sit thou on my right hand, till I make thine enemies thy footstool? If David then call him Lord, how is he his son? And no man was able to answer him a word, neither durst any man from that day forth ask him any more questions.*

1. Dear friends, in this Gospel our beloved Lord lays before us two points for us to heed, ponder, and practice. First of all, the Lord answers the question of the scribes, stating that the primary and greatest commandment is to love God with all your heart, with all your soul, and with all your mind; and also, to love your neighbor as yourself. In these words he has summed up all that one can preach, teach, and communicate, both to Jews and also to Gentiles, about good works; in brief and in summary, that we are to love God and our neighbor. Everything should emanate from, and flow back into, this source. The person who asks how he might serve God has his answer here from

God himself who says, You serve me when you love me, your God, with all your heart, and so forth, and your neighbor as yourself.

2. On Judgment Day this lesson will call forth a very stern judgment. For everybody knows well what has occurred under the papacy. Those who wanted to serve God did not keep in mind the Ten Commandments; instead, one became a monk, another went on a pilgrimage to Rome, invoked St. James, or some other saints, petitioning with fasting, ceremonies, and so forth. It was then known as spiritual devotion, and everybody conceived of it as service to God to go on a pilgrimage, to enter a monastery, to devote oneself to fasting, vigils, singing, and so on. But serving is when you do what God commands. It follows, therefore, that whoever wants to serve God aright must do as God commands and not as he himself thinks. Now, what does God bid us do in order to serve him? As stated here, if you want to serve God and do what he enjoins, you don't have to go far afield or contribute lots of money to some cause. Love God and your neighbor! Indeed, how could God make serving him any plainer and explain it any more simply? In other words, If you want to serve me, pay attention to me and I'll tell you all you need to know; just listen to what I have to say and do it; love me and your neighbor. For I want you to know that when you love your neighbor and do good to him, you have done me a valued service, and I shall look upon it as if you have loved me and done good things for me. It is a wonderful doctrine that what we do for our neighbor is regarded as service and work done for God himself!

3. This lesson, I say, will certainly cause a great stir on Judgment Day. For on that day the righteous will reply, "Lord, when saw we thee an hungered, and fed thee? or thirsty, and gave thee drink?" and so forth. But Christ will respond, "Verily I say unto you, Inasmuch as ye have done it unto one of the least of these my brethren, ye have done it unto me." In like manner the ungodly will say, "Lord, when saw we thee an hungered, or thirsty, or a stranger, or naked, or sick, or in prison, and did not minister unto thee?" To them Christ will also reply, saying, "Verily I say unto you, Inasmuch as ye did it not to one of the least of these, ye did it not to me." It is indisputably settled, therefore, that when you give a poor Christian a garment, a coat, a penny, yes, a cold drink of water, or help your neighbor out of

his misery, you have done it to Christ, for there is no distinction to be made here.

4. But now because of the accursed devil's prompting, we allow opportunities to slip away and do not realize that without great trouble we can serve our Lord God, and yet don't do it. We think, if Christ were right this minute to come to our door, or if we knew where he were to be found, we would go to him and give him all we had. How often we wish that if we had been at Bethlehem when the child Jesus was born, we might have picked him up, cradled him in our arms, and cared for him. But what is the good of such thoughts? The point here is that the second commandment is like the first, and it has to follow that our Lord God will cheerfully accept and regard what we do for our neighbor as being done to him.

5. Yes, you say, our Lord God is in heaven and doesn't need my service at all. It doesn't matter; he is here on earth as well. Therefore, when you see a Christian in distress, know that Christ is in distress and is in need of your help. As he himself says, on Judgment Day he will fault us for letting him hunger and thirst.

6. However, it is really sad that this lesson is so clearly taught us here, and yet we disregard it as if God were not there, whereas we could be serving him faithfully every day and every hour. We cannot excuse our disobedience by saying that we were unaware of this. For here it stands written: "The second is like unto it." For this reason the verdict on Judgment Day will read: Didn't you hear that whoever loves his neighbor loves God? Had you served your neighbor, you would have served me, and I would have richly rewarded you; but because of your neglect I had to die and perish. Let us beware of such a judgment, for it will result in eternal damnation.

7. In the papacy it was very common for all knights, soldiers, jurists, and people of this sort, who imagined they had been in an improper, execrable calling, to say, Up till now we have served the world, but now we want to begin serving God. For this reason many of them entered the monastery and became monks and hermits. However, this was a devilish deception. Is it serving God when you crawl into a corner where you help and bring solace to no one? What need does our Lord God have of the service you perform in a corner? The one who wants to serve God should not crawl into an isolated

cell but remain among people and serve them, where he can rest assured that thereby he is serving God, for he has commanded it and said, "The second is like unto it."

8. The same thing occurred also among the Jews. They did all manner of evil to their neighbor and thought if they merely slaughtered a lot of cows and calves it would make all things right. But what does the Lord say in Psalm 50:8–10? "I will not reprove thee for thy sacrifices or thy burnt offerings, to have been continually before me. I will take no bullock out of thy house, nor he goats out of thy folds. For every beast of the forest is mine, and the cattle upon a thousand hills." He says the same thing in many other passages: He does not need their gold, their temple, and other things; but if you want to serve me well, I direct you to your neighbor at your elbow. You have wife, children, servants, and other people with whom you have to do, and that will give you enough to do as you serve me. If your child does not want to be obedient and upright, immediately and without hesitation apply the rod. If the servant does not want to do what is right, discipline him or show him the door. If your neighbor is poor, distressed, or sick, help and minister to him, consoling him; if you obediently do your civic duty under those who are your rulers, you have done it to me.

9. It is sad that this doesn't sink into our hearts. For God does not want to impute to us the things we have done wrong against him; his desire is to forgive us. However, if we serve our neighbor and do good to him, God will look upon it as having been done to him; in addition, he will richly reward us. On the other hand, anything we did not do to help our neighbor, God will look upon as not having been done to him. If we hate and deceive our neighbor, we have hated and deceived him, and he will take just revenge on us.

10. Around us we see what the nature of the world is like and how it treats our Lord God. Everyone—peasant and burgher alike—does nothing other than shamefully oppose our Lord God to his face and trample him with their feet, concerned only with how to become rich and pile up treasures, regardless of what happens to the neighbor, whether he languishes or dies because of our neglect. If people would realize that what they do to their neighbor is doing it to God in heaven, they would be filled with terror at their wickedness and unfaithfulness.

But they don't consider that it is our Lord God whom they slap in the face, whom they hate, deny, persecute, and trample; and on Judgment Day they will say, We did not realize what we were doing. But the verdict in reply will be, You would have known if you had been willing to listen, for it was prescribed and preached to you often enough that what you do to the neighbor, you do to me personally.

11. The lesson, therefore, very closely shows (may God give us his grace so that we do not, like the world, get beyond its reach) that God looks on all the good and bad we do to the neighbor as being done to him. If, when we serve our neighbor, each one would consider it as being done to God, the whole world would be filled with God-pleasing service. A servant in the stable, a maid in the kitchen, a boy in school, they would be nothing but servants of God, were they to willingly perform whatever father and mother, masters and mistresses commanded. Then every home would be filled with godly works, indeed, every home would be a true church where nothing but truly God-pleasing works were done. It's just the opposite now in the world; false preachers and wicked tyrants do our Lord God great harm in his church. Peasants and burghers try to deceive their neighbors, and so also our Lord God; young people are disobedient to parents, elders, and magistrates, and so also to our Lord God. They shunt their service from him to the devil, who is therefore being served all over the world, while God, as a result, is not. Everyone serves the devil because they set little value on love to the neighbor. Everywhere false, unprincipled, deceitful people prey upon, exploit, gouge, steal from, and rob their neighbors. As a result, the whole world is not only full of devil worship but also full of the devil. But if a person does good and aids his neighbor, he is serving the Lord God; and every house and chamber becomes a church, where God-pleasing works prevail and where people uphold decency and morality. How could our Lord God make it any better? How could he bring godly service to his honor any closer to us than by building a church of pure gold out of our own homes and dwellings, adorned with emeralds and pearls?

12. We should, therefore, learn here that whoever does good to his neighbor and serves him well, whether in casual relationships of one person to another, or out of bounden duty, as children to their parents,

servants to their masters and mistresses, subjects to their rulers, that individual serves not merely his neighbor, but God in heaven; for he himself states that he acknowledges such service as if it were done to him. As Christ says here, "The second is like unto it." Whoever will not be persuaded that he is able to establish a kingdom of heaven on earth or make out of his own home or situation a house or temple of God is heading toward the devil. For where there is service to God, there is heaven. When I serve my neighbor, I am already in heaven, for I am serving God. Consequently, we are making for ourselves a paradise and heaven here on earth when we are obedient to God and serve our neighbor. But when we disobey God and do not serve our neighbor, we make earth a hell for ourselves; for we are serving the devil who belongs in hell. And it is not dependent upon whether a person sees or perceives this; the time will come when he will.

13. This is the first point in today's Gospel. May God grant that we take it to heart and remember that each of us loves and serves God when he loves and serves his neighbor. But what does it mean to love thy neighbor? To do good to him in everything. For loving, if done properly, does not occur solely in thoughts and words, but in deeds. Where love holds sway in the heart, it teaches and drives the body to rise up, sing, and speak about what it loves, yes, to be more concerned about what it is doing than about itself. Therefore, loving one's neighbor is followed by action, as when one teaches, instructs, admonishes the neighbor, assists, befriends him, and does everything possible for the benefit of body and soul, possessions, and honor. You see, then, that love is not a matter of outward appearance, but, as St. John says, it does show itself in deed and in truth.

14. Now, then, the second point in this Gospel, where the Lord asks the Pharisees whose Son Christ is, appertains to the life to come. The first point concerned the neighbor, to render our neighbor the service as though owed to God, constantly exercising ourselves in love toward him. God gave us mouth, tongue, eyes, ears, hands, feet, money, goods, reason, and all else, to be able to do this and assist our neighbor in this life. But when our life ends here, we have to live there as well. We need to know, therefore, that Christ is David's son. And not only that, but also why David in spirit calls his son Christ, a lord, and the one Lord, indeed, who sits at God's right hand until all his enemies are made to be a footstool under his feet.

15. Now David was foremost among men on earth because he was the one with whom God concluded a great covenant in fulfillment of a glorious promise; and yet this great man and king falls on his knees, humbles himself, and confesses that his son, Christ, is his Lord. If now Christ is David's Lord, it then follows that he is a greater Lord than the most exalted and mighty monarch on earth, since there could be no more exalted king in this world than David was. Therefore, by this question our Lord Christ means to say, You Pharisees and Jews do not know what and who Christ is; you regard him as a mere human being and David's son; but you are to know that he is not a mere human being and David's son, but also true God and David's Lord, the Lord who sits at God's right hand and under whose feet God subjects all his enemies to be his footstool.

16. This, then, is the second point, not about our neighbor but about Christ, not as regards this present life but about hereafter, when this life comes to a close. In this life we are to acquit ourselves by loving God and our neighbor. But once we die and are laid in the grave, the issue is not that we can say, I have loved God and my neighbor, but rather, I believe in Jesus Christ, our Lord, the Lord of the life which is to come, who can and will save all who believe on his name. This temporal, earthly life is not the inheritance Christ gives us; for God gave this temporal, earthly life to the whole world, long before Christ came, and stated that we are to love him and our neighbor. He then also gave the world his Son, Christ, so that through him and in him we might also have eternal life. We do not believe in Christ for the sake of this present, temporal life; for it was not for the sake of this existence that Christ died; but we believe in Christ for the sake of eternal life. And he died so that he might lead us out of this life into the life to come.

17. Accordingly, we need to understand these two points well and make this distinction: Moses and the Law belong to this life; but for the life to come we must have the Lord, who is called Christ, David's son, who is seated at God's right hand and under whose feet lie all his enemies. Through the Law and through our works we cannot achieve the life to come. For our works are not adequate to pay for our sins and to trample the enemies. God's Son had to come from heaven, become man, and with his death and blood pay for our sins,

seat himself at God's right hand, and trample the enemies under his feet. Moses teaches us how we are to comport ourselves in this life; however, for the life to come this is our treasure, namely, Jesus Christ, God's Son, who is the Lord of eternal life.

18. The temporal, perishable life in this world we have from God, the almighty Creator of heaven and earth, as we confess in the first article of the Creed. But the eternal, everlasting life we have through the suffering and resurrection of our Lord Jesus Christ, who even now is seated at God's right hand, as we confess in the second article of our Creed. It is essential that we understand these two points. The teaching of the first and greatest commandment, to love God and our neighbor, is necessary for this life; however, the doctrine and knowledge of who Christ is we need for the life to come, so that we might know our abiding place when this life comes to a close. In other words, when this life ends we must be able to say, I believe Jesus Christ is Lord of eternal life; he deals with me in a veiled and hidden manner through his Word, power, and Spirit so that I may enter it. Accordingly, a person lives a holy life in this world when he serves God properly in accord with the great commandment; and, in addition, through Christ has eternal life as a fruit of the gospel.

19. Surely God's fearful anger must hang poised over the human being who pays no heed to this crucial teaching, and there must be enormous vexation with God because these words are not taken to heart to move that individual. Where is there a greater, more vital lesson than these two points? First, we are taught how a man ought to create for himself a paradise and a kingdom of heaven here on earth, serving God, whether sleeping, awake, walking, standing, eating, or drinking. For, as stated, what we do for our neighbor is done to the service and pleasure of our Lord God himself. Ought one not be overjoyed with this one point alone and be prompted to serve God? This is not fabricated or trumped up, but spoken assuredly by him who cannot lie. Second, there is comfort in the face of death for a person who is about to die, to know and have Christ, be baptized, receive absolution and the Holy Sacrament, because eternal life must then follow.

20. However, since these words have, unfortunately, become so commonplace for everyone, so that almost no one pays attention to

them, we, therefore, must earnestly pray God not to let us sink to the point where our hearts become insolent and obdurate as the manner of the world unfortunately is. Neither peasant, burgher, nor aristocrat deserves to savor and taste these words, for they have become so insensitive and have failed to see or hear, like men groping in darkness, as though these words did not apply to them. This is a sure sign that they are repelled and rejected by God. If just once they would incline to think: I want to build God a church and make a paradise for myself; I also want to have a place in that heaven as I now serve God here on earth; I want to serve my neighbor, and so serve God; and, finally, I want to be with my Lord Jesus Christ in the life to come; I want to believe in him who is Lord of eternal life. But they refuse, becoming insensitive like blind and obdurate people.

21. We must, therefore, diligently pray that we might retain this lesson. Its words are so lofty and lovely that they exceed all bounds. Let each one of us worship fully and humbly and take these words to heart. For it is a bad sign if a person remains untouched by them, a sign that the devil has taken possession of his heart. But now the whole world is so obdurate, particularly the learned smart alecks, who, though they hear our Lord God speaking graciously, nevertheless, love the devil more than God.

22. Our Lord God places himself most graciously at our disposal, comforts us, gives us all that we need for body and life, and in return demands nothing more than our love; also, he promises us eternal life in his Son, Christ Jesus. And yet no one wants to serve him. The devil, on the other hand, who causes us all kinds of heartache, who harasses us daily with war, pestilence, famine, and all manner of evil calamities, everyone gladly serves unto eternal death. When by God's command, and to the glory of Christ, people are to give a penny, they find it so hard to do and they lock up tightly their strongbox, purse, fist, and all else. But when they should give a hundred gulden for the devil to use, then fist, purse, strongbox, and all else stand open. That's the way the world is, that beautiful, delicate, noble plant; and yet, it sees how poorly the devil rewards his servants, here in time with all sorts of calamities and there in eternity with the fire of hell. God, on the other hand, rewards his servants well and richly,

here in time granting paradise and good fortune, and there in eternity, eternal life in Christ Jesus, our Lord. But no one pays attention. Let us with all our hearts thank our dear Lord God for this lesson and earnestly call on him, praying that he graciously preserve it to us, so we may abide in it eternally. Amen.

EIGHTEENTH SUNDAY AFTER TRINITY

Second Sermon[*]

Matthew 22:34-46

1. Today's Gospel lesson primarily deals with two questions. The first one is raised by an expert in the Scriptures, who wants to know, Which is the greatest commandment in the entire law of Moses? The second is raised by our Lord Christ, who in return asks the Pharisees, What sort of person is Christ, since he is David's son, and yet David, speaking by the Spirit, calls him his Lord?

2. The first question shows that the Jews had fallen into such total blindness, that they had forgotten the Ten Commandments, which even little children understand. Therefore, a scribe (Scripture expert) and the Pharisees should certainly be able to answer such a question.

3. The first commandment, "You shall have no other gods," is certainly the foremost and greatest commandment. The Pharisees and scribes, however, have departed from it and have fallen into the folly of arguing about this commandment, one insisting, That means sacrifices; another, It means giving to the poor; a third, It means fasting, wearing a special garb, and so on. You see, that is what happens when you depart from God's commandments and his Word, substituting your own ideas about good works, ignoring what God's Word says. That is what also happened in the case of our monks and nuns. They have lost and forgotten what Christian faith and love really are, and have substituted for them their monasticism, going into cloisters, being obedient, renouncing all personal properties and rights. They call such a cloistered life "the estate of perfection," and to this day they still labor under that delusion, with the result that they still don't know what righteousness really is.

[*]Delivered at home on October 12, 1533.

4. But, praise God! now even a ten-year-old child can give you a better definition of righteousness than all the monks and nuns. The reason for that is that they think only in terms of their monastic way of life. But a Christian says, Being righteous means that you fear and love God, that you obey your father and mother, that you do not kill, but are always helpful to your neighbor. For God has not commanded us to do anything but just that. Our children know that now. When you ask, What is righteousness? they reply, If you want to be righteous, love God with all your heart, and your neighbor as yourself. But I know for a fact that no monk can tell you that, for they do not know the Ten Commandments, the Creed, the Lord's Prayer, and so on. If they did know them, they would not engage in such foolhardy things, but would devote themselves to truly obeying the Ten Commandments.

5. Such nonsense and blindness comes from doing external works that look and sound special, for example, observing special days, wearing special garb, not eating or drinking, and not getting married. That looks good and it puts people's noses up in the air. Meanwhile, however, they ignore the greatest works and commandments, loving God and being helpful to everyone. As we see from our text, it is the Pharisees and scribes who raise the question about the greatest commandment, because they don't agree among themselves on that point, each one having a different idea about which work is greatest.

6. That is why Christ is right in calling our attention to this example and warning us that we must always pay close attention to what God's commandment and Word say. Then we will know that if we love God and our neighbor, we are truly doing what is right and are truly worshiping and serving God. He jerks the scribes and Jews to attention by turning their thoughts away from their works, sacrifices, gifts, fasting, and the like, and directing them to God's works as indicated in the Ten Commandments. In effect he says, So, you're debating which is the foremost and greatest commandment in the Law? Well, I'll tell you, Moses himself answers that question when he says, "Love God with all your heart and your neighbor as yourself."

7. The fact that people of such great influence and power became so blind that they didn't know the difference between the smallest

and greatest commandment in the Law, should be a solemn warning to us. This expert in the Scripture is a doctor and teacher of the people, but he himself doesn't even know what a good life is, nor does he know which is the greatest commandment. Since he himself doesn't know, how can he teach other people and instruct them about the right way to worship God? After all, he clearly reveals his ignorance and lack of understanding by the question he addresses to our Lord. That's the kind of teachers our present-day foolish monks and priests are. Ask one of them about good works, and he will not direct you to the Ten Commandments, but will say, If you want to worship God and do good works, you must become a monk, hear confessions, go on sacred pilgrimages, fast, etc. That is directing people away from the Ten Commandments and the true way and to a nonexistent fool's paradise. What is the end result of man-made doctrines? When you advocate and glorify such works—which God has not commanded—you are blinding the people, so that they disregard the Ten Commandments and forget all about them. If that were not the case, a person should be wise enough to say, The greatest and foremost commandment is the one God has given. But Pharisees and scribes, priests, monks, nuns, and all those who promote man-made rules, are unable to do that.

8. That is why Christ is fully justified in exposing this expert's ignorance. In effect, he is saying, You are an expert in the Scriptures and a teacher in Israel, and you haven't even read the Ten Commandments and don't know which is the greatest and foremost commandment in the Law. What in the world are you stupid and ignorant fools teaching the people anyway? As we said before, that kind of stupidity is the result of man-made doctrines.

9. That is why we must be on guard against and avoid the doctrines of men and of our own ideas. We dare not neglect the catechism's teaching of the God-given Ten Commandments as an insignificant doctrine, but must diligently use it in teaching people how they must live in this earthly life. Of course, showing them how to be saved takes an entirely different doctrine than the Ten Commandments, namely the doctrine of Christ, which our Lord Christ presents a little later. But you must use the Ten Commandments to teach people how they must live in this life. They tell us that we must love God and not wor-

ship any other gods, that is, you must let God be your God and not allow anything to be more important than loving him. You must cling to him and his Word, even if it means suffering and sacrificing anything and everything else. When you do that, you will be a member of the highest estate, a truly righteous saint.

10. A monk says, Yes, the laypeople, the everyday Christians do that; I want to do something special! The ordinary Christian doesn't get up at night to pray; I want to get up for matins and pray; he eats meat, I want to eat fish; he wears ordinary clothing, I'm going to have a special garb made for me; he lives in the world, I want to escape from the world. When someone entered the monastery, that is what people said. It was just as if that person had overcome the world and everything in it: pride, envy, hatred, greed, and the like, even death itself, and as if he were already seated in heaven, loving nothing more than God. It finally gets to the point where these blind people are so preoccupied with their devotions, that they forget all about the Ten Commandments. That is why our Gospel lesson says: Whoever wants to know which is the foremost and greatest commandment in the Law, should learn God's Ten Commandments. They teach you which works are great and which are small, and that no work is greater than loving God; out of love use the gifts he gives us in order to glorify him, and gladly and willingly do without the things he does not give us.

11. The second question is the one Jesus addresses to this Pharisee, "What think ye of Christ?" In effect he is saying, You Pharisees are the masters and teachers in Israel; you should, therefore, be experts in the Scriptures, since it is your job to teach and instruct other people. In fact, however, you are ignorant people who don't know the Law, because you ask me, Which is the foremost and greatest commandment in the Law? Therefore, let me ask you a question: What do you know about Christ? Whose Son is he? You know his lineage well, that he is to be a descendant of David. Since you know that, you claim that he is nothing more than a human being, a descendant of David. But my question is: Do you really consider him to be nothing more than a human being, a descendant of David? Discuss it, and then tell me: How can Christ be David's descendant, since David calls him "my Lord"?

12. The fourth commandment does not make a son superior to his father, but rather ascribes authority and honor to the father, so that a son is to be obedient and subject to his father, as the commandment itself says, "Honor your father and your mother." Among the Jewish people, too, this discipline flowed from the fourth commandment. A father did not address his son as lord, but the son addressed his father as lord. That is why Christ is really telling us, It should be the other way around; it would be much more fitting if Christ, a descendant of David, were addressing David as lord, instead of David, the father, addressing his descendant as Lord. But David, though he is the father, calls his descendant "Lord" by inspiration of the Spirit. How can that be? If he is David's descendant, how can he be David's Lord?

13. Our Lord uses this question to make the Jews realize that they need to know who Christ really is. In effect he is saying, If you want to know who Christ is, you must recognize that he is more than merely a descendant of David. For, since David by inspiration of the Spirit calls him his Lord, he must be not merely a human being, but also true God, begotten of the Father from eternity. Otherwise David would not address him as Lord, if he were merely a human being, merely a descendant of David.

14. Now the Pharisees are in a quandary, unable to answer a single word, not daring to ask another question. For, you see, David is one of the greatest saints and the most learned and greatest king on earth, and he is the one who calls Christ his Lord! The only conclusion you can possibly draw from that is: Christ must be even greater and holier than David. So, when David calls Christ his Lord, he is obviously saying, Oh, my descendant, Christ, is far greater than I am; I, too, am a king and am called his father, but he is my Lord, and not merely my Lord, but the Lord of all the kings, prophets, and saints on earth, a Lord who sits at God's right hand of almighty power, and who, by God's command, rules over all his enemies.

15. Since Christ is such a great Lord, he must be not merely a human being, and according to the flesh David's descendant, but rather true God and God's Son, equal to the Father in majesty and glory, for it is not fitting for anyone to sit at God's right hand unless he is equal with God. But especially because God subdues all his enemies under

Christ's feet, Christ must be much more than a mere man. For, who these enemies are, we learn from St. Paul in 1 Corinthians 15:25–26 where he quotes from this Psalm (110:1) and says: "For he must reign, till he hath put all enemies under his feet. The last enemy that shall be destroyed is death." Now, if the devil and death are to be subdued by this son of David, so that he is their Lord, you can only conclude that divine power and omnipotence reside in this son of David; otherwise, like any other person, he would not be able to overcome death and the devil. Therefore, says Christ, you Pharisees will either completely ignore the Bible, or, if you do study it, you will ignore the heart and core of it, namely, Christ and the gospel.

16. So our Lord uses this question to direct us to the true way to eternal life. He teaches us that if we hope to be saved, we must know not only the Law, but must add to it a second doctrine, one that does not tell us which is the greatest of the commandments in the Law nor directs us to the works we must do, but a doctrine which tells us who Christ is, how, and in which way we can attain what the Law demands from us. That doctrine, however, is the gospel of Christ, who is both David's Lord and the Lord of everyone and everything. That teaches us an altogether different lesson. Since we were enslaved to sin and unable to keep the Law, Christ came and entered the cesspool of sin in our place, so that he might help us get out of that cesspool. As St. Paul says in Romans 8:3–4, "For what the law could not do, in that it was weak through the flesh, God sending his own Son in the likeness of sinful flesh, and for sin, condemned sin in the flesh: That the righteousness of the law might be fulfilled in us, who walk not after the flesh, but after the Spirit." We could not fulfill the Law because we were captive and handcuffed under the devil's power, sold into the slavery of sin. That is why Christ had to come and help us. He hoisted us up on his shoulders and bore our sins; he kept and fulfilled the Law which we were unable to fulfill, overcame sin, death, and hell in our stead, and through the gospel he now says to us, I want to be your Lord; just cling to me, confessing that I am the Lord who has conquered sin, death, and hell; then I will help you so that sin must depart from you and neither death nor hell can harm you.

17. Those are the pure, divine works of this man, who is called Christ, David's son and David's Lord. For, abolishing sin, overcoming death, buying us back from hell, and giving us eternal life, these are not the works of an angel, much less the works of the devil. They are, instead, the majestic, glorious works of the majestic God himself. When I now hear and believe, Christ is the one who redeems from sin, death, and hell and who gives eternal life, then I am truly calling him Lord. For that is how David and the prophets called him Lord, ascribing to him these divine, eternal works of God, saving from sin, death, and hell and giving eternal life. Of that, says Christ, you Pharisees know nothing. You are, indeed, called teachers and experts in the Law, and you bear the title and name, teachers in Israel, but you teach neither the Law nor Christ. You do not teach the people how they must live to worship God on earth, nor do you teach them how they can get to heaven through Christ and be eternally saved. All you talk about are your sacrifices: calves, tithes, fasting, ascetic rules, etc., but all those things are not a worship of God, either in this life or the next. That is how our Lord rebukes the Pharisees and scribes, accusing them of being totally blind, mad, and foolish.

18. This is a terrifying illustration of two blackouts. It shows us that the darkness and blindness among the people was so great, that even the most influential rulers and the most devout people, officials whose responsibility it was to direct others to the way that leads to heaven, were so ignorant they didn't even understand the first commandment, much less know anything about the gospel or about Christ. Under the papacy there was also such a blackout, one that still exists today in those places where the papacy is in control. I myself must confess that when I was a monk, I could not recite the Ten Commandments in proper sequence. And to this day no papist, be he bishop or the pope himself, can properly recite them. Things were so bad when Christ came to earth that they were not proclaiming either the Law or the gospel; and since the people knew neither of them, they didn't know how to live a God-pleasing life here or how to obtain eternal life. That is total blindness and total blackout.

19. In addition to this darkness, he found among the Israelites another group of contemptuous people, the Sadducees. They believed

and taught that man dies like any other animal. They denied the resurrection from the dead, did not believe in the existence of angels, evil spirits, the soul, the devil, hell, or eternal life. That is the awesome blackout our Lord Christ found among the Jewish people of his day. It was all he could do to dispel this darkness, and it especially taxed all his recreative powers to reestablish a correct understanding of the two doctrines: the Law and the gospel.

20. This same kind of darkness will also prevail at the end of the world, unless Judgment Day comes first. And, as we said earlier, we saw that kind of darkness under the papacy, as we went along doing good works devised by men but knew nothing about either the Law or the gospel. If Judgment Day doesn't come soon, the same conditions will return, except that they will be even worse than they were under the papacy. Then even the doctors and teachers of theology will no longer know anything about God and his commandments, much less will they know anything about Christ. Our dear Lord Christ will not be made a liar when he says in Luke 18:8: "I tell you that he will avenge them speedily. Nevertheless when the Son of man cometh, shall he find faith on earth?" Prior to Judgment Day the Sadducees, the Epicureans, and contemptuous unbelievers will control everything.

21. That is why our Lord Christ admonishes us in this Gospel lesson to have a reverent fear and to give careful attention to these two doctrines. In effect he is saying, Be on your guard, learn God's commandments and the gospel of Christ; God's commandments teach you what you are to do, which estates are pleasing to God and are ordained by him; but my gospel teaches you how to escape death and be saved. These doctrines will give you more than enough to study as long as you live, and no one will be able to master them completely.

22. And this is also most certainly true: Wherever these two doctrines—the Law and the gospel—remain bright and clear and are correctly understood, there are two great lights which God created to rule over the day and the night, the sun and the moon, will continue to shine, and there you can distinguish between light and darkness. The gospel of Christ is the sun, the Law is the moon. The moon is like a bronze kettle when the sun is not shining. If you do not have

the gospel, the Law inspires fear and terror. But when the sun's light is reflected by the moon it, too, is a brilliant and shining light. The moon rules by night, the sun rules by day; the Law guides us through this temporal life, while the gospel guides us to eternal life. So long as these two lights are shining, you can distinguish between day and night, between light and darkness; but when these two lights disappear, you have total night, complete darkness, absolute blackout.

EIGHTEENTH SUNDAY AFTER TRINITY

*Third Sermon**

Matthew 22:34–46

1. There are three things in this Gospel meriting our attention, each actually worth a sermon by itself. The first is about the Sadducees, whose tongues the Lord silenced; the second, about the two chief commandments, to love God and one's neighbor; the third and final point, about Christ, who he really is, and whence he comes.

2. The first point treats of the Sadducees, who maintained that there is no resurrection. They addressed this question to Jesus: We know of seven brothers each of whom, in turn and in succession, were married to the same woman and then died, and last of all, the woman also died. Now, then, the question is, Whose wife will she be in the resurrection? for they had all married her.

3. The Lord replies and rebukes them, jarring them as he says, You are fools, "not knowing the scriptures, nor the power of God!"

4. He reproaches them, first of all, for not knowing God's power. You Sadducees think, he says, that in the resurrection of the dead and in life to come there will continue to be marriages and children be born. In other words, you think God's creation of man and woman is as far as God's power extends. You think God has no more might and power than what he requires for governing this present earthly existence. If that is your opinion, as is plainly the case, then indeed you are most despicable individuals because you limit God's power to empirical, created things in the world around us. God's power is not limited in this way to things like constituting marriage, rearing children, and so forth. Such things won't carry over into the life to come; all that will come to an end. You are fools for restricting and limiting the power of our Lord God in this way, as though he were

---

* Preached at home on the Sunday after St. Michael's Day, 1534.

unable to do any more than what occurs in this life. You want to gauge God's power according to your reason, contrary to what is right. By so entangling yourself in gross error, you plainly show you do not understand God's power. True, in the resurrection men and women will exist, but there will be no marriages and domestic life. It will be an altogether different existence, a life in which no one will marry or be given in marriage. You believe that things will always be like at the present on earth, with its natural, physical, animal existence. But your thinking is pure folly. "Ye do err, not knowing . . . the power of God." There will be a spiritual, heavenly life, and the elect will be like the angels of God in heaven.

5. He rebukes them, secondly, for not knowing the Scripture, asking them whether they have never read that God (Exod. 3) called to Moses out of the burning bush and said (v. 5): "Draw not nigh hither: put off thy shoes from off thy feet, for the place whereon thou standest is holy ground"; and further (v. 6): "I am the God of thy father, the God of Abraham, the God of Isaac, and the God of Jacob." In other words, You Jews read the Scripture every day and, therefore, you ought to comprehend these things. However, just as you do not understand God's power, so you also do not understand the Scripture. This was an extremely sharp and severe rebuke because they ostensibly were the doctors and teachers of the people, and yet did not comprehend the Holy Scripture, which they read every day, nor God's power. If you were learned and versed in the Scripture, says Christ, you would realize that if God is the God of Abraham, the God of Isaac, and the God of Jacob, then Abraham, Isaac, and Jacob must still live. For God cannot be a God of dead people who don't exist; he is a God of the living. Were God a God of the dead, he would be like the husband who has no wife, or the father who has no son, or the master who has no servant. For if he is a husband, he must have a wife; if a father, he must have a son; if a master, he must have a servant; or he would merely be an imaginary husband, father, or master—in reality, nothing! That is the case here also. Were Abraham, Isaac, and Jacob dead, or nonexistent, God could then not be their God. You should have come to that conclusion yourselves, were you really well versed in the Scripture. But since you disagree, you show that you really don't understand it.

6. Thus the Lord stops the mouths of Sadducees and validates the article on the resurrection from the Scripture, stating, "God is not the God of the dead, but of the living; God is the God of Abraham, Isaac, and Jacob." Hence, it follows that Abraham, Isaac, and Jacob are not dead before God but live forever; else God could not be their God. For he is not a painted or sculpted God, or a phantasm, but in very truth and essence, the eternal, omnipotent God. If, now, he is the God of Abraham, Isaac, and Jacob, then Abraham, Isaac, and Jacob must be alive before him; otherwise he would not be their God.

7. Indeed, had the Sadducees said, as the Epicureans of our day do, But we don't see Abraham, Isaac, and Jacob in the flesh; how can it be that they are still alive? Hold on, you base individuals, you don't see the holy angels alive either, but does that, therefore, mean the beloved angels don't exist? If that were true, then nothing would be alive which you and I do not see. But the rule you ought to follow is not just to believe in what you see, but what God tells you in his Word. Now, in his Word God says that Abraham, Isaac, and Jacob have a God; and, moreover, that Abraham, Isaac, and Jacob are the people of God. So, if Abraham, Isaac, and Jacob are the people of God, and God is their God, it then follows that Abraham, Isaac, and Jacob are not dead but alive. For God is not a God like heathen idols, nor a figment of the imagination, unconnected to reality, with no one to call upon and serve him.

8. A person ought to know what "a God" denotes and what it means "to have a God." God signifies the one from whom we should expect and receive every good thing. Accordingly, "to have a God" is nothing else than to trust and believe in him with all our hearts, call on him in time of need, worship, and serve him. Otherwise, were he utterly to himself, completely unconcerned with anything and anyone, we could expect nothing good from him; he would be a god of stone and straw. However, it is in his nature as God that we may expect and receive from him every good thing, and call upon him to deliver us in every need. Were he to sit in heaven like a solitary block of wood, he would not be God. But Scripture says that God is the God of Abraham, Isaac, and Jacob; therefore, Abraham, Isaac, and Jacob must expect and receive from God not only this temporal life, but life eternal as well. If Abraham, Isaac, and Jacob now have eter-

nal life from God, they must also be alive with God. To the world they are dead, but with God they are not dead.

9. Therefore, this Gospel emphatically affirms that with God there is life, even though before the world everything has died. God looks upon the death of all men like the sleep of an infant slumbering at rest in its cradle. It is not eating, then, or drinking, and doing things like a living person, but sleeping like a log, dead to the world, except for the sound of its breathing. Of course, the mother does not think of the child as dead, but alive. Now someone who's alive is supposed to eat, drink, stand, walk, and be active in the way a living person ordinarily is. We must not confuse the issue. For although a man who is asleep is not busy with things like a person who is alive, yet we do not say, This man is dead, but, alive, even though all his activity as a living person has ceased. Now, in the selfsame way, as we think of those who slumber, God speaks about those who have died. He says, To me those lying in the grave are not dead; to you humans they are, of course, but in my own time I shall awaken and raise them from the dead.

10. That means that the resurrection is firmly established in Holy Scripture. Had you examined Scripture closely, Christ says to the Sadducees, you would have found in it the article of the resurrection. And had you given any thought to God's power, you would not have had such insolent thoughts nor asked so stupidly about marrying and being given in marriage in the resurrection; but you would have realized that life then will not be as it is now on earth; Abraham will not marry Sarah again, nor will Isaac take Rebekah again in marriage. To the glory of our God, you should have believed that he was able to create more than this life here on earth. But you raise the kind of questions which doubting fools do, who understand neither God's Word nor God's work. Now then, this is the first point: the Lord silences the Sadducees by means of God's Word and mighty acts.

11. The second point in this Gospel is about the Pharisees. They hear that the Lord has squelched the Sadducees; for this reason they put their heads together in order to preen themselves and their reputation by asking this country bumpkin of a teacher a biting, sarcastic question. But they trip over their own feet, and, like the Sadducees, prove themselves dunces and insolent smarties. They, however, regard themselves as sharp and subtle, addressing the Lord with a test

question: Dear sir, master and teacher, we would like you to hear us out; we are not as insolent as the Sadducees. We know God's Word and acts, things which the Sadducees do not comprehend. We understand the Scripture and God's power; we are the recognized teachers of the people. Now, then, tell us, "Which is the great commandment in the law?"

12. This is the question they pose to him. They think he won't really be able to handle or answer it. For among them the question of the first and greatest commandment or work was an issue of debate, just as in the papacy the greatest question has been, What is the highest estate? As a result, the pope's law has been more highly regarded and feared than God's commandment and Word, and monks adhere more firmly to the scapular than to God's fourth and fifth commandments. Similarly, among the Jews, it was not God's commandment about loving God and the neighbor that was foremost, but human traditions, the temple, the gold ornamentation in the temple, the altar, sacrifices, fasting, washing of hands, and so forth. They had fostered and promoted these traditions above everything and forsaken God's commandment and Word. The first and greatest in their thinking was to offer sacrifice to the Lord God in the temple, to adorn the temple with gold, and so forth. For if there were no temple and no sacrifice, God's glory and service would be tarnished. Therefore, to them, the first and foremost had to be the temple and the sacrifices.

13. Harboring such presuppositions, they now interrogate the Lord, thinking: If he names something other than the temple and sacrifice as the first and greatest, we can then say that he doesn't know how to answer our question. Just like today, if someone were to ask the pope what is better, to build churches or to give a poor man a coat? the pope would answer: In the church there are many good things happening, preaching, praying, singing, saying of Masses, and so forth; accordingly, to give alms is nothing compared to building churches or other works performed in the church. The Pharisees, too, thought that the Lord would surely answer: The first and greatest commandment is to maintain and adorn the temple and to offer sacrifices in the temple.

14. But Christ gets right to the point—he is an especially adept communicator—and immediately responds: The first and greatest

thing one can do is not adorning the temple or offering sacrifices, but to love God with all one's heart and the neighbor as oneself. I know that you Pharisees would have been very happy if I had answered that what the priests perform in the temple is the highest thing. But I will not do that; rather I shall cite as foremost the basic, ordinary things which God has commanded for everyone to do, namely, to love God and one's neighbor, in keeping with what he commanded through Moses.

15. The Lord's reply is especially irksome, that the everyday routine works which people are commanded to do, namely, that they are to love God and the neighbor, supersede all other works, regardless of how they shine and glitter. The fact is, not only the Pharisees among the Jews, and the hypocrites under the papacy, have regarded human traditions as more important than God's commandments; for there is a little monk that sticks in all of us from youth on. We, too, regard the ordinary works God has commanded as insignificant, but the special, diverse works done by the Carthusians, monks, and hermits, about which God has commanded nothing, as especially noteworthy.

16. However, our Lord God is averse to such distinction. He does not prefer one before another, nor does he exclude anyone from serving him, no matter how lowly he might be. Instead, he enjoins upon everyone to exercise love to God and his neighbor. Since God seeks nothing extraordinary from us and tolerates no distinctions, we must conclude that when a maid, who has faith in Christ, dusts the house her work is more pleasing in service to God than that of St. Anthony in the wilderness. That is Christ's meaning here. This is the highest commandment: to love God and one's neighbor. God is not concerned about the rules of the Franciscans, Dominicans, or other monks, but wants us to serve him obediently and love the neighbor. They may consider their monastic rules to be something wonderful and special, but before God they are nothing. The very highest, best, and holiest work is when one loves God and the neighbor, whether a person is a monk or nun, priest or layperson, great or small.

17. If that is not speaking German, I don't know what German is. It is the Lord's own mouth and word, the master and teacher of the whole world who says this. Therefore, we dare not gainsay it. The only thing that counts is whether a person believes in Christ and is

God-fearing; that is the issue here; not whether he is a tailor or shoemaker, farmer or burgher, aristocrat or commoner. If he believes in Christ and is God-fearing and serves his neighbor, he is a living saint and abides by the greatest commandment, and does the highest and best work.

18. This, however, is something most people refuse to see. They always look for something special and impressive. You have to strive for this and that, says the monk; you must dress this way, you must distinguish between the things you eat and drink. Loving God and the neighbor are ordinary works which also the laity can do. But if you want to be perfect, you must strive for higher things and undertake something special. Indeed! may your fortune be bright, you shameful fellow! Is Christ our Lord lying to you? Does he not know as much as you, and what the first and highest commandment and work are? Christ states, There is no greater commandment or work than loving God and the neighbor. Accordingly, in this way these shameful fellows make their attack, accuse him of lies, contradict him, and say, Not so! Monasticism, monastic discipline, privation in the wilderness, and so forth, these are the best and greatest works.

19. We, therefore, must learn to think and answer like this: Not something extraordinary, but to love God and your neighbor, that is the best way of life! If I do that, I don't have to be searching for another way. It is so very true that loving God and the neighbor is the greatest and best work, even though it appears to be so very ordinary and insignificant. Such acts occur quite spontaneously without special and deep cogitation. But people always reach for something different and want to be something special in the sight of others, meanwhile neglecting what God has commanded, leaving these undone, without even lifting a finger. But our Lord God says, Act contrary, if you will, but know that whatever you yourselves purpose and propose to do is unacceptable to me since I have not commanded it. The end result is that when you prefer your own way, no matter how devout and earnest, you are departing more and more from the way and life which I hold to be best.

20. But that's the way it has always been, and is so today yet; the world assays to do things its own way and disdains the excellent works about which Christ speaks here. The Pharisees were unable to

decipher this text; they were like blind people, who didn't comprehend or see even though they read the words. The pope and his band are doing the same thing today. If you ask him what the greatest commandment is, he replies, The best work is to build churches and chapels, to read the psalter, to wander in the wilderness, befriending and serving no one, but becoming a hermit or monk. That's the way to peace and quiet; you can read the Bible, pray, and serve God. However, that is not the way it should be! We must here listen to the master and preceptor of the whole world, the one who is to be hearkened to before all others. What he says is this, The greatest work, the noblest life, and the holiest walk is for one to exercise love to God and the neighbor.

21. Therefore, what will happen on Judgment Day is that many a maidservant who did not know whether she had done anything good all her life will be preferred before a Carthusian monk who has the appearance of great holiness and yet has loved neither God nor his neighbor. There God will pronounce this sentence: This maid has served her mistress in harmony with my commandment, has looked after the house, and so forth; since she has done this in faith, she shall be saved; but, Carthusian, you did what you wanted to do, serving no one but yourself and your own idol; therefore, you are damned. That will be the verdict on Judgment Day. And it serves the world right. It considers our Lord God a fool, who does not know what a holy life is all about, and fancies that it knows everything better than what God has enjoined in his Word. Isn't it right that lightning and thunder strike there? Since the world will have it no other way, it serves the world quite right to be deceived and misled when it renounces the works which have been commanded by God and prefers other, foolish works which have not been enjoined by him. Why does it not listen to God's Word and follow his commandment obediently?

22. We should mark well that on Judgment Day our Lord God will not judge the world according to each person's opinion but according to this commandment which is the first and highest in the Law. When a person assays to judge by externals in his life as to which work is the best, he ought not measure it in line with his own self-chosen devotions (how he fasts, prays, and so forth), but according to what he does out of love for God and his neighbor's benefit. The one

who proceeds according to this rule occupies the highest estate. This is what Christ teaches here, and on Judgment Day he will judge accordingly. Then it will do no good to say that so many holy fathers taught and lived differently. For here is the master and preceptor who excels by far above all popes, fathers, and saints; and this is the way it should be. For he is the one whom God the Father sent down from heaven to be preceptor and teacher, upon whose head he has placed the biretta and said, "Hear ye him." Therefore, we too should be pupils of this doctor and approve what he says. Whatever is done contrary to his Word and doctrine is condemned.

23. The third point in this Gospel is about faith, how and whereby we should achieve love toward God and the neighbor, namely, alone through Christ who is David's son and Lord, and who sits at God's right hand until he makes all his enemies his footstool. But it would take too long to discuss that at this time; therefore, we shall leave it at this. Amen.

NINETEENTH SUNDAY AFTER TRINITY

1533*

Matthew 9:1–8

And he entered into a ship, and passed over, and came into his own city. And, behold, they brought to him a man sick of the palsy; lying on a bed: and Jesus seeing their faith said unto the sick of the palsy: Son, be of good cheer; thy sins be forgiven thee. And, behold, certain of the scribes said within themselves, This man blasphemeth. And Jesus knowing their thoughts said, Wherefore think ye evil in your hearts? For whether is easier, to say, Thy sins be forgiven thee; or to say, Arise, and walk? But that ye may know that the Son of man hath power on earth to forgive sins, (then saith he to the sick of the palsy,) Arise, take up thy bed, and go unto thine house. And he arose, and departed to his house. But when the multitudes saw it, they marvelled, and glorified God, which had given such power unto men.

1. From today's Gospel we learn about the wondrously gracious ministry of the word which God has given to mankind here upon earth, a word we can speak to one another, namely, Your sins are forgiven unto you! Wonder of wonders to every God-fearing person and something for which to thank God from the bottom of our hearts, because he has given such power unto people! It truly is a mighty power when one Christian can say to another, Dear brother, be unafraid, God is gracious to you; only believe what he promises, as I declare it to you in Jesus' name, for it is as valid as if God himself were saying to you, Your sins are forgiven.

2. Such power began, as we hear in this account, with Christ himself, and it continues for mankind, especially with those who occupy the pastoral office and are duty bound to preach repentance and the forgiveness of sins in Jesus' name. Nevertheless, every Christian has the command, not only that he can, but should, say to you when you

---

*Preached at home, October 19, 1533.

are troubled by your sin: Why are you troubled? As your fellow Christian, I say to you, you are not fair to yourself, for God is not ungracious toward you; you ought to trust these words just as surely as though God were speaking to you personally from heaven, never questioning them because of the person of the one from whom you hear them.

3. Everything depends on your receiving the promise as true, that God, for Christ's sake, wants to be gracious to you. That is why the Lord, in the first place, exhorts the man sick with palsy to believe, saying, "Son, be of good cheer, thy sins be forgiven thee." Immediately, as soon as the afflicted man believed, he had the forgiveness of his sins.

4. Similarly, when the pastor or another Christian declares to you, God is not angry with you; now don't you be angry with him, for he has forgiven you all your sins for the sake of his Son, Jesus Christ, and so you should believe this pledge with all your might. Better to be torn apart rather than to doubt it! For if you doubt and do not believe, the absolution is of no benefit, even if God himself with all his angels were to speak it with his own mouth over you.

5. For the fact is that when we refuse to believe, we disdain God as a deceiver, as though the things he declares to us were not true, that he can and wants to do them for us. May God graciously keep us from such unbelief and sin. The devil is an extraordinary master at getting us to call God a liar and refuse to believe his promise. An unbelieving heart dishonors God and makes him a liar.

6. A believing heart, on the other hand, honors God with the highest possible honor due him, for it regards him as trustworthy, as incapable of lying, as one who certainly fulfills what he promises. That is why Christ is very pleased with these people who brought the man sick with palsy to him, because they showed their confidence in his ability to help the man. Tenderly he addresses him, My son, you are ill; the devil has afflicted you with crippling palsy, and God has permitted it to happen to you, a sinful human being; as a result your conscience is troubled and you think, God is angry with me; what can I do? It is but natural that we fear when we perceive God's judgment.

7. But, my son, Jesus is saying, Don't let such thoughts sink too deeply in your heart. Don't think thoughts like this: What does God

care about me? Who knows whether he will be gracious to me, or not? What, after all, am I to God? Don't look at your illness but listen to me when I say, Your sins are forgiven you. Therefore, say rather, Palsy, so what! My sins are forgiven, and I'll not let palsy or any other illness divert me from this faith.

8. Word and faith are correlatives; the one is never without the other. If a person has faith without the Word, he believes like the Turk or the Jew; they believe that God is benevolent and good, but they are without the promise, for God will not be gracious apart from Christ. Contrariwise, whoever has the Word but no faith, for him the Word avails nothing. Therefore, both belong together, Word and faith, like marriage partners, and they must not be separated.

9. Now, M.S.* believes that the Apocalypse, Christ's return, is to occur today, on this very day. Such belief is pure delusion; indeed, there is not a grain of truth in it. A Turk expects to enjoy Mohammed's salvation, but it is a pure lie; there is not a grain of truth in it either. Well, now, the pope believes that a Christian must be raised to heaven by his works, but this is a false faith; for missing are the Word and the promise. Thus it can well be that one has faith, but, since it is lacking the Word, it is not true faith, but a mere delusion since nothing will ever come of it.

10. We Christians do not lack for the Word. God's grace has given it to us purely and unadulterated. But we are lacking in faith. We who have the Word at times do not believe and trust as firmly as those who don't have the Word. This is the devil's doing, the result of original sin which causes us to be drawn away from the Word and the truth, toward believing the lie rather. In short, it is the devil's fraud and our flesh's deception because our natures are so corrupted by original sin. When the Word is absent, we have faith galore; but when we have the Word, it is only with great difficulty that we ward off unbelief. That's because our flesh and our reason want to have

---

*The reference is to Michael Stifel, a pastor at Lochau, who had predicted Christ's imminent return for October 19 of this year, 1533. He caused considerable stir among the people of his parish and neighboring regions, and had to be censored and relieved of his post. Luther dealt with him in kindly manner, seeking to show an otherwise faithful preacher the error of his ways in trying to be a date-setter of the Apocalypse. (Cf. M. Brecht, *Martin Luther,* Vol. 2, pp 8-9.)

nothing to do with the Word; they are willing to believe only what they want to believe.

11. It is also the evil spirit's doing that we find ourselves dead in the water spiritually; otherwise our hearts would be joyful and comforted. For think what it would mean if we rightly and truly believed that what Christ here says to the man sick with palsy, he is saying to you and to me every day in baptism, in absolution, and in public preaching, that I must not mistakenly think that God is angry and ungracious toward me. Shouldn't that cause me to stand on my head with joy? Wouldn't that make everything sweet as sugar, pure as gold, sheer everlasting life? The fact that this doesn't happen for us proves that the "old Adam" and the devil drag us away from faith and the Word.

12. Therefore, let us learn that both things need to be there: You must have the Word, and faith must cling to the Word, never questioning it in any way. You then have everything the Word promises and which you require for support of body and soul. Those who don't have the Word are strong in faith too, but they believe only as much as by nature they're inclined to believe, preferring to believe a lie. That's the way it is with the human heart ever since the devil corrupted our nature in Paradise.

13. Accordingly, the pope and his adherents believe very strongly in Masses, in the merits of saints, in intercessions, in monastic vows, singing, fasting, and the like. The Turk believes steadfastly in his Koran; but it is a false faith, and for this reason it is so steadfast. Speaking with propriety, harlots and scoundrels are together at this point: the heart is the harlot; false faith is the scoundrel. We, however, we who—praise God!—have a chaste bride (for the Word is ever pure and good), are unable to believe so firmly and steadfastly. And, yet, by rights we ought to because we have the Word; contrariwise, the others ought not believe steadfastly because they do not have the Word. The fault, you see, lies with our "old Adam" and the devil that, on account of original sin we turn away from the Word and the truth, to believe the lie.

14. First, therefore, we are to learn from today's Gospel lesson that we must possess the Word; and, then second, that we must firmly believe it. It is by divine power that we have forgiveness of sin and

salvation here and now. If the Word is not there, then faith is like that of the Enthusiasts, Zwingli, Carlstadt, the Anabaptists, Turks, Jews, and the pope. That's a faith inherited out of the fall of Adam, that is, a lying faith, bereft of the Word, a fraud to which people cling more tightly than to the Word.

15. But now, as our dear Lord Jesus addresses the afflicted man and forgives him his sins, the scribes begin to speak among themselves, "This man blasphemeth," saying that he can forgive sins. This is an important point, which we must duly note. For we see the same thing in Zwingli, the Enthusiasts, and all the fantastic spirits, how they err and fail to understand in what way forgiveness of sin comes about. Similarly, the pope and all his doctors of theology fail to understand what absolution is, for all of popedom rests on this article: Grace is infused into people in a mystical way, and whoever wants to have it must be sorry, be contrite, and make satisfaction.

16. But if you ask, What do absolution and the keys accomplish? then they answer that it is an external power belonging to the church. So, forgiveness of sins is not grounded upon the Word and faith, where it ought to be, but upon contrition, confession, and making satisfaction.

17. The Anabaptists say the same thing: What can baptism do for the forgiveness of sins? A handful of water cannot wash the soul, stated Nicolaus Storck. Thomas Muentzer argued similarly, How can water cleanse the soul? The Spirit must do it. The pope and his monks, likewise, fail to see what power has been given to mankind to forgive sins.

18. Also, the Enthusiasts and Sacramentarians chime in, The Sacrament gives only bread and wine; therefore, one cannot find forgiveness of sin there; the Spirit must give it, the flesh profits nothing. In short, no fantastic spirit, no papist or monk, is able to discern this, that the power to forgive sins is a power God has given to mankind, as stated in this Gospel lesson.

19. You must learn, therefore, to speak of the matter in this way: I know very well and acknowledge that God alone forgives sin. But I must also know and discern the manner, or the means, by which I can be sure that my sins are forgiven. The Scriptures teach every one of us Christians as follows: If I am to have forgiveness of sins, I must

not sit in some corner and say, My God, forgive me my sin, and then, as it were, wait for an angel from heaven to come, to say to me, Your sins are forgiven; but God has deigned to draw near to me by ordaining holy baptism and his Word, that I should be baptized in the name of the Father, and of the Son, and of the Holy Spirit, and he attached his promise along with his command, saying, "Whoever believes and is baptized will be saved."

20. Yes, you say, but isn't baptism just water? True, but not water only, for the Word is connected with it. Therefore, when you go to the parish pastor, who has been given his office or to some other Christian, asking that he comfort you and absolve you from your sin, and he says to you, In the stead of God, I declare to you the forgiveness of all of your sins through Christ, then you may be certain that through the external word your sins are really and truly forgiven. For baptism and the Word do not lie to you.

21. This was not being preached in popedom, nor do papistic preachers understand it even now. Thank God, therefore, for such grace, and learn that God wants to forgive sin. But how? As the text says, in no other way than that he has given such power into men's hands, even as he here declares, and then also commands that it should so be done in his church unto the end of the world.

22. Listen to his mandate (Luke 24:26,46–47): "Ought not Christ to have suffered these things . . . and to rise from the dead the third day: And that repentance and remission of sins should be preached in his name among all nations?" and Matthew 18:18; John 20:23: "Verily, I say unto you . . . whatsoever ye shall loose on earth shall be loosed in heaven," and so on, indicating that we are to seek forgiveness among men, and nowhere else.

23. Therefore, if you want to have forgiveness of sin, do not try to climb into heaven, but go and be baptized, if you are not already, or, if you have been, remember the promise God has made to you in your baptism, be reconciled to your neighbor, and ask that the absolution be declared unto you in Jesus' name. Believe the Word, receive the most venerable Sacrament of the Body and Blood of Christ, so that you may be sure that such priceless treasure is meant for you to have and to enjoy.

24. We must not despise baptism, absolution, preaching, and the Sacrament, but seek and receive forgiveness of sins in this way. That

is why God has ordained that there be pastors, fathers and mothers, and fellow Christians, and he places his Word in their mouths, that we might seek comfort and forgiveness of sins through them. Even though it is just people who speak, nevertheless, it is not just they who speak, but it is God's Word. Therefore, trust it implicitly and do not despise it.

25. When the pastor baptizes a child, think of it this way: God is baptizing that child. When the pastor absolves, it is God speaking, and he has declared this verdict upon me, that I should be free and forgiven of my sin.

26. These are things we must surely learn well, so that when we encounter the shameless, fantastic spirits who cry, What is water? What is the laying on of hands? Do you think that water and the hands can make you clean from sin? Then we can answer, True, water and the hand don't do it of themselves, but the Word of God which is with the water and the pastor's hand. The pastor and servant of the church does not give the water, but God has ordained and given the water, whereby we can be born again into the kingdom of God and be free from our sin.

27. God does the same with the Word, for it is not our Word; and he also gives the faith that trusts the Word. So both are God's work, the Word and faith, that is, the forgiveness of sins and faith. We are to seek the forgiveness of sins in the Word which is spoken by human mouth and in the Sacrament administered by men, and nowhere else.

28. Is there anyone who does not see that the works which I do are far different from the Word and works of God? How can it possibly be that the godless papists seek for the forgiveness of sins in their own works? Therefore, when on the Last Day they parade their works and merits, Christ will put the question to them, But where is my Word? Have I not provided my church with baptism, the Sacrament, absolution, and preaching, so that men might come to have forgiveness of sins and be assured of my grace? Why did you not hold on to these? They would not have failed you, as your works must and will fail you.

29. This is the lesson I wanted you to learn, in order that you might know what forgiveness of sins is and where to find it. You need

not scramble here and there for it, except to the Christian church, for it possesses the Word and Sacrament. There you will certainly find it, and not up in heaven, as the Pharisees thought. They charge Christ with blasphemy against God because he forgave sin, something only God could do. Guard against such thoughts and reply, God has placed the forgiveness of sins in baptism, the Lord's Supper, and the Word; in fact, he has placed it in the mouth of every Christian, to comfort and pronounce to you God's grace for the sake of Christ's vicarious satisfaction. You can receive it nowhere else, for this is tantamount to Christ himself speaking it with his own mouth as he does here to the palsied man.

30. For this reason the fanatics and enthusiasts, Zwingli, Oecolampadius, and their adherents, and, similarly, also the Anabaptists, err perilously when they sever the forgiveness of sins from the Word. One might do such a thing if it were the word and water from man. But here it is God's Word and God's water. However, since they turn away from God's Word, they deprive themselves and others—who let themselves be influenced—of all the blessings, the forgiveness of sins, baptism, the Lord's Supper, the Lord Christ, and retain nothing but the mere husks of baptism and the Lord's Supper. In like manner, since the Anabaptists repudiate their neighbors, run away from wife and children, condemn government, reject Christian estates and offices, they thus deprive themselves also of all Christian, godly works. For whoever repudiates his neighbor retains no one on whom he could exercise Christian love.

31. Accordingly, fanatics and enthusiasts have lost Christ, baptism, the Lord's Supper, the pulpit, the Christian church, and all else. They do not want to hear public preaching of the Word. Preaching by men, they esteem no higher than the bellowing of a cow. If then God chose to speak through a cow or another animal, what would be wrong with that? He once spoke through an ass, you know. Should one for this reason despise his Word and refuse to acknowledge its validity? No! He is now speaking to us through men; but even though it is the voice of a man, it still is God's Word and, at the same time, the forgiveness of sins is certainly present there.

32. We need to learn this, so that we are prepared when we meet enthusiasts, like Muentzer, Zwingli, and the like; also the pope, who

in all of his books teaches none of this, nor even understands it. According to his doctrine, when a man falls into sin, his baptism no longer avails. If he seeks forgiveness, he must do penance, be contrite, and make satisfaction for his sins through good works. This is how they teach concerning repentance. A fine theology, indeed, over which the devil laughs, because it does him no hurt!

33. True, I must be repentant and sincerely endeavor to leave off from sin. But I don't come to forgiveness of sins thereby. What is the way? Only by trusting the Word and promise, by believing in Christ who is preached to me by his ordained servants, yes, even by all Christians. To their mouths I look, and not to my contrition and doing of penance. Whatever God imposes upon me, I must bear, but the Word should alone console me, which Christ has entrusted to the parish pastor and brethren to speak.

34. That is how they subvert things: They abandon the Word, do not consider the fact that the ministers of the church or a fellow Christian speaks at the command of our Lord Christ, and they are concerned only with their own contrition and confession. But in so doing they lose Christ and all that Christ means for them, so it is impossible for them properly to comfort and assist a troubled soul. For the Word, which alone can be of help, they have lost, and they point people instead to their own contrition and piety.

35. You, however, are being instructed here that you can speak thus about the forgiveness of sins and can teach others that in baptism, in absolution, from the pulpit and in the Holy Supper, God is speaking to us through ministers of the church and other Christians. We should believe this, and then we will find the forgiveness of sins, which under the papacy was covered in silence, for in all the papal bulls there is not one letter written about it; they focus only on contrition and make forgiveness of sins contingent on that. What we have said here pertains to the fact that God has given to mankind the power to forgive sins. Now we would also like to take a brief look at the narrative in our text.

36. The palsied man serves as a paradigm of all sinners, for it is the nature of this illness that it incapacitates the members of the body; one can no longer flex the foot or hand or draw it upwards to oneself, but these become rigid and stretched out. Aristotle in his

Ethics, for example, compares the physical condition of such an afflicted person to an ill-bred, unruly youth who, likewise, is uncontrolled in his actions.

37. By nature we are all palsied. The more we try to draw close to God and be reconciled with him through our works, the farther from him we get; and the more our hand pushes him away, the greater becomes the trepidation in us. I must confess concerning myself that when I think I can do things very well on my own, I'm actually making things much worse, because I'm not acting in faith.

38. If, therefore, we want to be helped in this dilemma, we need to look away from our works and trust in Christ who is able to help us wondrously. He says to us, "Be of good cheer, my son, your sins are forgiven you." With such word the limbs again become strong and sound, capable of helping us to carry a load, as happened here with the palsied man whom Christ healed physically, having bestowed the forgiveness of sins upon him.

39. The palsied man lay before him helpless, as is the nature of that illness, much like a slaughtered pig with all fours stretched out straight. But at Christ's word he immediately stood up, sound and healthy. And in order that people might know that the Son of man had power on earth to forgive sins he said to the man, "Arise, take up thy bed, and go unto thine house." By this wonderful miracle he demonstrated to them that he had power on earth to forgive sins.

40. Very plainly he says, "on earth," in order that we should not gaze to heaven, or, as the pope has taught, hope for forgiveness of sins through other people's work and merits after we have died and are in purgatory. He clearly states that power has been given to men on earth to forgive sins, when a person baptizes, administers the Sacrament, absolves, and preaches from the pulpit. He declares that whatever is loosed or forgiven on earth is loosed in heaven. Contrariwise, whatever is bound upon earth (that is, apart from baptism, absolution and the Sacrament) is bound in heaven.

41. God's glory is not taken from him, nor other gods created, through the exercise of this power, as some uninformed people assert, for we are simply carrying out this office. If you believe his Word, then you have the power of the Word; reject his Word, and you have nothing. God has bound us together through this office, so

NINETEENTH SUNDAY AFTER TRINITY

that one Christian can comfort another as a concerned friend, and the other by his faith can know that he has the forgiveness of sins in Christ's name, as long as the Word is rightly proclaimed. That's what leading a man to God and the forgiveness of sins means. Whoever dies in such faith dies well and will be saved.

42. However, as in the papacy, the one who dies invoking the saints, his own merits, and those of other men, that person dies a wretched and sorry death. For he has no attendants assigned and given him by God, that is to say, he has no devout pastor, no faithful brother, no true Word and absolution. And even though he has been baptized, he does not know how to derive comfort from it. It is the devil who, through the pope, has given rise to this calamity—and now advances it further by the help of the fanatics—for he cannot tolerate the Word; it is offensive to him.

43. As a result the pope has silenced it and, instead, instituted monastic orders, Masses, pilgrimages, indulgences, and the like. These things the devil can well tolerate, for they do him no harm. Into the bargain, the Anabaptists lend aid when they speak so contemptuously of baptism; in the same way, also, the Sacramentarians, Zwingli and his adherents, who speak so contemptuously about the Lord's Supper, as though nothing but bread and wine were there.

44. All of them are striving to take these blessed doctrines away from us. Therefore, be wary of them and learn that forgiveness of sins exists only where the Word is found, and nowhere else. However, this Word is in baptism, in the Lord's Supper, in absolution, and preaching. Accordingly, forgiveness of sins is there as well, notwithstanding what someone might say to the contrary. Where now the Word is, there faith must be; and there the elbow, which before this the palsied man could not bend, he now flexes easily and surely. But where the Word is not present, there the palsy remains, and as a result there can be no grasping rightly to hold.

45. I have spoken at length about this because the pope and the bold fanatics have caused so much havoc that everyone must be on guard. The pope directs neither to the Word nor to the sacraments; so also the fanatics can do nothing but speak contemptuously of the Word and sacraments and merely cry, Spirit! Spirit! But we know that the Holy Spirit does not want to carry on his work apart from the

Word and sacraments. For this reason we dare not disdain the Word and sacraments, but we should cherish them as the very best and noblest of treasures.

46. May God grant us his grace to hold fast to this doctrine, persevere in it to the end, and finally be saved. Amen.

TWENTIETH SUNDAY AFTER TRINITY

First Sermon—1532

Matthew 22:1–14

And Jesus answered and spake unto them again by parables, and said, The kingdom of heaven is like unto a certain king, which made a marriage for his son, And sent forth his servants to call them that were bidden to the wedding: and they would not come. Again, he sent forth other servants, saying, Tell them which are bidden, Behold, I have prepared my dinner: my oxen and my fatlings are killed, and all things are ready: come unto the marriage. But they made light of it, and went their ways, one to his farm, another to his merchandise: And the remnant took his servants, and entreated them spitefully, and slew them. But when the king heard thereof, he was wroth: and he sent forth his armies, and destroyed those murderers, and burned up their city. Then saith he to his servants, The wedding is ready, but they which were bidden were not worthy. Go ye therefore into the highways, and as many as ye shall find, bid to the marriage. So those servants went out into the highways, and gathered together all as many as they found, both bad and good: and the wedding was furnished with guests. And when the king came in to see the guests, he saw there a man which had not on a wedding garment: And he saith unto him, Friend, how camest thou in hither not having a wedding garment? And he was speechless. Then said the king to the servants, Bind him hand and foot, and take him away, and cast him into outer darkness; there shall be weeping and gnashing of teeth. For many are called, but few are chosen.

1. In this Gospel lesson our Lord Jesus Christ warns us to guard against the sin of despising and opposing God's Word. He also gives us an example of those who do, and how horribly God has punished them for scorning his Word and killing his servants. Especially, however, the Lord warns us against the false security which not only causes people to despise God's Word but, at the same time, makes them so cocksure in their own minds about things continuing to go

well with them. That's what is described here concerning the invited guests who did not wish to come to the wedding, and who scorn the wonderful banquet, each going his own way, one to his farm, another to his business. We would not have been surprised if fire from hell had rained down on them; but they go their way and become rich.

2. It's still the same story today. When the precious gospel is expounded, the world plays its little game, becoming worse than it was before, as everybody bustles around with activity. Earlier, before the gospel's advent, they did not carry on like this; but now that they are invited through word of the gospel, they have so many things to do that they cannot attend the wedding banquet. Peasants, burghers, and noblemen alike, with the gospel light beaming, become more avaricious, proud, and arrogant; they show more wantonness and wickedness than before under the darkness of the papacy, cause their parish pastors, who have invited them to this kind of supper, all manner of grief, and become ten times worse than they were under the papacy.

3. Let no one fret about the fact that godless peasants, burghers, and nobles become so proud and cocky, and even trample on God's Word and their parish pastors. It is, of course, upsetting that we have to see, hear, and experience things like this, and some pious folks might think to themselves that since the majority of people in the world despise God and his Word in this way, and yet are prospering, I shall do likewise, for I see that they lack nothing, have enough of everything, are completely at ease, convinced that their conduct is right. Not on your life! Let them despise and ridicule God's Word and cause their preachers all sorts of heartache, but don't you veer off and follow them. Now they are secure, and they do not regard our Lord God as one to be feared. But be on your guard. Our God is, indeed, a gracious host who will dish out goodies for a time, but he does not go on being host to those who do not mend their ways. Today he is biding time, letting burghers and peasants pursue their wantonness, despise the gospel and every bit of earnest admonition and teaching, accumulate money, overcharge people for everything they need—wood, grain, butter, eggs; and yet he remains silent, as if he did not see what was going on. But what about the time when—today or tomorrow—he comes with pestilence and causes people to fall in droves, or with a war and Italian and Spanish mercenaries who

barge into your home, plunder what they find and, in addition, beat you to pulp, literally strangling you, violating your wife and children right in front of your own eyes? while you cry out, Bloody murder! Oh, how could God deal so horribly with us?*

4. Then you will see what kind of pleasure God harbors toward your greed, wantonness, and pride; and the answer will be very plain: Friend, if earlier you got by with being greedy, proud, and wanton, and despising my Word, so now take stock and look behind you at the notches chalked up against you. You have caroused a long time, friend, so now pay up, with your neck here! That's how it will ultimately end. For that reason it would have been well to have desisted beforehand and amended your life, as we are admonished by the Word. But we much preferred despising God's Word and doing what we pleased, and still not have God punish us. Yes, that was the way we preferred it to be.

5. However, some who are invited do not let it rest at disdain, but are so wicked that they seize the servants, treat them shamefully, and finally kill them. With this the Lord is referring especially to Jerusalem; she slew the prophets and ultimately killed the Son of God himself.

6. But what happened? The king became angry and sent out his army—the Romans! They had to be in his service, put to death the murderers, burn the city, and manhandle the Jews so horribly that they were sold more cheaply than sparrows, thirty Jews for a penny, when for a penny one could buy but one sparrow. Pitiful wailing and lament went up from the Jews; how great the injustice, to be so tormented by the heathen! But that is the way they had wanted it; they had caroused for a long time and let preaching fall on deaf ears. Then came the time of accounting for the bill; God no longer was willing to listen to them; he, the father of the house, dealt with them as with serpents and toads. Guard yourself against this.

7. Of course, apart from that, there is a great deal about us that is contrary to our Lord God and justly displeases him—things like anger, impatience, greed, belly-serving, sexual voyeurism, evil lusts,

---

*A prophecy partially fulfilled, according to the editor, in the Smalcald War of 1547, following Luther's death.

fornication, hatred, and other vices which are nothing other than abominable mortal sins—rampant everywhere in the world. But such sins are nothing compared to the terrible disdain of the divine Word, disdain that is so deep and so pervasive, that in truth, greed, stealing, adultery, whoremongering, and so forth, cannot even compare; yes, indeed, these sins would be as nothing if people would only love and esteem God's Word. However, sad to say, the opposite is the case and, as a result, the whole world is inundated by such sins. Peasants and burghers could care less about the gospel; they snarl against it and don't regard that to be sinful. Truly, I am shocked to see how people in the church, on the right and on the left, yawn away, so that out of a great throng there are hardly ten or twelve who are actually present in order to learn something from the preaching.

8. But worse still is the fact that this disregard of God's Word is now so commonplace that this truly terrible, hellish, devilish sin is not even regarded as being sin at all, like other sins. Everyone simply dismisses it as a trifling matter that people fail to listen diligently to preaching; yes, the majority hold that opinion, believing that wine and beer taste just as good when listening to preaching of the Word as at any other time. Nobody is bothered by this, much less does anyone make it a matter of conscience for having such little regard for the beloved Word. This does not happen in connection with other sins, like murder, adultery, and robbery; for with them there is remorse, if not sooner then later, because the heart is horrified and wishes it would never have happened. For no one can regard these things as right. But, for inattention to God's Word, yes, for despising and ridiculing it, for this no one has conscience scruples. But the fact is, the horror of this sin becomes manifest when country and people end up ultimately destroyed as a result of it; for because it remains unrecognized, there can be no repentance or amendment that follows. Witness, for example, what has happened to Jerusalem, Rome, Greece, and other empires.

9. For this reason Germany must also yet pay the piper, for this sin screams continually to heaven, giving God no rest, but causing him in anger to say, I have given you my beloved Son, my greatest and dearest treasure; he would gladly have spoken with you, taught and instructed you unto eternal life. But there is none who will listen

to me; therefore, I must let punishment fall. So the Lord himself testifies in John 3:19: "This is the condemnation, that light is come into the world, and men loved darkness rather than light, because their deeds were evil." In other words, I would gladly have held my tongue relative to all the other sins; however, this is the judgment which breaks the world's neck, because I have sent my Word, but the world does not give a rap about it. That is what deeply displeases me. People are otherwise so full of sins that I would gladly have delivered them from them through my Word; but they do not want this. Now, if they will not listen to my Word, they will then have to listen to the devil's word. I have no other option beside this; and even now they are witnessing what the outcome will be for them.

10. This was the fate of the Christians also in countries lying to our east, e.g., in a great, beautiful land like Hungary, which the Turk brought under his control; it is virtually lost. We Germans, and other nations as well, are barely willing to listen to or tolerate the gospel; as a result, people have to deal with and listen to the devil's sects, the Anabaptists and the Sacramentarians. It is bound to happen. Whoever despises and refuses to hear God's Word will then have to listen to the Turks, the factious spirits, and the devils who proclaim all manner of error. For because it is the worst and greatest sin, it, therefore, also calls for the greatest and severest punishment.

11. Our Lord God would gladly have us fall on our knees before the Word and write it with letters of gold, not only in books but in our hearts. But that's the last thing of all which the world is willing to do; in fact, it can hardly tolerate it being written in books and ringing out from the pulpit; in its heart it wants the devil, and ultimately that will also be the world's fate.

12. Let this, therefore, be a warning. God has plenty and enough reason, because of other sins, to be angry and to punish. But the greatest sin of all is when his Word, wherein forgiveness of sins is proclaimed, is despised and its invitation to his wedding feast is scorned. May everyone who is guilty of this sin be jarred in his conscience, that he is entrenched not in some trivial sin, but in the worst and greatest of sins, one which God will absolutely not tolerate, but will punish most severely.

13. Everyone yammers about the enormous unfaithfulness and the greed now prevailing in the world—how much peasants, burgh-

ers, and noblemen wrangle, scrimp, steal, and rob. This is not a minor matter and cannot, in the long run, be left unpunished. But worse still, surpassing all the rest, is that we who have the gospel snore away during the sermon and then in the same hour amble off to the marketplace by the gate, then into the alehouses, or sit and loll around in the amusement park. Our fellow citizens are steeped in sin up to the ears, despising not only the Word, but also scoffing at the preachers and saying, Our pastor preaches about nothing else but faith, about love, about the cross! And meanwhile they shuffle off to destruction. It breaks my heart to see this happening. God will surely punish them horribly because of this, letting false doctrine and factious spirits engulf them, causing dissension and defection of countless people from God's Word. This has happened in Greece and other countries, where Mohammed now is in control, who teaches them to believe the rubbish offered by the devil, where before they had God's Word but despised it.

14. The same thing happened in Italy, at Rome. At first the doctrine there was right and sound; but when the people opposed it so foolishly and ungratefully, God punished their sin accordingly, causing some to go into monasteries, to become monks and nuns, who tortured themselves to death in the name of the devil, and others to pilgrimage themselves to death and, instead of divine truth, to believe gross, shameful, and pernicious lies until everything was dismantled and corrupted. Such punishment is again on the way (for this sin must be punished, physically and spiritually, physically with sword and fire, spiritually with error and seduction). Today the devil tosses in the Sacramentarians and Anabaptists, who virtually eliminate baptism and the Lord's Supper, all of it so nicely contributing to total erosion of doctrine. Why is it that people do not want to stay with the Word and gratefully cling to it?

15. We must, therefore, learn to guard against this sin, esteem God's Word highly, and hearken to it diligently and gladly. In fact, we have to do this if for no other reason than God has commanded it and by it we show our love and service to him. For serving such a mighty Lord is no small matter and he is able to reward us richly. Each Christian, therefore, should diligently devote himself to such service and think: Since my Lord and God so wants me to hear his

Word and regards this service so highly that he readily accepts it as a service pleasing to him, I shall gladly render it, proclaim, hear, read, and learn his Word, so that I also may be able to boast that at least for a day or an hour I have served my God. This should be reason enough to draw us to the Word. For to serve such a great Lord, as God is, is a wonderful thing. All of us, therefore, ought be ready to say, Dear God, daily you shower countless kindnesses on me; therefore, since you want me to give ear to your Word, I shall in service to you and to your glory diligently and earnestly do so and be careful not to despise it. That would be reason enough.

16. But, in fact, there are still other and greater reasons. For God promises: If you diligently hear and keep my Word, you will vanquish the devil; he will have to flee from you and will not dare to draw near you. For where my Word is, there I am also; moreover, where I am, there the devil cannot be but must make himself scarce.

17. Further, by this you will also be benefitted in having your sins forgiven you, and your heart regenerated and enkindled with true devotion and rightful obedience. For there you will hear nothing but good tidings, how you may overcome death and obtain eternal life. In short, my Word will show you the way to heaven and bring you to eternal life. That is why I bid you thus to serve me, because the fruit and the benefit are all yours. Yet, apart from that, you would be obligated, if I ask something from you, to do it for my sake. In fact, right now I am doing it for your sake and bid from you the kind of service, which for the most part you will enjoy doing. It is similar to what we experience when we occupy ourselves for a time with the Ten Commandments or the Lord's Prayer; we always discover new benefit, finding and learning something we were not aware of before.

18. And if there is no other blessing, at least there is always this, that the devil cannot abide with you, nor is he able to harm you. For this reason no Christian should think himself so smart that he says he already knew the Lord's Prayer and the Ten Commandments very well before this; rather, if such a thought crosses your mind, then rather cross yourself and say, May my God preserve me, so that I am not without his Word for a single day! For if that should happen, then the devil will for sure come at me; and so, although I have already prayed today, I shall now pray again. For you need always to drive

the devil and sin away, and render service to our Lord God. If you do not do that, you do our Lord God a grievous disservice; and who wants to be exposed to the wrath of such a mighty Lord?

19. But, unfortunately, most people are headed that way, paying virtually no attention to the Word. If today or tomorrow the plague or war comes, our Lord God will say, I am not listening to you again; since you do not want to listen to me when I speak, I shall no longer listen to your screaming and howling, as it is written in the Proverbs of Solomon (1:24–30): "Because I have called, and ye refused; I have stretched out my hand, and no man regarded; But ye have set at nought all my counsel, and would none of my reproof: I also will laugh at your calamity; I will mock when your fear cometh; When your fear cometh as desolation, and your destruction cometh as a whirlwind; when distress and anguish cometh upon you. Then shall they call upon me, but I will not answer; they shall seek me early, but they shall not find me: For that they hated knowledge, and did not choose the fear of the LORD: They would none of my counsel: they despised all my reproof." In other words, this sin will be fearfully punished.

20. When on some future day you come up with a bloody head, our Lord God will laugh up his sleeve and say, Yes, indeed! You didn't want it any other way. I preached to you in all seriousness, but you would not listen to me. So now listen to the devil! If you do not want to listen to my Son, Jesus Christ, who says, "Come unto me, all ye that labor and are heavy laden, and I will give you rest," then listen to your fellow compatriot who swears by mighty oaths and curses by St. Valentine against you, and runs you through with a spear, which is what you deserve. Why do you despise God's Word in this way, the Word to which you ought to be hearkening and be guided to your most sacred treasure? Instead you run off to your farm, where you have things to do, preventing you from listening to the preacher's sermon. Don't you think this grieves God? Besides he has given you six days in which you may work and earn your livelihood; he desires no more than the seventh day, when you should glorify him and serve him with the best you have; instead, he is unable to get this service from you.

21. We must, therefore, mark this Gospel well. Very earnestly the Lord says, "[The king] was wroth: and he sent forth his armies, and destroyed those murderers, and burned up their city." This indicates

how deeply our Lord God is grieved when his Word is despised—surely it ought not surprise anyone!

22. If a powerful prince were to send his son to set free some captives from a dungeon, and they responded by not only refusing to welcome him with joy, but also killing him, and, on top of it, ridiculing the father, do you think that the prince will laugh this off? In one fell swoop he would smash the dungeon and prisoners, and be justified in doing so. So also with our Lord God, who seeks to free us from sin, death, and the devil, and in order that we might inherit eternal life, has the gospel preached and says, Believe in my Son, and you shall have eternal life. Reasonably, we should accept and believe in him, but we turn our backs on him and say, Nonsense! and in the meanwhile go to our farm and to our business, which we deem to be more important to us.

23. Ah! then comes lightning, thunder, pestilence, Turk, mercenary troops, and calamity of all kinds, and it serves us right! To complain and cry murder then will do no good; for, dear fellow, remember how much it pleased our Lord God when you for so long a time robbed him of due service and glory. Squaring one against the other, he should also let you experience the fires of hell for not according to him his glory.

24. It is tantamount to killing the murderers. The king punishes all despisers, but murderers he punishes more severely, as warning to us, not to be scandalized by the common crowd—peasants and burghers, or wicked rogues—into following their example. For nowhere in this world are things any different; the world does not want or desire the Word; it loves its farms and markets more. But woe to the world! We see in the case of the Jews and others the judgment and punishment which will follow in due time.

25. Let us, therefore, not follow their example but gladly and diligently hear the Word and in all good faith regard those who invite to the wedding feast as dear and precious, for the sake of the Lord who sends them out. Then the Lord will be with us in every need, help and protect us, and finally give us eternal life for the sake of his Son, our loving bridegroom, Christ the Lord. What more should he do? He offers us his grace and also faithfully warns us against harming ourselves. If we then are lost, the guilt is not his but ours. May our loving God grant us grace to receive this such faithful admonition and diligently guard us against despising his Word. Amen.

TWENTIETH SUNDAY AFTER TRINITY

Second Sermon—1533

Matthew 22:1–14

1. Dear Christians, in today's Gospel you hear that the kingdom of God is likened to a marriage festival to which guests have been invited. Some of the guests disdain the invitation and stay away, while others deliberately and insolently kill the servants who were sent to invite them to this beautiful wedding.

2. Here, first of all, we are to learn what the words "kingdom of heaven" mean. This is not an earthly but a heavenly kingdom, where God alone is King. It is what we call the Christian church here on earth. The Lord is comparing the kingdom of heaven to a royal marriage, because the Lord Christ, the King's Son, chooses the church as his bride. He is the bridegroom; the Christian church is the bride. God the Father, the King, gives her in marriage to his Son, Jesus Christ, and invites many guests to the wedding. For this reason we say that the kingdom of heaven is also on earth; however, it is not a worldly or temporal kindom, but a spiritual and eternal kingdom. For it so happens that we Christians on earth are more than halfway in the kingdom of heaven, namely, as to soul and spirit, or according to faith.

3. So, whenever you hear of the kingdom of heaven, you should not only gape up to heaven, but keep your eyes fixed right here on earth and look for it among people, everywhere in the world, wherever the gospel is preached, wherever people believe in Christ and the holy sacraments are properly used. In plain words, the "kingdom of heaven" is the kingdom of Christ, the kingdom of the gospel and faith.

4. For where the gospel is, there is Christ. Where Christ is, there are the Holy Spirit and his kingdom, the true kingdom of heaven. It is called the kingdom of heaven because all who believe the Word

and have the Sacrament, and through faith remain in Christ, are heavenly princes and children of God. All that still needs to be done is for our Lord to tear down the wall that still separates, that is, for us to die, whereupon all will be heaven and salvation.

5. So, the first thing we ought to understand is that the kingdom of heaven is the kingdom of our Lord Christ, a kingdom where the Word and faith are to be found. We are in this kingdom through the Word and faith, and have a living hope, cleansed from sin and delivered from death and hell, notwithstanding the habitation that still houses the body and the evil flesh. This tabernacle has as yet not been pulled down; the sinful flesh has not been laid aside. This must first take place. Immediately after that there will be nothing but life, righteousness, and salvation for us.

6. To such a marriage, says Christ, our Lord God invited his people, the Jews, through the prophets, before Christ made his appearance. The main function of the prophets was to bid the Jews to this marriage, that is, to comfort their people by proclaiming that the Son of God would become man and by his death pay the debt of sin for the entire world, and by his resurrection destroy the kingdom and power of death and the devil. Thereafter, he would send the gospel to the entire world and have forgiveness of sins and eternal life preached to all in his name. The prophets directed the people to wait for such blessed preaching, to find consolation in it, and to hope for forgiveness of all sins, and eternal life through Christ.

7. But, as Christ says here, they refused to come. They stayed away, just as did the Jews in the wilderness, who wanted to return to Egypt. Thereupon, he sent out other servants, for the time was now at hand for Christ to come, to let people hear his preaching and witness his miracles. There were John and the disciples of Christ who announced that the wedding feast was prepared, and nothing was lacking, save that the guests should drop everything, dress up, and prepare to celebrate the marriage. But all was in vain. They paid no attention, says the Lord, and went their ways, one to his farm, another to his business. Greed, money, and possessions meant more to them than the kingdom of Christ. Just as today many are being invited to this marriage but do not want to come, allowing greed to get the best of them; and as a result they do not come to Christ and obtain eternal life.

8. Some are truly religious fanatics; they seize the king's servants, mistreat, and kill them. Such were the Jews, who killed the prophets, the apostles, and the bridegroom himself. But note what happens to them. "When the king heard thereof," says Christ, "he was wroth: and he sent forth his armies, and destroyed those murderers, and burned up their city." This is what happened to the city of Jerusalem and the Jewish people. Because the Word was scorned and the prophets, apostles, and Christ persecuted, the entire Jewish nation was destroyed, and the Jews, who had been God's people, were brought into disgrace. They perished and died miserably, not as God's people, or as holy people, but as deceivers and evildoers. Now then, they have their reward. They have been ravaged and scattered, and set forth by God as an example for later generations. By such an example the Lord Jesus Christ wants to warn us to hearken with thankful hearts to the preaching of his gospel, believe it, and joyfully await his return, when he will come in his glory and gloriously raise our mortal bodies, just as, according to soul and spirit, he has already placed us into the kingdom of heaven.

9. In short, the Jews have had their reckoning. Let us see now how the Gentiles fare. They lay outside on the streets, had no Law or Word of God as did the Jews. There were no walls for them, but they stood there exposed like an open field, so that the devil could rip them right and left as he chose. These now the king also invites, impartially, just as he finds them, husband and wife, young and old, rich and poor, just as we see today still that God gives baptism, the Word, and the Lord's Supper freely and upon even terms to each one who desires it.

10. Go, says the king to his servants, into the highways and invite to the marriage whomever you find there. This means: Call everybody without discrimination and say to them, Come to the marriage, believe in Christ, be baptized, hear the gospel, love one another; you are to be the guests of the Lord God, to eat and drink at his table to your heart's content; that is, you are to have forgiveness of sins, eternal life, and victory over the devil and hell. Accordingly, we Gentiles are all invited to the wedding. None can say that he has not been invited into the fellowship of the gospel. The servants have gone out and are still going out today, inviting out of all lands and peoples whomever they find.

11. When now all the tables are filled—it is clear then that the good and the bad have been invited without discrimination—the king enters the room and looks over his guests, and finds many who are not wearing wedding garments, for as the saying goes, There are always mouse droppings mixed in with the pepper. So in every Christian group there will be some—and their number is large—who are evil, and yet bear the Christian name because they are baptized, partake of the Sacrament, and listen to the preaching. Yet they evidence nothing but the name, since they hold nothing of what they profess to be true.

12. We will have to get used to this. By our preaching we shall never convert an entire city, town, or home. It will not happen, but, as the text says, there will be both good and evil. We must endure this and allow them the name Christian. True, they are all invited guests, but they are not all dressed alike. This is something that continues until Judgment Day, at which time the verdict will be altogether different.

13. Before Judgment Day, sitting among the guests is the person who does not have on a wedding garment, meanwhile doing little else than to ridicule the bridegroom. At a marriage a person ought to dress up out of respect for the bridegroom and the bride; it is a great insult to both if he does not. If a blacksmith arrives from his forge dressed in his long overgarment and skullcap, with coal-black beard and face covered with soot, and wants to mix with the wedding guests and be a part of the marriage procession, everyone, particularly the bridegroom, would think that the man was either out of his mind or that he was doing this to spite the bridegroom. This is exactly what the improperly dressed guest was doing. That is why the king addresses him, saying, Friend, how do you come to be here without your wedding garment? In other words, By coming without proper dress you dishonor and spite me! These are the kind of people you will find also in the church. They listen to the preaching, are baptized, partake of the Sacrament, and yet do not wear wedding garments; that is, they do not believe, do not demonstrate any serious intent, make believe they are Christian, and use the name Christian, just as the pope and his band, in order to fill their stomachs and have a good living. They do not become Christians for God's sake or for the sake of their soul's salvation, but only because the name puts food into their stomachs. And there are such despicable people also

among the Christians, such as today's factious spirits, fanatics, and all false Christians, who are looking for something in the gospel other than God's glory and their salvation, namely, for their own glory, wealth, and power.

14. The king catches sight of such a guest here, pulls him aside, and says, Friend how did you get in here? That will happen either at the point of death or on Judgment Day when the king will call such despicable guests and false Christians forward and say, Is it so that you are here because you have the name, because you are called a Christian, and you don't even believe what a Christian is supposed to believe? In all your born days you never were serious about how to rid yourself of sin, or how to become righteous and attain salvation. All you thought about were possessions, prestige, good days, and so on, and you come now as a guest covered with soot. Away with you! You do not belong among those who have come properly dressed; your dirt might soil them.

15. When either in conscience or on Judgment Day such roguish Christians are addressed in this way, then, says the Lord, they will have nary a word to answer; they will be unable to offer any excuse. For what can their excuse be? God did what he was supposed to do. He gave you holy baptism; he gave you the gospel and allowed you to have it in your home; likewise, absolution and the Lord's Supper; in the church he ordained his servants for you; in the home, father and mother, master and mistress, to teach you what to believe and how to order your life. As a result you will not be able to plead ignorance, that you might otherwise have believed. But you will have to confess, Yes, I am baptized, I have been preached to and told often; with my fellow Christians I have received the Sacrament, but I did not take anything seriously; I did not believe; I loved the world more. In this context, this means that the improperly dressed guest, covered with soot, is struck dumb when in his final hour or on Judgment Day he will have to hear the words, You went to the marriage, you allowed yourself to be counted among the Christians within Christendom, you died without faith. Who, indeed, would then be able to respond to the Judge, of whom we must ourselves testify that he sent his Son to us, in baptism, in the Holy Sacrament of Christ's Body and Blood, and in the Holy Gospel pledged us all grace? It is our fault

that we do not hold out our hands and take what he so gladly wants to give us. At that point a person would be left without defense.

16. And how will the improperly dressed guest and unbelieving Christian be judged? "Bind him hand and foot," says the king to the servants, "and take him away, and cast him into outer darkness; there shall be weeping and gnashing of teeth." This means that with the devil they will be confined forever in hell and in the fires of hell. For to be bound hand and foot means never to be able to disengage oneself from his works. In short, he will be deprived of all help and of everything whereby he might be saved, and besides, he must lie in darkness and will be separated from God's light. "Light" in Holy Scripture means joy and comfort. Consequently, the unbelieving will be cut off from all comfort, in everlasting torment, agony, and wretchedness, in hellish anguish and bonds before God, never to see a flicker of light. In all seriousness, it is a horrible affliction thus to lie in torment and hell, and be deprived of all comfort and joy for eternity.

17. But we also read, "There shall be weeping and gnashing of teeth." The father explained this as follows: Weeping, because of the heat; and chattering of teeth, because of the cold. By this the Lord wanted, in general, to indicate all the torment and agony man could think of; for fire and cold are two of earth's worst visitations. In other words, Those who attend the wedding and are not wearing wedding garments will have to endure more than what one might suppose, far beyond what words or mental pictures could portray.

18. The punishment for not recognizing or attending to the time of visitation—we had the Word, the Sacrament, baptism, gospel, absolution, and yet did not believe in or benefit from them—is that we shall have to endure everlasting captivity, darkness, torment, weeping, and gnashing of teeth. Therefore, the dear Lord would gladly have us recognize what great grace has been showered on us by being invited to such a blessed feast, where deliverance from sin, devil, death, and from eternal weeping and gnashing of teeth are to be found. But if we refuse to partake of this blessed feast and scorn this grace, we shall instead receive eternal death. It has to be one or the other: either accept and believe the gospel and be saved, or refuse to believe and be damned eternally.

19. This Gospel lesson agrees with what Paul said to the Jews, who strove against and blasphemed him (Acts 13:46): "It was necessary

that the word of God should first have been spoken to you: but seeing ye put it from you, and judge yourselves unworthy of everlasting life, lo, we turn to the Gentiles." Since the Jews did not wish to listen, God had them destroyed and sent his gospel to us Gentiles. Now it has come to us Gentiles; and if we, too, are found without wedding garments, we certainly shall have to face what is recorded here, that God will reject the improperly dressed wedding guests and say to them on Judgment Day: Since you preferred the curse, you shall have it; Since you did not want blessing, it shall be kept far from you; Since you did not want everlasting life, eternal death shall be yours. By his inviting and exhorting, our Lord wanted so dearly for us to accept the gospel as our greatest treasure and gladly hear and believe it. By means of the promise, he tugs at our hearts. Oh, how great is his grace! By means of judgment and punishment, he threatens with earnest warning! But nothing helps the obdurate world, neither invitation nor threat, neither grace nor punishment. Now if these two things will accomplish nothing, death and the devil will!

20. Were our Lord God to rain down money, there would be no lack of people whose desire would be to obtain heaven. However, since he promises eternal life and threatens with eternal death, no one wants to pay heed and mend his ways, until too late they realize what they have done.

21. So now the gist of today's sermon is that the Lord most earnestly invites us, but also earnestly warns us, as regards his Word, that we sincerely embrace it, believe and comprehend it, and so look forward to his joyous return, when he will come again on Judgment Day to deliver us from all suffering, and succor us, body and soul. May the merciful God grant us this through Christ, his Son, and the Holy Spirit. Amen.

TWENTIETH SUNDAY AFTER TRINITY

Third Sermon—1534

Matthew 22:1–14

1. With the parable of the wedding our Lord has pictured his holy Christian church and his beloved holy gospel. He expresses dismay over the contempt shown for his Word and the gospel, and also rebukes those who willfully despise it, persecuting and killing those who minister the Word.

2. He portrays his gospel in beautiful, lovely tones, comparing it to a wedding, not a time for work or sadness, but a time for festivity and joy, when people dress themselves specially, sing, play, strike up the music, dance, feast, drink, and are happy all around and in good spirits. It would be no wedding, certainly, just to work, be sad, or mourn. Christ, accordingly, describes his Christendom and the gospel in terms of earth's happiest occasion, namely, a wedding. And by this he teaches us that his gospel is a proclamation of love and joy, a truly joyous wedding celebration where Christ is the bridegroom and the Christian church, the bride, and our mother. Beautifully, magnificently the Lord portrays the kingdom of heaven, that is, his kingdom on earth, or the gospel, as a wedding, in order winsomely to urge and coax us to come to him in his kingdom, to accept his gospel. We are to bear in mind, that it is to the wedding we want to go; it will be beautiful and delightful; we will be truly happy, our hearts and spirits lifted up in song. In this way our Lord seeks to urge us to regard the holy gospel as the choicest of treasures and greatest joy on earth.

3. He then makes it still more beautiful and wonderful by calling it not simply a wedding, but a royal wedding, since the bridegroom is a king's son and the bride, a king's daughter, and everything is most magnificent, not only the food and drink, as at a wedding, but royal fare and royal happiness, evoking in us the sincere desire and longing to attend this wedding. When a high and mighty earthly king cele-

brates a wedding, with lavishly prepared wedding feast and many invited guests, throngs of people come from everywhere to gawk—Hans from Jena, and who knows who from everywhere—eager to see the royal pomp and splendor. If now that's what happens at the wedding of a mortal king, and even at weddings of lesser importance, why wouldn't that be true also at this royal wedding, since God's eternal Son is the bridegroom? Our loving Lord, you see, earnestly wants to urge us to come to him, so that we might learn eagerly to accept the gospel. That is why he calls his kingdom a royal wedding, to indicate that his gospel is a loving proclamation for hungry and thirsty souls everywhere. In short, this royal wedding is Christ's gracious realm, where there is sumptuous food and drink, comforting proclamation, genuine joy, and everlasting bliss; where the poor sinner finds redemption from death, where the sorrowful are comforted, and there are glad tidings, singing, praising, and giving of thanks.

4. This is not under the law of Moses or an earthly kingdom. The law of Moses is not a wedding feast, but it works terror and fear, and prompts to wrath (Rom. 4:15). The secular realm has murder, depravity, and villainy; for the world knows nothing but lying, deceiving, murdering, and all sorts of vices, and secular government is occupied with controlling and restraining these things. In the political order, therefore, there is neither rest nor peace, neither pleasure nor joy. In short, the world is the devil's realm, and yet everybody flocks to it, also the uninvited. In fact, even though God forbids it with deepest displeasure and threat of punishment, that is, with the fires of hell, people still show no concern. So totally is the world devoted to the devil, to his wedding, and to his kingdom, that it kills the prophets and apostles through whom the invitation to the Lord Christ's wedding comes to them and all other invited guests. To highlight how great a difference obtains here, Christ portrays his kingdom most engagingly and beautifully in this parable, calling it a wedding feast, a royal wedding no less, as if to say, The devil's kingdom is tantamount to Babylon, *confusio*, "a mixed mess of disarray," a disordered society through which all manner of shameful things flow together, where murder, unchastity, robbery, and all manner of vice reign. But my kingdom is called a wedding, a royal wedding, where genuine peace, joy, and delightful living prevail. This should so deeply move us that with heart and soul

we are ready to accept the gospel as a gracious, comforting proclamation and eagerly gather around Christ in his kingdom, where pure, eternal joy, heavenly glory and splendor reign; in short, where everything happens in regal fashion.

5. But is it not due to the accursed devil that they who are being invited to this royal wedding do not want to come? We may indeed vaunt ourselves against the devil's name and say that original sin is a small infraction and a trifling misstep. But is this not clear evidence of human blindness, a terrible effect of original sin that man thinks so despicably of God's Word? What more appalling thing could be said than that poor, sinful human beings, who lie captive in the devil's kingdom, do not want to come to a wedding through which the bridegroom, Christ, wants to rescue them from sin and from the power of the devil? Is this not a terrible calamity that they do not want to listen to the Word of life and the proclamation of their salvation?

6. Christ certainly does not call his gospel a word that leads to hell, or the hangman's gibbet from which a person is inclined to flee, or menial drudgery or work, but he calls it a wedding; in other words, gladsome tidings that open up on happy times. That a person, therefore, would be unwilling to listen to this word must certainly be regarded as a most shocking thing, prompted by devilish venom. Yes, it is not merely the result of original sin and Adam's failure, but it is also the mighty power of the devil who is able to blind and harden men's hearts so completely that they are unwilling to listen to the loving voice of their gracious, heavenly Father and the honey-sweet tongue and mouth of their beloved Saviour. As a matter of fact, it causes them not only to be unwilling to listen, but to draw the sword and challenge the invitation to this royal wedding even being tendered.

7. The invitation to the wedding is nothing else but this proclamation: Whoever hearkens and clings to the gospel of Christ will be saved; by faith in Christ he has forgiveness of sins, is absolutely free of God's wrath and judgment, has a gracious God, a faithful Redeemer, who rescues him from eternal death and from the devil, is a child of everlasting life, an individual whose sin will not overcome him! God wants to say to him, My dear son! and he in turn, confidently believing that he has access to God, will be able to say, My dearly beloved Father!

8. Isn't that a sweet proclamation? a magnificent, royal wedding feast? a more lavish and delectable meal than the choicest banquet on earth? What could possibly be a more gracious, sweet, and comforting message than the gospel's proclamation to me, that God wants to be my gracious God and take me into heaven and that in his kingdom I am to sing and leap for joy forever? Shouldn't a person hurry to get there? and be happy about the fellowship of the gospel and say, Praise and thanks be to God who has invited me to his royal, heavenly wedding!

9. The most delicious food, the glorious splendor of this wedding is the message Christ's kingdom proclaims: Whoever believes in the Son of God has forgiveness of sins. So wonderful and glorious is this proclamation that even the angels in heaven rejoice to hear it and long to inquire into it, as St. Peter attests (1 Peter 1:12). The beloved, holy angels are not in need of it; nevertheless, they are very eager and have great joy and pleasure, longing to hear about and share in the word about our great fortune and blessedness that Christ has become our bridegroom. If we, then, are ungrateful and violently oppose God, his Holy Word, and the faithful ministers who proclaim his Word and invite us to this wedding, we will find out, as the text also states, "The king was wroth: and he sent forth his armies, and destroyed those murderers, and burned up their city."

10. We see, then, that our dear Lord Jesus Christ calls the kingdom of heaven a royal wedding, because in his kingdom there is eternal joy, the fullness of heavenly blessings. The preaching of the gospel is for that reason such a glorious proclamation, not merely in terms of the words, but in its reality, that even the angels yearn to see it. These same holy, blessed spirits stroll about at this wedding, observing how happy we are, sitting at the table, eating and drinking of the eternal, heavenly food laid before us in the Word; and they wait on us at the table as ministering spirits, sent out to serve (Heb. 1:14) those who are to inherit salvation. They are always around us, observing with delight that we are gladly hearing and learning the proclamation of the gospel. They rejoice that we are so happy and are sharing in this heavenly calling. Christ portrays his kingdom so very beautifully as he here calls the proclamation of the gospel a wedding celebration, a day of rejoicing which begins here in time and continues afterwards in eternity.

11. Now, then, what do we do when we are invited to this wedding? When the gospel is proclaimed, no one comes running, but they all turn their ears elsewhere. But when the proclamation is about pilgrimages, indulgences, and other nostrums of the devil, everyone tunes in and people come running in droves, some barefoot, others dressed to the hilt, and they think they are coming to a wedding, while in reality they enter the devil's headquarters. Original sin has so blinded us, and the devil so taken hold of and bewitched us, that we would rather listen to the preaching of lies than to the preaching of Christ; and we swallow the poison that results in death rather than eating the heavenly food at this royal wedding which results in life.

12. For where one suppresses the gospel of Christ and proclaims instead human merits and works, what else is this but poison for the soul? Just as has occurred under the papacy, where virtually nothing has been proclaimed about the Lord Christ, but people have been counseled to neglect the duties which God had commanded them in their calling, conscientiously to look after wife, children, and servants; and instead they have opted for other works which God has not commanded. In those fabricated and self-chosen works they have sought comfort and aid over sin and death, but found none. For the heart is filled with joy only when it hears that Christ Jesus is our only Lord, our King and bridegroom. Apart from that our heart cannot receive any comfort.

13. Since now the gospel has again come to the light of day, so that people are taught where to find comfort and help against sin and death, namely, in Christ alone, and how, after coming to faith, to live a Christian life and serve God, each in the calling and station wherein God has placed him, let us, therefore, also note very carefully how firmly the "old Adam" still adheres to each one of us, and diligently, attentively, and obediently hearken to God's Word, and faithfully fulfill the office committed to him. For we see every day how the eyes, ears, and heart of the entire world are turned away from this preaching and everyone prefers to swallow his own venom, and as a result dies eternally. Too, the whole world is filled with murder, robbery, unfaithfulness, treachery, and so forth, and no one faithfully carries out the duties of his station. The Lord, in our lesson, deplores the fact

that men despise his royal, heavenly wedding festival, and instead run in droves to the devil's wedding. Isn't that a deplorable situation? he asks. My wedding is all ready, the guests are invited, and yet no one wants to come to it. The whole of Scripture, Old and New Testament, and all of church history from beginning to end bear this out!

14. The invitation to this wedding began in the earliest days of the world. Initially, the servants who invited the guests to this wedding were the patriarchs and prophets. The very first was Adam, who as a true bishop, yes, as a true pope above all others, proclaimed to his children the King's Son, our Lord Jesus Christ, who would crush the serpent's head and be the true bridegroom. After Adam came Seth, Enos, Enoch, and so on, until Noah. These, one after the other, were wedding hosts and preachers who summoned the world in those early days to the wedding. But what did the invited guests do? In early history it went exactly like it is going today in the later world—some despised it, and others killed the servants and wedding hosts as well.

15. After the patriarchs came the prophets. Among the people of Israel there were Isaiah, Jeremiah, and other prophets, sent out by God as messengers to invite the people, to the wedding. But how did the people of Israel respond to the prophets' invitation to the wedding? They despised this festive meal and, on top of it, killed the prophets.

16. Finally came the bridegroom himself. Christ was born in the land of the Jews, preached, performed miracles, came riding into Jerusalem, and invited the Jews to the wedding. But what did these privileged people who were the cousins and kinsmen of our Lord Christ, do? They killed the bridegroom and drove the bride out of Jerusalem. In his anger our God then sent out his armies, the Romans, and had the city of Jerusalem destroyed, so that not one stone was left upon another, and slew these murderers, the Jews, who had slain the prophets and the Son of God.

17. And as he punished the city of Jerusalem, so he also punished the other despisers and ridiculers of his gospel. The early world, which despised the patriarchs and Noah, the preacher of righteousness, he destroyed by means of the flood. Sodom and Gomorrah, which despised the righteous Lot, God destroyed by means of fire and brimstone. The people of Israel, who despised and killed the prophets, he punished with the Assyrian and Babylonian captivity and countless

other calamities. In many different ways he punished the large countries and cities of the heathen, as noted in the Prophets. He punished Greece through Mohammed and the Turks. Italy and Rome he punished through the Goths and the Wends, finally also through the pope.

18. The first despise the Word and cast it to the wind, with the excuse, I must tend to my farm and my business. The landed squires say, What are the five books of Moses to me? Would that they were five towns! And the peasants, What is heaven to me? Would that I had flour! Many among the peasants, burghers, and nobility arrogantly despise God's Word in this way. Others are even much worse; they deride and kill the servants. It is especially reprehensible to kill, and, in addition, to ridicule. Criminals don't even resort to that. Even the executioner has a good word left for the thief, around whose neck he has put the noose, even though he has already strung him up on the gallows. Surely, those servants who do the inviting to the wedding feast don't deserve to be murdered, nor maligned and derided, thus having both their honor and life taken from them! Our Lord God, however, keeps his silence the meanwhile, as regards these things, until his time comes.

19. That is the situation today still. In the Netherlands, in France, and elsewhere, much Christian blood is being shed. Our Lord God for the time is silent, acts as though he does not notice, and allows it to continue. Not far from us the same thing is happening; B.V.M. and H.G.* revile and persecute the Christians; our Lord God is silent here also. But in his time he will come and lash out, as the text here states, "The king was wroth and destroyed those murderers." One must not even think that he would bestow a gift on someone who despises his Word and kills his servants. If he destroyed the first world by means of the flood, if he wiped out Sodom and Gomorrah which was situated on very choice land, like Cain was privileged to be the first among the children of Adam; if he rejected his chosen, beloved children of Israel at Jerusalem, so that today they still lie in misery; yes, and if (as St. Peter says in 2 Peter 2:4) he did not spare the angels who sinned; if all these things are true, we can then be sure that he will not spare us if we despise and oppose his Word.

*Apparent reference to Albert, the Archbishop of Mainz, and Duke George of Leipzig, opponents of the Reformation.

20. It does indeed appear as though our Lord God lets the despisers and opponents of his Word go unpunished. But he does not let them go scot-free or leave his servants unavenged, as Christ teaches with the example of the unjust judge and the poor widow (Luke 18). The widow, says he, did not give up, but plagued and wearied the judge by her persistence, so that he finally vindicated her. If now a mere human being—one without fear of God and who kowtows to no man—indulges a suppliant in her plea, should not a faithful God bestow his help? If an unjust judge, a scoundrel, hears and vindicates, should not then the righteous Father in heaven hear and vindicate his elect who call upon him day and night?

21. Our tyrants and wicked bishops, therefore, who despise and ridicule the Holy Gospel, will not escape God's wrath, even though punishment is delayed for a time. For they do not let up opposing God and his Word; meanwhile, we also continually call on God for help, and the shed blood of our fellow Christians cries out as well. Therefore, as Christ states, God will come before long and justly avenge the blood of his elect and punish his enemies beyond imagination. For God loves his elect and will not forsake them, except that we must still wait for his time of deliverance, persevere in prayer, and beseech him to restrain the devil with his minions and vindicate us.

22. Now, once more, it is very necessary for us to pray diligently, since our adversaries have evil in mind and would gladly begin shedding blood. We must, therefore, pray God that he would plunge into their hearts the sword which they are drawing. They brandish the sword, as Psalm 37:14 states, and want to strike; and they draw their bows in order to bring down the poor and needy, and slay the righteous. But the just judge and avenger will come; he will cause the sword to pierce their own hearts and break their bows. He has never exonerated anyone who despises his Word, and torments and persecutes his Christians. Let us then pray and gladly hear, learn, and esteem the Holy Gospel. Let each of us also be diligent in his calling to be obedient to God and serve his neighbor, a woman in tending to her house, a craftsman to his work, each one happily performing the duties of the calling entrusted to him. We need not be concerned as to how God will vindicate us and avenge himself on his enemies.

23. We have the wedding invitation and are already seated at the table with the guests. We should, therefore, not only rejoice inwardly in spirit but also outwardly, with joy and delight, doing what we are commanded. While the devil and the world don't like it, our Lord God is smiling at us, and the dear holy angels are piping their tune. Though we do not actually see them, God's Word still attests to it, as Christ himself says (Luke 15:7): "I say unto you, that likewise joy shall be in heaven over one sinner that repenteth." If now angels rejoice, then surely we are hapless losers, if we do not repent and share in this joy. Consequently, also, even though we do not see how God vindicates us and how the beloved angels protect us, we learn about this in the Word, as for example in the story of the prophet Elijah and his enemies (2 Kings 6). So we, too, can be sure that the beloved angels are around us. Though we do not see them, we believe God and his Word. He has said so in Holy Scripture and also attested to it with instances galore. So let us come to the wedding and not stay away or be ungrateful, like the Jews, nor be concerned at all how God will vindicate us and the beloved angels protect us.

So much in connection with the first half of the Gospel.

Then saith he [the king] to his servants, The wedding is ready, but they which were bidden were not worthy. Go ye therefore into the highways, and as many as ye shall find, bid to the marriage.

24. We Gentiles are those people. Among them the king also finds people who are not upright. These are the counterfeit Christians and hypocrites who by the gospel seek merely to satisfy their greed and achieve approbation. They will be cast into hell where they will suffer grief and reproach forever. The words Christ utters are especially fearsome, "Bind him hand and foot, and take him away, and cast him into outer darkness; there shall be weeping and gnashing of teeth," that is, endless lamentation with no letup; that is where false Christians must go. They do, indeed, have the Word and really think they are Christians, but what condemns them is that they do whatever they please and, at the same time, want to have the name and be called Christians.

25. The hypocrite in our lesson is such a false Christian. He dishonors the bride and bridegroom by not dressing in a wedding garment. Were I the bridegroom, I, too, would take it as an insult and judge him to be making a farce out of the wedding. That is the way

with false Christians; they want to take in the festivities and yet do not partake of the wedding food, even though they sit at the table; they lack true faith, nor do they do what is their duty to do; they remain whoremongers, adulterers, gluttons, drunkards, usurers, haters, enviers, and so forth. Yes, says Christ, such hypocrites and counterfeit Christians I will deal with in due time, even though the meanwhile they continue to mingle with the wedding guests; but they will not escape me. Out, out into the abyss of hell with such false Christians, who boast of being a part of the wedding and yet are not wearing wedding clothes! They bear the name of Christian, pretending to be Christians, and yet are without faith, nor do they wear a wedding garment; they only bring shame on the gospel and cause offense.

26. Thus this Gospel concerns both Jew and Gentile, and rebukes the one as well as the other on account of unbelief and ingratitude. It rebukes the Jews because they have not believed but absented themselves from the wedding through unbelief and disdain, besides killing the prophets, apostles, and God's Son. The Gentiles are rebuked because not all of them are wearing wedding clothes, even as today there are many among us who boast that they are evangelical and Christian, and yet remain in their old garb.

27. Let us bestir ourselves, obey, and follow our beloved Lord, who coaxes us so tenderly and lovingly. He says that he wishes to invite us to this joyous wedding feast, for which the angels are to be our stewards. Therefore, let us come to the wedding and not despise the invitation. Then let us also apply ourselves, that each one performs what is his duty to do. If we do that, we shall be of good cheer and blissful. If we have to suffer a little because of God's name, it's all to the good. Such gracious words should fairly motivate us to hear and learn God's Word gladly, to feed our souls daily at this banquet, so that we do not disdain the Lord who so graciously urges us to come, and assigns us a place at his royal wedding celebration, which begins here and continues there forever. Let us be careful not to fall into the devil's den of murderers because of our ingratitude. May our dear Lord God grant us his Holy Spirit that we may learn to cling tightly to these things, truly believe, lead a Christian life, and ever be found wearing the proper wedding garment and adornment, for the sake of Jesus Christ, our Saviour. Amen.

TWENTY-FIRST SUNDAY AFTER TRINITY

First Sermon—1533

John 4:46–54

> So Jesus came again unto Cana of Galilee, where he made the water wine. And there was a certain nobleman, whose son was sick at Capernaum. When he heard that Jesus was come out of Judæa into Galilee, he went unto him, and besought him that he would come down, and heal his son: for he was at the point of death. Then said Jesus unto him, Except ye see signs and wonders, ye will not believe. The nobleman saith unto him, Sir, come down ere my child die. Jesus saith unto him, Go thy way; thy son liveth. And the man believed the word that Jesus had spoken unto him, and he went his way. And as he was now going down, his servants met him, and told him, saying, Thy son liveth. Then inquired he of them the hour when he began to amend. And they said unto him, Yesterday at the seventh hour the fever left him. So the father knew that it was at the same hour, in the which Jesus said unto him, Thy son liveth: and himself believed, and his whole house. This is again the second miracle that Jesus did, when he was come out of Judæa into Galilee.

1. St. John tells us that this was the second miraculous sign Jesus did when he had come out of Judaea into Galilee. He performed the first miracle soon after his baptism, when he changed water into wine at the wedding feast in Cana of Galilee. Now then, in this second miracle he restored the health of the royal officer's son at Capernaum. All of this took place in the first year of his public ministry. After our Lord's baptism in the Jordan by John the Baptist, he immediately began his ministry, preaching and performing miracles, and among these wondrous signs, the aforementioned two were the very first.

2. The Evangelist has recorded these marvelous works to show what kind of person this preacher really was, and to indicate also how he was to be heard, namely, with the confidence that everything he taught was

"Yea" and "Amen!" We do not really know whether this royal official was a Jew or Gentile, nor does that really matter. He was some sort of provincial ruler or magistrate serving King Herod. It's more important that we discover the reason why the Evangelist has reported this miraculous healing, so that we may all realize how very important it is for us to respond to God's Word with the proper sort of faith.

3. This royal official had a young son, lying sick in Capernaum with a dangerously high fever. It was the kind of illness we label pestilence, very life threatening. The officer had heard that a new prophet had arisen whose powerful teaching was being backed up by mighty deeds. It's even possible that he had personally heard Christ preach, since the Lord had begun his Galilean ministry at Capernaum, as St. Matthew reports (4:13). It's also possible that he may have heard how Jesus made water into wine at the Cana wedding feast. All of this may have so moved him, that he had become a believer, and now, in the desperate situation of his boy's illness, he hurries to Christ and pleads for help.

4. What a receptive heart! After just one sermon and one miracle he had faith enough to go immediately to Christ in his time of need. Here surely the king's officer becomes a wonderful example for us. What ought we learn? First, that we have God's Word in richest measure, yes, the Holy Scripture itself, and that it was written aforetime for our learning and comfort. In addition, of course, God's Word is preached to us every day. And yet, how slow we are to believe! Now look at this royal official: one sermon and one miracle, he believes, and comes to Jesus begging help for his dying boy! Did the Lord perhaps think to himself: Who was it that told this man I could help? Here I've preached only a few messages and have only a dozen or so disciples; I haven't yet healed even one person and did only that one miraculous sign at the wedding in Cana of Galilee; how then did it happen that this royal official now comes to me seeking help, eyes pleading with me to restore his son's health?

5. Yes, here we surely have an exemplary faith! It's true, of course, the Evangelist does indicate what might be considered a weakness in the faith of the king's officer, namely, that he asks Christ "to come down and heal his son," a weakness which led Christ to reply, "Except ye see signs and wonders, ye will not believe!" In spite of this, however, it was nevertheless a great thing on his part that after just one comparatively easy

miracle, he nourishes the hope for a much greater one. After all, to make wine out of water—an astounding act in itself indeed!—is not as marvelous as healing one who is close to death, or bringing back to life someone who has actually died. And so, if this royal officer had concluded from the Cana miracle that this Christ could do even greater things, such as restoring health and life to his dying son, that was surely not a small or weak faith! Precisely, here is where the king's officer is way ahead of us. We've heard so many sermons and seen so many wonderful signs and yet we do not have his strong faith in Christ. On the contrary, we often are so evil and stubborn that we not only despise the Word, but even persecute those who proclaim his gospel.

6. And so the Evangelist presents the example of this royal officer's faith both to make us blush with shame and then to stimulate our faith. Indeed, on the Last Day the king's official will step before all unbelievers and judge them as follows: Shame on you despicable people! I heard only one sermon and saw only one solitary sign, namely, that the Lord made wine out of water, and yet I learned enough, so that I believed he had power to do all things. You, however, have heard the gospel for many years and have seen many mighty acts of his, and yet your life does not show it and you make little progress in spiritual growth.

7. At the outset it did seem as though the royal official was weak in his faith, in that he asked the Lord to "come down" and heal his boy. He wanted very much to have the Lord come personally to help his son so that he could witness the miracle with his own eyes. For that the Lord did indeed chide him, Why don't you believe without signs and wonders? Nevertheless I will grant what you have asked; "Go thy way; thy son liveth!" To this word of Christ the official clung so strongly that all other thoughts were driven out of his mind; he went on his way in the sure confidence and blessed hope that his boy would live—just as Christ promised him! Moments before, he may indeed have thought: My son is sick unto death and will surely die if the Lord does not come with me right away to help. But now that he has this word from Christ, Go, your son will live, he has different thoughts entirely. When I left my son at home he was very sick; but now, when I return, I will find him alive and well!

8. This, then, is the faith which the Evangelist now praises; "The man believed the word that Jesus had spoken unto him and he went

his way." Or, putting it another way, the officer possessed a very wonderful, excellent faith, trusting Christ completely at his word, never doubting that when he got home he would find his son alert and well. The hope in his heart was as certain as if he had already experienced the reality. And so, as he clung to the mere word in true faith, the miraculous work took place—his boy became well, and soon his servants came running with the great news: "Thy son liveth."

9. Surely a great wonder, indeed, that Christ's word should have power to effect such a miracle. Here a child, close to death, nevertheless lives and is restored to good health! This is a lesson especially for the Anabaptists with their disbelief about holy baptism, denying that it bestows forgiveness of sins, life, and salvation. They regard only the water and do not consider the word which is connected with that water. That's why they do not rightly value baptism. Here is the word which Christ spoke, "Baptize them in the name of the Father, and of the Son, and of the Holy Spirit. He who believes and is baptized shall be saved!" It is to this word that we must cling, for it is truly an almighty power. What it promises, it will surely deliver; neither the devil nor the world can hinder or prevent it.

10. They operate the same way also with absolution, refusing to believe the word which God speaks to a poor sinner through the called pastor, "Be of good cheer, my son, your sins are forgiven!" Instead of believing that simple word, they say, How can any human agency contribute something to forgiveness? Answer: When God speaks his absolution to us through the word, "Your sins are forgiven," this is just as sure and valid as was the word which Christ spoke for the healing of the royal officer's son!

11. It follows, then, that we are to have the highest regard for God's Word, never doubting any part of it, but steadfastly believing that what God promises is most certainly true and cannot possibly fail. That's why St. Paul had such high praise for Abraham, "He staggered not at the promise of God through unbelief; but was strong in faith, giving glory to God; And being fully persuaded that, what he had promised, he was also to perform" (Rom. 4:20–21). So also the king's official is here praised because he simply depended on the word of Christ, without debate or wavering. And that's why the Evangelist also presents him to us as an example, so that we too may learn to val-

ue the Word very highly, and confidently believe that God will bring to pass what he promised. After all, God cannot lie!

12. The same applies also to what God will say on the Last Day to us who lie in our graves: Arise all you dead! Immediately we will arise from the ground and come forth—no grave, worm, or rock can prevent it! Here stands the word of Christ (John 5:28–29): "The hour is coming, in the which all that are in the graves shall hear his voice, And shall come forth; those that have done good, unto the resurrection of life, and they that have done evil unto the resurrection of damnation." This word neither lies nor will it fail.

13. Christ's gospel and Christian teaching are powerful and capable of great wonders, for it is a power of God unto salvation for all who believe it (Rom. 1:16). God's Word is an entirely different word than man's word. When a mortal man gives a command, a lot of things have to happen before that word becomes effective and accomplishes what is intended: walking and running, riding and journeying, toil and labor, expenses and living costs—all are necessary to activate a human word or command. The Word of God, on the other hand, executes everything posthaste. It brings you forgiveness of sin, offers eternal life, and costs you nothing more than that you hear and believe the Word. Believe it and you have it—without a lot of toil, cost, delay, or hardship.

14. It is thus that the gospel of Christ and Christian doctrine accomplish their purpose with a minimum of words. Because it is God's Word, it has an almighty power, before which nothing is impossible—as we see here in the case of the royal officer's son. Christ speaks to the father, Go, your son will live! and at the first spark of faith on the father's part, his son was restored to health! There was neither cost, nor toil, nor hardship; one little word from Christ and it was done! Just so, God also rules his Christian church—yes, so rules the entire world without laborious effort. He accomplishes it all by one word.

15. How necessary, then, that we always have the highest regard for the Word, accepting it in simple faith. We have that same Word today in the gospel message, in baptism, in the Holy Sacrament, in absolution. Never should we think lightly of any of these but, instead, value and treasure them highly. By so trusting his Word, we shall always receive what the Word has promised, as was the case in the story of the king's officer.

TWENTY-FIRST SUNDAY AFTER TRINITY

Second Sermon—1534

John 4:46–54

1. This is one of the miracles which our dear Lord Jesus Christ performed shortly after he was baptized in the Jordan. The first miracle after his baptism—once he began to preach and perform miracles—was changing water into wine at the wedding at Cana in Galilee. The second was curing the nobleman's son.

2. The Evangelist says that Jesus had come from Judæa into Galilee. When the nobleman hears this, he goes to him, begs him to come down and heal his son. He is very confident that Jesus will cure his son. He has that kind of faith in Jesus and yet has not heard much about his preaching and miracles; for the Lord had just begun to preach and had performed only that one miracle at Cana. Here we should not think that Jesus had come only once from Judæa into Galilee but that he had often traveled back and forth, from Capernaum to Jerusalem and again from Jerusalem to Capernaum. For during the three years of his ministry he did not stay in one location, but moved from place to place and traveled all over the Jewish land, preaching and healing the sick.

3. In any case, we have an extremely fine example of faith on the part of this royal official, whose faith is so highly extolled that we, too, should learn to believe the gospel of Christ. For to believe is not an art achieved as easily as many people think. Indeed, the word "faith" has now become so common that many scorn faith and say, Ha! what is faith? I have heard so much about it. Who doesn't know what faith is? But verily to such people the gospel has an empty ring to it, and faith is merely a dream they concoct. For this reason one should learn to know what faith really is.

4. This nobleman was an official of King Herod, and possibly a Jew. He knows nothing more about Christ than what he has heard from other people, and has, perhaps, not heard him personally; nevertheless, since his son was at the point of death because of the fever, he goes to him and begs him to heal his son. In those lands at that time fever that resulted from the plague was of great concern because the victim lying ill with it faced certain death—for, fever with them and the plague in our day are one and the same thing. When the father now sees that his son will die, he becomes very despondent; he wants badly to help and console his son but cannot. But when he hears that Jesus is coming from Judæa into Galilee, he becomes excited, meets up with him after a two-day journey, and firmly believes that he will cure his son.

5. Such faith probably grew out of the public outcry and report made by everyone about how Christ readily cured everyone who came to him. He does not presume in any way to be deserving of Christ healing his boy. For even though he has been a pious person, nevertheless, he does not bank on his piety, nor does he approach Christ in such self-esteem; but the public report has influenced him, and he has heard that Jesus readily helps, whether people are ungodly or godly, just as the heavenly Father makes his sun rise on the evil and on the good and sends rain on the just and on the unjust (Matt. 5:45). So, he thinks like this: Even though I might be a wicked scoundrel, this man, nonetheless, is so kind that he turns no one away; therefore, I shall lay it on his merciful heart, which is minded to assist everyone, and plead hopefully and confidently.

6. This example is recorded for our sakes, so that we too might summon up courage to come to God. For faith is nothing else than sincere trust in God. Whoever has deliberate trust in God and comes to him with courageous heart possesses a true faith. In temporal matters among people, faith is a different thing; as, when one entrusts another with a thousand gulden, he says, I am placing this money in your care. But in spiritual matters, when one deals with God, faith is something else; as, when I say, The official here has a beautiful faith in Christ, that is, he is very confident that Christ will grant him mercy and help. Accordingly, his thoughts are: Even though I am a wicked scoundrel, he still allows his loving kindness

to govern over the evil and the good; and, therefore, he will help me just as he has helped others.

7. Reason opposes such faith; flesh and blood speak like this: Yes, I really do believe that God is kind and gracious; but St. Peter, St. Paul, and others, they are devout; but I am a wicked scoundrel, I am unworthy, and for this reason he won't be gracious to me. The person who is of such a mind does not believe but is a heathen and reasons like this: Ah, it is doubtful whether God would help me. Miserable unbelief, you see, doubts God's grace and mercy. Such a person God does not help. Faith is necessary if you are to be helped. Our Lord God, as Psalm 18:25–26 states, shows himself holy with the holy, upright with the upright, pure with the pure, ill-disposed with the perverse. As you twist and turn, so also God twists and turns; if you think he is angry with you, then he is angry; if you think he is unmerciful and would send you to hell, then he is that also. Whatever you believe God to be, that is the way it is.

8. If now you say, I am not as upright as Peter, for this reason God will not help me—if that is what you think—then woe betide you! For by this you are building yourself a hell and making yourself a damnation. St. Peter did not exalt himself as highly as you exalt him. St. Peter does not say, I have been upright, therefore, God, give me eternal life; but he talks like this, "Now therefore why tempt ye God, to put a yoke upon the neck of the disciples, which neither our fathers nor we were able to bear? But we believe that through the grace of the Lord Jesus Christ we shall be saved, even as they" (Acts 15:10–11). As if to say, God did not look with favor on our fathers, Abraham, Isaac, and Jacob because of their uprightness, but for Christ's sake; thus we do not look at how holy we are, but acknowledge that we would rather not bear the burden of the Law—just as Abraham and the fathers were unable to bear it—and rely on God's mercy and grace promised us in Christ. Therefore, you must not rely on how upright St. Peter may have been, but you should pay heed to his doctrine and faith, when he says that he believes he will be saved by the grace of Jesus Christ. For that is primary, to believe on Jesus Christ, that he alone can and will forgive sins and grant eternal life.

9. We see, then, that faith is the kind of mind-set in which a person looks to God for every good thing. Such a faith, where the heart

places complete confidence in God alone, God demands in the first commandment when he says, "I am the Lord thy God," and defines and explains what kind of God he is when he adds, "which have brought thee out of the land of Egypt, out of the house of bondage"; that means, I alone want to be your God; you shall have no other god; I am ready to deliver you out of all trouble. You are to trust in me with all your heart and believe that I want to be your helper; you are to seek no other help and comfort. You are not to think that I am at enmity with you and do not want to help you. When you think of me in that light, you make me out to be a god different from the one I am. Therefore, rest assured that I want to be gracious to you and that you are to obey me in all my commandments. This, then, is faith, when a heart looks to God for all help, mercy, and comfort in all trouble. This is what the first commandment teaches.

10. And there Christians and heathen part company. However, in outward works they do not. For a heathen can fast, keep vigils, and so forth as well as a Christian, but he does not believe like a Christian. If a man does not have faith, and, particularly, faith in Christ, there is no difference between him and a heathen. Yes, fasting and watching can be done also by a dumb animal. However, what distinguishes a Christian and a heathen is that a Christian has recourse to Christ as his only Saviour and looks to him for all good things. On the other hand, a Turk and heathen has doubts and says, Yes, if I were upright like St. Peter I would want to believe that God would be gracious to me and help me; however, I am a poor sinner.

11. Monks do the same; they disregard the picture which God has painted for us in the first commandment, that is, that he wants to be our God, to whom we should look for all good things; also, they disregard the mediator between God and man, namely, the Saviour Jesus Christ. That very picture of divine grace and mercy they put out of sight and think their own thoughts; St. Peter may well have looked forward to grace and mercy from God, but not they. That is what the devil and unbelief say to them. Since now they have such thoughts, they gravitate farther towards their own works and say, I want to enter a monastery so that I may pursue piety. Well now, go wherever you want, you will accomplish nothing. Whoever wants to become truly upright must not start with his self-conceived works,

but with the first commandment and with Christ, that thus the heart might first become upright, that is, trust and believe in God. If the heart is not upright, how can works please God? With man the situation is still this: Were you to give me a thousand gulden and do so from an evil heart, in order that such money would redound to my harm, then I would say, Be hanged, you and your money too! If a person acts like that, it will be all the more displeasing to our Lord when he then seeks to do all manner of works from an evil, unbelieving heart. Therefore, see to it, above all things, that you have an upright heart; then, that you do good works, for these will please God if done out of a pure heart.

12. In keeping with what the first commandment teaches us, therefore, about the nature of faith, so this Gospel lesson holds before us a living example of faith exhibited in this nobleman; he truly believes that Christ will cure his son, even though he does not deserve it. He does not think like this: I am unworthy and, therefore, my prayer will not be heard; he does not question the purposes in Christ's heart, nor does he say, He could cure my son if he but wanted to. For were he thus to have doubted, he would not have gone to meet Christ but simply remained a heathen. But because he believes, he goes to Christ and thinks like this: Even though I am unworthy, he still is merciful and will not deny me his help. His faith drives him on. A heathen would not have done this because he knows nothing about faith. Nor would a monk do it, for he wants to appease our Lord God first with works.

13. For this reason we should thank God with all our hearts for having delivered us from the darkness and error of the papacy, since we poor, blind human beings have pursued so many different idolatries. We should pray diligently that he would graciously shield us, so that we do not fall into greater darkness and error, or desire still other strange gods. Let us gladly hear God's Word and learn what faith is so that our hearts may learn to build on God, and trust in him.

14. Thus, a Christian and a heathen are to be differentiated, not according to clothing or some kind of work, but according to heart and faith, that is, a Christian trusts in God; a heathen does not. A heathen, also, does outward works; yes, it often happens that the heathen, according to outward appearance of works, are considered

holier than Christians; but faith makes a difference. A hound and an ass also can fast and keep watch, and soldiers suffer even more privation than Carthusian monks. For, as the saying goes, The devil's martyrs will gain hell with less effort than true martyrs heaven. No man, however, believes and trusts in God unless he is a Christian.

15. Whoever does not possess the confidence of this royal official, whoever is not absolutely sure that Christ will be gracious to him and help in every need, that man is a heathen. Moreover, if a Christian does not have such faith and confidence, he does not belong to him whose name he bears. In short, a Christian must persevere in this faith, that, whether he lives or dies, God will justify and save him and help in every need. Such hope we should never let go of, even when God at first causes us to be tested, as Christ here does with the nobleman, as he first is abrupt with him, even harsh and says, Why don't you believe without seeing signs and miracles? Thus he puts him to the test at the beginning and then straightway strengthens him in faith. For just as we initially lead children by the hand when they learn to walk, and then gradually withdraw the hand and say, Come here, come here, so that they learn to walk by themselves; so does Christ here to this nobleman; he tests him first to see if he will hold on tightly, then strengthens him.

16. When the nobleman now says, "Sir, come down ere my child die," the Lord responds, "Go thy way; thy son liveth." The nobleman believes that word so firmly and holds onto it so tenaciously, as though he could already see his son standing before him hale and hearty. And as he goes on his way, his servants meet him with the news, "Thy son liveth. Yesterday at the seventh hour the fever left him." Then he notes that this was the exact time when the Lord had said to him, "Thy son liveth." Since he believed that word as spoken, he was convinced in his mind: The man will not lie to me; when I return home, my son will certainly be restored to health; and so it also was, just as he believed, and he finds his son alive and well.

17. We see here that faith is that kind of confidence, where the heart does not doubt God's grace and mercy, just as Psalm 34 describes faith in verse 4: "I sought the Lord, and he heard me, and delivered me from all my fears"; also, verse 6: "This poor man cried, and the Lord heard him, and saved him out of all his troubles." That

was the thinking of this official: This is a gracious man, from whom no one has ever departed without receiving what he desired; therefore, he will not let me go away empty-handed. If you, too, have this kind of sincere trust in God and are able to say, Has anyone ever come to God and been left in the lurch by him? Therefore, he will not let me down either! Then you have true faith also.

18. The one who does not believe will be justly damned, especially since God draws us so gently to himself, also promises, first of all, in the first commandment that he wants to be our God, that is, our comfort, helper, life, and all that is good, and will fend off all that may be bad for us. On the other hand, he also threatens very earnestly that if we do not come to him or trust him with our whole heart, he will wipe us off of the face of the earth (Deut. 6), and wreak his vengeance unto the third and fourth generation (Exod. 20). But then he also has given his Son and in him promises forgiveness of sins, eternal life, and blessedness. Whoever does not pay heed to such a gracious promise, such an earnest threat, and, at the same time, to the Son of God, is not wrongfully dealt with when he is damned. For it is a great affront to God if we do not believe or trust in him; for it is also true that all sins spring from unbelief. Therefore, as we believe, so shall our lot also be; if we believe him to be our God, then, of course, he will not be our devil; if we do not believe him to be our God, then, of course, he will not be our God, but be like a consuming fire; as he said to the Jews through the prophet Hosea (13:4–8): "Yet I am the LORD thy God from the land of Egypt, and thou shalt know no god but me: for there is no saviour beside me. I did know thee in the wilderness, in the land of great drought. According to their pasture, so were they filled; they were filled, and their heart was exalted; therefore have they forgotten me. Therefore I will be unto them as a lion: as a leopard by the way will I observe them: I will meet them as a bear that is bereaved of her whelps, and will rend the caul of their heart, and there will I devour them like a lion: the wild beast shall tear them."

19. For no greater affront exists than unbelief before our God through which we make God out to be a devil! On the other hand, no greater honor can be done to him than by believing him to be a saviour. For this reason he cannot tolerate a doubting heart; as the Turk

doubts, and a monk enters a monastery out of despair, and says, O how hot hell is; I want to do so many good works, in order that I may reconcile God! But with works no one becomes a Christian, but remains a heathen. A Christian becomes a Christian when his heart believes, and says, Christ is a kind, gracious Saviour of all men; for this reason I shall come to him confidently and in full assurance call upon him for help. Such a person leads with the head and not with the tail. Therefore, we should make it a habit to put our faith into practice. Faith is solely the Christians' art wherein they are to exercise themselves daily. And it is not as easy as so many people think, who demean and ridicule faith. May our dear heavenly Father grant us grace through his Holy Spirit, that we learn to believe and daily give evidence of our faith, grow and increase therein, and truly glorify God in Jesus Christ, our Lord. Amen.

TWENTY-SECOND SUNDAY AFTER TRINITY[*]

Matthew 18:21–35

Then came Peter to him, and said, Lord, how oft shall my brother sin against me, and I forgive him? till seven times? Jesus saith unto him, I say not unto thee, Until seven times: but, Until seventy times seven. Therefore is the kingdom of heaven likened unto a certain king, which would take account of his servants. And when he had begun to reckon, one was brought unto him, which owed him ten thousand talents. But forasmuch as he had not to pay, his lord commanded him to be sold, and his wife, and children, and all that he had, and payment to be made. The servant therefore fell down, and worshipped him, saying, Lord, have patience with me, and I will pay thee all. Then the lord of that servant was moved with compassion, and loosed him, and forgave him the debt. But the same servant went out, and found one of his fellowservants, which owed him an hundred pence: and he laid hands on him, and took him by the throat, saying, Pay me that thou owest. And his fellowservant fell down at his feet, and besought him, saying, Have patience with me, and I will pay thee all. And he would not: but went and cast him into prison, till he should pay the debt. So when his fellowservants saw what was done, they were very sorry, and came and told unto their lord all that was done. Then his lord, after that he had called him, said unto him, O thou wicked servant, I forgave thee all that debt, because thou desiredst me: Shouldest not thou also have had compassion on thy fellowservant, even as I had pity on thee? And his lord was wroth, and delivered him to the tormentors, till he should pay all that was due unto him. So likewise shall my heavenly Father do also unto you, if ye from your hearts forgive not every one his brother their trespasses.

1. Today's Gospel lesson deals with the doctrine of the two kinds of kingdoms, the spiritual kingdom and the civil kingdom, about which you dear people have often heard me speak. But for the sake of those who are not yet familiar with the distinction between the

---

[*] Preached publicly at St. Mary's, the parish church, 1530.

two, I must needs speak about it again. Now there are two kinds of government—spiritual government or kingdom, and civil government or kingdom—which are quite different from one another as we shall see. The civil government or kingdom has been ordained and established by God for the purposes of defense, of levying taxes, and the punishment of crimes in the world. This is not to say that civil government can punish every wrong, because its power is much too limited to accomplish that. No, it is intended to punish the gross, manifest crimes that people commit, so that no one is free to commit crimes against his neighbor's body, wife, property, and so on. Civil government is authorized to preserve external peace, so that each person may be able to preserve what belongs to him.

2. In this civil kingdom or government there is no forgiveness of sin, but rather punishment for sin. That is why Holy Scripture calls it the sword in Genesis 9 and Romans 13:4. God did not put a useless piece of paper into the emperor's hand, but rather the hardest and sharpest sword with which to execute punishment; not a pen, but a sword. God gave the emperor a sword to indicate that civil government is not to forgive but rather to use the edge of the sword to punish crimes. If civil government were to forgive crimes, you and I would lose everything. When a thief steals everything there is in a house, when a murderer robs and kills whomever he meets on the street, if the prince of a territory and the judge of a city were to ignore and forgive crimes, we would all lose our property, our bodies, and our lives.

3. When thieves insist on stealing and murderers insist on killing, then the emperor and his agents have a responsibility to address the problem in a different way than I or some other preacher of the Word and servant of peace would address it. It is not appropriate for us preachers to wield the sword; our job is to proclaim grace, to forgive, and to announce forgiveness in the name of Christ. To repeat, the job of the emperor and his forces is to punish evildoers, not to forgive them (Rom. 13:4).

4. Unfortunately, what is happening today is that officials in the civil government, who are reminded of their responsibility to punish, not only are indifferent and lazy about punishing crime, but actually aid and abet the criminals. We must diligently teach this doctrine, so

that people will learn and know that civil government must be stern and severe. The Turks know how to discharge this responsibility; they waste no time in disciplining. Whoever disobeys given laws loses his head. The result is that there isn't nearly as much unrest or rebellion among the peasants, city folk, knights, and household servants as there is in our country.

5. This negligence in regard to secular government is to a large extent the result of the monks, who in their sermons taught that princes and lords should always be merciful and should not practice capital punishment. By doing this, they brought secular government to the point where rulers pleaded conscientious objection when it was their duty to execute criminals. Our Lord God could easily enough have instituted that kind of civil government if that had been his pleasure, or if such government would have been good and useful for the world. But God deliberately commands civil government to make use of the sword; they are to use it in punishing criminal evil.

6. God ordered King Saul to eradicate and totally destroy the Amalekites along with all their property, people as well as animals, young and old alike. Some people might object: That is a cruel command; shouldn't they have spared at least the little children, the wives, and the old people, which is what even rational heathen do? But God doesn't want them to spare anyone or anything in this case. He says, "Spare them not; but slay both man and woman, infant and suckling, ox and sheep, camel and ass" (1 Sam. 15:3). Saul should have carried out that command of the Lord and not spared any of the Amalekites despite their pleading, weeping, and begging. Saul, however, did not obey, but captured alive Agag, the king of the Amalekites, nor did he destroy those sheep, cattle, and lambs that were fat. This made the Lord so angry that he took Saul's kingdom away because he had not obeyed the command of the Lord (1 Sam. 15).

7. As we learn from 1 Kings 20, the same thing happened to King Ahab. God allowed Benhadad, king of Syria, to be defeated by King Ahab in a great battle that involved 100,000 Syrian foot soldiers, all of whom were slain in one day. When Benhadad and his army had been defeated, he begged King Ahab, "Please, let me live!" Ahab replied, "Since he is still alive, he shall be my brother" (v. 32), and Ahab propped him up in his own chariot, made a treaty with him, and re-

leased him to resume the rule of his own kingdom. After these things had taken place, a prophet came and told Ahab (v. 42): "Thus saith the LORD, Because thou hast let go out of thy hand a man whom I appointed to utter destruction, therefore thy life shall go for his life, and thy people for his people." That made Ahab sullen and angry as he thought, Should not I, being king of Israel as I am, spare a defeated prisoner? But that turned out very badly for him. Three years later an arrow from one of Benhadad's men pierced King Ahab's heart, and so this king, whom he had spared against God's will in untimely mercy, destroyed Ahab and his whole family.

8. Therefore, secular governments must punish, not spare, criminals. However, the fact that secular officials often neglect this duty is the fault of the pope, the monks, and the false preachers who fail to teach the proper distinction between the spiritual kingdom and the secular kingdom. In the latter, evil must be punished with the sword. The spiritual kingdom and the civil kingdom have been totally confused, as is evident from the fact that present day bishops want to be secular princes, while at the same time they are neglecting their spiritual duties. Consequently, this is a very timely doctrine and those nations which properly distinguish between the two are very wise because there everyone will be taking care of his specific duties. A prince and secular lord will stringently carry out God's command against criminals by punishing them with the sword.

9. Unfortunately, however, I'm gravely concerned that it may already be too late, and that our preaching about the difference between the two kingdoms can no longer correct this problem because there no longer is any timidity, fear, respect, or obedience in the world. Everyone knows full well that governmental laws and officials ought to be obeyed, but no one does it. The very opposite is what people do; they lie, deceive, steal, and rob with abandon. There is no longer any fear or timidity among subjects over against government and its officials; and the government no longer punishes crimes or evil. It's possible that the world may stumble and bumble along till then; but to hope for the day when secular government really functions as it is supposed to in providing peace and order, that is a mere pipe dream. Let that suffice for the present, so far as the secular kingdom is concerned.

10. Christ also speaks about the spiritual kingdom in today's Gospel lesson and teaches us that in the church it is not the sword of the secular kingdom that is to be used, but rather grace and forgiveness. That is why everyone who claims to be a Christian must remember that he is to forgive his neighbor's shortcomings. The kings of this world have a kingdom that is to be ruled by vengeance and punishment, as God has commanded, but Christian people also live in a totally different kingdom in which there is to be no vengeance or punishment, but where everyone is to be friendly and merciful, as we shall explain very shortly.

11. This servant owes his lord ten thousand talents, such a huge sum that it will be impossible for him ever to repay it. In the course of the king's accounting with his servants, he comes across the figure of the huge debt which the servant will never be able to repay. So the king commands that the man is to be sold, along with his wife and children and everything else he has, until he has paid off the entire debt; and yet, that servant, even with his wife, children, and all his other possessions counted in, will not possibly be able to repay his debt because of its overwhelming size. Now when that servant is caught in this pitiful situation of not being able to repay, his lord does not punish him; instead, he takes pity on him, taps his shoulder with the sword, releases him personally, forgiving his debt, huge as it is. Just as that lord treated his servant, this servant should also have treated his fellow servant and should have thought: My lord has just canceled a huge debt for me; why shouldn't I also forgive my fellow servant's debt of a few hundred dollars? But he doesn't do that. Instead, he has his fellow servant thrown into prison till he will have paid every cent he owes. What the ultimate result of this is for him we shall learn shortly; for he is again summoned by his lord and is himself thrown into prison till he shall have paid every cent he owes. This illustrates the fact that only in the spiritual realm or kingdom is forgiveness to be the guiding principle.

12. Now we must diligently continue to study what forgiveness of sins is. It's a simple thing to mouth the expression "forgiveness of sins," just as it is a simple thing to repeat the basic truths of Christian doctrine. Ah yes, if all we had to do was to mouth the words! The problem is that when it comes to putting that expression into prac-

tice, we don't know the first thing about it! You see, it is such a tremendous truth, a truth that I am to believe wholeheartedly, that all my sins are forgiven, and by that faith I am righteous before God. Oh, what a marvelously astounding righteousness this is! How totally different this is in contrast to the righteousness of this world as proclaimed by all its lawyers, intellectual giants, and philosophers! For they all reach the same conclusion, namely, that righteousness must be an inner, inherent characteristic of the human heart and soul. But this Gospel lesson teaches us that Christian righteousness is not a universal characteristic of the human heart which all share. No, Christ is teaching us that we become righteous and are freed from sins through the forgiveness of sins!

13. During my early days when I was still under the papacy, I myself taught that anyone who wishes to be rid of sin must do this or that, build a chapel, erect an altar, pay for Masses, and the like. That attitude prevails among us to this day as we see in the case of the servant in our text. When he is called to account and told to pay up, he gets down on his knees, but does not ask for forgiveness or release from his debt, but pleads instead for patience and time. So this rascal assumes responsibility for his sin and promises to his lord that he will pay the whole debt himself, which is clearly an impossibility. We react in exactly the same way. When we hear that we have been promised forgiveness of sins, we really cannot grasp that, and take this position: I have committed this and that sin; to pay for them I will do thus and so, fast "x" number of days, say "x" number of prayers, fund "x" number of poorhouses, and pay for all my sins. It's because human nature is proud and always wants to be in control, pulling its own water bucket from the well, wants to have the honor of laying the first stone, of being Number One.

14. That's why this is a majestic message of divine wisdom: We must believe that our righteousness, salvation, and comfort lie outside of ourselves, namely, that we are righteous before God, acceptable to him, holy and wise, even though there is nothing within us but sin, injustice, and stupidity. In my conscience there is nothing but an awareness and feeling of sin and of the fear of death; and, therefore, I must look elsewhere for help, and must believe that there is no sin and no death. A person who refuses to see what he

does see, and who refuses to feel what he does feel must be completely bewitched. My eyes see a bronze gulden, a sword, fire, and yet I'm supposed to say, That is not a bronze gulden, no sword, no fire. That's how it is with the forgiveness of sins. I feel that I have been a bad boy, that I still am a bad boy, and yet I'm supposed to say, All my sins are forgiven; for this is the message that has been proclaimed to me: "Your sins are forgiven."

15. That is why this servant will never pay the ten thousand talents out of his own pocket, treasure, check, or bank account, for the debt is too great and the servant doesn't have what it takes to pay that debt. Someone else, however, does have the power to pay that debt, namely, the king; he takes pity on the servant and says, I feel sorry for you; therefore, I shall tear up the bill, so that you no longer owe me anything; not that you've repaid me, but I have simply forgiven you your debt.

16. But I repeat, flesh and blood have this affliction, that they are always trying to bring up something on which they can depend. Human nature is defenseless against a bad habit; it cannot avoid an awareness of sins and yet cannot believe in pure grace and the forgiveness of sins. If you have developed this skill, of not seeing what you do see, and of not feeling what you do feel, then let me tell you about something nobler and more majestic. But I warn you, it will take you a long time to develop this artistic skill! For this business of faith in the forgiveness of sins is just as if someone were aiming a loaded gun at your face and was ready to pull the trigger, and yet you are to believe and to say, Not to worry!

17. I myself must confess that it's contrary to my nature and is hard for me to believe this article, for I see before me a long catalogue of sins. And even if I had committed no other sin against God, I did for sixteen years live in the wicked and abominable monastic system, conducted Masses, preached errors and misleading doctrine, and led myself and others astray; and yet I'm now asked to overlook all those sins just as if I had never committed any of them. In addition to that, every day I still feel that I lack a proper fear of God and also lack in faith. I'm plagued by laziness, by the "old Adam" who tells me nothing but evil. I don't love God with all my heart or my neighbor as myself, and so I am filled with sin. Yet I'm to believe that I have

no sin at all. I must confess, it's hard for me to believe this article. For by nature I'm inclined to do what we practiced doing under the papacy, wanting to fast, to go without sleep, to pray, to go on pilgrimages, and to do good works, in order to pay for my sins. Because that is my natural inclination, this wicked servant in our text does exactly what I'm inclined to do by saying, "Have patience with me, I'll pay back everything I owe you!"

18. Now there is no way of receiving forgiveness of sins except to simply close my eyes and believe that my sins are forgiven, as we pray in the Christian Creed: "I believe in the Holy Spirit . . . the forgiveness of sins." But by nature my reason would prefer to have this article avoid calling sin "sin," and would instead describe it as an apparent but imaginary sin; in other words, that sin would be a word used only in a self-deprecating way to indicate humility. In short, I would prefer to present myself to the Lord as a falsely accused sinner, and to confess myself to be a sinner but without feeling guilty of sin. To me that would be the ideal kind of sinner. However, these words that say, "I believe in the forgiveness of sins," are the words of the Holy Spirit. Whatever the Holy Spirit calls sin can, therefore, not be an imaginary or apparent sin, but must truly be actual, genuine sin, such as adultery, fornication, stealing, and so on. These are sins that I have committed and that I still commit every day, just as the debt which this servant owed was not an imaginary debt but one he truly owed, ten thousand talents worth! So, whoever wants to truly confess that he is a sinner must see to it that he is not confessing any dreamed up or imaginary sins. He must confess that his sins are just as real as adultery, theft, murder, and the like, that is, that these sins are so great that they will take you to hell unless they are forgiven. For even if we don't commit all the gross, outward sins like adultery, theft, or murder, nevertheless, unless we have this benefit of believing in the forgiveness of sins, our sins will damn us to the abyss of hell.

19. I still have not mastered this skill but am constantly in the process of learning this art. The uneducated masses have no idea of what either sin or the forgiveness of sins is. But we who assume that we do know what forgiveness of sins is will have to keep on learning what it is as long as we live. For it is our natural inclination to try to erase our sins by our own efforts and to minimize our sins by saying, I'm not

aware of having committed any special sins; I'm not an adulterer, or a thief, or a murderer, and so on. Our confession of sins, however, must be genuine, so that before God we plead: Dear Lord, if you enter into judgment with me, what you will find is not imaginary, but genuine, great sins, just as this servant owes a genuine debt. Those are not artificial pennies, nor are they make-believe coins but actual coins, gulden, Joachim dollars,° ten thousand pounds of them. That is the kind of confession of sins that is required, for if the forgiveness of sins is to be genuine, then the sins themselves must also be genuine.

20. That is why the Creed includes those most precious words, "I believe in the forgiveness of sins." We believe that sin exists and that at the same time it has been forgiven. Forgiveness devours sin. On the other hand, whoever believes in and confesses forgiveness must also believe in and confess sin. That is why we are all burdened by sins, sins that are constantly propelling us toward hell, unless we have been called into the state and regimen of the forgiveness of sins. For we have been baptized into the name of Christ; thereby we have received forgiveness of sin and are pure. The guilt is still there, but it is forgiven. By itself it is guilt, but our blessing is that the guilt has been remitted.

21. So Christ created this article, forgiveness of sins, in us through baptism but he also continues to maintain it through the Word, Sacrament, absolution, and the Holy Spirit whom he sends into the heart. Sin is indeed present in us, but is forgiven, just as the snakes which some people carry about in their bosoms are indeed reptiles, but nonpoisonous ones. That's how it is with the sin that weights us down; it is truly sin, but it is not a damning kind of sin, because it is forgiven. It is like death which destroys the Christian physically; it is truly death, but a death that has already been overcome. Now, because this article is begun through baptism and is preserved through the Word, we shall never in this life be able to comprehend fully what forgiveness of sins is.

22. We see this clearly illustrated in this servant. Before the king calls him to an accounting, he has no guilty conscience, no sense of

---

° Prince Joachim of Brandenburg was one of the seven electors of the holy Roman Empire. Hence, major coin of the realm!

wrongdoing. He would have continued his dishonesty, made more debts without any conscience scruples. It is not till the king demands a settlement of his debts that he begins to feel his guilt. The same thing is true of us too. Most of us are unconcerned about our debt of sin, living along blithely, not the least bit concerned about God's wrath. Such people cannot receive forgiveness of sins, for they never reach the point of even realizing that they have any sin. If they took their sins seriously, they would sing an altogether different tune. Before his lord called him to an accounting, this servant also blithely admitted, I owe my lord ten thousand talents, and then laughed about it. But when he is hailed into court and his lord orders him, his wife, his children, and everything he owns to be sold until the whole debt is paid, then he suddenly is aware of his guilt and debt. In the same way we feel the seriousness of our situation when our hearts realize their sins. When we are confronted with the total record of our sins, the laughter dies on our lips. Then we are ready to confess: Of all men I am most wretched; there's not another person on earth who is as wicked as I! That kind of confession indicates a truly humble person, enables a person to truly receive forgiveness of sins. And unless there is such humility, there can be no forgiveness. Therefore, the gospel of the forgiveness of sins is only appropriate for true Christians, for those who truly recognize and feel their sins. Other crude people who neither recognize nor feel their sins don't belong in the same group, nor do they understand this teaching of the forgiveness of sins. And even if they listen to sermons about it, it remains a mystery to them.

23. However, true Christians who feel their sins have the comfort of believing in the forgiveness of sins because they have been baptized, they hear the gospel, they have absolution, and the Holy Sacrament; they believe that selfsame word in each of these. For you see, God has invested the same treasure, forgiveness of sins, in his Word and Sacrament and has commanded us to believe that Word. That is why Christians don't appear before God the way the wicked servant did, saying, "Have patience with me and I'll pay you everything I owe," nor do they minimize their sins, but confess that they are truly genuine and grievous, and so they plead for forgiveness. Such people truly receive what they believe, namely, the forgiveness

of sins. This kingdom of grace and forgiveness began for us in baptism and remains ours till we die. God instituted the preaching of the gospel, baptism, absolution and the Sacrament, so that we would be able to continually strengthen our faith in the forgiveness of sins.

24. We should diligently note this, so that we may know how to get rid of sin, namely, in no other way than the means indicated in the third article of our Christian Creed: I believe in the forgiveness of sins. That is the same as saying, I acknowledge and feel my sins; I quake and shake in dread because of them. But how can I get rid of them? I can get rid of them only by believing that even though sin is there and though I feel its presence, nevertheless, it is not sin, because it is forgiven. But if the sin is forgiven, then the forgiveness is not earned because "to forgive" does not mean to reward or to pay, but rather to give as a free gift, out of grace. That is why it takes genuine faith to receive forgiveness of sins. You see, the two go hand in hand: recognition of sin, or humility, and faith. Just as we must truly recognize and feel sin, so we must also truly feel the forgiveness of sin in the Word. It is not something that can be seen or grasped or touched, for it is a high and holy matter of faith. We hear and feel it in the Word, and God, who speaks that word, is greater than heaven and earth. Now, because it is God who speaks, because the word of forgiveness is God's word or promise, therefore, every creature in heaven and on earth must agree with that promise, and no creature dare overlook the importance of the forgiveness of sins.

25. Therefore, a Christian should cling to this article and not doubt it, but should firmly believe and always trust in the forgiveness which he has in the Word. Don't waste any time denying your sins. For if you do that, you quickly reach the point where you want to repay your debt, as did the servant in our text. That is why we should refuse to listen when our heart speaks to us in terror and unbelief. We should, instead, listen to what God says, for he is greater than your heart or mine. If we believe the Word, it will open heaven to us, and we shall know that God's Word is greater, more majestic, deeper, longer, and broader than any of God's creatures.

26. We also hear about this wicked servant that, after he had experienced grace at the hand of his king, he became proud and obstinate, stirring up the king's wrath once more. That's the way the

godless world is which horribly misuses this doctrine of the forgiveness of sins. Some refuse to admit their sins; even though they are wallowing in sin over their heads, yet they refuse to admit that they are sinners. For such people there is not forgiveness; for as we said earlier, If there is no sin, neither can there be any forgiveness. Some keep right on sinning after receiving forgiveness, believing that the gospel allows everyone to do just as he pleases. But the gospel is a message for the depressed, for people with a guilty conscience, not for those who keep on defending their sins, nor is it for those who deliberately sin against a gracious God.

27. After this wicked servant's debt had been canceled, he forgot all about that great grace, went out, accosted one of his fellow servants who owed him a few hundred dollars. He begins to choke the man, demanding that he immediately pay every cent of his debt. The fellow servant pleads and begs, but the more he pleads, the more obstinate and inconsiderate the wicked servant becomes. This is characteristic of most worldlings; when they are forgiven for their sins, they immediately forget the forgiveness and grace of God and become more wicked and rebellious than before. It is my opinion that those who boast of being evangelical are worse sinners after hearing the gospel than they were before hearing it. It is not a case of the gospel being at fault, but the fault lies with the people who so horribly misuse the gospel.

28. The nature of the gospel is such, that those who misuse it, become more wicked than they were before. Christ himself says (Matt. 12:43–45): "When the unclean spirit is gone out of a man, he walketh through dry places, seeking rest, and findeth none. Then he saith, I will return into my house from whence I came out; and when he is come, he findeth it empty, swept, and garnished. Then goeth he, and taketh with himself seven other spirits more wicked than himself, and they enter in and dwell there: and the last state of that man is worse than the first. Even so shall it be also unto this wicked generation." There you have it, black on white! Any person to whom the gospel is proclaimed and who then misuses that gospel, becomes seven times more wicked than he was to begin with, and it would have been better for him if he had never heard the gospel. That is why I have often said that if I could accomplish things by wishing, I would

wish that peasants, burghers, and nobles, who now horribly misuse the gospel, might still be under the papacy, for they are nothing but a hindrance, a shame and a disgrace to the gospel.

29. You see that illustrated here in this wicked servant too. After having experienced such great mercy, this scoundrel leaves and becomes more wicked than he had been before. This is not just my own personal judgment or opinion; it is the judgment of our Lord Christ himself. In crystal clear words he asserts that those who become evangelicals turn out to be more wicked than they were before. Experience, too, teaches us that this is so. Sad to say, we daily experience the fact that people who are under the gospel now bear greater and more bitter hatred and envy in their hearts; they are more greedy and materialistic now than when they were still under the papacy. As Christ says, The reason for this is that they have again opened their heart's door to Satan, and he has brought with himself seven other spirits, more wicked than he himself is. We, who proclaim the gospel, must simply put up with the fact that under the gospel people become more wicked than they were before. But it is not the fault of the gospel, but of the devil and those people who return to serving Satan, allowing him to reenter their hearts and rule there along with seven other, more wicked spirits. This really depresses and angers the rest of the servants, so they come and report to the king the sordid conduct of their fellow servant. We, too, experience the same kind of disappointment when those who have the reputation of being "evangelical" conduct themselves so disgracefully and abominably that we really wish they were still under the papacy. But here we follow the example of these fellow servants by bringing their disgraceful abuse of the gospel to the attention of God and of the public.

30. What happens next? The king summons that servant and says: You wicked servant! I've canceled that huge debt of yours just because you pleaded with me; should you not likewise have had mercy on your fellow servant, just as I had mercy on you? In effect, the king was saying, What a contrast in forgiveness! I canceled your multi-million dollar debt, but you are unwilling to cancel your fellow servant's piddly debt of a few hundred dollars! What can the wicked servant say in response? He just stands there speechless, with not a word to say. Similarly, the Lord God will soon bring down upon our

false "evangelicals" plagues, hard times, and war. Already we hear complaints on every hand that things are so expensive. But the world won't have it any other way; it is completely materialistic, misuses the gospel in the most disgraceful way possible; and that is why God will have to send some sweeping catastrophe. It is just as we read in Proverbs 30:21–23: "For three things the earth is disquieted, and for four which it cannot bear: For a servant when he reigneth; and a fool when he is filled with meat; For an odious woman when she is married; and an handmaid that is heir to her mistress." We are such sated servants. Through the gospel we've been freed from the pope's tyrannical rule of law and, therefore, we have become intolerably proud and feisty; and that is why God will have to punish us by throwing sand into our gears.

31. This wicked servant horribly mistreats his fellow servant, chokes him, and has him put in prison. And what happens to him? The king becomes furious with him and turns him over to the torturers until he shall have paid every cent he owes the king. That's what will also happen to us; we will become the objects of God's wrath and both his physical and spiritual punishment. For God will avenge and severely punish the haughty rebellion of all who misuse the gospel, rich or poor. Would to God, that the punishment could be delayed for a while by our prayers! But things cannot be allowed to continue as they are now. Rebellion is so great and widespread that God will have to put a stop to it. No amount of warning or admonition, pleading or begging, no amount of threats or punishments by either spiritual or secular authority will do any good; God himself will have to step in with avenging judgment to punish and put an end to such wickedness.

32. All right, if people want to risk forcing God's hand, shamefully misusing the gospel and stirring up God's wrath, I will venture to see which of us can better stand the heat of his wrath. I have one head to lose, just one. Even if I lose it, I will still know where I end up; but you'll just have to wait to find out where you end up. For we see from our text that these servants meet different fates. The wicked servant is punished, but the rest of the servants have a gracious lord. He doesn't treat them the way he treats the wicked servant. Similarly, you who are misusing the gospel so shamefully will meet a different

fate from the one that is reserved for us, whom you are mistreating and depressing so severely.

33. Therefore, we should not misuse God's grace and forgiveness. Our Lord God has given us more than enough proofs that our sins are forgiven, namely, the proclamation of the gospel, baptism, the Sacrament, and the Holy Spirit in our hearts. Now, it is important that we, too, give proof by which we testify that we have indeed received the forgiveness of sins. The proof that is expected of us is that each of us forgive the faults of his brother or sister. Of course, there is no comparison between God's forgiveness and our forgiveness; for what is a few hundred compared with ten thousand talents! There is no equivalency. Similarly, we do not by our forgiveness deserve to have God's forgiveness for our sins; instead, God offers us forgiveness of sins out of sheer grace. Nevertheless, we should also forgive the brother who has sinned against us, so that by that forgiveness we prove and testify that we have indeed received and accepted forgiveness from God.

34. Brotherly forgiveness, however, also includes that the brother whom I am to forgive admits his shortcomings. For, any sin that is not admitted, I cannot forgive. If the brother keeps right on doing me wrong and becomes more offensive from one day to the next, I must, of course, put up with that, but I should not pronounce absolution for such an offense. Instead, I must put a burden on his conscience by telling him, Brother, by doing thus and so, you have sinned against me; I want you to know that you have wronged me. If he disregards my rebuke and laughs it off, I'll have to bear with that; but then I cannot forgive him for it because he refuses to admit that it is a sin. But if he honestly admits his fault by saying, Brother, I have sinned against you; please forgive me, then I must reply, With all my heart, dear brother, I forgive you.

35. You see, brotherly forgiveness is not like the forgiveness of the peasants, burghers, and nobles who deliberately make trouble for their pastors in every way they can, because they know that the pastor is powerless to do anything about it. So they bank on that and say, Nonsense! Our pastor has to forgive us for there is no one who can punish us. The pastor is a preacher who is supposed to be patient and just put up with us. He can't take anyone to court, and even if he

complains loudly, no one listens to him. They give him whatever they please, and then steal back from him corn, rye, oats, whatever they wish. And especially the nobles treat their pastors like a fire stoker, lackey, messenger boy, or bootblack. They rob him of his share of the rent and of the taxes with which he is supposed to provide for his wife and children. And they all claim to be fine "evangelicals" who can do no wrong that might bother their conscience. They operate on this formula: That poor fellow, our pastor, it's his duty to forgive! Yes, my dear squires, we are obliged to forgive you, if you admit that your actions are sins and if you intend not to commit those sins again. But if you refuse to admit that such conduct is sinful and if you go right on doing the same things, then it is our duty to inform you: You are dealing unjustly with me, and you refuse to admit that it is sin; therefore I cannot forgive you. If you laugh it off, my response is: May your sin be a fire in your soul! And when plagues, hard times, and the grim reaper come, and when you ultimately are confronted by hellfire, then God will hold an accounting, just as he hailed the wicked servant in our text into court.

36. That, in brief, is what I wanted to share with you for this time in regard to this sublime and important doctrine, the forgiveness of sins. This doctrine is so important that we could preach about it every Sunday for a whole year. May our dear Lord God grant us his grace to correctly understand this doctrine, comfort ourselves with it, and may we joyfully put it into practice. Amen.

TWENTY-THIRD SUNDAY AFTER TRINITY

First Sermon*

Matthew 22:15–22

Then went the Pharisees, and took counsel how they might entangle him in his talk. And they sent out unto him their disciples with the Herodians, saying, Master, we know that thou art true, and teachest the way of God in truth, neither carest thou for any man: for thou regardest not the person of men. Tell us therefore, What thinkest thou? Is it lawful to give tribute unto Caesar, or not? But Jesus perceived their wickedness, and said, Why tempt ye me, ye hypocrites? Shew me the tribute money. And they brought unto him a penny. And he saith unto them, Whose is this image and superscription? They say unto him, Caesar's. Then saith he unto them, Render therefore unto Caesar the things which are Caesar's; and unto God the things that are God's. When they had heard these words, they marvelled, and left him, and went their way.

1. The most important thing our Lord Jesus Christ teaches us in this Gospel lesson is the distinction between the two kingdoms, that is, the kingdom of God and the kingdom of the world. We must carefully differentiate between the two, allowing each its own purpose and function, so that neither infringes upon the other, as happens regularly in the case of the factious spirits. The kingdom of God, which is the greatest and most sublime of the two, often finds itself opposed by its adversaries. But so also the kingdom of the world. The devil is always working through his lackeys to destroy both kingdoms on earth.

2. However, God has ordained and established them both, and has built a wall around them to protect them against all fanatics. What this wall is, Christ tells us in the words, "Render unto Caesar

---

*Preached at the parish church, 1529.

the things which are Caesar's, and unto God the things which are God's." This is addressed to all people, so that they pay attention to it and do it. If they do it willingly, well and good. If not willingly and gladly, they will have to do it anyway. Whoever gives God what is God's and Caesar what is Caesar's does so willingly and receives special commendation. If he does it grudgingly, he still has to do it. For since the word "give" is appended to each kingdom, it becomes the kind of moat, wall, and buttress that compels all people to give.

3. The devil would like to stop this. He gives rise to many factious spirits and sects within the church in order to check this giving to God what is God's. But to no avail. The more the devil rages and fumes against God's kingdom and the church, the stronger it becomes. And the more that Christian blood is shed, the more martyrs there will be. In the secular realm or kingdom this is what happens: The more vigorously the devil plants himself against it, the more firmly God asserts his ordinance; and historians attest to the fact that God never lets rebellion go unpunished.

4. With the words, Give Caesar what is Caesar's, Christ validates and establishes the civil state. If civil government were not warranted and ordained by God, Christ would not say, Give Caesar what is Caesar's. For he is a preacher and teacher of truth; he cannot lie and always speaks absolute truth. So, if we are to give to Caesar, we must consider him to be a man of authority and power. Now, at that time Caesar was a Gentile, knowing nothing of Christ. His kingdom was founded on principles of common sense and good order, and governed according to the dictates of human reason. Accordingly, Christ says here that because Caesar has the authority, he is to be obeyed. And even if persons were to disagree with him, they still were obligated to obey him.

5. This word, Give Caesar what is Caesar's, Christians gladly and gratefully accept, yielding Caesar what is his without complaint. For they are taught and enlightened by God's Word to understand the value of the political state. This is the reason they are not ungrateful as are the Anabaptists, who disdain the civil state. A Christian, first of all, looks at the word "give" and willingly acknowledges the implications of the word because Christ himself has spoken it. He carefully notes that Scripture calls the civil state God's ordinance and

considers the purpose which the political state serves on earth. For, as long as God upholds it, there is peace on earth and wicked scoundrels do not, by and large, get away with murder. This peace is such a great treasure that no one, except the Christian, is able to grasp its true significance. Furthermore, a Christian looks at the obligation involved, realizing that everything he possesses has been received from God and belongs to Caesar, or to the magistrate to whom Caesar has delegated authority. When swearing allegiance, each citizen pledges wholeheartedly to obey the existing authorities as required.

6. So the word, Give unto Caesar what is Caesar's, also signifies that life and property are removed from the citizen and given to Caesar. First Samuel 8 clearly states what the king's right is. Samuel says to the people who were requesting a king (vv. 11–17): "This will be the manner of the king that shall reign over you: He will take your sons, and appoint them for himself, for his chariots, and to be his horsemen; and some shall run before his chariots. And he will appoint him captains over thousands, and captains over fifties; and will set them to cultivate his ground, and to reap his harvest, and to make his instruments of war, and instruments of his chariots. And he will take your daughters to be confectioneries, and to be cooks, and to be bakers. And he will take your fields, and your vineyards, and your oliveyards, even the best of them, and give them to his servants. And he will take the tenth of your seed, and of your vineyards, and give to his officers, and to his servants. And he will take your menservants, and your maidservants, and your goodliest young men, and your asses, and put them to his work. He will take the tenth of your sheep: and ye shall be his servants." And to Nebuchadnezzar, the king of Babylon, the prophet Daniel says (2:37–38): "Thou, O king, art a king of kings: for the God of heaven hath given thee a kingdom, power, and strength, and glory. And wheresoever the children of men dwell, the beasts of the field and the fowls of the heaven hath he given into thine hand, and hath made thee ruler over them all."

7. Christians know this from Holy Scripture. They are provided with spiritual understanding. So that peace may continue on earth, they are content with the political state. They are ready to do Caesar's bidding. They serve him even if it means life and property. Because of this they will have approval. As St. Paul says (Rom. 13:3):

"Wilt thou then not be afraid of the power? do that which is good, and thou shalt have praise of the same." It is this minority, made up of true Christians, which is cognizant of this word, Give Caesar what is Caesar's, and consequently think: Because God has commanded and so wants it, thus shall it be. These are the ones who uphold the civil government. If Christians did not engage in prayer, there would be no civil state on earth to maintain peace. Only Christians take up the challenge of this word, Give unto Caesar, and on account of their obedience they are approved of God and men.

8. But the majority, the restless rabble, do not do this. Though they have been told, they do not believe that the secular state and government officials are instituted by God. They do not believe that God's Word rightly teaches that the state is an ordinance of God. They look upon civil government as an affliction, a yoke around their neck. The godless do not set store by God's ordinance, ordering, and command. Their only thought is to fill their purses and have a good feast time, regardless of whom God constitutes as head of state, and whether peace or unrest prevail.

9. Ah, dear friend, were our Lord God always to allow peace to reign in the land, to let you dance and frolic, and you were not obligated to thank him for it and pay taxes, you would rejoice. You do not believe that your possessions belong to Caesar and the state. You think they are yours, and you forget that you have sworn to obey your country with life and property. This is the way the wicked think. They give no thought to prayer in behalf of their government, nor that peace is a precious treasure. Still less do they think of the homage they have pledged their country. People today generally raise their voices against the state because they have to pay taxes. This happens because they do not believe that God has said or commanded anything as regards Caesar. They think that what they possess is theirs, even though the Lord says here, Give Caesar what is Caesar's. What is Caesar's? The life and property which you swore to him when you made your vow of allegiance. However, you oppose your head of state as if you yourself were he, and the head of state had sworn allegiance to you.

10. This is the group of people who do not understand this word, Give unto Caesar, and so on. Nor do they understand what a needful, precious thing earthly peace is, but are like swine that think everything

is theirs. These constitute the majority of the people; they are ready to destroy the state were they not walled in on all sides by God's Word and command. That Word compels the godless masses; for it says, You will have to obey your government whether you want to or not; and Master Hans will teach you in due time. If you were unwilling to obey government, you should never have pledged allegiance, but should have said instead, I refuse to render obedience with life and property. But face up to it, you swore allegiance and vowed obedience; and despite this you would endanger yourself by contesting whether you are going to obey and give Caesar what is his, or not.

11. And as we read in this Gospel lesson, that is exactly what the Jews did. They allowed Caesar to come in; they paid him homage and vowed obedience. And now, first, they ask Christ whether they ought to obey Caesar. The Lord replies, This coin is used to pay taxes due Caesar, and you have sworn loyalty to him; so bear this in mind and give him what is his. Let me also say, Why did you accept Caesar as your ruler if you do not want to obey him? Hence, I tell you: If you have sworn obedience to the state, you must render that obedience; and if the government is tottery and unstable, Master Hans and the Turk will teach you soon enough. At the moment you have peace and are confident that body and possessions are yours; the thought never enters your mind that just maybe you have these things because God and Caesar gave them to you. God tells you in his Word, Give Caesar what is Caesar's, but you respond, Not so! It is I who tell Caesar what is his. And so you mock God. And he will in consequence send you the Turk to be a noose around your neck, who will not leave your wife, child, home, or possessions untouched for long, just as recently happened to the Viennese peasants. The Turks despoiled them and in two days carried off 90,000 women and children. Thus our Lord God taught those poor people that neither house nor home, neither wife nor child, are yours but Caesar's, through whom God gives them.

12. We Christians should not be influenced by how the godless world thinks. We should willingly and gladly yield to Caesar what is his. I have nothing of value but four or six goblets. Yet, if necessary, I would gladly let him have them and my life as well. No matter what you think, you will never tear down this wall whereby Christ firmly establishes Caesar in his position. If you are unwilling to give Caesar

his due in God's name, be assured you will have to give to some tyrant in the devil's name.

13. Many revile us because we obey the state, but we do not give a rap about their slanderous words. Whoever wants to be a Christian knows that he is not living in paradise, where only good prevails. He knows that he is living in the midst of Sodom and Gomorrah, where there are people who neither know nor understand, nor do they want to know and understand, what God has commanded. We are not saying these things for their sakes; but we do not want them to be left unsaid either. If they demur and refuse to obey God, the Lord will nonetheless have his way. Meanwhile, we will have to live with their sins, and for ourselves with ready heart and spirit do what God has commanded, not looking at their disobedience, but at God's command. For the sake of a righteous man, God often tolerates a whole country's sinfulness, as in the case of Lot who pleaded in behalf of his countrymen and by his prayer succeeded in forestalling the destruction of the cities. However, no sooner was he gone from Sodom than it was destroyed. So, while we are living on earth, let us, as obedient people, pray that God will not impute their sins to the ungodly. However, once we have departed, they will come into hell in the name of the devil. The die is cast; they will not escape. I say this to those who love the gospel. The rest are not worthy to hear a single word of what I am saying.

14. This, then, is the reason why we are to know that God has commanded to give Caesar what is Caesar's. But what is Caesar's? Let's talk about duty. You pledge loyalty to the civil magistrates and the prince, and he in turn pledges with life and property to serve the emperor. When the time comes that you are approached by the state, then remember your pledge. If you do not want to do what is asked, then go to your civil authority, to Caesar, and say, Dear sir, gracious prince, benevolent emperor, in times past I have sworn and pledged allegiance to you, but I do not wish to obey you any longer; for this reason I am now retracting my vow. You will hear soon enough what your magistrate, prince, or Caesar will have to say about this! On the other hand, if you want to keep your pledge of loyalty, then with heart and soul do what you promised when you publicly

vowed allegiance, and be on guard against those who refuse to give what they owe, for in the end it will cost them their life.

15. Pious Christians heed the words, Give unto Caesar, and give Caesar what is his. In turn, a just government accepts what subjects give, not only that it might enjoy esteem, but that citizens may live in peace, sleep securely in their homes, and the world be kept in line. We should recognize blessings like these and be thankful for them. God will visit the ungrateful in his own time. This is Christ's meaning in Matthew 21, the parable of the landowner. A landowner planted a vineyard, let it out to tenants, and then went abroad. But the tenants greedily grabbed the fruits of the vineyard for themselves, as if the vineyard was theirs. They forgot that the vineyard was leased to them, that in due course they would have to account for the fruits thereof. In short, they dealt with the vineyard as if it were their own property. And when the landowner, demanded his share of the vineyard's produce, the tenants killed not only the servants, but also the son of the landowner so that they might get his inheritance. How do you think, says Christ, the owner of the vineyard will deal with these tenants? He will bring those scoundrels to a sorry end and lease his vineyard out to other tenants, who will give him his share of the crop at harvest time.

16. I wonder whether you could tolerate such mischief on your estate? If you would cultivate your land and entrust your property to a servant who swore that he would take care of everything for you, but then, while you were gone he would break to pieces everything in the house, what would you do about it? Verily, you would deal with the servant just as the Gospel lesson says the landowner will deal with his tenants. Why shouldn't our Lord God do the same? Who can fault our Lord when he sent the Turks to plague the ungrateful and disobedient?

17. Our Lord God has given you possessions through Caesar, and you have sworn loyalty to Caesar. And now you are disavowing your allegiance and acting as if the possessions were yours and not Caesar's. For this reason you need someone like this tyrant, the Turk, to threaten and give you a thrashing. Something of this sort is going to happen. Whoever will not accept this word, "Give unto Caesar," by fair means will have to accept it by foul. That's what happened to the Jews: They

had accepted Caesar as Caesar, as they themselves admitted, We have no king but Caesar. While wanting nothing to do with Caesar, they had to accept him. Emperor Titus came and taught them this to their destruction, for he smashed them completely.

18. On the other hand, when Christ adds the words, Give God what is God's, he establishes and confirms the spiritual polity, called the kingdom of God. There is not the same and immediate urgency to establish and confirm this kingdom as for the civil state, for God is Lord over the whole world, whether it acknowledges this voluntarily or involuntarily. Moreover, this kingdom endures forever, even though there are many who defy it. Just the same, it requires as much explanation as does the worldly kingdom, if we are properly to understand it. Human reason grasps and comprehends the political kingdom, but this spiritual realm or kingdom lies beyond human reason's competence.

19. This spiritual kingdom is a realm in which those are gathered whose hearts are united in trust of God. For the citizens of this kingdom have sworn allegiance to God in baptism. Just as a citizen and subject swears allegiance before the bench of the civil state, so all Christians solemnly pledge and promise fealty in baptism, that Christ is their Lord and God. Is not this exactly what we do prior to our baptism when we disavow the devil, all his works and all his ways, and say that we believe in God the Father, Son, and Holy Spirit, pledging with all our hearts to believe in the one true God and in none other, and to bring forth good works, to be patient, meek, and loving toward our neighbor? Our Lord God requires of us the vow to cling to Christ alone, to listen to no other word, and to accept no other belief than the gospel of Christ and believe in him. This is what is meant when Christ says, Give God what is God's. What is God's? Nothing other than faith in God and love of the neighbor.

20. Many contend against this faith in one way or another. Some give God what is God's; many do not. Just as in the civil state there are some obedient citizens, so also in the spiritual realm there are some upright, righteous Christians, even though others may merely bear his name and be intermingled in the external fellowship. A handful willingly give God what is his. Pious hearts call and cry unceasingly to God to have their faith made stronger and to produce fruits commensurate

with their faith. These are the righteous Christians. God does not look for our money, life, and property. These he has given to Caesar, and to us through Caesar. But the heart, the greatest and best that man has, God has reserved for himself. We owe this to God in faith.

21. However, the majority of people in the world—by far the greatest throng—do not give God what is his. The mass of humanity is constituted by so many factious spirits and sects that we are unable to count them. In each of these the devil attempts to create new and strange beliefs, as those spawned by the enthusiasts, Anabaptists, and Sacramentarians. Just like the papacy, they, too, have torn Holy Scripture to shreds and robbed the people of God's Word. One and all, they are guilty of subversion within the kingdom of God. Like those within the civil state who are rebellious and think that everything belongs to them and do not give Caesar what is Caesar's, rebellious people exist within the spiritual realm. They think that spiritual blessings and God's Word belong only to them. They feel that these things are theirs to adapt, bend, and pervert to suit themselves, to adulterate Christian belief, and design good works according to their way of thinking. In short, they wish to be masters of their faith and lords over all of Holy Scripture, even though in baptism they have sworn allegiance to remain true to the Christian faith and to the pure Word.

22. Pious Christians, however, who pledge loyalty to the true faith and pure doctrine, meanwhile, continue to pray, and bear with such rebellion, thereby staving off God's anger, until God, once he has threshed out and gathered the wheat into the heavenly granaries, finally eliminates them from this earth and sets fire to the granaries along with the chaff. If the ungodly will not with heart and soul give God what is his, they must suffer the penalty. So God upholds his Word and the faith, despite the obstacles created by factious spirits. He will purge his threshing floor and burn up the chaff. Christians and those who fear God are mindful of such divine vengeance and punishment, and for that reason pray and stave off God's anger as long as possible. A righteous Christian must be like Lot in this world. Because of such people the Word remains pure and unadulterated. But as for the rest, the Word does not stay pure and unadulterated for even a moment. Yes, as indicated, they do much to impede God and his Word and strive to obliterate it quickly and completely.

23. Therefore, it is Christians alone who by their prayers sustain these two kingdoms on earth, God's and Caesar's. Were it not for the Christians and their prayers on behalf of these two realms, it would be impossible for them to continue to exist. In short, it is for the sake of the Christians that God spares the world. For his thoughts are these: My Christians give me what is mine and give Caesar what is Caesar's, and for this reason they must have peace, peace which it is mine to provide and bestow. When God now grants Christians peace, this same peace also spreads over the ungrateful, who benefit from what Christians enjoy.

24. That fruits now spring forth and peace reigns on earth does not happen for the sake of the godless masses, but for the sake of pious Christians; and often it is true that the godless have more peace than the Christians. God is a Lord who abounds in mercy and goodness. He scatters his blessings throughout the world, even among the ungodly, as Christ himself says (Matt. 5:45): "He maketh his sun to rise on the evil and on the good, and sendeth rain on the just and on the unjust." Nevertheless, all this occurs for the sake of the upright and the grateful, even though the wicked and the ungrateful also enjoy the blessings, until ultimately the upright have all entered heaven and the chaff is set ablaze and consumed. This is what happened in Jerusalem. Once the apostles and the Christians were gone, along with them went grain, wine, bread, and meat. And upon the multitudinous mass of Jews came pestilence, hunger, and sword, to the point that they killed and devoured one another. For what was left was chaff; the wheat was gone. This is the way it ultimately ends. As long as there are upright Christians living in the world, so long will there be peace and abundant blessing. But once the faithful depart this world, they take all blessings with them—food, life, and property. Like with the Jews, all will be gone.

25. We must, therefore, be aware of this distinction between these two kingdoms, God's kingdom and Caesar's. When a person hears the word, Give God what is God's, he should call to mind the vow he made to God in baptism and be on his guard against alien and false belief, heeding God's Word so as not to be deceived and led astray. When he hears the word, Give Caesar what is Caesar's, he should be thinking of the magistrates and the ruling prince, and

should recall the pledge and the oath he made to the civil authorities. In this way he will give each his due, as St. Paul says in Romans 13:6–7. The one who does this with heart and soul will be repaid by God many times over and, in addition, will receive honor and praise from the civil authorities. The one who does not do so will run headlong into the verdict: In the name of a thousand devils hand it over!

26. Solomon says (Eccles. 3:1): "To every thing there is a season." Up till now it has been a time for peace; but now it is time for conflict. Up till now a time for laughing and dancing; now it is time for crying and lamentation. For so long a time God graciously granted his mercy and a day of salvation, time during which to hear and learn his Word. But the time of his fury and wrath is now here. The time of gathering now gives way to scattering. If until now you have scorned God and Caesar, for this you will now shed tears in captivity. If before you have revelled and lived in abundance, you must now take up arms and march against the foes. For this reason I pray that you will give God what is God's and Caesar what is Caesar's. And do this not for my sake, but for the sake of him who has so commanded. If you do it with thanks, you do well. But if you do not do it with thanks, you will have to do it with ingratitude, and as a result suffer not only shame and disgrace, but also harm to body, possessions, and soul.

TWENTY-THIRD SUNDAY AFTER TRINITY

Second Sermon[*]

Matthew 22:15–22

1. The first portion of this Gospel tells how the Pharisees and hypocrites gathered to hold counsel as to how they might trap Jesus in what he was saying. It provides us with a helpful picture of how we should respond when spiteful people in this world use all their resources to persecute us. If they cannot suppress the gospel with their fists and physical force, they resort to evil spite and poisonous devices. They are especially malicious sorts.

2. It is a particularly disturbing situation that they misconstrue meaningful words, as do these hypocrites when they stealthily sneak up on Christ with flattering words, "Master we know that thou art true, and teachest the way of God in truth." They act as though they were his dear disciples, supporting his message and his preaching as true, and that it was a shame and sin that people did not accept his teaching. With such words of praise they approach him thinking he will entrap himself. Christ unmasks what they have in mind and answers, "Why tempt ye me, ye hypocrites?" Their words sound gracious but their intentions are mean-spirited. But no matter, however clever their approach and poisonous their thoughts, Christ makes fools of them with all their hypocrisy, cleverness, and venom.

3. Christians have always been vexed by hostile confrontation with counterfeit spirits and poisonous hypocrites like this. David felt their venom and complains vehemently about them as the Psalms give evidence. The apostle Paul also frequently encountered such individuals and called them false brethren. We, too, have plenty and enough of such hypocrites around today, who cozy up to us, as though they

---

[*]Preached at the parish church, 1530.

agreed with us, learn to talk our language, but only in order later to be able to condemn us.

4. Against such venomous evil we take comfort in this, that our teaching, which is so on target—no matter how spiteful and malicious the devil and the world may be—confidently forges ahead, looks everyone in the eye, and disdains to use force or cunning. This Gospel shows how these hypocrites failed against Christ. So let our adversaries grease their shoes with the measure by which they outdo us! Whoever seeks to harm us had best look to the final end to see who has been harmed most. In short, we do not want to be deceived or bested; but if it nonetheless happens, let the attacker be aware of a boomerang. At the present meeting of the Reichstag at Augsburg° the devil has been nicely twisting facts on all sides. But what has he accomplished? Nothing more than that our adversaries are put to greater shame, and the truth still stands.

5. This Gospel lesson, therefore, presents a unique teaching which can never fail. In everyday affairs it happens that people betray each other. But that's not the way it is with the gospel; for whoever tries to do it damage will find that he harms himself the most. If someone takes my cloak, my life, my property, or obstructs me in this way or that, so be it; as long as I cling to Christ, I am merely a spectator of what may be taken from me. Our dear Lord Jesus Christ cannot be bested by the world because he is too powerful and too wise to permit himself to be overcome. God has promised us this very thing, as St. Paul states (1 Cor. 1:30): "But of him are ye in Christ Jesus, who of God is made unto us wisdom, and righteousness, and sanctification, and redemption." It is nothing but utter folly when the world turns against Christ and his gospel, and against those to whom the gospel is dear. Even though a Christian may be cheated in temporal affairs out of house and property (as the godless dukes and tyrants are now doing when they drive off their subjects because of the gospel), yet he remains invincible. Our unscrupulous peasants cheat us and raise the price on everything which people need to subsist, and then, in addition, laugh at us. But what do they accomplish with that? Nothing, ex-

---

°Reference to the Diet of Angsburg, 1530, at which the Luthern party presented their confession in defense of the faith.

cept that we laugh at them. And, indeed, we have the advantage over them, to be able to laugh at them rather than they at us. They laugh at us because by hook or by crook they relieve us of our money with their overpriced wares. We laugh at them because their payment will be the fire of hell. Indeed, what a difference this is!

6. The advantage a Christian has is that with his teaching he cannot be swindled, because his teaching is godly wisdom. Also, the Holy Spirit supports him and reminds him what he should say and do as Christ says (Matt. 10:19–20): "But when they deliver you up, take no thought how or what ye shall speak: for it shall be given you in that same hour what ye shall speak. For it is not ye that speak, but the Spirit of your Father which speaketh in you." Therefore, a Christian does not permit himself to be deceived. Yes, even if one of the elect (were that indeed possible, as Christ says, in Matthew 24:24) would be misled into error, nevertheless, in the end he will prevail.

7. It is a Christian's firm conviction to know that even though I lose the temporal, nonetheless, I am sure the eternal will remain, simply because Christ, my Lord, sits at the right hand of the Father. Because he sits there, what power indeed is there that is able to dethrone him? Through him I have eternal righteousness, peace, and life. Even though on earth I suffer shame, ignominy, strife, and persecution, yet is my conscience free and my heart joyous. Such a treasure far exceeds all crowns, glory, and riches of earth. But the godless peasants, burghers, nobles, and princes who venture to harass the Christians will have a bad conscience and in due time will hear what they do not want to hear, namely, "Depart into hell fire"; you disdained to have eternal life, so now eternal death is yours!

8. We see, then, that no stratagem or trickery, no power or might, can prevail against Christ and his gospel. These hypocrites handle this very cleverly, fogging over their intentions with a smoke screen of chatter trying to shield what sort of rascals and knaves they are. They hope to babble on till he inadvertently says something to compromise himself. "Tell us," they say, "is it lawful to give tribute unto Caesar, or not?" Their strategy was to trap him, however he answers. He will have to answer "yes," or "no." But what if he answers nothing and remains silent? We'll take care of that, they think, by offering a little bait so that he will have to answer. We will address him as Mas-

ter, to remind him of his position, duty, and obligation, so that he cannot leave them without an answer. In other words, they are saying, You are a master, you represent yourself as qualified to teach and give answers to everyone; now, therefore, you cannot leave us without an answer and remain silent, or brush us off.

9. What should poor Jesus do? They figure they have him ensnared. If he says "no," Herod's deputies will be there to say, Are you trying to teach people not to pay tribute to Caesar? If so, then you are a rabble-rouser and we will throw you into prison. If he says "yes," we have him right in our trap. For that would be in opposition to the law of Moses. He would be a heretic and foe of the entire Jewish nation in that he endorses and upholds an alien, a foreign king who was not born of Jewish lineage and blood. If he says one should pay tribute to Caesar, the Jews will take him on. If he says one should not pay tribute to Caesar, the heathen will take him on. Either way, we will be rid of him.

10. Note the excellent, clever wisdom in these people! They are certain their strategy cannot fail and no one can outwit their cunning. But let them be wise, cunning, and clever, let them lie and deceive; it will not help them. It is true, human reasoning might easily become confused here, wondering whether to answer "yes" or "no," particularly if we note the great danger threatening Christ. If he says "yes," he will be ensnared by the Jews; if he says "no," he will be in trouble with the heathen. So also today matters can become so confused that we don't know what to say or advise. But Christ, "in whom are hid all the treasures of wisdom and knowledge" (Col. 2:3), and whose gospel is the hidden wisdom of God, 1 Cor. 2:7, gives the following answer. "Shew me the tribute money," he says. And as they hand him a penny he asks, "Whose is this image and superscription?" Now they cannot remain silent. Just as they forced him to answer, he now forces their hand. Were they to have remained silent, he would have said, If you won't answer my question, I will not answer your question. Therefore, they answer and say, "Caesar's." Then he pulls the noose tight and says: Thank you, dear sirs. You asked me if one ought to pay tribute to Caesar? Here you have the answer. You acknowledged with your own mouths that you have already done that. Now I ask you, What kind of people are you that you do something and then after you have done it

ask whether it is right? If you have accepted Caesar as your lord, and if you are under Caesar's jurisdiction, then you give him what you owe him. If that is Caesar's imprint and picture, as you have acknowledged, then you are Caesar's subject, and already have given to Caesar what is his due, and I will not deny his right.

11. Thus the Lord drives the Pharisees' question into their own bosom. Now, then, this has been written for our comfort that we may know that the same thing will happen to all who oppose Christ and his gospel. God, through his Holy Spirit, will provide us the kind of answers that will heap great shame upon our adversaries. We have, in fact, already seen this happen, not only with the pope and his minions, but with all who oppose themselves against the truth. All our adversaries drive the Scripture against us head-on, allowing us to take it out of their grasp and hit them over the head with it and thus plunge their own sword through their hand and belly. Moreover, it is impossible for them to bring up a single word in truth to oppose us, for the Holy Spirit is much too wise for them and his position much too secure, so that they become unsure of their own. Thus he knocks the sword out of their fist and drives it into them. We have seen this happen in all the books of the fanatics, Anabaptists, and Sacramentarians, how their own arguments are of such a nature that when turned around they condemn themselves. And while they have one thing against us, we have a hundred against them. Where they try to trick us with one word, we have a hundred against them. Solomon sums it up well (Prov. 21:30): "There is no wisdom nor understanding nor counsel against the Lord."

12. Since our teaching is God's Word and teaching, I advise you not to be entangled in it or you will get smeared. But the world can't leave it be; it has to attack Christ and the gospel. For it thinks that those are poor, simple people, who can easily be tricked and ripped off. But just how easy it is we see here in the case of Christ and the question of the Pharisees.

13. Now, that is the first part of this lesson, namely, a helpful example given for our assurance that we not be frightened when our enemies attack the gospel with power and cunning. No matter how wise and powerful, they will not be able to outdo the wisdom and

reasoning on our side. Even though it cost us our heads and our lives, they cannot and will not destroy us.

14. The second lesson of this Gospel, and most important, are the words, "Render therefore unto Caesar the things which are Caesar's; and unto God the things that are God's." With these words God's realm and that of Caesar are distinguished, indicating what our obligation to God is, and what it is toward Caesar. Why did the Evangelist not first say, Give to God what is God's, but instead turns it around and first says, Give to Caesar what is Caesar's? Answer: because the Pharisees' question was whether or not it was right to pay tribute to Caesar. That's why the Lord first answered what they were asking, namely, to give to Caesar what belongs to Caesar. For the coin, the inscription, and the picture, were of Caesar. Because, therefore, the coin was Caesar's legal right, it should be given to Caesar, Christ says; but then reminds at the same time that we should not forget to give to God what is God's.

15. There is a distinct difference and a specific teaching as to one's obligation to God and to Caesar. But the world is so evil that all this is turned topsy-turvy. Today no one wants to be obedient to the government. Moreover, if a few devout Christians want to be obedient, the government is not satisfied to limit itself to its realm, but interferes in the realm which is God's and uses its power against Christ and his gospel, overtly vaunting itself to hold and to rule over the kingdom of God and Christ. That's what the power hungry rascals, the princes and the lords, are doing now, when they learn that people are to be obedient to the government, even to suffer injustice, according to the dear Gospel, where we are taught that it is God's will to be obedient to government.

16. Thus, our dear emperor, Charles, is now surrounded by so many devils—wicked priests, godless bishops and dukes—who get him to proclaim something really unwelcome to him, namely, that one ought not give to God what is God's. Government has been ordered and instituted by God to rule over life and property. Now it proposes to venture into territory where it has no authority, namely, requiring obedience to the pope. Where does the emperor get the authority to rule my faith? He is a mortal man who should rule over temporal affairs. How does it come about, then, that he reaches

higher, into matters beyond this temporal life? It is no longer a matter of this earthly, temporal life when I believe in Christ, but it appertains to another life, above and beyond the life which is subject to the emperor. Nevertheless, the emperor wants to be lord over, and have jurisdiction over, that very life which is not subject to him. If he were lord over that life and then died, who would then be in charge of eternal, heavenly life?

17. Therefore, when the emperor and the princes require of me to believe so and so, I reply, Dear emperor and lords, you are reaching too high. If they reply that I must be obedient because they are the government, I answer, Yes, you are lords over the temporal life, but not over eternal life! They go on to say that it is their duty to maintain peace and unity, and for that reason we must believe as do the emperor and princes. Do I hear right? Then the Turk could also say, Listen, dear emperor, listen, you princes, you are to believe as the Turks believe so that peace and unity might prevail. If it applies to one, it should apply to all. If the Roman emperor has the power and might to require people to believe as he wills, then the Turkish ruler also has such power and might, and the magistrate of every village has the power to force his subjects to believe as he does, also every father in the home. If this were the case, there would be as many varieties of beliefs as there are varieties of heads on earth. That's why our opponents are crazy mad when they so misuse their power. They have their power from us and because of our gospel, but they cannot acknowledge this and tolerate that we give to God what is God's. Is that the thanks they give to God for his Holy Gospel, through which they enjoy the honor to which they have come?

18. Accordingly, Christ defines and gives the emperor his power, and at the same time places a cap on the extent of this power when he says, Give unto Caesar what is Caesar's. He doesn't say to give to Caesar what is God's. We must not, therefore, give everything to the emperor, only that which is his. What then is the emperor's? That over which he has legal right and power. This we should give him heartily; but anything beyond that which is his, we should not give him. It should be a matter of common knowledge that Christian faith, baptism, the Sacrament, or Lord's Supper, the gospel, the Lord Christ at the right hand of God, and eternal life are not the emperor's to do with as he pleases. Therefore, if the emperor and the

government want to rule in these matters, I must say, No, dear emperor, dear prince, dear nobleman, dear lord, dear lady, I cannot and will not grant that, because Christ has ordered me that I give Caesar what is Caesar's, but I must not give him what is God's.

19. Life and goods I should yield to the emperor, but when the emperor is not satisfied with that, but demands my soul as well, I must say, Dear emperor, it is not in your domain to demand this! Produce document and seal to prove that such has been entrusted to you! If the emperor considers this an act of disobedience then I will have to suffer. In truth, though, it is not rebellion or disobedience if I am not obedient to the emperor in this matter where he has no power or jurisdiction. Has not the emperor sworn obedience to the same God and Lord as I have? How does it come, then, that he presumes to give orders about this same God, his gospel, Sacrament, baptism, and so on, and that he wants to be lord and command whatever he pleases? But nothing helps; they are callous and stubborn and do not hear. They will someday experience a counter-reaction themselves.

20. Yes, you say, but the emperor cannot do otherwise. He gave his oath to the pope at Rome, by whom he was crowned, that he would bring about return to the way things were under the old order and that he must honor this obligation. Answer: The legal counsel of the pope and the emperor's judiciary, however, both mandate that one may not say or praise anything which is in conflict with the first commandment. If today I would reverence the pope, so that his idolatry and abominations were reinstated, swearing this in so many words, a person would still have to understand such an oath to include this, that Christ and his gospel must remain without diminution. For we are also indebted to God, as this text teaches, Give unto God what is God's. I cannot promise any man something in violation of my baptism and faith, for constraint is always present that it not be anything contrary to God and Christ. If it is against God and Christ, it cannot be binding. Therefore, all vows and oaths which pertain to the pope are of no validity apart from this understanding and this annotation, namely, that it not be contrary to God. Those who insist on these vows and oaths are mad, foolish, and blind because they do not see how one ought to understand such vows and oaths.

21. Therefore, let us carefully bear this in mind when they say, What you have promised, that you must do, and then remember these words of Christ, Give to God what is God's. Thus such thinking is countered with the question: Did you not in your baptism swear that you want to believe in God, serve him, and accept his gospel? This we must hold to be paramount, for this vow must take precedence. What is the emperor or the pope compared with God? For that reason their premise is nothing but a lie when they say the emperor has sworn to the pope to be beholden to him, as though all that matters is one's oath toward the pope; but what one has sworn in baptism, namely, to remain true to the gospel, to keep one's christening robe clean, that is of no consequence.

22. Indeed, such matters (the oaths promised to God) don't belong on the agenda of the Reichstag, but only how to carry out what one has promised the pope. For this reason I feel the harvest is near of which Christ spoke (John 4:35): "Look on the fields; for they are white already to harvest." I do not know what to make of those who want to drive the emperor to this. The point is that they insult God when they elevate the emperor above the station that is his due, placing him in Christ's position. He forces the people to believe whatever he prescribes. Warfare may result, but whoever wishes to be a Christian must be ready to say, I will not fight against God and it is not in my heart to rob God of what is God's; rather, I will obey and do my duty, so that the emperor has what is his, and God has what is God's. If the emperor isn't satisfied to take from you what is his and leave to God what is God's, another will come to teach him a lesson, one who will not let himself for the sake of the pope be talked out of what belongs to him. He will be as protective of his own as is the emperor, as Psalm 2:9 states: "Thou shalt break them with a rod of iron; thou shalt dash them in pieces like a potter's vessel." If the earthly kings are not willing to honor and serve Christ, he will strike hard, sending the pieces flying in all directions.

23. If, now, our adversaries do not understand the difference between the two kingdoms, God's and the emperor's, then we will explain it to them. In matters that are temporal and transitory, one should be obedient to the emperor. In matters that pertain to eternal life, one cannot and should not be obedient to the emperor. God did

not give the emperor power and might over eternal heavenly life, which we have in Christ. We want no part in taking from God what is God's and giving it to the emperor. The worldly lords, of course, do not believe that God will be provoked. That is why the iron scepter falls upon them to teach them what they do not want to acknowledge. It has always been this way, that those who oppose the gospel are smashed and destroyed. The Roman emperor at the time of the apostles was as proud and mighty as our adversaries are now. But where is he now? The Jews depended on their holiness, power, and might, but they have been crushed, so that one hardly knows where Jerusalem stood. Our adversaries, therefore, will not outrun our God, for they are much too insolent. We may, perhaps, perish with them, but God can rescue a Lot from the midst of Sodom, and, before he would abandon a Christian, he would build him an ark. He has the expertise to maintain his own while wiping out the rest of the world.

24. With these words, Give to God what is God's, our dear Lord Christ challenges the tyrants who want to supersede him, to take from God what is his. God has defined their duties and jurisdiction. They should be satisfied therewith and not try to grab for more. But that they don't do. The subjects, for their part, want everything for nothing and are unwilling to give anything to anyone. As we see, out of freedom of the gospel, they make a freedom of the flesh, to do as they please. Thus both rulers and subjects shuck off their duty. Temporal authority, emperor, princes, and lords would have enough to do seeing to it that good government prevailed in Germany; but they just go merrily along and command what one's faith is to be. The duties which belong to a doctor of Holy Scripture, a bishop, or a parish pastor, these the emperor wants to carry out; the bishops, in turn, want to be worldly lords; and so everyone does what suits him best.

25. In the lower echelon of society things are the same; the peasants and burghers profiteer with their buying and selling. They do as they please, raising prices on everything people need to buy from them. They incline to nothing but wantonness. When the farmer is obliged to pay what is due to the prince, the parish pastor, and the like, he would rather give chaff, if he could, especially to the parish pastor. Everyone lives as though he were the emperor. There no longer is any kind of justice, nothing but wantonness. If a farmer brings wheat, bar-

ley, and so forth to market, he sets his own price, unconcerned for others. To sum it up, everyone does his thing, grabs for himself, even what belongs to the emperor, leaving the emperor out in the cold. They understand very well what belongs to the emperor's rights and duties, how one ought to comply with these obediently, pay taxes, and other obligations. They don't inquire into this, but do as they please, and their conscience doesn't bother them. In the same way the emperor, princes, and lords want to take hold of Christ's kingdom to reign over the church and matters of faith. They, likewise, have no conscience pangs about this. The common people the same, even though it's against the emperor's command. They don't ask themselves whether it is wrong, but laugh into their fists and think, Hey, what am I doing? Is it proper? What if the emperor finds out and throws me into prison? No way, they think, because I, John Kunz, lord peasant himself, am emperor; that's why I can do what I please. So, there's no such thing any longer like magistrate and subject—no further need for that!

26. This gospel, however, points out an unequivocal difference as to how one should serve God with one's spiritual life and how to serve the emperor with one's temporal life. But, as has been said, the world mixes the two together. The temporal authority interferes as it pleases with the spiritual rule which belongs to God. The subjects do as they please with the temporal realm which belongs to the emperor. That is why neither God's kingdom, nor the emperor's kingdom, can possibly survive in the world. Eventually someone will arise to avenge both God and emperor, to punish both rulers and subjects.

27. Conditions everywhere are so shameful and lamentable that I no longer really care to preach, for, in spite of the gospel's bright light, both rulers and subjects are becoming worse day by day. The more the bishops and princes heard our confession of the truth at the Diet of Augsburg, the more they demonstrated and raved against the gospel and the truth. The peasants, burghers, domestics, and maidservants understand well enough that they are to give to the emperor what is the emperor's, but they don't respect the emperor or let loose of their purse strings, just as though they were not indebted to him. No one any longer thinks: This acre which I occupy is not mine, but the emperor's, or that he places me here for service to him, and not that I should do as I please. No one thinks that he owes the government or

his parish pastor income, but says that he will do as he pleases about that; I will give him a handful of chaff for the taxes! They do this without compunction, as though they themselves were emperor. If this is the existential reality for both government and its subjects, then he who said, "Render therefore unto Caesar the things which are Caesar's; and unto God the things that are God's," must have been lying.

28. I have prayed and I have implored that we ought maintain this distinction and each perform his duty. I have also warned of God's anger and punishment. But to no avail everywhere! The peasants, burghers, nobility, princes, and emperor want it that way. Very well, I have done my best and can do no more. I hope our dear Lord God will take us away before we have to experience what they are asking for. Our Lord God has differentiated these two kingdoms, so that he keeps what is his and at the same time the emperor has his modest portion. He will see to it that this division remains. In short, he will not permit the emperor to usurp what is God's, nor will he permit the emperor to be robbed of what is his. The emperor may be supremely powerful, but God will teach him that in heaven he is God and Lord, even over the emperor. The peasants, burghers, and nobility may be as proud and wanton as they wish, but God will teach them that the emperor is lord and they are subject to the emperor.

29. Everyone ought to know, first of all, that he owes his soul to God. That is why he should diligently study God's Word and in firm trust and faith commend his salvation to God. He should demonstrate his faith as he diligently and faithfully instructs his children and domestic servants in God's Word. Moreover, he also is beholden to the emperor for his life and material possessions. For that reason, whoever possesses money and goods should consider they are not his, but the emperor's. For the emperor gives property in fief to the prince; the prince, to the land barons; the nobles, or the prince himself, gives you this or that acre. For that reason no one should say, This property is my own; I may use it as I will. Whoever does that uses his possessions sinfully and disobediently and is a thief. Such sin will cry to heaven. So this is what we should learn from today's Gospel, namely, that we have two masters, God and the emperor—the emperor as regards this temporal life, God as regards eternal life. We should give each master what is his. I have stated this as emphatically as I can, and there is nothing more to add to what I have said. Let us call upon God to give us his grace.

TWENTY-THIRD SUNDAY AFTER TRINITY

Third Sermon—1533

Matthew 22:15–22

1. The reason for today's Gospel stems from a promise to the Jews in the Writings of Moses, that if they served God and were obedient to him they would have their own kingdom, with a king of their own people, and not be subservient to a foreign king. They clung firmly to this promise, forever hoping they would not meet with distress. When the Romans came and subdued them (even though there had been resistance which caused the Romans much bloodshed), it grieved the Jews greatly and caused a great deal of misery and want in the country. Their hope was to be rid of this oppression. But they were subjugated and humbled to the extent that they did not dare to oppose the Romans.

2. The Jews remembered very well that according to this promise they were to have their own kingdom. However, as is the bad habit of all humans, they failed to observe the conditions, namely, that they should serve God, be obedient to him, and observe his commandments. That, they soon forgot, being unwilling to lift a finger. For the kingdom, they said, is our due; it was promised to us and that is why we want to be free and have a king from our own people. Their attitude was akin to a disobedient maid saying to her mistress, You promised me a certain reward; now, therefore, give it to me, while I go on doing as I please. The answer was, No! That was not the agreement for your reward, but you are to work and do as I direct. That's the way it was with the Jews. They were a disobedient and stiff-necked people, who weren't concerned about God's commandments, yet wanted to be free.

3. For that reason they debated among themselves whether they had to be under the jurisdiction of the Romans and pay taxes to the

Roman emperor, a heathen. They felt they had a firm promise, that they were to have their own king. Thus they twisted the facts in an effort to corner Christ and at the same time ingratiate themselves with Herod's deputies, as they now ask Christ whether it is lawful or not to pay taxes to the emperor. No matter whether he answers "yes" or "no," they feel they have him entangled. If he says "yes," he will stir up the people's animosity and they will call him a blasphemer and a liar who contradicts the teaching of God and Moses. For there the promise stood, that they were to be a free people, under bondage to no foreign, heathen lord. If he says No, he would place his head on the block, because Roman authority would not tolerate insurrection. This was their strategy, that regardless of whether he said "yes" or "no," he would be apprehended and killed. So, would this simple fool escape and save his neck? It was an especially cagy tactic on their part, to accost him with this poisonous question.

4. But what happens? How does he handle it? In the following way: The Lord turns the spear around, with which they purposed to pierce him, stabbing themselves with their own sword. Let me see a coin, he says. They comply with his request and hand him a coin. He then asks, Whose image and inscription are on the coin? thereby outwitting them with this simple maneuver. They answer that it is the emperor's. Very well, my dear sirs, he says. The emperor's, you say? The people say, Yes! Very well, if you have the emperor's property and coin, then give him what is his; for when they admitted that the emperor's coin was required, they had already admitted that they accepted the emperor as lord. Thus by their own words the conclusion has to be: If the emperor is your lord, as you yourselves acknowledge, then I shall not take him from you, nor will I withhold what is the emperor's.

5. That's the purpose of today's Gospel, which is truly a masterpiece. The Pharisees wanted to betray and dispose of the Lord Jesus. However, their scheming backfired on them. They wanted to catch him with his own words, but instead they trapped themselves. They thought they could catch him no matter whether he said "yes" or "no." They themselves remind him by their answer what they expect him to say. Thus they put the sword for slaying them into his hand, just as if a person committed suicide with his own sword.

6. From this incident we should garner two lessons. The first is that from the example of the Jews we should recognize our own bad habit, that we all without exception, are especially inclined to complain over something that causes us grief. We, too, think injustice is being done us. Of course, by human standards we often do experience injustice which is undeserved from our fellowmen who deal unjustly with us. Then in our thoughts we are riveted only on our rights and the wrongdoing of our adversary, causing us then to cry out and complain, just as the Jews did here about the Romans. By exercising authority over the Jews, who were God's people, the Romans were perceived by the Jews to be opposing God and acting unjustly. In fact, the Jews argued, the Romans had no right to subjugate and set themselves over the Jews. For the Romans were heathen and did not have God's Word or the correct form of worship like the Jews. That disturbed the Jews very much, causing them to believe they had correctly perceived and upheld their rights. But they failed, just as we fail in a similar circumstance. Even if your fellowman does you an injustice, you should not consider retaliation, but ask yourself what you are doing. What? Have I not already sinned so grievously against our Lord God that I have long ago deserved to have not only my rights taken away, but also my body and life?

7. The Jews looked upon it as very execrable that they should be subjected to a heathen emperor. They reasoned: We are God's people; the heathen know nothing of God, and, what is more, live in all manner of idolatry and shame. How, then, can it be right that we should serve them and they should be our lords? The kingdom was promised and given to us by God. It is wrong for the Romans to have taken it from us. What God-fearing, pious people they were as they lifted their hands to God and prayed for mercy! However, they didn't drive the issue of justice very hard, because they well knew that they had earned their lot. The facts were that what was taught and preached publicly didn't amount to much (as we see from today's Gospel); so government, too, was of no real significance. Covetousness, usury, fornication, self-pleasure, and other sins were in abundance. What, then, was our Lord God to do about that? Should he protect them in view of the fact they were not concerned about him and his Word? Should he be supportive of them

in their rights even though they lifted not a finger for his sake or for his service? Yes, that he was jolly well to tolerate! Now, since they did not want to observe his rights, he had good reason for not regarding and upholding their rights. Moreover, God had not promised them a temporal kingdom in perpetuity. Rather, God had a tether around the dog's neck, having promised the kingdom with these conditions, namely, to be pious, obedient, and respectful of his commandments. Such covenant matters they ignored, unconcerned about God's commandments; yet, they still wanted their kingdom, with no strings attached by God, whether they were pious or not. It was the same as if a servant demanded his wages whether he has earned them or not. Indeed, immediate accounting! The principle, however, is: Do what you are told, and then you will get paid what you deserve. If a farmer is not pious, obedient, and ready to pay his taxes, it is no injustice to him if his feudal lord relieves him of both his property and rights, and gives them to another who is pious and does what is required of him by his lord.

8. We need, therefore, to mitigate our complaints and evaluate things fairly, not only looking out for our own rights with others, but also our rights before God; and then humbly and patiently raise our hands to God and say, Indeed, it is true that injustice has been done to me which I have not deserved from this person. But I need also to look behind and before myself to see how I stand before God. There I find that there is a very long list and register of wrongs that convince me that I am ten times worse and have sinned against God ten times more, yes, a thousand times more than my fellowman has against me. That is why it behooves me to straighten out these distortions and say, O Lord, forgive me! I will also forgive.

9. For it would be wrong for us to remain adamant about our so-called rights when we have committed such great wrongs against God. It is true that a person who contends for his rights by legitimate means and procedures does not do wrong. Since law and justice have been ordained by God himself, we ought to respect these and make use of them. But where we cannot justify our right, let everyone be aware that he does not become contentious and impatient. Instead, we should turn things around and say, I definitely deserve justice, and those who offended against me ought to be punished; but I must

confess that before God I deserve such injustice. Then we would not act like the Jews. They set a bad example with their behavior and demeanor. They wanted to maintain their right while our Lord God was not to have his right from them. It was the same as if the wicked peasants wanted protection from the government, but also wanted to be free from taxes and under obligation to no one. But God opposed such wantonness by ordaining to put the sword in the hands of government. If they are not willing to pay up freely, one whack on the head will straighten them out.

10. Our poor clergy do not have this option. They have no authority to force those who do not wish to pay the dues for which they are obligated. Consequently, the ill-tempered burghers and peasants think they are in the right when they give nothing, or very little of any value, the very meanest. But what finally happens? If the parish pastor cannot punish them or exact from them what is his due, God will intervene, sending pestilence among the people and the cattle; also thieves and land stewards will strip you of what you have. He programs things in such a way that, because of unfavorable weather, grapes, grains, fruit, turnips, and cabbage rot in the field. When that happens the bottom line is: Friend, villages, or farmer, do not complain that you have been dealt injustice. You may well think you have gotten the shaft unjustly, but before God you receive justice; in fact, you deserved even more severe punishment long ago. Therefore, don't complain that you have been treated unjustly, but rather lament about your sins, your unrepentant life, your avarice, your pride, your overconfidence, your despising of God's Word, and the like. Such sins make of your right nothing but unrighteousness.

11. Thus the Lord here wants to remind the Jews that even though they lost their right and were subdued by the Romans, they ought not lament, but rather chalk up their debts and remind themselves that they are indebted to him. They should, therefore, be ready to bear with anything. But the Jews weren't willing to do that, but adamantly insisted on having their kingdom back and their titular rights. To that our Lord God said, No! The emperor at Rome will serve me very well to force you who are unwilling to accept the punishment you deserve, to endure it in spite of all. The kingdom was promised the Jews on the condition that they would remain God-

fearing; otherwise, they would lose the kingdom and their rights in one fell swoop.

12. Today the situation involving the Turks is similar. To our thinking the situation is unjust that the Turk, who is more malicious than the heathen, has scored such great victories against us Christians. But let us not look at who the Turks are, but at ourselves, who we are, for we oppose God; and then we will understand that we have received no injustice. Why are the papists so adamant in their idolatry and persecution of the gospel? Why don't we who have the gospel improve how we behave and live, as it behooves Christians? That, now, is one of the lessons which we ought to learn from today's lesson.

13. The other point of the lesson is that we are to differentiate between the secular kingdom and the kingdom of our Lord Christ; also, that our Lord God does not denounce the earthly kingdom, but establishes it with house, property, sustenance, matrimony, civil laws, peasants, burghers, nobles, and other stations of life, all under the authority of the emperor. For as Christ says, Give unto Caesar what is Caesar's. In other words he is saying, If you are a villager or a farmer, a nobleman or a prince, male or female, manservant or maid, remain in your calling and don't try to unsettle the emperor's realm. You servant, serve your master; you child, obey your father and your mother. These stations of life I will not disturb or tear apart, for they belong to the emperor, and he cannot be without them, nor do they conflict with my kingdom which is not a kingdom of the world.

14. This serves to show us that for a Christian to pursue his calling he does not have to withdraw or be free from the secular realm or exchange his calling for some new lifestyle like the monks. They thought that if they remained in the worldly realm and vocation they could not be saved. No, says Christ, that is not so; I do not intend by my preaching to tear apart the empire. Therefore, remain in your calling and give what is due to the emperor; God does not inhibit you in any way.

15. In addition, you should also give God what is his due. For God has his separate realm, namely, that you believe in Jesus Christ, hear and accept the gospel, are God-fearing according to his commandments, merciful, kind, and patient. Such are the offerings that you bring to God, and with that he will be pleased. Whatever pertains to

your body, your property, your vocation, and calling belongs to the emperor. But whatever concerns your soul, your faith, and your Christianity belongs to God. Thus God and the emperor can remain side by side even though the Jews would like to tear them apart; yes, they wanted to give neither God nor the emperor what was rightly theirs. However, that is too complex for you children in a house sermon. It belongs in the church and is meant for the learned people. Therefore, we will now leave it for such a time and place.

TWENTY-FOURTH SUNDAY AFTER TRINITY

First Sermon—1532

On Sunday we ought to listen to God's Word as he commands in the third commandment, "Remember the sabbath day to keep it holy," that is, honoring it and thus keeping it holy. Now, that happens when we hear and learn from God's Word, how we are to believe and trust in him. Accordingly, St. Mark writes as follows:

Mark 5:21–43

And when Jesus was passed over again by ship unto the other side, much people gathered unto him: and he was nigh unto the sea. And, behold, there cometh one of the rulers of the synagogue, Jairus by name; and when he saw him, he fell at his feet, And besought him greatly, saying, My little daughter lieth at the point of death: I pray thee, come and lay thy hands on her, that she may be healed; and she shall live. And Jesus went with him; and much people followed him, and thronged him. And a certain woman, which had an issue of blood twelve years, And had suffered many things of many physicians, and had spent all that she had, and was nothing bettered, but rather grew worse, When she had heard of Jesus, came in the press behind, and touched his garment. For she said, If I may touch but his clothes, I shall be whole. And straightway the fountain of her blood was dried up; and she felt in her body that she was healed of that plague. And Jesus, immediately knowing in himself that virtue had gone out of him, turned him about in the press, and said, Who touched my clothes? And his disciples said unto him, Thou seest the multitude thronging thee, and sayest thou, Who touched me? And he looked round about to see her that had done this thing. But the woman fearing and trembling, knowing what was done in her, came and fell down before him, and told him all the truth. And he said unto her, Daughter, thy faith hath made thee whole; go in peace, and be whole of thy plague. While he yet spake, there came from the ruler of the synagogue's house cer-

tain which said, Thy daughter is dead: why troublest thou the Master any further? As soon as Jesus heard the word that was spoken, he saith unto the ruler of the synagogue, Be not afraid, only believe. And he suffered no man to follow him, save Peter, and James, and John the brother of James. And he cometh to the house of the ruler of the synagogue, and seeth the tumult, and them that wept and wailed greatly. And when he was come in, he saith unto them, Why make ye this ado, and weep? the damsel is not dead, but sleepeth. And they laughed him to scorn. But when he had put them all out, he taketh the father and the mother of the damsel, and them that were with him, and entereth in where the damsel was lying. And he took the damsel by the hand, and said unto her, Talitha cumi; which is, being interpreted, Damsel, I say unto thee, arise. And straightway the damsel arose, and walked; for she was of the age of twelve years. And they were astonished with a great astonishment. And he charged them straitly that no man should know it; and commanded that something should be given her to eat.

1. This incident teaches us that our Lord Jesus Christ is a helper and rescuer from life's worst extremity, death. We are aware that all men must die, from the first human being, Adam, to the last; from the beginning of the world until its end. One individual drowns, another loses his life in a fire, or in an epidemic, or some other illness; and those presently alive can anticipate nothing more certain than death. The question presses: What must be done to overcome death?; or, if it's inevitable, how can we learn the magic of restoring life again? Christ teaches us this art here, not how to become rich, but rather how to be rescued from death.

2. While death is an ever present threat to all mankind, mankind nonetheless despises what Scripture teaches about death, and in particular about the Lord who can rescue from death. This is no mere human frailty, but a devilish maliciousness, since young and old know that they must die. Yet they march along in bold security, bucking the wind, despising him who wants to rescue mankind from death. For less urgent needs and lesser harm, everyone seeks help. If someone has an injury, he seeks a medical doctor, incurring whatever it costs to obtain relief. If one has nothing to eat, he will go over land and water, through fire and hazard, to fill his belly. In any distress and misery, people race and run to be rid of the burden. Now, people know that death is the greatest evil of all, greater than all the

rest, simply because if there is no help, we die not only in this life, but eternally.

3. Now comes Jesus, our dear Lord, the true physician and trusted helper, who says, Listen, dear man, to what I wish to do for you. You are saddled with death and there's no way you can outrun it. No one else can help you. But I can, and not only will I rescue you from death, but I will also give you eternal life. Only cling to me and believe my Word; then you will be freed from death. Just as I live, you too shall live. Such a message, however, should be preached only to those who see their need, who confess, feel, and know that they must die. The rest, who do not feel that death is inevitable, go their merry way, bucking the wind, just as peasants, burghers, and nobles do today, having more regard for a blade of straw than for this sermon in which we learn how to escape death and come to eternal life.

4. It is an especially abominable and atrocious situation that the Lord, who can and wants to rescue from death, is so despised, and that individuals become vexed at hearing God's Word, as though it were a great burden. Imagine, if an experienced and highly esteemed physician came to a sick person suffering from a throat infection and said, I will give you a specific medication for your ailment if you will listen to me, and the sick person responded, Stay away from me; I don't like your medicine; I'd rather die than take your medicine. Everyone would consider such a sick person out of his mind, and would tell him, Very well, go ahead and die, in the devil's name, because you have refused to listen to the physician. Similarly, in this situation, if you opt for death rather than our Lord God's help, then go ahead, into hellfire as well. Death marches on. Today it tears this one from life, tomorrow another. People see this right and left, and yet pay no attention, and feel no fear. Even though men know that they must die, they refuse to mobilize against death that they might escape it.

5. Christians, who desire comfort and help, and who anticipate living eternally, have in this lesson a good picture of what sort of man Christ is and how he seeks to help mankind at the hour of greatest need, as a man faces death. Then, when everything comes to an end, when friends forsake, and the whole world cannot help, there still is a helper, namely, Jesus Christ, who can trample death before our eyes, and rescue us from death's power.

6. Christ's words and deeds bear this out. He states that the maiden is not dead, but is sleeping, takes her by the hand and raises her up. It is as though he said, To you the maiden is dead, but to me she is not dead, but rather sleeps. Therefore, if you truly wish to know me, you must realize that I am master over death and that the dead for me are not dead, but asleep. What he says, he proves with his deed. It is impossible for the entire world to raise anyone from the dead. For the Lord Christ, however, it is not only possible, but a light and easy task, hardly more than rousing a sleeping individual by thumping his bed and saying, Hey, get up! So Christ does here. As a matter of fact, it is easier for Christ to awaken someone from death than for us to arouse someone from sleep.

7. The Lord here solicits our faith and does not want us to coast along thoughtlessly like swine, like careless clods who spend their Sundays and workdays sitting in the beer halls guzzling beer like cattle drink water. They say, Heck, what do I care about God, or about death? Miserable swine! They will reap what they sow. They will die and go straight into hell. Because they despise the Lord God, who not only created them but also wants to give them eternal life, they will be punished with hellfire. Nor will this in any way be an injustice.

8. If we wish to be Christians, we must be circumspect, guarding against false security and despising of God. We realize that we must die and that we will have to suffer shame and death, with no one to help us. Therefore, we should learn that God is our Lord and that he wishes to help us and rescue us from death. The first commandment teaches us: "I am the Lord your God who led you from Egypt." That is to say, I am your God who guides you and rescues you from every distress, will resurrect you from death, give you good health and heal all your diseases, and, who will finally draw you out of the earth to make you alive. That is all summed up in the first commandment. In Matthew 22:32, Christ states: "God is not the God of the dead, but of the living." Because God states in the first commandment that he wants to be our God, it follows that he wants to help and rescue us from death. It is tantamount to his saying, Only believe in me; I will lead you out of your Egypt; I do not look for my advantage, but your advantage. Why else would I ask about you! For I was God long before you came into existence and will be God long after you have

died. Whatever I do, I do for your benefit. Therefore, you should learn to have faith that I can and want to help where no one can help, namely, to lead you out of your Egypt, that is, sin and death. On Judgment Day I will knock on your grave, in order that you need no longer remain there, but come forth to eternal life.

9. This is what we should learn. That's the purpose for preaching, that listeners may understand God's Word, especially the first commandment: "I am the Lord your God." God wants to be our God, just as Christ here for the maiden. The little girl was near death when the father came to Jesus and said, O Lord come, prove the first commandment, lay your hands on her that she may be well and live. The Lord Christ recognized his office, under the promise of the first commandment; gets up and follows the father, that we might learn that the first commandment is true. He resurrects the maiden, takes her by the hand, and says to her, Little girl, I say to you, get up! Immediately the little girl responded, moving about as though she had just awakened from sleep.

10. Christ thereby demonstrated that he can and wishes to rescue us from death. He doesn't do it at all times and for everyone, for then no man would lie in the grave, but all who die would immediately arise and live. It is sufficient that he has done it for some; the rest he saves for the Day of Judgment. That he did it in this and other instances is a mighty proof of the first commandment. We learn thereby that he has the power to resurrect from the dead. What he did for this maiden should be proof for me that I might believe that he will do the same for me on Judgment Day. In the meantime, I will rest content in God's grace, until I am resurrected on the Last Day.

11. We are, therefore, to differentiate between the general exodus out of Egypt on Judgment Day, that appertains to all mankind, and the miracles which were performed and which, if he deemed necessary, could happen today to bring about understanding of, and faith in, the first commandment, namely, that God is our Lord who will rescue us from death. As yet we have not witnessed the general resurrection, but his word stands true, which God himself affirms: "I am the Lord your God." In the raising of the little girl to life, we have the evidence and the proof that he can and will resurrect us. In this conviction I can die and permit myself to be buried, saying: Now I

must pass away, but at the appointed time I will be raised to life, because God has told me that he is my Lord who promises to rescue me from death. I have his word for this and, to verify his word, proof in the resurrection of the nobleman's daughter. Just as he did with this maiden, so he also did for Lazarus who had been in the grave for four days, whose body, no doubt, had already begun to decompose.

12. You might ask, why doesn't he awaken all the others from death as he awakened the maiden? The answer is that he spares the rest until his appointed time. Meanwhile, he awakens a few to undergird our understanding of the first commandment. If no one had ever been raised from the dead, the first commandment would be hard to believe. But because this maiden, as well as Lazarus and the son of the widow at Nain were awakened from death, this should be evidence for us to learn, understand, and believe the first commandment. That is why God states in Exodus 3:6: "I am the God of thy father, the God of Abraham, the God of Isaac, and the God of Jacob." That is as much as to say (as Christ explains in Matthew 22): Abraham, Isaac, and Jacob live; though they are dead to the world, they are alive to me. That is how one should speak of the dead, that they are not dead to our Lord even though they are dead to us. This God will make clear on the Day of Judgment. Just as here Christ brought forth the maiden from death, so God will bring forth Abraham, Isaac, Jacob, and all of us. For there stands his word: "I am the Lord, your God." And here are the miracles accompanying his word, by which we may learn to believe and say: If Christ has resurrected so many who were dead, it is evident that he is able and will do it, as he states in the first commandment, "I am the Lord, your God." In other words, he will help in every need, and if you die, nevertheless, you shall live again. Thus you learn to know who I am, Christ says.

13. It is God's command to preach, so that people believe in him and cry out for his help: O Lord, preserve me from death! Be my Lord and God as the first commandment promises! The Sunday sermons are intended to proclaim this so that we might learn these truths. Moreover, that would be serving God acceptably when we laud and praise him, when we learn to have faith in him and speak of him according to the first commandment. We ought not act like thoughtless, brutish clods, like the peasants, burghers, and nobility

of today who, though they see that they must die, nevertheless despise God and his Word, and succumb to death like cattle.

14. Surely an alarming attitude in the face of death's reality! They brashly despise God who offers them his grace. What? say these knaves, should I listen to the parson? Pass the beer, let us have a drink! O you shameful, miserable swine! Can you thus despise your Lord and God who so kindly invites you? You are impressed when your servant does something special for you, when your cow gives milk, when your horse gives you a ride, when your needs are met. But when your God and Lord wants to give you life, you despise and reject him, and try to keep him from speaking any longer to you in sermons; you have no desire to learn how to call upon him in time of need. I say it is disgraceful that our Lord God offers his help uselessly to people who beat against the wind, but have no other source of help. The result of such false security and despising of God will be that they coast along in the devil's name, until they come into hell and are lost eternally.

15. For this reason, you young people, you children, you servants, you boys and girls, should diligently learn to fear our Lord God from early youth, to learn to love his Word. You do have recourse in every need, especially for the terrors of death, namely, by the assurance that God is our Lord who wants to rescue us from death. This is the first and paramount lesson in today's Gospel.

16. The other part of the lesson has to do with the fife players and wailers, and how we ought rather act at such time. The professional pipers at a funeral were the Jew's bells. They went to the door of the deceased and wailed songs of sorrow, of mourning, and of lamentation. They stood at the bier and bewailed death. Here now Christ asked that they be removed, saying, Why all this commotion and wailing? The child is not dead, but asleep. They laughed at him, just as today the world considers our dear Lord Jesus a fool. But even though they mocked him, he persisted and drove out the fife players. The same thing will happen to all those who foolishly pipe lamentations over death, whether they are false teachers or those who live an un-Christian life. So, also, all preaching that is not Christ-centered is tantamount to piping unto death, as is also a life of despising and disobeying God.

17. Jesus wants to get rid of all this. He drives them all out, as though to say, Away with all false teaching and all un-Christian living; take note of what I have to say and do as I bid you. I will pipe the right tune for death. And what is that tune? "Little girl, I say unto you, get up! Just as the first commandment states, "I am the Lord your God!" If you are a Christian, you should know that you are to believe in God, trust in him, call upon him in every need, also at death. Then he also said to the maiden that she should eat, drink, and be an obedient girl. He asks nothing of her but obedience. Life is a sheer gift, not a reward. It is Christ's gift to the little girl, out of grace, freely, that she may know that he is her God. After that he commands her to eat, drink, be pious, and obedient. That is to pipe a tune for death!

18. Christ is our helper and our rescuer, as he states in Psalm 68:20: "Our God is the God of salvation; and unto GOD the Lord belong the issue from death." Therefore, we should recognize him, call upon him, and do what is our duty to do. He didn't suggest that the maiden enter a cloister, but told her to eat, drink, and help about the house, as requested by her father and mother. If Christ is our personal Saviour and we have faith in him, we demonstrate this sufficiently by our personal attention to duty. We are God's people for eternity.

19. When the hour comes for us to die, we proceed, assured of our salvation and that, once placed in the grave, we will be awakened in eternity. A thousand years will be no longer than if we had slept in the grave for half an hour. This is how it seems in sleep. Even more so, that will be our experience in death! A thousand years will pass as a night's sleep. Before we realize it, we will be like beautiful angels and soar with Christ in the heavens.

20. This is what our dear Lord Jesus wishes to picture for us here. It is as though he said, My dear people, learn from me who I am, so that you may know what a powerful God you have in me who can raise you from the dead. In the meantime, be pious and obedient. When death comes, cheerfully rely on me; then you may be assured of eternal life, for I was your aid in the exodus from Egypt and I am your rescuer from death. May God give us his grace that we believe. Amen.

TWENTY-FOURTH SUNDAY AFTER TRINITY

Second Sermon—1533

Mark 5:21–43

1. In today's Gospel, beloved, we learn of two miracles, both of them great and without parallel. The first, of the sick woman, who had such a firm faith in the Lord Jesus, that she hoped to be healed immediately if she could only touch his clothes secretly, without his knowledge; the other, of the ruler of the synagogue, who also believed that, although his daughter had died, the Lord could restore her to life. Therefore, in both miracles faith is honored as an excellent thing and held up to us as an example. Because faith in Christ accomplishes such great things, let us also bestir ourselves by it, that we might cleave to this man, to whom no one ever entrusted any good thing without it certainly happening as he had believed.

2. The first miracle was performed on the woman, who was sick with a bloody flux, or dysentery—a disease so critical and so dangerous that many died from it. Mark makes special note of the fact that she spent all that she had on doctors, and that she had the disease twelve years, and her condition worsened from day to day. This was a most extraordinary case of dysentery, lasting as long as it did, for anyone who contracts this disease in these lands, does not survive very long before death must ensue. With this in mind, the miracle is all the greater, since the malady had lasted twelve years; and still the woman was healed so readily, though she did no more than touch Jesus' garment. She had heard that some had been healed who did no more than that. She thereupon decided that she could also be healed the same way, and so she forced her way through the crowd to the Lord; but, hesitant to petition him outright, in her great humility, she thought within herself: If I can but touch his robe without

him noticing, I can perhaps snatch healing from him. Just as she expected, no sooner had she done this, the flow of blood ceased and the dysentery disappeared, which had caused her so much trouble and on which she had frittered away so much money, trying all kinds of things to no avail and with no improvement; in fact, they worked to her great detriment, for she had gotten worse as time wore on.

3. Christ immediately perceived in himself that power had gone out from him, and therefore turned around in the midst of the people and asked who had touched his clothes. To the apostles this seemed an utterly ludicrous question: he wanted to know precisely who touched him, with the crowd thronging him on all sides? But the Lord was determined to find out who had touched him. For it was not a touch with the hands merely; she had touched him with her heart and with her firm trust in his grace and omnipotence; hence, he also felt the power that had gone out from himself. Such a touch as this the Lord was not willing to let go unnoticed, as an example to us. Therefore, he so probed the woman with his questions, that she had no choice but to come forward, show herself, and relate all that had happened to her, to stand there before them all and confess it, in order to give him an opportunity to extol a faith such as she possessed. For faith is the most acceptable, most precious, and highest service we can render him, and the most pleasing to him too. Therefore, he commended the woman and addressed her tenderly, My daughter, be of good cheer, thy faith hath saved thee. And the disciples themselves had to admit that the Lord did not inquire into this for nothing; it was not simply a question of touching, but something out of the ordinary, of no small import to the Lord and to us all.

4. This is an amazing speech which the Lord made here, if we but consider it. He confessed that a power had gone out from himself, and yet he ascribed the work and the power, which issued from him, not to himself, but to the woman and to her faith. He had saved her, as he himself felt the power, and the woman, likewise, confessed that she had been healed by touching his clothes. In any case, he said, Thy faith hath saved thee. This is the right way to praise faith. For the Lord intended by this means to show how greatly he is pleased when you expect all good things from him, and turn to him for help. The woman did not desire that the Lord touch her, or lay his hands

upon her, as the ruler of the synagogue wished; instead, she said, "If I may touch but his clothes, I shall be whole." It was a faith which even the Lord himself would not allow to remain hidden, but extolled it publicly in the presence of all the people. As if to say, Consider carefully and learn to believe confidently, in whatever extremity you find yourselves. For my desire to help is actually much greater than you could possibly desire. Is it the peril of death? My desire to rescue you from death is even greater than the life you now have. He demonstrated this very thing here in this miracle. It happened so simply and he allowed the power to go forth so willingly, in order to heal the woman.

5. So let us learn from examples like these to believe in the same fashion and to expect all good things from Christ in all our distresses and in all our petitions. But what happens? We hear it in sermons, we are told it at home, we discern the miracles which he performs on a daily basis; and, for all that, faith does not follow. He whose cupboards and cellars are full, he believes—although barely—that he will have enough food and drink to last him a year. The healthy man believes that God can heal. But when we are impoverished and ailing, then faith is at an end. We do no more than complain and cry, and persuade ourselves that there is no deliverance, though we hear day in and day out that God longs to be gracious to us through Christ and is willing to help.

6. But how does all that square with this woman here? She had heard of the Lord Christ and his mighty works once or twice maybe, and yet accosted him with a faith so great that if Christ had been seated above over all heavens, she, with her faith, would have torn heaven to pieces to bring him down and compel him to heal her. For, as we said, he cannot turn away from any who seek him earnestly and with true faith.

7. Before God, let us admit it: Of a truth, we are an accursed people, who have God's Word in such abundance, and nevertheless refuse with faith to storm the heavens. It is the fault of the devil and our damned "old Adam." Otherwise, we would always believe on Christ and hope all things through him if we earnestly desired to be justified and saved, and to have what we needed. For, as we hear, faith cannot fail. Therefore, the Lord here praises it to the skies and

says, Thy faith hath saved thee. That is how it ought to be with us too: your faith has raised you up from the dead unto life; your faith has overcome the devil, sent sin packing, and saved your soul. Such works—granted that Christ does them—are nevertheless the works of faith, for without faith they can never happen. Just as in the proclamation of the gospel and the holy sacraments, faith has to be at work if we are going to get any of the good things which are offered to us and distributed among us. That is the first miracle.

8. The other miracle concerns the little girl who had died, who was as old, according to Mark, as the woman's illness lasted. They were sure of nothing else than that the little girl was certainly going to die, for she was in the throes of death. But the girl's father went to him thinking strange and wonderful thoughts. He hoped that if he had Christ, his daughter would surely be restored to health, and live. But before Christ got there, the little girl was dead, and everything had already been arranged and the preparations made which were customary for the dead. The pipers stood in the house (for the Jews did not have bells) and played a mourning song at the door to her chamber, just as we toll the bells for the dead. The people were gathered about the body; there was much wailing, and goings in and out, as was normal in such situations when someone of high social standing had died.

9. Now when Christ arrived and saw the pipers and the wailing of the people, he set upon it as something ridiculous. Away, he said, with the piping and wailing! The child is not dead, but sleeping. Note these words well. It was a venturesome thing to say, and I would give a hundred gulden to understand it and retain it in my memory as the Lord meant it. The little girl had died, the pipers had been ordered, and the pallbearers who were to carry her to her grave were all present; and the Lord came and said, Get out of here, you pipers of death and pallbearers! The maiden is not dead, but asleep. Oh? She is not dead? She is lying on the bier, as you can plainly see; isn't that death, when you're lying on the bier? No, Christ said, she is not dead, but rather asleep, and then proved it by his action. He went up to her, took the little girl by the hand, no differently than we would do with a sleeping child when we wanted to wake him or her up. Then the girl got up and walked.

10. Now the one who could believe this, who could look at a dead body as if it were lying on a bed asleep, who could so shape his words and what he sees with his eyes, so as to look upon death as sleep, and suppose that a corpse could as readily rise from death as one asleep readily arises from sleep—such a one might well boast that he could so something unique, that no one else can.

11. But what we experience in our own lives and see in others is that the greater a man's reason is, the less he believes such things and the more he laughs at it. As we see them here ridiculing the Lord and thinking: Is he going to raise the dead or something? He is out of his mind if he thinks a dead person is only asleep and can be roused with the touch of a hand. But this is what the heavenly wisdom of God is like; it is so sublime that it is considered sheer nonsense by human reason. For consider, if your own child had died, and I said to you, Oh, he's not dead, don't you see that he is only asleep and I can wake him up with the tap of a finger? You would think I was mocking you in your time of grief, and you would tell me to leave you alone. And that is just what these people here have done to the Lord.

12. Therefore, learn this from today's Gospel lesson: For the Lord death is nothing more than sleep, as we see him here awaken the little girl who had died by placing his hand on her; and that a sick body is for him no different than a healthy one, as is demonstrated in the previous example with the woman. She was very sick, but as soon as she came to Christ and touched his garment, the illness had to give way and depart from her.

13. The Lord showed himself no less powerful against other afflictions and infirmities as well. The blind who sought healing from him received their sight, sinners were justified, the lost were saved. He can do marvelous things for us too. What he speaks is the exact opposite of what we see with our eyes. As, for example, the little girl was dead in the eyes of all the people, but in my eyes, Christ said, she was alive and sleeping. David was in his own eyes and in the eyes of the world a poor shepherd, but in my eyes he was a king. All of you who believe on me are in your own eyes miserable sinners, but in my eyes great saints and as the angels of God. For I need speak no more than a word, and sin, death, and disease must flee away, and righteous-

ness, life, and health shall be in their place. As I speak, so it must be, and it can never be otherwise.

14. Also here, therefore, our Lord God spoke a very marvelous word, which to the world is a big lie, when he said of the little girl, She is not dead, but sleeping. If he had simply said, She is asleep, then they might have said, It is the sleep of St. Michael which people sleep until the Day of Judgment. But he added to it, and said outright, She is not dead! Yet surely he had to acknowledge that she had died, and was not alive any more. He said in so many words, Measuring by what you can do and by what you can know, she is no longer alive, but to me she is alive; and so that you may see that this is true, I will awaken her just by touching her with my finger, just as you awaken your children from sleep.

15. So to sum up, all this happened so that we might not look upon our distress according to our reason, with fleshly eyes, but with the eyes of Christ. These are eyes which can look upon death, sin, and hell and can say with certainty, I see no death, I feel no sin, I am not damned; but I see through Christ nothing but holiness, life, and blessedness. So if I am poor, I feel no poverty; rather, I believe I have enough; for I have Christ, who can give me hour by hour everything I need, although I have nothing.

16. Anyone endowed with such sight may well boast of having the eyes of Christ. In times of famine or pestilence this person would see things quite differently than the way the world customarily does. In times of famine everyone looks to see what is in the cellar and in the garden; what he finds there determines his mood. If he finds a lot, he will be merry; if he finds little, he is troubled and close to despair.

17. It is the same in times of the plague. Those who can flee do so, thinking they will be safe in another place. But a Christian who has firm faith in Christ would think: Even if I had a thousand plagues in my body—were that possible—still I refuse to be fearful; for I have Christ. If he so wills, the pestilence will do me no more harm than a flea in my armpit; though it bite me and eat at me, it won't kill me. And this is for certain: Those who could take heart in this way would abide securely and fearlessly, in anticipation of good things. But since we don't believe and do not possess such spiritual eyesight as this, we fear and are fainthearted and find ourselves thinking we can

tiptoe past the wrath of God, or flee ten or twenty miles away, or some such nonsense.

18. Now the Lord Christ testifies that not merely this little girl, but also those who have died before our very eyes, are buried, and long since decayed, live unto God. Therefore, the Lord says in the Gospel of Matthew (22:32): "I am the God of Abraham, and the God of Isaac, and the God of Jacob. God is not the God of the dead, but of the living." Therefore, Abraham, Isaac, and Jacob must be alive, not dead, since they were laid in the ground over three thousand years ago, and have long since been reduced to dust, and neither hide nor hair is left of them. But Christ offers a strong proof that they are alive because God is a God of the living, and not of the dead! Therefore, everything must be alive to him, but to us everything is dead. For the world and reason cannot see anything other than death. But the Christian's eyes should see that which they do not see and hear except in the Word, as Christ here saw the little girl who had just died.

19. With sin it is just as I say here about death. I ought to know and confess that I am a sinner, and, nevertheless, believe and hope for nothing short of holiness and righteousness. For this is the word of our Lord in baptism: "He that believeth and is baptized shall be saved"; and in the Lord's Supper: "Eat, this is my body which is given for you for the forgiveness of sins." I am supposed to believe words like this, that they are true, even if I see and feel in myself the very opposite. I am to give no regard to that, but to look and hearken alone to the word which he speaks to me. So if you see a Christian dying, your eyes see a dead man; but close those fleshly eyes, open the spiritual eyes which look to the Word, and you will discover that this man is not dead but alive in the eyes of God. For Christ's word is: "Whosoever believeth on me shall never die."

20. So from today's Gospel let us learn that all adversity, no matter how great it appears in your eyes, is in the eyes of our God less than nothing. For if death has no part of a Christian, then even less so blindness, deafness, leprosy, and pestilence; they are of no significance. Therefore, if you see in your situation sin, illness, poverty, or other such things, do not be afraid; close the fleshly eyes and open the spiritual ones, and say, I am a Christian, and have a Lord who

with one little word can bring all this chaos under control. So, then, why do I insist on worrying myself to death about it? For this is certain: As readily as Christ helped this little girl from the bodily death in which she lay, so readily does he desire to save us, if we only believe and look to him for it.

21. Furthermore, we ought to consider that this little girl was not saved by her faith (for the dead cannot believe any more than they can hear or see), but her father believed, and besought Christ to help his daughter. For the sake of his faith this miracle happened. The little girl came back to life; as Christ said in another place: "All things are possible to him that believeth."

22. So faith really is a very powerful thing. Let it be ever so great, you can believe and look to Christ; the answer will be "yes" and neither the devil nor death shall prevail against it. Just as we see in these two miracles! It is for this reason that they are held up before us, and, therefore, faith is so highly extolled by Christ himself, to cause us to look upon his creation in a wholly new way, through his eyes and not through our own.

23. So whether we seem to be poor and dead to ourselves, or in sin, or lying prostrate before the pestilence or some other sickness, let us, in spite of all this, believe that in God's eyes things look quite different. And let us say with a merry heart, Though poverty, pestilence, and death are before me, yet as a Christian I know no poverty, no death, no pestilence. For in the eyes of Christ my Lord there is nothing but riches, health, holiness, and life. But if I do not see this yet, it is only for him to speak the word, and I shall see it even with my very own eyes that it is true, and the end of all things shall certainly be as he has said.

24. May God, for the sake of Christ, our Redeemer, and his Son, through his Holy Spirit, grant us also such spiritual eyes, that we may look upon all adversity differently than the world, hold fast to this consolation, and at last be saved. Amen.

TWENTY-FIFTH SUNDAY AFTER TRINITY*

Matthew 24:15–28

When ye therefore shall see the abomination of desolation, spoken of by Daniel the prophet, stand in the holy place, (whoso readeth, let him understand:) Then let them which be in Judaea flee into the mountains: Let him which is on the housetop not come down to take anything out of his house: Neither let him which is in the field return back to take his clothes. And woe unto them that are with child, and to them that give suck in those days! But pray ye that your flight be not in the winter, neither on the sabbath day: For then shall be great tribulation, such as was not since the beginning of the world to this time, no, nor ever shall be. And except those days should be shortened, there should no flesh be saved: but for the elect's sake those days shall be shortened. Then if any man shall say unto you, Lo, here is Christ, or there; believe it not. For there shall arise false Christs, and false prophets, and shall show great signs and wonders; insomuch that, if it were possible, they shall deceive the very elect. Behold, I have told you before. Wherefore if they shall say unto you, Behold, he is in the desert; go not forth: behold, he is in the secret chambers; believe it not. For as the lightning cometh out of the east, and shineth even unto the west; so shall also the coming of the Son of man be. For wheresoever the carcase is, there will the eagles be gathered together.

1. In today's Gospel lesson our dear Lord Jesus Christ foretells the devastation of the city of Jerusalem and the Jewish homeland, as well as the end of the whole world. St. Luke (chapters 17 and 21) gives this prediction even more clearly and pointedly, item for item; St. Matthew blends both together, the end of the Jewish kingdom and the end of the world, and, as a result, is not quite as simple and clear as St. Luke. Both Matthew and Mark concentrate more on the world's end than on the devastation of the Jews, telescoping the two things together. But for better understanding we need to look at

---

*Preached publicly at the parish church, 1537.

each separately, in order to see what pertains to the end of the Jewish kingdom and what pertains to the end of the world.

When ye therefore shall see the abomination of desolation, spoken of by Daniel the prophet, stand in the holy place, (whoso readeth, let him understand).

2. Here Christ speaks of the devastation of the Jewish people, citing the prophet Daniel who foretold the same in prophecy long before (Dan. 9:27): "And for the overspreading of abominations he shall make it desolate, even until the consummation, and that determined shall be poured upon the desolate." On the basis of Daniel's "overspreading of abominations," Christ is saying that devastation shall come upon the Holy City, that is, upon the temple where the cherubim stand in the innermost sanctuary, where the ark of the covenant rests. By saying that the abomination will pinpoint on these sacred precincts, Christ is emphasizing the severity of the devastation, as a definite token of how Jerusalem and the Jewish kingdom would be destroyed, and forever remain so.

3. This occurred during the reign of Caius Caligula who had his likeness set up throughout the Roman Empire for people to worship as a god. He not only wanted to be worshiped as a god in Rome alongside the heathen gods and throughout the heathen lands, but he also ordered his image to be set up in the temple at Jerusalem, to be worshiped as a god by the people of God. The Jews protested vociferously, since they were opposed to all images. But they had to endure it. When they attempted to remove the images, the governor, Pilate, had them installed again, quietly by night, causing great public uproar.

4. Christ's meaning is that when this happens, they would understand the abomination of desolation, the abomination spoken of by the Scriptures. For the worship of idols is known in Scripture as an abomination. It is so not merely before God, but is also a terrible, detestable thing for all pious hearts to behold, when they have to see the devil worshiped instead of God. When this comes to pass in the Holy City, that an idol or image is to be worshiped by the poor, miserable people, then be aware of what is happening, Christ says very plainly and simply. He calls it an abomination of desolation, not only because it portends the destruction of Jerusalem, but also because God would no longer dwell in Jerusalem as heretofore. The city

would be given over to the devil and his minions who rightly are an abomination before God and all godly persons.

5. St. Matthew speaks in somewhat veiled terms with the phrase "abomination of desolation," whereas St. Luke is more straightforward in speaking of its destruction (21:20): "When ye shall see Jerusalem compassed with armies, then know that the desolation thereof is nigh." A little further on (v. 24): "And they shall fall by the edge of the sword, and shall be led away captive into all nations: and Jerusalem shall be trodden down of the Gentiles, until the times of the Gentiles be fulfilled." The prophet Daniel adds that this devastation would never end, something borne out in history. The destruction of the Jewish kingdom has lasted for 1500 years now. They have often endeavored, sometimes with the help of foreign rulers, to reconstruct the temple, but in vain. It will not happen, as the Scriptures state. Daniel states that this will be Jerusalem's fate until the end, and St. Luke adds that the Gentiles will tread over the city until the time of the Gentiles is fulfilled. Jerusalem will not be reconstructed but must remain subject to the Gentiles until the Gentiles are converted, and so, until the world's end. That is the meaning of Christ's words here. St. Matthew has given this somewhat briefly, while the prophet Daniel and the Evangelist Luke make it very plain.

Then let them which be in Judaea flee into the mountains: Let him which is on the housetop not come down to take anything out of his house: Neither let him which is in the field return back to take his clothes.

6. Jewish homes were not gabled like ours, but the roofs were flat, four-cornered decks, allowing people to stand and sit on them, with steps giving access up and down. What the Lord wants to say is this: Whoever at that time is in Jerusalem and the land of Judaea, let him hurry down and away at top speed, allowing nothing to delay him, for the time has come when Jerusalem and the land of the Jews will be devastated.

And woe unto them that are with child, and to them that give suck in those days! But pray ye that your flight be not in the winter, neither on the sabbath day: For then shall be great tribulation, such as was not since the beginning of the world to this time, no, nor ever shall be.

7. This ties in with the preceding. Before the Lord's eyes, Jerusalem is a devastated city, never to be rebuilt, for this is its last and final

devastation. And that is the first part of today's lesson which we will now let rest. We already heard in the lesson for the tenth Sunday after Trinity what it means. So, now, we want to take up the second part, which is also the primary lesson that Christ treats here.

And except those days should be shortened, there should no flesh be saved: but for the elect's sake those days shall be shortened.

8. St. Matthew now leaves off speaking about the demise of the Jewish kingdom and focuses on the end of the world, devoting the whole discussion to that subject. I tell you, Christ is saying, when that time comes, if the days are not shortened, no one would finally be saved. He himself explains, showing what would befall with the world's end, stating:

Then if any man shall say unto you, Lo, here is Christ, or there; believe it not. For there shall arise false Christs, and false prophets, and shall shew great signs and wonders; insomuch that, if it were possible, they shall deceive the very elect. Behold, I have told you before.

9. This pertains not only to the Jews, but also to the whole world and, especially, the Christian church, which has been illumined by the light of the gospel. What will be its lot at the end of the world? When once the gospel has come into the world, Christ is saying, the devil will multiply the enthusiasts and the sects, false prophets and false teachers around the believers, so that those who view the world through spiritual eyes will wonder whether anyone will finally be saved. The seduction will be so pervasive and the false prophets will perform such great signs and wonders, that even the elect—were that possible—succumb to error.

10. For that reason the Lord warns so earnestly, Lo, I have told you beforehand, thereby stating that there will be no room for excuse, since I have warned you before it happens. They will perform such great wonders and signs, along with a very pious life, that everyone will draw the conclusion: God must dwell here, for how could they otherwise have done such miracles? For that reason, I say, be on your guard. I've told you in advance. I have given ample warning. No excuse will avail if you blindly blunder along.

11. That is the tragic picture prevailing before people's eyes, day in, day out, even among the best and most respected people of the world. It is a tragedy in which many of us, too, are deeply involved.

Consider the story which history tells from the time when the tyrannical Turks and Moslems took over, and after them the papacy, and you will begin to understand what Christ is talking of here. In all of the Turkish Empire (it is actually larger and mightier than Spain, France, England, Germany, Italy, Bohemia, Hungary, Poland, and Denmark taken together), there is no knowledge of Christ except among the poor Christian captives who must do the Turks' bidding. That multitude cares nothing about Christ, denying and despising him, pointing to him derisively and saying that the gospel of Christ is kaput, now that Mohammed and his Koran are in the picture. They consider themselves the beloved and chosen children of God because God has granted them victory over the Christians and made them his dear children instead.

12. They do not understand that the Christians must suffer because of sin in the world, the innocent becoming martyrs, as the prophet Daniel long ago foretold, and that the Turks would fight against and triumph over the godly. Therefore, as a result of their victories over the Christians in battle and their supremacy generally, they have become proud, arrogant, and secure in their beliefs, in no wise doubting that their faith is right and the Christian faith wrong. There can be no mistake, they reason, because God gives them so many victories, allows them to conquer so many kingdoms and forsakes the Christians. Therefore, they are the people of God, with the true faith, while the Christians are not and do not have the truth. The Moslem seduction has swept over and destroyed many kingdoms, and countries, like the flood, the result being, says Christ here, that even the elect are drawn to and almost engulfed by the delusion, if that were possible.

13. And what was the situation under the papacy with regard to this? Nothing less than that none were coming to salvation. For at that point in time, the world was full of all kinds of orders and sects, and this had such an effect on people that emperors, kings, and the best people on earth gave enormous amounts of money, not merely to promote the preaching office and advance false doctrines and lies (as was done early on when the papacy came into existence), but also monasteries and convents (as others did later on), so that the dear holy fathers, monks, and priests might pray for the people and share

their good works with them. That's why the great bishoprics Wuerzburg, Bamberg, Cologne, and others, and so many monasteries and convents came into being everywhere. When you see such goings-on emanating out of the papacy, what else is it than what Christ says here: There will arise false Christs, and false prophets who will say, Lo, here is Christ, or there. For this is what the pope teaches: Whoever obeys the Church of Rome and fasts, celebrates, eats, and attires himself in a certain way, will be saved.

14. Here, too, we see how completely this text is fulfilled. There is no other way, no other name whereby to be saved, than Christ's alone, through whose death and shedding of blood we are delivered from sin. The Lord himself declares (John 14:6): "I am the way, the truth and the life: no man cometh unto the Father, but by me." The apostle Peter states (Acts 4:12): "Neither is there salvation in any other: for there is none other name under heaven given among men, whereby we must be saved." Whoever does not see this light bumbles along blindly in darkness, leading and being led into error. In popedom we not only did not see this light, but actually had it extinguished, and we ourselves helped to make it so. I myself had no other understanding of Christ than to think of him as sitting on top of a rainbow and regarding him as a stern judge. We did not really understand holy baptism. When a person became a monk, people said of him that he was newly born. Monkery was elevated high above baptism. As a result baptism in popedom was not only held in low esteem, but its significance was also lost. Since we had no proper understanding of Christ, we forsook him and turned to the saints, praying to them, that they might be our patrons and intercessors. We especially ran to Mary, petitioning her, Oh, holy Virgin Mary, show your breasts to your Son, Jesus Christ, and procure grace for me from him. Ultimately people also ran to the cloisters, petitioning the monks to pray for them, went on pilgrimages, and importuned the saints, in the hope of obtaining grace and absolution. It was just as Christ here says, They will say to you, Lo, here is Christ, or there. People were directed to this saint and that, to go on this and that pilgrimage, to scurry to this and that shrine and holy place—Cologne, Rome, wherever. The world became so full of monastic sects and orders that the person who assesses the darkness and horror of popedom would have to conclude that no one could have been saved.

15. It is, therefore, foolish for people today to say that they will follow in the footsteps of their fathers and grandfathers. Do you think that God should let the whole world sink because they did not understand the way to salvation? Friend, if you refuse to heed the words which Christ here speaks, that is what will happen to you. He says, "There shall arise false Christs, and false prophets, and shall shew great signs and wonders; insomuch that, if it were possible, they shall deceive the very elect." Also: "Except those days should be shortened, there should no flesh be saved." Therefore, don't be swayed by their numbers, nor by the wise and learned of the world, but heed Christ's words: The days will come, if the time is not shortened, when no man will be saved. The papists, indeed, think that their regime is very precious and free from all error. They also claim: The Church cannot err and it will endure forever. They don't see, nor do they want to, that this prophecy of Christ must also stand.

16. In addition to that, we must also add that they will perform great signs and wonders, and yet they will be false Christs and false prophets. This, also, has been fulfilled under the papacy in a very graphic way. A great many supernatural healings occurred at Eichen, Grimmethal, and elsewhere, so that the churches overflowed with crutches and were saturated with wax. Yes, I am going to tell you even more. The pope's doctrine is buttressed with all manner of great, supernatural happenings, so that it is simply impossible to tell them all. In Hessen a child was caught in a mill wheel, was critically mangled, and lay dead in the water for three days. But after the child was finally pulled from the water, he was commended with prayer to St. Anna and restored to health. Many books have been written about such miracles. People have gone out in droves to see them and have believed the lie. Why, they have said, should I not believe? I can see with my own eyes that St. Bastian, St. Anna, St. Benno, and others, have cured this or that sick person who commended himself to the saints. Christ is issuing a warning here, so that people might be aware of it when it comes to pass. False Christs and false prophets, he says, will come in my name, will prophesy in my name, cast out devils in my name, and perform many deeds in my name, so that even the saints, who are truly filled with the Holy Spirit, and the elect might be misled—were such a thing indeed possible.

17. So, what is the bottom line? Listen to what Christ says: See, I have told you beforehand. When they say to you, Lo, here is Christ, do not believe it. That's what you should do. Pay no attention, don't believe the false Christs and the false prophets, even if they prophesy in the name of Christ, drive out devils, and do miracles. From Christ's revealed Word and gospel we must learn that we are not to believe such signs and wonders, not even if a man dead for ten days were raised from the grave. Even if I were to see a papist or a monk resurrect a dead person in the name of St. Anna, I would still have to say that it was done by the devil's power. St. Anna is not to be my advocate and intercessor; Christ alone is to be that! (1 Tim. 2:5; 1 Jn. 2:1). One warning ought to be sufficient for those willing to be warned. Christ says that "false Christs and false prophets will arise, and shew great signs and wonders." St. Paul also states (2 Thess. 2:9–12) that the coming of Antichrist will be "with all power and signs and lying wonders, And with all deceivableness of unrighteousness in them that perish; because they received not the love of the truth, that they might be saved. And for this cause God shall send them strong delusion, that they should believe a lie: That they all might be damned who believed not the truth, but had pleasure in unrighteousness."

18. That is an earnest warning, and St. Paul clearly states that God will send the ungrateful and unbelieving strong delusions, that is, the kind of delusions which will greatly disturb and capture people's minds, that is, affecting them deeply and misleading them into believing a lie, as I described just a moment ago, that St. Anna in Hessen restored to life a child that had lain in water for three days. That was an overpowering deception, inflicted by God as punishment for ingratitude, because people have had God's Word and yet refused to accept the truth; and as a result had to believe that lie. That was also the significance of a story connected with Mary at Loretto. It was a very gross, brazen lie, which claimed that this very same Mary was to have sailed across the sea in a ship constructed of stone. The legends of the miracles of St. Francis, in particular, are a bag full of selected, great, base lies!

19. That's why I say that one ought never accept such "signs," once the gospel has gone out into the world and has been vindicated

sufficiently by signs and miracles. Even if one were to see an apparently dead man resurrected, we must not believe it, for God has threatened to allow false and lying wonders to come unto the world through the devil, in punishment upon those who reject the truth. Therefore, we must not believe them, but be wise and listen to what Christ earnestly warns, "Then if any man shall say unto you, Lo, here is Christ, or there; believe it not; Behold, I have told you before." And even though protest is made that these are pious people, prophets with sterling reputations and convincing powers, you should answer that it's not a matter of signs, wonders, prophets, and christs that count, but Christ's word here, When they say to you, Lo, here is Christ, or there, don't believe it.

20. But how can we keep from being deceived, since some of the deceptions which come our way are very compelling. How can we keep from being misled? To learn such mastery or art requires that we truly be Christians. First of all, we must recognize that the devil is a very crafty and powerful lord—that's why he is called lord and ruler of the world!—and that if our dear Lord and God does not counter and thwart his craftiness, cleverness, and power, there would be no one on earth wise, strong, and holy enough to withstand and survive against him. That is to say, with his knowledge, smartness, and power the devil far exceeds all human understanding and mental power. If God, therefore, were to withdraw his hand, the devil would quickly contrive an apparition before our eyes and take us in before we know it.

21. We see this in the case of Job, how the devil brought him to the point of cursing and blaming God for the day he was born. David was a great and outstanding individual, but when God withdrew his hand, David succumbed to adultery and murder. We simply have to be aware that before the devil's wiles and power, no man is ever safe. If God permits, the devil can deceive even the most godly, and, in fact, others through the godly. We dare not be secure, but must continue humbly in the fear of God, petitioning him that we not be misled into temptation or succumb to trials. The devil uses the same craftiness and power to keep people from believing the truth, as he does when he makes them foolish and gullible, so that they believe a lie, swearing that it is the very truth of God, even though it is nothing

more than the devil's lying deception. Similarly, he pulls the wool over people's eyes, so that they think they see, hear, and grasp what is not even there to see, hear, or grasp. It's no big trick for him to so blind a man's mind and reason that he thinks he has God's Word, when all the while he has only the devil's lies. The devil gets him to think that he truly possesses Christ and a trustworthy prophet, while all the while it is a false Christ and false prophet. He is able to blind the physical senses to such an extent that you imagine something is happening right before your very eyes while nothing at all is really happening, as he did in the case of the child in Hessen, which had not died, and yet the devil so blinded the eyes of the people that they all actually thought the child was dead. The devil had (as he indeed is able to do!) kept the child from breathing so that everybody thought the child was dead.

22. Thus we read how on one occasion the devil dressed a man in the garb of a king, so that both he and also the rest of his brothers, who were present there too, were led to believe that it truly was a king's garb. When they looked at it, touched and fingered it, it was like velvet and silk and exquisitely woven. Thus the devil had cast a spell upon their eyes, ears, and fingers in such a way that they all became disconcerted and bewildered. But when they then entreated the brother and said to him, Dear brother, go to Bishop St. Martino, so that he too may see the beautiful garb, the devil himself took notice. Not on your life, said the bewitched brother with the royal garb, I will not go to St. Martino; for the angels which gave me the garb have forbidden me to do that. When the others now insisted that he must go and wanted to compel him to go, the royal garb vanished before their eyes. The devil knows all sorts of tricks.

23. There is a report in *Vitis Patrum* (Lives of the Fathers) that a pious couple had a beautiful daughter. The devil so bewitched the couple that they thought their daughter had become a cow; their eyes were so blinded by the devil that in their eyes there was nothing there but a real cow and they could feel nothing but the horns, neck, legs, and hide of a cow. Isn't that a wondrous power the devil possesses that he is able to bewitch people into thinking that they see and feel nothing but a cow, while all the while it is not a cow but their daughter? They then go to the holy man, Marcarius, and bewail so

plaintively to him about their daughter, whom they had brought with them, as if she had become a cow. Then Marcarius said (for his eyes had not, as had the eyes of the parents, been blinded by the devil): Dear people, I see no cow but a fine young lady. But the parents persisted and said that it still was a cow. Then Marcarius besought our Lord God to open the eyes of the parents, and God heard the prayer of the pious man and opened the eyes of the parents; they then saw their daughter truly as before.

24. The devil knows his trade. For if he can blind the internal senses, he is more than able to blind the external senses. He is a veritable master, and one who knows a thousand tricks. If he can harden our heart, he is more than able to restrict the bodily eyes so that they are unable to see what they should be seeing. What did he do to Thomas Muentzer? He misled him so totally that he neither saw nor heard but stood there like a boulder in a clouded landscape. So, the first thing we ought to note is this, that many false signs can occur through the devil when God withdraws his hand and empowers him to punish the world on account of sin. Then he can make the blind see, yes, even raise the dead, and yet these are not true signs, but simply apparitions whereby the devil bewitches people. Just as he caused that young woman to appear as a cow, so he can also make people blind and dead, and again give them sight and life. Not that he is a creator like God; but that he draws such illusionary cover over things that people think they are seeing true signs.

25. Second, one should very diligently bear in mind the purpose of signs and wonders. For the *causa finalis*, "the ultimate intent," of all false signs is that thereby the devil wants to substantiate his deception. Thus one reads that many miracles were performed by Anthony and others, merely with the intent of substantiating the legends of the saints, monasticism, pilgrimages, and adoration of the saints; in short, for the purpose and with the result that people fell away from the true and only way of Christ and worshiped the creature instead of Christ. We must note this very well, so that we can fend off those who extol miraculous signs so highly and respond, I know the devil. He can imitate God (for he is God's ape); he can perform all manner of miraculous signs, except that they are false miraculous signs. People think they are real signs; also, those who

experience them actually feel like they are really blind or dead, as that young woman herself thought that she was a cow. But they are false signs, whose intent is to get the person involved to fall away from God and to entrust himself to this or that saint. When people have been convinced, then the devil removes the apparition. Thereupon, these people say, This or that saint has cured me! and they are strengthened in idolatry. Such false miraculous signs, which the devil has performed, to strengthen his lies and errors so that idolatry can become all the more extensive in the world, the pope has endorsed and reinforced by means of his indulgences.

26. All such false signs and wonders, even when they occur among the godly, must be evaluated and judged in line with Christ's words here, that we should not believe them, even when they say, Lo, here is Christ, or, lo, there. We are to say, Yes, I see that they are fine, pious people, even prophets, who can perform wonders; but, no matter, that doesn't count with me, since if one looks at the end result of such wonders, they end with a denial of Christ. The Christian faith instructs me to place my trust only in Christ and not in any false god. These signs and wonders seek to divert me, so that I believe my salvation lies in doing pious works and service. They make "Christs" out of the saints and try to turn my heart away from Christ who alone is the true rock and fortress upon which my faith can build securely. For that I don't need to go on pilgrimages or seek out holy shrines, but can stay at home, go to church, and pray to my God through Christ, who is able to help me far better than any saint or other holy person.

27. Whoever takes this stance will rightly discern the difference between genuine and counterfeit signs and wonders. The apostles, too, were able to do many signs and wonders, but always for the purpose of confirming the gospel, that Christ might be made known and believed in the world. The devil immediately got into the act and duplicated what they were doing, especially when he saw that people were becoming lax and indifferent; and God allowed it to happen in punishment for the world's ungrateful disregard, for God cannot tolerate that the treasure of the gospel by which he gives us Christ, his dear Son, should be despised. In the moment that men despise him, God withdraws his hand. If you are wearied and filled up, he says, then I am, too, with you. Then is when the devil comes with his won-

ders and signs, casting a spell by means of his charms and supernatural wonders, counseling people to pray to this or that saint, and lighting up all kinds of wax candles. And should it be that someone regains his health, they then think that so-and-so saint was the reason. The devil has then accomplished what he set out to do.

28. The whole of the pope's kingdom is shot through with this sort of idolatry, where people say, Lo, here is Christ, or there. But a true Christian does not pray to the saints or sing their praises. On the contrary, he says, I believe on Jesus Christ, who is my only helper, to whom I come in every need. When I am sick, I say, If it is your will, Lord, you can help me; if not, I will bear my cross or burden willingly for your name's sake. That's the way of a Christian. The non-Christian or unbeliever does not act that way, for the devil stirs him up to call on the saints, to seek help from creaturely beings, and to fall away from God and Christ.

29. Whoever wishes to remain safe from temptation should stand firm in true faith on Christ, fervent in prayer, eagerly and obediently listening to God's Word, thanking him from the bottom of his heart for that, lest God be angered and withdraw his hand, allowing the devil to slip in. The devil, as said, is such a crafty, powerful spirit that, even though you once understood everything and knew the whole Bible, you would fall and be lost, were God not supporting and upholding you. That is certainly true should the Turk continue as he began, that the whole world would fall victim to the Mohammedan faith. And if the papacy had continued unchanged, the whole world would have become replete with monasticism and superstition. For the papacy has concerned itself with, and promoted more diligently, the legends of the saints than the gospel of Christ. For this reason it would have come to the point finally that, as is written here, no man would have been saved.

30. However, the judgment has to come at some time and break the staff in two, about which Scripture says that Antichrist must be revealed. By God's grace we have indeed curbed papal abominations, so that to some extent they were forced to a halt and Christian doctrine cleansed and purified; otherwise, we all would have remained under the papacy and been suffocated. See to it now that you do not overlook this grace of God or become ungrateful to God. We

always preach and warn you about this; for the devil is a powerful foe, who is continually vying for your soul.

Wherefore if they shall say unto you, Behold, he is in the desert; go not forth: behold, he is in the secret chambers; believe it not. For as the lightning cometh out of the east, and shineth even unto the west; so shall also the coming of the Son of man be. For wheresoever the carcase is, there will the eagles be gathered together.

31. "Deserts" are the pilgrimages and monasteries, as at Eichen; "secret chambers" are the spiritual cloisters, like the Carthusian monasteries. The Lord means, See to it that you do not wander off the right way, as I have preached and taught you; no matter who approaches, performing whatever miracles and signs, just pay no heed. If you hear something other than what you have heard from me, be it pope, church, fathers, or councils, don't probe any farther or pay attention to them. Remember what I have told you, "I am the way, the truth, and the life." I am faithfully warning you and telling you before it happens that the devil will come through his prophets and produce false signs and wonders in order to mislead you. Things will be so frightful in the church that it will be almost impossible for the saints and elect to remain faithful and be saved. However, God will sustain his own, according to the proverb: "Wheresoever the carcass is, there will the eagles be gathered together."

32. I, too, believe, therefore, that our dear God has preserved many of our forefathers under the great darkness of the papacy. For in that very blindness and darkness the practice, nonetheless, survived of holding the cross up before the dying and that some of the common folk said to the dying man, Look to Jesus, who died for you on the cross! In that way many a dying person again clung to Christ, even though prior to this he believed the false miraculous signs and indulged in idolatry. These are the elect who also were led away into the prison of error and would have remained there had such a thing been possible. Accordingly, we can take comfort in this, that to those who have died under the papacy God has ultimately granted grace, that through recollection of the crucifix they departed and died in Christ. These very ones were misled into error, but it was not possible for them to remain in it.

33. I believe that Bernard (of Clairvaux) was also saved. For when he was about to die, he said, I have lived an evil life and confess that

I cannot obtain the kingdom of heaven by my own merits; however, my Lord Jesus Christ has a twofold jurisdiction as regards heaven. First, by inheritance from the Father, that he is the only begotten Son of God, born of the Father from eternity, and has inherited the kingdom of heaven. Second, through the merit of his sufferings, that he is the Virgin's son, and has won the kingdom of heaven by his holy, innocent sufferings. The first right to the kingdom of heaven, that he is its natural, eternal heir, he retains for himself. The second right, however, that he has won it through his sufferings, he grants to me. That very gift I take to myself, and I shall not perish. Through this word Bernard has been saved. For even though he had led an austere life and had so strenuously exerted himself in fasting and vigils that the air smelled foul to him, and he could no longer because of weakness, stand in the choir with his brothers, nevertheless, he did not die in that way but took comfort in Christ and in his suffering. This man was also one of the elect, a man who had been led into error but who did not remain in it. And there have been many more like him.

TWENTY-SIXTH SUNDAY AFTER TRINITY

Matthew 25:31–46

When the Son of man shall come in his glory, and all the holy angels with him, then shall he sit upon the throne of his glory: And before him shall be gathered all nations: and he shall separate them one from another, as a shepherd divideth his sheep from the goats: And he shall set the sheep on his right hand, but the goats on the left. Then shall the King say unto them on his right hand, Come, ye blessed of my Father, inherit the kingdom prepared for you from the foundation of the world: For I was an hungred, and ye gave me meat: I was thirsty, and ye gave me drink: I was a stranger, and ye took me in: Naked, and ye clothed me: I was sick, and ye visited me: I was in prison, and ye came unto me. Then shall the righteous answer him, saying, Lord, when saw we thee an hungred, and fed thee? or thirsty, and gave thee drink? Or when saw we thee sick, or in prison, and came unto thee? And the King shall answer and say unto them, Verily I say unto you, Inasmuch as ye had done it unto one of the least of these my brethren, ye have done it unto me. Then shall he say also unto them on the left hand, Depart from me, ye cursed, into everlasting fire, prepared for the devil and his angels: For I was an hungred, and ye gave me no meat: I was thirsty, and ye gave me no drink: I was a stranger, and ye took me not in: naked, and ye clothed me not: sick, and in prison, and ye visited me not. Then shall they also answer him, saying, Lord, when saw we thee an hungred, or athirst, or a stranger, or naked, or sick, or in prison, and did not minister unto thee? Then shall he answer them, saying, Verily I say unto you, Inasmuch as ye did it not to one of the least of these, ye did it not to me. And these shall go away into everlasting punishment: but the righteous into life eternal.

The editor of *Luther's Saemmtliche Schriften,* St. Louis edition, volume 13a, from which our translation has been made, explains at this point that Georg Roerer, who originally gathered and published selected works of Luther in 1559, including the HAUSPOSTILLE, was unable to find a sermon preached by Luther at the Lutherhaus for the twenty-sixth Sunday after Trinity. No doubt the explanation simply is that usually there are not this many Sundays after Trinity in a given church year. Of course, during Luther's lifetime an occasion like this did occur, and the editor of the St. Louis edition notes that we have a sermon by Luther extant for this Sunday dating from the year 1543. The reader may find an English translation of this sermon on Matthew 25:31–46 in Lenker's edition of the KIRCHENPOS-TILLE, or Church Postils. We refer the reader here to *SERMONS OF MARTIN LUTHER*, edited by John N. Lenker, Baker Book House, reprinted 1983, volume 5, pp. 379–395.

FESTIVAL OF CHRIST'S NATIVITY

*First Sermon**

Isaiah 9:1–7

Nevertheless the dimness shall not be such as was in her vexation, when at the first he lightly afflicted the land of Zebulun and the land of Naphtali, and afterward did more grievously afflict her by the way of the sea, beyond Jordan, in Galilee of the nations. The people that walked in darkness have seen a great light: they that dwell in the land of the shadow of death, upon them hath the light shined. Thou hast multiplied the nation, and not increased the joy: they joy before thee according to the joy in harvest, and as men rejoice when they divide the spoil. For thou hast broken the yoke of his burden, and the staff of his shoulder, the rod of his oppressor, as in the day of Midian. For every battle of the warrior is with confused noise, and garments rolled in blood; but this shall be with burning and fuel of fire. For unto us a child is born, unto us a son is given: and the government shall be upon his shoulder: and his name shall be called Wonderful, Counsellor, The mighty God, The everlasting Father, The Prince of Peace. Of the increase of his government and peace there shall be no end, upon the throne of David, and upon his kingdom, to order it, and to establish it with judgment and with justice from henceforth even for ever. The zeal of the LORD *of hosts will perform this.*

ABOUT THE CHILD JESUS AND HIS SIX NAMES.

1. People are presently celebrating the beautiful and delightful festival of the birth of our Lord Jesus Christ. And it is fitting, indeed, for us to celebrate God's glorious grace with a truly wonderful festival and to ponder it well, so that the article in which we confess and pray in our Christian faith, "I believe in Jesus Christ, conceived by the Holy Ghost, born of the Virgin Mary," may be remembered not just within Christendom, but also that distressed, sorrowful hearts

---

*Preached Christmas Eve, 1532, at the parish church.

everywhere might find comfort and be strengthened over against the devil and every misfortune.

2. We celebrate this festival, first of all, because of what we confess in the Creed. For it is a great, unspeakable endowment that we have in faith to regard this as God's consummate wisdom that he, who created heaven and earth, is born of a virgin. Among Jews and Gentiles this has been judged as a particularly foolish proclamation, when first it was preached to the world. It was considered to be absurd, just as today still so very many regard it to be ridiculous that sublime, divine majesty, God himself, should lower himself so deeply, not only to create, nourish, and sustain mankind, but also himself to become a man. To sum up, human reason does not understand it; the devil, the world, and human reason object to it, exclaiming, Nothing more foolish has ever been foisted on people in the world! For this reason we must diligently preach and study this article, so that we become well versed in and strengthened by it, in no way entertaining any doubts about it, but becoming ever more sure that God sent his Son into the world, to become man and be born of a woman. For this is solely the gift and wisdom belonging to us who are Christians, that we are able to say that no greater wisdom, no more sublime truth, has appeared in the world than that God, who created heaven and earth, was born of a virgin, that he, therefore, has such members as eyes, ears, hands, and feet, body and soul, just like any other human being. Indeed, it is ridiculous to human reason; but we celebrate this festival in order to become firmly persuaded of it and entertain no doubts about it.

3. Second, we also celebrate this festival because of the great good connected with it. For where we firmly believe this and want to know nothing more than that God, born of the Virgin Mary, has nursed at his mother's breast, eaten from her hands, received care and attention from her just like a child is wont to have, and that this is our greatest good and wisdom, then the benefit follows of itself, and we draw from it this comfort, to apprehend, perceive, and reach out our hands for this act of grace, that God is not at enmity with us human beings. For if God were against and hostile to us, he certainly would not have assumed the poor, wretched human nature into his person. For, the fact is that he not only created the human nature but himself

becomes a creature, and is called, and is, true man. Since he does this, there is no anger and displeasure in him. For if he were at enmity with the entire human race, as to some extent he is with angels and men, namely, with the evil angels and ungodly men, he would instead have assumed an angelic nature, which is closer to God than is the human nature and become not man but an angel. God now passes over the angels, who are of a holier and more exalted nature than are we humans—we who are a vile, base, stinking sack of worms—and assumes not the angelic but the human nature and becomes man. This is extolled in the Epistle to the Hebrews (2:16–17): "Verily he took not on him the nature of angels; but he took on him the seed of Abraham. Wherefore in all things it behooved him to be made like unto his brethren, that he might be a merciful and faithful high priest in things pertaining to God, to make reconciliation for the sins of the people."

4. At this the Gentiles have taken offense and said, Is it possible that his pure nature, God himself, should have sunk into such foulness, misery, and poverty? That is impossible! Truly, God would not have permitted himself to become involved in such misery and poverty. He could well have assumed an angelic nature, or created and assumed a nature that was neither divine nor human. However, he did not wish to do that, but assumed the human nature and became man, just as you and I are, suckled at the breast of his mother, the Virgin Mary, just as you and I did when we lay at our mother's breast. From such knowledge every believing Christian must take joy and exult: This my God and Lord assumed my nature, flesh and blood and was tempted and suffered everything just like me, yet was without sin! For this reason he is able to sympathize with my weakness (Heb. 4:15).

5. Because faith then goes farther and thinks: If it is true that God became man, like unto us in all things, yet was without sin, it then follows that as far apart as God and man formerly were from each other, namely, farther than heaven and earth are from each other, they now belong closely together; therefore, no kinsman, however closely related, brother or sister, is as closely related to me as is Christ, the Son of the everlasting Father. For it is absolutely true, if apart from Christ we consider how far God and man are from each other, it will

be seen that they are farther apart from each other than heaven and earth. However, if we reckon in connection with Christ, true God and man, we discover that we are much more closely related than a brother to his brother; inasmuch as God, the Creator of heaven and earth, has become true, natural man; the Son of the everlasting Father has become the earthly son of the Virgin.

6. It is for this reason that in Holy Scripture Christ often calls himself our kinsman and brother, just as the Epistle to the Hebrews (2:11–13) draws this from the Psalms and Prophets, stating: "He is not ashamed to call them brethren, Saying, I will declare thy name unto my brethren, in the midst of the church will I sing praise unto thee. And again, I will put my trust in him. And again, Behold I and the children which God hath given me." And St. John writes (20:17) that soon after his resurrection Christ commanded Mary Magdalene to tell his disciples: "Go to my brethren, and say unto them, I ascend unto my Father, and your Father; and to my God, and your God."

7. Yes, what is more, Scripture says that Christ, God's eternal Son, is not only our brother but also our flesh and blood (Eph. 5:28–30): "So ought men to love their wives as their own bodies. He that loveth his wife loveth himself. For no man ever yet hated his own flesh; but nourisheth and cherisheth it, even as the Lord the church: For we are members of his body, of his flesh, and of his bones." This, indeed, is to be closely related. Husband and wife become one body, one flesh, more closely related than father and mother, son and daughter, brother and sister, as Scripture teaches (Gen. 2:24): "Therefore shall a man leave his father and mother, and shall cleave unto his wife: and they shall be one flesh." That closely, also, is Christ related to us. Yes, he is more closely related to us than husband and wife are related to each other. For God and man are here united in one person. Thus Christ now says to us, My body is your body and your body is my body; my bone is your bone and your bone is my bone. He considers himself and us to be one body, blood, flesh, bone, and soul.

8. This is truly great, sure, and overwhelming comfort. Whoever is able to apprehend it confidently, never doubting, will fare well. Whoever does not doubt but firmly believes that this child, Mary's son, is true God has to be filled with joy, knowing that this applies to me; for he came in my flesh and blood. I did not come to him, but he

came to me; he came down from heaven and did not go to the devils in hell, or into a forest or wilderness to the wild animals, but into the world to us humans, as St. John says: "The Word was made flesh, and dwelt among us" (1:14). He assumed all that I am and have, yet was without sin. Accordingly, St. Augustine states: "In Jesus Christ, our Lord, everyone among us is *portio* (i.e., a part of) flesh and blood." Therefore, where my body holds sway, there I believe that I myself rule. Where my flesh is transfigured, there I believe that I myself receive glory. Where my blood prevails, there I believe that I myself prevail. For though I am a sinner, I have no doubts in the communion of this grace. That is a most intimate graciousness, when we bear in mind how far God previously was separated from us before Christ became man. Therefore, we celebrate this festival, so that we may truly learn to recognize and lay hold on this kinship we have with God and God has with us, and the communion of this grace, comforting ourselves with it and rejoicing over it.

9. The worldly-wise and Epicureans set no store by such things. When they hear it repeated that God became man, as the Christian faith attests, they say, Oh! if that's the gist and nothing else is written in the Christian faith than that God became man and was born of a virgin, we perforce must leave it as an open question. You see, the world never ceases to look upon it as absurd that God became our flesh and blood and was crucified for our sins. As St. Paul says (1 Cor. 1:23): "We preach Christ crucified, unto the Jews a stumblingblock, and unto the Greeks foolishness." That's the route the world takes; it pays no attention to preaching and, meanwhile, is absorbed in thinking: We would rather have our belly full of beer, gorge ourselves, and carouse.

10. Of a truth, that's the way it might well have been, with the whole world rejoicing and in high spirits because of this birth. The beloved, holy angels respond this way, regard it as a wonderful happening, and never cease being astonished over it. And it would not have been surprising if the beloved angels had been resentful and hostile toward us; for if he had assumed the form of another creature, they would have looked askance. If he had assumed the nature of an eagle or lion, they would have become indignant and asked why God would take such a lowly nature. However, because he assumes

our human nature and becomes man, they do not become indignant and begrudge us humans such honor, but sing and rejoice over it, with high esteem for Christ, our Saviour, even though they are in no need of him. And we dissolute people hear of it, are baptized into it, and are called by the gospel to accept the treasure and to rejoice over it. But instead we pass it by and scorn it, preferring a mug of beer, and besides, many among us disdain it.

11. I selected this text from the prophet Isaiah, because in it we see how assertively the prophet speaks about this article, preaching so many years beforehand about it, as if Christ were already born. He rejoiced over it and so anxiously longed for it. In contrast we, who have this treasure before our eyes, must realize how godless we are. When we hear how the mother bathes and tends to this child, we can still be such thankless wretches that we ignore it and find no joy in it. But we are to pay no attention to such wanton fools, for we must still preach the story for the sake of those who receive joy and delight from it. The vast majority hear it and yet don't hear it; they touch it and yet do not feel it. Therefore, just as they are haughty and scorn our preaching, so, in turn, we will preach proudly and scorn such insolent despisers. The beloved prophets, indeed, had sincere delight and joy in it. For their sakes it is being preached; the other crowd, made up of Epicureans and swine, we will let be.

12. There are beautiful, precious words in this text, so beautiful and excellent, that none of the Evangelists could have expressed it more beautifully. For the prophets appropriated the best of the promises concerning Christ for whom they had great longing and sincere yearning. As the saying goes: Hunger is a good cook, and thirst is a good bartender. But one who gorges himself gets tired and drowsy, just like satiated and well-fed swine get tired of eating husks. But because the prophet has a great longing and yearning for Christ, he also sings a very lovely and beautiful song; no Evangelist has composed another like it in such clear, beautiful, joyous words. And this, indeed, is right and proper, for the child deserves to be written about in this fashion.

13. He gives this child the greatest and most beautiful names; that should cause us not merely to ponder him as he lies in his mother's lap, having body, eyes, ears, and members, and looking just like any

other human being, but also to see and recognize him as being the true, eternal God. It is as though the prophet were saying, Lend your ears and pay heed; I want to tell you exactly what sort of a child this is. We must not look balefully at this child, seeing how he is born of a woman and is a son of a natural mother. That, indeed, is how the Jews thought of him, dismissing him as in no way unusual. They say, I, too, have seen this child; other children are just like him; he is wrapped in swaddling clothes and circumcised on the eighth day; these things happen to other children too. What's so special about that?

14. The prophet, therefore, wants to rouse us, and get us to look properly at this child and recognize who he is. We must, therefore, open our ears and listen to what the prophet foretells concerning the child. For he praises him so highly that, by comparison, heaven and earth are as nothing. He brings everything into comparative relation with this child, all creatures, yes, God himself. To our eyes there's nothing special here, for the child needs to be handled just like other children, to be fed with porridge, bathed, swaddled, sung to, cradled, and nursed, and so on. And yet this child is more exalted than other children. True, the prophet says, a child is born; but on the shoulders of this extraordinary child the power of government will rest, and he has six titles and names, namely, Wonderful, Counsellor, Mighty God, Conqueror, Everlasting Father, Prince of Peace.

15. These terms had been generally known under the papacy; for they had been read and sung in the Masses in connection with the epistle. But no one had ever understood a single letter or tittle of them. Now we are preaching about them—praise God!—and without ceasing clarify their meaning; but no one pays any attention to them; instead most people disregard and refuse to take them to heart. Nevertheless, we're not going to stop preaching because of such despisers and swine.

16. The first thing to learn in this prophecy of Isaiah is that a child is born to you and is your child, just as we sing, "A child so praiseworthy is born to us today." We must accentuate the word "us" and write it large. That is, when you hear, A child has been born to us, make the two letters US as large as heaven and earth and say, The child is born, it is true; but for whom is he born? Unto US, for us he is born, says the prophet. He was not born solely to his mother, the Virgin

Mary, nor solely for his compatriots, his brethren and kinfolk, the Jews. Much less was he born to God in heaven, who was in no need of the birth of this child; but he was born unto us humans on earth. Thus the prophet wants to say to you and to me, to all of us in general, and to each and every one in particular, Listen, brother, I want to sing a joyous song to you and proclaim the joyous news to you. There, in the manger at Bethlehem, lies a young child, a fine little boy; this little child is yours, he is granted and given to you.

17. Ah, Lord God, everyone ought open his hands here, take hold of and joyfully receive this child, whom this mother, the Virgin Mary, bears, suckles, cares for, and tends. Now, indeed, I have become lord and master and the noble mother, who was born of royal lineage, becomes my maid and servant. Ah! for shame, that I do not exult and glory in this, that the prophet says, This child is mine, it was for my sake and for the sake of us all that he has been born, to be my Saviour and the Saviour of us all! That is the way in which this mother serves me and us all with her own body. Really we all ought to be ashamed with all our hearts. For what are all the maids, servants, masters, mistresses, princes, kings, and monarchs on earth compared with the Virgin Mary, who was born of royal lineage, and withal became the mother of God, the noblest woman on earth? After Christ, she is the most precious jewel in all Christendom. And this noblest woman on earth is to serve me and us all by bearing this child and giving him to be our own! It is about this that this beautiful festival preaches and sings:

> To you this night is born a child
> Of Mary, chosen virgin mild;
> This little child, of lowly birth,
> Shall be the joy of all the earth.
> This is the Christ, our God and Lord,
> Who in all need shall aid afford;
> He will himself your Saviour be
> From all your sins to set you free.

Simply, but eloquently, this hymn tells of what the prophet Isaiah foretold, but though it is sung over and over again, no one, or very few, understand what it is they are singing.

18. The prophet's foretelling and the Christmas hymn proclaim: "Unto us a child is born." Who are the "us" unto whom this child is born? or who are we people that we should receive this child? The philosopher categorizes man as follows: *Homo est animal rationale,* "Man is a rational animal." That is how we humans see ourselves, in comparison with swine. But what is man essentially when compared with God or with the angels? If we examine and classify man properly, we will find out exactly what man is. True, compared with lions and swine, man is a higher, superior animal. So much for what is taught in the schools by heathen philosophers and other scholars! But in theology we must compare man with God and say, God is eternal, righteous, holy, and truthful; in short, God is all that is good; on the other hand, man is mortal, unrighteous, deceitful, replete with vice, sin, and depravity. God is the epitome of all that is good; with man there is only death, devil, and hellfire. God is from eternity and lives into eternity; man is caught up in sins and lives every moment in the midst of death. God is full of grace; man is full of impiety and is under God's wrath. That is what man is compared with God. Therefore, when comparing God and man over against each other, closely examining and describing what God is and what man is, the little word "us" becomes important, as does also the comfort that he brings. For when we portray ourselves correctly, relative to what we are before, and compared with God, we find that there is a great difference between God and us humans, a distance greater than between heaven and earth. Yes, it is impossible even to make a comparison. And it is to this that the prophet Isaiah wanted to lead us, to recognize and consider how deeply God humbles himself for us poor creatures and how fatherly and affectionately he receives us.

19. For this reason we have to note well what the little word "us," or man, means. The world looks upon man from on high, as the heathen poet says: *Pronaque cum spectent animali caetera mundi, os homini sublime dedit, coelumque videre jussit;* that is, "it views the various animals of the world and notes that, different from an animal, man proceeds upright and is a rational, thinking, intelligent being." According to Holy Scripture, however, man is a creature who has turned away from God, and is godless and evil, subject to the power of the devil, under the wrath of God, and guilty of eternal death. It

is for the sake of such desperate scoundrels, that is, for the sake of mankind that was lost and condemned, that Christ was born.

20. Hopefully, may everyone lay hold on this! I shall say one more thing: God allowed this child to be born for the sake of condemned and lost sinners. Therefore, hold out your hand, lay hold of it, and say, True, I am godless and wicked, there is nothing good in me, nothing but sin, vice, depravity, death, devil, and hellfire; against all this, however, I set this child whom the Virgin Mary has in her lap and at her breast. For since he is born for me, that he might be my treasure, I accept this child and set him over against everything I do not have. Since I am not godly and righteous, I find in this child pure righteousness and godliness. Within me are death and all that is adverse, but in this child I find life and every good thing. And this is as sure as if I were already beholding it with my own eyes. That's what it means to lay hold of him, when by faith we receive this treasure for our benefit.

21. But such faith is lacking everywhere. If you were 100,000 florin in debt and had nothing with which to repay, and someone were to give you enough to be able not only to pay off the debt, but also to have something left over, everyone would reach for it and spread wide their bag and pouch. But here—where the treasure is so great that it could not be any greater—no one reaches out his hands for it and holds his pouch open. Yes, and what is even more distressing, there are many who despise and disdain it. It is only the upright Christians who accept this child and say with all their hearts, I am a condemned human being; I am eternally guilty in body and soul; but I know that Mary, this child's mother, gladly gives me this treasure and assists thereto with her virgin body and all its members, bears the child within her body, delivers him into the world, and after he is born, she nourishes and cares for him. In short, she does everything that a mother would do. Thus the child is born for my sake; salvation is intended for me and for all of us.

22. This is how true Christians respond. But shame on the world because it is filled with scoundrels who simply will not accept this treasure and yet need him so desperately. The whole world should crawl toward him on all fours if it had no other way to go. Our Lord God is still delighted when there are some who desire this treasure.

It forever remains an awful shame that we have to cast such preaching before swine and dogs who despise, scorn, and disdain it, not to mention that they ought to hear and accept it. Were one to preach to such people about a rich man who was willing to give a lot of money to everyone who came and brought a pouch with him, the entire world would come running from all directions. But since we are preaching about the child Jesus, who offers eternal life and salvation to the whole world, there is hardly anyone who covets this treasure.

23. Whoever, therefore, wants to be a Christian ought to listen with joy to this preaching and believe that it is true what the prophet says, "Unto us a child is born." For what can the devil with all his evil tricks do to the Christian who lays hold on these words in all seriousness and firm faith? For though such a Christian be tempted by the devil, he can easily oppose him and say, Devil, are you listening? do you know that a child has been born? Yes, indeed, do you know that he was born for us, that is, for me? That's when the devil has to back off. For this reason we ought to think highly of this word "us," in order to tie together in faith the "child" and "born unto us!" Then a person is well armed against all the assaults of the devil.

24. Under the papacy only the mother has been praised and extolled. True it is, she is worthy of praise and can never be praised and extolled enough. For this honor is so great and wonderful, to be chosen before all women on earth to become the mother of this child. Nevertheless, we should not praise and extol the mother in such a way as to allow this child who has been born unto us to be removed from before our eyes and hearts and to think less highly of him than of the mother. If one praises the mother, the praise ought to be like the wide ocean. If either one is to be forgotten, it is better to forget the mother rather than the child. Under the papacy, however, the child has all but been forgotten, and attention riveted only on the mother. But the mother has not been born for our sakes; she does not save us from sin and death. She has, indeed, begotten the Saviour for us and the whole world; but she herself is not the child and Saviour! For this reason we are to wean ourselves away from the mother and bind ourselves firmly to this child alone!

25. So, for the present, that's enough about the words, "Unto us a child is born." It is a message that should evoke in us a more vital tie

to this child than to our own body and life. For he is as close to us as are our body and soul. That person is blessed many times over who is well taught and firmly grounded in this wisdom. To find neither comfort nor joy in it is a sure sign that we either do not believe it at all, or that our faith is little and weak. We keep this festival and preach about it in order that we might learn that our labor is not in vain or useless, and that at least for a few people, comfort and joy will follow. Amen.

Festival of Christ's Nativity

Second Sermon*

Isaiah 9:1–7

1. Yesterday you heard the prophet Isaiah singing a very beautiful hymn about the birth of our Lord Jesus Christ. That hymn has remained in Christendom, also under the papacy, and it is still being sung today by young and old, except that not all grasp its meaning. The prophet, however, stresses that we should receive this child as the one who is born UNTO US, and should be and is our child.

2. We preach and continue to preach this diligently year after year in such a way that we learn to understand these two articles: "conceived by the Holy Ghost" and "born of the Virgin Mary," adding to each phrase that little word "us," conceived unto us by the Holy Ghost, born unto us by the Virgin; and then continue: "suffered under Pontius Pilate, was crucified, died, and buried." Unto whom? Us! And, therefore, the Christ is entirely ours and remains ours. The fathers, too, did not overlook this but intentionally and purposely added the little words "us" and "our" to the Nicene Symbol or Creed: "Who for us men and for our salvation came down from heaven and was incarnate by the Holy Ghost of the Virgin Mary, and was made man; and was crucified also for us under Pontius Pilate; he suffered and was buried." The common Symbol, or Apostles' Creed, also states: "I believe in Jesus Christ, his only Son, our Lord." These words "our Lord" we must direct not only to Jesus Christ, but also to all other parts of the Creed, as Jesus Christ, our Lord, was conceived for us, was born for us, suffered for us, was crucified for us, died and was buried for us; our Lord rose from the dead for our comfort, sits

---

*Preached Christmas Day afternoon, 1532, at the parish church.

at the right hand of the Father Almighty for our sakes, will come again for our comfort at the Last Day to judge the living and the dead. What the holy apostles and fathers wanted to indicate by the words "us" and "our Lord," is that Jesus Christ is ours, and that his mission was to save us, enabling us to say, You are our Lord. You were conceived and born for our sakes, suffered for us, were crucified for us, and died for us.

3. In similar manner, the prophet Isaiah here refers to this and says, "Unto us a child is born." Just as in the Christian faith we repeat the expression "I believe," and repeat the same with reference to each person of the Godhead, "I believe in God the Father," "I believe in Jesus Christ," "I believe in the Holy Ghost," even so we must also continually repeat the words "our Lord," since they belong to each part, just as we believe and confess concerning Christ. We say, I believe in Jesus Christ, our Lord, conceived by the Holy Ghost, born unto us through the Virgin Mary, suffered for us, and so forth. The point is that we must not merely recite or say the words and apply them solely to Christ, but to ourselves as well. For he did not stand in need of this for his own person. If he had not been conceived and born, or had not died or risen from the dead, he, nevertheless, would have remained Lord; but because he has been conceived and born, suffered, died, was buried, descended into hell, and whatever else is stated about him in the Christian Creed, all of this is designated as ours, and is ours. Now it is of all this that we preach on this festival, so that we learn well the power and fruit of this article, and know that Christ is our Lord. Yesterday we dealt with the words "Unto us a child is born." Now the prophet continues: "Unto us a son is given."

4. Women are accustomed to ask: Whose child is this? To which the prophet Isaiah responds: It is a son, and this very same son is ours. It is an extraordinary thing that you and I and the whole world should become the mother of this child, since neither you nor I conceived or gave birth to this child. For just as you heard yesterday how by being born this child becomes our blood, flesh, and bone, we, each and every one, become this son's mother by virtue of the fact that the son has been given unto us. This is inexplicable. For, do you, whoever of you is able to think deeply about it (let alone express it in

words), do you reckon that we poor, miserable sinners should so presume to receive this child and not doubt but believe with certainty that he not merely is born unto us, but also this very same son is given unto us? No human heart can fathom it, no human tongue is able to explain it.

5. For "to give" means to grant freely, gratuitously, without price. The prophet now says, This son is given to us, which means as much as, he is a present, a free gift unto us; he is yours and mine in such a way that we do not purchase or pay any money for him, but that he is absolutely a free gift.

6. The world really does not deserve hearing even a single word about this because of its shameful unbelief. The pious Virgin and noble mother does indeed bring this son into the world, so that that very same son is your and my son and gift, just as surely as if he were put right into your and my hand. And for this we have positive and sure signs, God's Word and the holy sacraments. The prophet Isaiah stands as a witness of this and says that this son is given unto us. And yet we do not believe it, nor do we thank God for it. In truth, because of our great ingratitude and shameful unbelief, we do not deserve to hear a single word about it.

7. But the prophet Isaiah ties "born" and "given" together, in order to indicate that this child is true God and true man. He is true man, for he is born to us; he is true God, for he is given to us. These two things are clearly stated in the text: a child who is born and a son who is given. But what sort of a son he is the prophet indicates when he states, "Of the increase of his government and peace there shall be no end, upon the throne of David, and upon his kingdom, to order it, and to establish it with judgment and with justice from henceforth even for ever." What the prophet sings is that this child is a true, natural human being, born of a virgin into the world, and is a son; and this is given and granted to us as a sign. Consider now how the son is further described: "The government shall be upon his shoulder."

8. One sermon is hardly enough for this. Do you want to know, the prophet says, what sort of a child is born and what sort of a son is given? Listen, I shall draw his picture for you. The child that is born and the son that is given is a Lord and has a government; and his govern-

ment rests on his shoulder. That is the kind of child and son he is. As a result, he is called a Lord, because he carries his government upon his shoulder. If you want to paint him correctly, that is the way you should do it.

9. This is to portray the child and the son correctly. The angel of the Lord, who appears to the shepherds out in the fields and preaches about the newborn child, also paints a beautiful picture of him when he says (Luke 2:11): "Unto you is born this day in the city of David a Saviour, which is Christ the Lord." The Saviour who is born, he says, is Christ the Lord, not simply as a father of a family is Lord in the home and over the domestic servants; but he is also Lord over heaven and earth, over all things, visible and invisible. For the one whom the angels call a lord is, to be sure, not some inferior lord but a Lord over all. Were he not a Lord over all, including also the angels, the angels would not then have called him Lord. But now the angel says to the shepherds, That newborn child is your Saviour. Now, then, that very same Saviour of yours is Christ and Lord of us all. This, you see, is to paint the picture properly, for this child, born at Bethlehem, is a Lord to whom all the angels of God pay homage (Heb. 1:6).

10. But the prophet Isaiah does not in his prophecy speak from on high, as does the angel, but remains here on earth. The angel places the government of the newborn child to include also the heavens, saying in effect that the Saviour, born at Bethlehem and laid in the manger, is the Lord over all creatures in heaven and on earth. The prophet, on the other hand, lets the government of this child remain on earth, saying that the child who is born to us and the son who is given to us is a Lord, but his government lies on his shoulder. Who, indeed, can plumb the depths of what this means: The child is a Lord, and his government lies on his shoulder? Who can really understand this—to have a government and to be Lord over it, and yet have the government on the shoulder? to be a Lord and at the same time a servant and a burden bearer? That has to be an amazing and truly extraordinary Lord, to carry his government up around his neck. He controls and administers his government, and yet is a servant and burden bearer of his government, raises and bears his government upon his shoulders. How shall we understand this? What, indeed, is denoted thereby?

11. The prophet wants this, first of all, to be understood, that this Lord's dominion is a government altogether different from that of this world. As Christ states in Luke 22:25, the dominion of the world is that "The kings of the Gentiles exercise lordship over them, and they that exercise authority upon them are called benefactors." So secular government's authority is that kings and those in authority govern strictly, as lords, with authority to administer justice. In secular government, the form of rule is like this: A prince in the land, a burgomaster in the city, each has his officers and administrators skilled in protecting the upright and punishing the evildoers. In secular government, dominion and authority belong to the lord. A magistrate must rest on the shoulders of the citizens and he says, Do this, and the citizens must support the magistrate and obey him.

12. Accordingly, in the home father and mother must govern children and servants; and children and servants must shoulder their parents, and their masters and mistresses. Secular government cannot endure unless rulers press heavily upon their subjects. If they oppress and deal unjustly with them, they had best watch out. However, I am not speaking now about such tyranny; I speak rather about a just, orderly government. There it cannot be otherwise; government must support those in authority. The person subject to secular government is not borne by his ruler; but he must offer his back and be supportive of his ruler. But here the matter is reversed. The child born to us and the son given to us has a government and is a ruler. However, the government does not bear the ruler here, but the ruler bears the government. But now this ruler's government is his kingdom, his people, his church, you and I, and all who are baptized into him and believe in him. Therefore, this ruler bears us. In secular government we must bear our kings and lords, and they rest on our shoulders. But in the spiritual government and kingdom of Christ this King and ruler bears us, and we rest on his shoulders.

13. Second, by this the prophet wants to point out where the government of this King and ruler is to be found. His government, he says—that is, his kingdom, his people, and his country—rests upon his shoulder. The government of our ruler is in Thuringia, Meissen, Saxony, and so forth. But the government and people of this King is all Christendom. Wherever Christians are in the world, there you

find his government. We and all who believe in him are his government. For thus says the angel: "Unto you this day is born a Saviour." And so we confess in the second article of our Christian faith: I believe in Jesus Christ, our Lord. If now he is our Saviour, as the angel says, and our ruler, as we confess in the Creed, then we are his kingdom, government, and people.

14. Exactly where are Christ's government and kingdom? "On his shoulder," says the prophet. It is unprecedented that Christ's government, kingdom, and people do not lie under his feet, at Rome, or at Babel, as if restricted to a certain locale, but lie on his shoulder. In my dialectics I cannot define or locate the Christian church as well as the prophet does here with such few words. If you ask, What is the Christian church? or, Where is the Christian church to be found? I shall tell you. You must not look for the Christian church at Rome, at Nuremberg, or at Wittenberg, nor among peasants, townspeople, or nobility, but as stated here, his kingdom lies upon his shoulder.

15. When artists want to paint this text, they paint a child who carries a cross on his shoulder. But if I were to paint this text, I would not paint a child with a cross but a child who carries a church on his shoulder. Then this text would be properly depicted. For the child carries his government on his shoulder, that is, the church and all Christendom. If you want to find the Christian church, you will never find it where you do not see Christians resting upon Christ's shoulder. That the pope, the factious spirits, and enthusiasts have this same text we have, and carry the title and name of the church and boast of being Christians, is something we will have to tolerate; but this does not, by a long shot, mean that they are the Christian church or Christians. For no one is a Christian unless he lies on Christ's shoulder, that is, trusts and puts his confidence in Christ, and permits himself to be carried by him, just as a strayed, lost sheep must let itself be carried by its shepherd if it is to get on well. This is what the parable in Luke 15 teaches. In short, whatever the faith be in the world, by whatever name, Jewish, Turkish, popish, no one is a Christian unless he lies on Christ's shoulder.

16. What the prophet Isaiah saw and wished to emphasize by these words is that the Christian church rests on Christ's shoulder and that a real Christian and true member of the church is one who

believes that he is carried on Christ's shoulder, that is, all his sins lie on Christ's shoulders, so that the heart says, I know no other comfort than that all my sins and transgressions lie on Christ's shoulder. They, then, who lie on Christ's shoulder and allow themselves to be borne by him are called, and are, the church, and genuine Christians.

17. A pastor should painstakingly preach on and apply this text, so that people may understand it correctly. Christ must carry us, must make payment and satisfaction for our sins, or we are lost. He had to suffer on the cross for us, and he must still constantly carry us and bear with us. We cannot and dare not carry him; he must carry us. In no way can we help him pay off our debt, but he says to me, I want to forgive you all your sins; your guilt lies on my shoulder; yes my entire government and all my people lie on my shoulder, regardless what their names might be—Isaiah, Peter, Paul—from the greatest to the least. These whom I carry are my country, people, and kingdom; those whom I do not carry are not my kingdom, church, or people!

18. Thus, now, we hear how wonderfully and lovingly the prophet Isaiah describes Christ. He is a child and son, he says, who is born and given to us, is a Lord and possesses a government. But what kind of a Lord is he? He is a Lord who bears us and on whose shoulder we lie. If he does not bear us, we are lost. If pope, bishops, monks, and priests believed this, they would deal much differently with this matter. However, they do not want to be borne by Christ; instead they bear Christ, as they seem to think, and to them Christ is merely a painted Christ. For in their thinking they believe they are to live in this or that manner, fast and pray, do enough to pay for their sins and appease God's anger. But that sort of carrying is contradictory. If Christ does not bear you but you try to bear him, that will be a very heavy load for you, just as if a lost and strayed sheep would say to its shepherd who wanted to carry it: No, dear shepherd, you are not to carry me; I wish to carry you; sit on me! Obviously, that sheep would be crushed by the load. But if the sheep is to be helped, the sheep must speak like this: Accept my thanks, dear shepherd, for seeking and wanting to carry me; I cannot carry you, but I shall let you carry me. So, also, in Christ's kingdom! Christ wants to carry his sheep, just like a shepherd carries a poor, wretched, strayed sheep. He speaks to

a poor sinner in this manner: You are conceived and born in sin, you have angered God by many sins and are condemned to death; but you are not to suffer anguish on account of this, for your sins are forgiven you; simply lie on my shoulder; I want to carry you before God.

19. One ought to accept this preaching joyfully and thank God with all his heart for it. But, unfortunately, most people in the world do not only not accept this preaching, but despise and disdain it. Truly now, it is no lie but eternal divine truth. The prophet Isaiah years earlier proclaimed it through the Holy Spirit. God has faithfully kept and fulfilled his promise, has borne and still bears us; just as the apostles and the entire New Testament attest, it is an accomplished fact. Therefore, let us receive this preaching, thank God for it, and be confident that Christ will intercede for and give answer for us, so that our sins will not accuse and condemn us before God. Now, indeed, this preaching is going out into the world; but how it is being received, that's another story, as we see!

20. After the prophet has said that Christ bears his government on his shoulder, he continues by showing how this carrying is effected. He has stated that the child has been born to us and the son been given to us and that on him lie all our sins, distress, misery, sorrow, and heartache, and that he would save us from all that by his bearing the load. But how this occurs, he now explains by means of the six names that are given to this child and son. We will continue this the next time. Amen.

Festival of Christ's Nativity

*Third Sermon**

Isaiah 9:1–7

1. This is a truly golden text of Scripture in which so aptly and eloquently the prophet presents a portrait of Christ as to his person and his lordship, whose "government shall be upon his shoulder." We have previously heard the meaning of this, that he bears you and me and all who believe on him, with all of our sins, troubles, and grief. And this was true not only for that time, the time of his advent upon earth when he took our sins upon himself and carried them to the cross, as St. Peter says (1 Peter 2:24), "Who his own self bare our sins in his own body on the tree," but also now, as he daily does so through his Word and gospel. Precisely, this is the distinction between the spiritual realm and the physical. The physical realm has to do with the government under a ruler and king. For in the world there is need for coercion and force. But the spiritual realm and kingdom of Christ is also called, and is, a government wherein we are under our Lord and King's rule. For just as the unruly, wild rogues in the world require the ruler's hand on their necks to get them to fear and respect him, in similar manner there is need that the heavily burdened hearts and consciences be lifted up and relieved of their heavy loads. The worldly realm requires thousands of people to support one head, one king and ruler. But in the spiritual realm one head or king, namely, Christ, upholds countless people, indeed bears the whole world's sin, as the prophet Isaiah states, (53:6): "The LORD hath laid on him the iniquity of us all"; and John the Baptist declares: "Behold the Lamb of God which taketh away the sin of the world."

*Preached on St. Stephen's Day, December 26, 1532, at the parish church.

And in our day he provides for the proclamation of the gospel, that he is a King of grace and mercy. This is the heart of this prophecy.

2. Here now follow the six names which the prophet attributes to this King. With these names he portrays further the nature of his kingdom. To this point he has portrayed him as a Lord and King who bears his government upon his shoulders. Now he teaches us the significance of the prerogatives belonging to the holy Christian church. If we are to picture the Christian church rightly, it must be defined as resting upon Christ's shoulders and being borne by Christ. Now as to how Christ bears his church, how the church is upheld, is something that depends, first of all, on the fact that his name and work is "wonderful."

AND HIS NAME SHALL BE CALLED WONDERFUL

3. Christ is named "wonderful" because of his work performed in behalf of his holy Christian church. Human reason is really incapable of fully understanding the nature of that which Christ governs, namely, the church. He ties it to no particular location, time or person, does not let its identity be recognized by any external thing, garb, or appearance by which to tell where it is, whether it is big or small. If you want to locate it, you'll find it nowhere else than on Christ's shoulders. If you wish to possess it, then you will have to focus your eyes and mind solely and alone on the way in which the prophet here portrays and denominates it.

4. Christ is and bears the name "Wonderful" because he is a wonderful King and possesses a wonderful kingdom. To the world he is a despised King, as he himself states, (Ps. 22:6): "I am a worm, and no man; a reproach of men, and despised of the people"; similarly, also (Ps. 118:22–23): "The stone which the builders refused is become the head stone of the corner. This is the LORD's doing; it is marvellous in our eyes." His church is a despised people before the world, before the devil, and even also by us ourselves, as St. Paul states concerning the apostles (1 Cor. 4:9): "We are made a spectacle unto the world, and to angels, and to men"; and (v. 13): "We are made as the filth of the world, and are the offscouring of all things unto this day." Holy Christendom is truly the beloved, lovely bride of Christ, and yet must appear and seem to be the devil's bride.

5. For the devil and the world to have such a perception might be expected and tolerable, but for the church to appear so also in our eyes would be something hard to square with. The devil, indeed, is skilled at diverting the eyes of a Christian away from his baptism, the Sacrament, and Christ's word, causing him to think that he has been rejected by God, like David, who was greatly troubled with inward anxiety and lamented (Ps. 31:22): "For I said in my haste, I am cut off from before thine eyes." Conditions in the church's backyard, or in our own, often appear as though it is no longer the holy Christian church, or I, a Christian; and both are blanketed with the blunt charge of being heterodox and of the devil. Yes, and my own heart chimes in and says, You are sinner. This heavy mantle of sin, death, the devil, and the world hang over the church and the individual Christian in such a way that nothing is seen of them except sin and death only, and nothing is heard except the devil's and the world's slandering. The whole world and everything in it that counts for anything, including my own reason, write me off as nothing, and yet I am to persevere and say, I am a Christian, righteous and holy.

6. That is so because Christ is named "Wonderful," because the mission he fulfills for his church is singular and wonderful, something beyond human reason's capacity to comprehend. The Christian church is righteous and holy, even though it may not appear so. For the truth is that Christian righteousness is outside of us, alone in Christ, and by our faith in him. Accordingly, the church and every believer in it confesses: I know that I am sinful and unclean, bound in sin and shame, subject to death, knowing nothing but sin, and yet I am righteous and holy, not of myself, but in Christ Jesus who has become my cloak of righteousness before God, my sanctification and redemption. This Christian righteousness surpasses all human knowledge, reason, and wisdom, being completely beyond reason's competence and judgment. That is why the wise of this world argue that righteousness is a quality or outward form, a kind of virtue, holy or pious conduct, that must be found in a person if he is righteous or pious. It is like the color of the wall, or of the bread, or of one's skin, light or dark; so, they say, righteousness and holiness must be a personal characteristic. Moreover, our own reason chimes in with the same conclusion, that righteousness must be something we see and

feel; and yet all I feel and see is nothing but unrighteousness. How can I, therefore, be righteous?

7. Thus, as stated, the devil, the world, and my own heart line up against me and say, I am unrighteous. What am I to say? Nothing else but what is here stated: My Lord Jesus Christ, who was given and born for my sake, is named Wonderful. He wonderfully rules his church and Christians, so that they become God's righteous, holy, enlightened, pure, strong, living children, all appearances to the contrary, both before the world and also in our own minds. How can we countermand the contrary impression? By the Word! Christ himself in his own person is a paradigm here for us. His goal is eternal life with his Father; but he enters death. He seeks to take sin, death, and the devil captive, and yet allows himself to be assailed by them, defamed, despised, condemned, throttled, and finally killed. Similarly, we need to open the eyes of our hearts, so that we discern things not by outward appearance, but by the Word.

8. Accordingly, I must conclude that all Christians—and I myself—are holy, not by reason of personal righteousness, but by holy baptism and the Sacrament, for the sake of Christ, my Lord, on whom I believe. When I look at myself apart from baptism, the Sacrament, and the Word, I see only sin and unrighteousness, indeed, only the devil who plagues me without letup. The same is true if I look at you apart from baptism, the Sacrament, and the Word; I see no holiness. You might attend the church's worship, listen to the Word and pray, but you still cannot be counted righteous apart from the Word and Sacrament. It's not external appearance that matters. What counts is to be able to say, This person is baptized, gladly hears God's Word, and believes on Christ. These are genuine earmarks by which to tell whether a person is a truly sanctified Christian individual.

9. External appearance and covering are not of the essence; what matters is that the gospel is clearly and purely proclaimed, the blessed Sacrament rightly administered, and every individual carries out his calling and work in life. God's people and true Christians will then surely be found there. Don't judge, therefore, by outward appearances, but by the Word; otherwise you will surely be mistaken, if you judge according to external criteria. The fact, simply, is

that a Christian does not differ markedly from other people; yes, it's even possible that unbelievers and the heathen surpass a Christian in upright conduct and behavior. Hence, outward appearance can be misleading.

10. Yet the godless, fanatical monks and papists like to fancy and picture the Christian church according to external things and trappings, the result being religious orders of all kinds with distinguishing garb and hoods. We priests and monks practice celibate, ascetic lives and wear distinctive robes, they say, so that people might know we are holy. You lay folks, on the other hand, follow the world's lifestyle, get married, work at your job, and, thus, cannot be as holy as we are. And the whole world is taken in by this, by the devil's trickery which focuses on the external things. I know for sure that right here in Wittenberg barely ten people wouldn't be fooled were I once again to affect the sort of piety I practiced as a monk under the papacy. Baptism, the Sacrament, and the Word are not as impressive to the mind's eye as are monkish garb and demeanor—be it Franciscan or Carthusian—and our reason nods assent and says, That man is a monk; he lives by such severe regimen of fasting, vigils, and prayers, that he looks like a mere shadow; he certainly must be a holy individual. The rest are just common folk—tailors, shoemakers, husbands, and wives—hardly holy, therefore.

11. It's necessary, therefore, really to discern the true nature of the Christian church, not by looking at external trappings but by the Word. A woman who is baptized, receives the gospel, believes on Christ, lives with her husband, and brings up her children, fulfilling her vocation in life, is blessed even though people don't discern her holiness; for my eyes cannot see her baptism and faith which cloaks her before God as one who believes in Christ. My eyes merely see how she goes about her work in the house, caring for her children, sewing, spinning, and cooking. None of this is unusual, and yet when the gospel and faith in Christ are present, she is a sanctified member of the Christian church as she goes about her routine duties, not because of her piety, but because of her baptism and the gospel which she holds in her heart for Christ's sake who dwells there. No one takes note of her as a specially holy individual or Christian. But let a nun or sister of one of the orders appear, genuflecting and of sober

demeanor, then everyone regards her as very holy, in contrast to the ordinary woman who is baptized, trusts in Christ, and is a faithful wife. Thus God traps the world in its folly and faulty judgment, so that it is unable to discern and recognize a true Christian. We have to be on guard, therefore, when it comes to external veils or habits and learn that the Christian church is constituted by those who have been baptized and believe on Christ in their hearts, pursuing after godly works as they go about the routine tasks of their station or calling. This is how we ought to view and discern the Christian church. We will then not be mistaken in our quest. If we don't, we will err, like the rest of the world and human reason.

12. Christ, therefore, bears the name "Wonderful" because all that he does in behalf of his Christian church is singularly wonderful. His church, as said, possesses a wonderful righteousness and holiness that is hidden to human reason. It becomes even more wonderful and singular in time of cross-bearing. For the baptized Christian who confesses Christ will bear suffering and persecution in the world because of Christ and the gospel, and to the world and to himself it will appear as though God has forsaken him, at least so it seems. God allows his church to be blanketed with cross, persecution, and all manner of trouble, thus highlighting the folly of the world; for thereby its reasoning is once again fooled and fails to understand things. But a Christian holds tight to the Word and thinks as follows: Though despised and persecuted, I still am baptized, possess the gospel, believe on Christ; and I count my baptism, the gospel, and Christ in my heart to be so great that the whole world is but a splinter in comparison.

13. And this is certainly most true: Whoever has the gospel and Christ in his heart possesses righteousness before God, and though he had all the world's sins laid upon him they would be like a drop of water compared with the whole ocean. It is no trifling matter when a person looks and clings to God's Word, for its power makes all other creatures pale in insignificance, like a dust particle. The Christian church is, therefore, righteous and holy, even though before the world it does not appear to be so but, in fact, bears cross and trial. And if anyone cannot by his reason fully fathom the church's righteousness and holiness, nor believe it, let him hold his tongue be-

cause it is impossible for human reason to ascertain or comprehend it. Whoever wants to know the church and Christian believers must discern them by the Word, gospel, faith, and the fruits of the gospel and faith. When you have the gospel, are baptized, and believe on Christ, you are a Christian and are holy. Moreover, whatever your calling in life, if you are faithful to your spouse, honor your father and mother, obey those who are over you, such things are fruits of the gospel and faith.

14. Should trouble, meanwhile, erupt, do not be overcome. Think of your baptism, hold tight to the gospel, receive absolution, and the Sacrament. Readily admit: Evil thoughts have engulfed me, I have stumbled and done this and that wrong, but I am baptized, I have the Word, absolution, and the Holy Sacrament, and these things provide me greater holiness than the whole world and all creatures. Christ Jesus is the very best, most merciful advocate, and when the devil seeks to frighten me, he is but a trifling spark in comparison with him.

15. From this we now see why Christ is named "Wonderful," because everything he does in behalf of his church is grounded in his Word and lies beyond our eyes, reason, and feeling to comprehend. Righteousness, holiness, power, life, salvation, everything the church has in Christ, are incomprehensible to reason and hidden to the world. If you judge the church by reason and outward appearance, you will err, for then you will see people who are sinful, weak, fearful, sorrowful, suffering, persecuted, and hunted down. But if you look at this, that they are baptized, believe on Christ, bear out their faith with godly fruits, carry their cross with patience and in hope, that is a true picture, for these are the true colors by which the church can be discerned. Reason looks on baptism as simple water, and the Word as a mere sound, and for that reason fails to find or discern the Christian church, because it despises baptism and the Word. But we Christians should esteem baptism and the Word so highly that we count the world's goods as nothing in comparison. When we do so, we will discern the church and we will be able to comfort ourselves, saying, In myself I am a sinner, but in Christ, in baptism, and in the Word, I am holy.

16. We must, therefore, treasure this name "Wonderful," so that we're not misled by external trappings, but safe from all enthusi-

asts. This is extremely important, because in due time monkish spirits will again appear, not those we have known under the papacy, but others. For the world cannot do otherwise; it always paints or conceives of the church in terms of usages and external trappings. The church, however, does not allow such distortion, as we have said, but must be seen in terms of the gospel, the Word, baptism, Sacrament, faith, and fruits of faith. Baptism is, indeed, pure white, and by it we put on the pure, white, beautiful christening robe. The Word and faith are the blue mantle of heaven, and the fruits of the gospel and faith are many colored; with these we are cloaked, each according to his calling and station.

Festival of Christ's Nativity

Fourth Sermon*

Isaiah 9:1–7

1. Earlier we heard concerning the first name by which the newborn child, our dear Lord Jesus Christ, was named; "Wonderful," a title designating the lordship and kingdom he bears upon his shoulders in this world, a truth unrecognized and not understood by all the world's wit, wisdom, and learning. It is and always will remain hidden to the world, known and experienced only by a person through faith and the Holy Spirit. Only in this way does anyone come to understand what the church is and whether he himself is a Christian. We come now to his second name:

COUNSELLOR

2. The child and son is named "Counselor" because he is a faithful advocate who provides good counsel in every situation of need where help, advice, or comfort are required. As he wonderfully governs and guides his holy church that is blanketed with sin, cross, sorrow, ignominy, shame, and persecution, so, too, he stands by her with good and faithful counsel when in need of help in troubles of any sort. The precious gospel is his good counsel in all situations; it is able to relieve our hearts and consciences in every assault that seeks to deceive or lead us astray.

3. Wonderful he is called because of the wonderful way in which he leads us, while allowing us to be buffeted as heretics and sinners hated of God. This defamation continues all the while the church is on earth. But it is difficult for Christians to bear, not only to be disparaged this way by the world as the worst, most shameful people

---

*Preached St. Stephen's Day afternoon, December 26, 1532, at the parish church.

under the sun, but also to be tortured by their own flesh to feel and think in their hearts that God is angry with them and rejects them. Here good counsel is needed to help Christian believers bear up, for if I, forever and a day, am called a heretic and my teaching is disparaged as having misled the whole country and people, fearing and feeling always with trembling heart that God will slay me, I would not be able to survive for long. Then I need to have Christ stand by me with his good counsel, putting a staff in my hand, enabling me to endure it.

4. This is how (St.) Christopher is pictured in the water, holding onto a tree branch that God has put within his reach whereby to steady himself. Without this support he would not have been able to go through the deep and wide body of water with his load. Likewise, I would have been unable to survive the world's threatening, fuming fury and tyranny, in addition to the devil's cunning and fiery arrows, if Christ had not stood by me. Early on I would have succumbed to the pope had not Christ afforded me good counsel in my heart.

5. So, also, now when the burden becomes too great for Christendom or for us individually, Christ comes to our aid with his counsel, speaking his word into our hearts: Be of good cheer, cling to me, let the world rage and fume, let them rebuke you as a heretic and condemn you; if they oppose you they also oppose me. Through the prophet he states (Zech. 2:8): "For he that toucheth you toucheth the apple of his eye." He counseled the apostles similarly (Matt. 10:16–20): "Behold, I send you forth as sheep in the midst of wolves: be ye therefore wise as serpents, and harmless as doves. But beware of men: for they will deliver you up to the councils, and they will scourge you in their synagogues; And ye shall be brought before governors and kings for my sake, for a testimony against them and the Gentiles. But when they deliver you up, take no thought how or what ye shall speak: for it shall be given you in that same hour what ye shall speak. For it is not ye that speak, but the Spirit of your Father which speaketh in you." And John writes (15:18–19): "If the world hate you, ye know that it hated me before it hated you. If ye were of the world, the world would love his own: but because ye are not of the world, but I have chosen you out of the world, therefore the world hateth you." And in Acts 4, as the apostles are called to account before the

council of the high priests in Jerusalem, Christ stands by them so that they lifted up their voices to God with great unity (vv. 24–28): "Lord, thou art God, which has made heaven, and earth, and the sea, and all that in them is: Who by the mouth of thy servant David hast said, Why did the heathen rage, and the people imagine vain things? The kings of the earth stood up, and the rulers were gathered together against the Lord, and against his Christ. For of a truth against thy holy child Jesus, whom thou hast anointed, both Herod, and Pontius Pilate, with the Gentiles, and the people of Israel, were gathered together, For to do whatsoever thy hand and thy counsel determined before to be done."

6. This is genuinely good counsel and support which is ours through Christ to be able to say, In the name of the Lord, if I am despised and labeled a heretic before the world, so be it; my consolation, however, is that this happened because of my Lord Jesus Christ, not because of me, for his sake, not mine. If I am branded a heretic before the world, God above knows very well that I am faulted and condemned because I have proclaimed and confessed him before the world. I did nothing more than this, nothing but good, and hence the world had no ground for faulting me. But because I was condemned and persecuted for preaching and confessing Christ, I will let him help whose concern it is. This is also the consolation he bespeaks in Matthew 5:11–12: "Blessed are ye, when men shall revile you, and persecute you, and shall say all manner of evil against you falsely, for my sake. Rejoice, and be exceeding glad; for great is your reward in heaven: for so persecuted they the prophets which were before you." That means we have the staff in hand when Christ bestows consolation in our hearts, and we can say, Dear emperor, dear pope, dear princes, if you don't want to laugh, then may you rage, the matter is not mine but Christ's. Because of him you persecute me; so now I put it in his charge. Moreover, our accusers cannot sustain the charge of murder, robbery, theft, or insurrection against us, but persecute us for preaching the gospel, which the pope condemns.

7. When the devil initiates turmoil and attacks me with his fiery arrows, causing my own heart and conscience to stand against and accuse me, I am ready to confess that I have sinned and offended God. The devil, meanwhile, comes along and builds up the sin like a

roaring fire to engulf me. Now, indeed, I am baptized, have the gospel, believe that Christ is my Redeemer and Saviour, possess the seal of his Word, absolution, and Sacrament. But the devil seeks to push all this aside, trying to make me forget my baptism and Christ my Saviour and Redeemer, tenaciously driving the thought into my heart that God is against me. What am I to do? Christ affords me good, genuine counsel and points me to his Word, that I am not to trust or follow my thoughts but cling to his Word, as spoken to the palsied man (Matt. 9:2): "Son, be of good cheer; thy sins be forgiven thee." Likewise, as in Psalm 42:5: "Why art thou cast down, O my soul? and why art thou disquieted in me? hope thou in God: for I shall yet praise him for the help of his countenance."

8. If the pope and the world want to scare me off from confession of God's pure gospel and truth, so that I turn away from God's name and church, saying to me, Aha, you are a heretic, you preach against God and his church; recant and return again to the mother, the Roman church, and you will find grace, at that point Christ speaks cheering counsel to my heart and says, Don't listen to the clamor; God is not behind it. He does not want to drive you away from the truth; the devil and the world are trying to make you weak and afraid, so that you fall away from the faith; so be of good cheer and stand firm. God spoke this comfort to the prophet Jeremiah (1:17–18): "Thou therefore gird up thy loins, and arise, and speak unto them all that I command thee: be not dismayed at their faces, lest I confound thee before them. For, behold, I have made thee this day a defenced city, and an iron pillar, and brasen walls against the whole land, against the kings of Judah, against the princes thereof, against the priests thereof, and against the people of the land."

9. So Christ bears also this name, and is called "Counselor" because he will stand by and comfort us in all circumstances, when the world shames, mocks, and persecutes us; or when the devil terrifies us with his fiery darts into our hearts because of our sins, or through our accusers, under the pretense of the name of God, and seek to divert us from confession of the truth. In such and similar straits I find counsel and comfort in the Scripture, cling to it, and never let go. If I do that, then neither my sins, nor the tyrannical scandal mongers of

this world, nor evil thoughts and fiery darts of the devil will cause me to be afraid, even less to despair and be overcome.

10. Very simply, therefore, he is called "Counselor" for the reason that he brings true comfort to the heart, specifically his Word, for Christ stands by those that are his, not with mighty armor, but alone with the Word. We Christians must learn and remember what this means. When persecution comes from the world, don't try to repel it with physical might, like the world, but find comfort in the Word. For Christ permits his followers on earth to bear adversity, lets the devil and the world trample over them, allows them to be thrown into prison, and appears to be dead and without power to help them. He gives them nothing but his Word and tells them, See, here is my Word, comfort yourselves with it. If the world terrifies you, be not afraid. If the devil assails you, hold onto my Word and believe it; it will sustain you and provide good counsel in every time of need. Thus states Isaiah (50:4): "The Lord God hath given me the tongue of the learned, that I should know how to speak a word in season to him that is weary." In other words, I am a faithful Counselor and true Comforter, and I perform this with my tongue, which is taught of God, that is, which possesses God's Word. To be sure, it doesn't free you completely of all tribulation but allows it to come; however, it will put a staff in your hand with which to steady yourself.

11. This is a message meant solely for Christians, that they might learn that when our Lord God allows them to be set upon by peril, shame, grief, and need, they must not despair but declare: These things happen to me not for my sake, but for Christ's sake, and, therefore, I will be patient, cling to God's Word, and there find consolation. This is so very true: No one labels me a heretic nowadays for any other reason than for Christ's and his gospel's sake. That the world and the devil seek to frighten and do me harm happens for no other reason than that, thereby, they seek to get me to believe as the world does. It is not a message for unbelievers, for they don't want to be in the realm of him whose first name is "Wonderful," but flee away from the cross, or struggle mightily to be free of it. They want no part of his counsel, which seeks to comfort and strengthen them by the Word and gospel. Were Christ's kingdom and gospel to offer gold and material, earthly things, people would soon write off hope

of heaven, and the heaven they hoped for would be too narrow and too crowded. With such a message that promised gold and silver to everybody, I could bring the whole world into Christendom. But because Christ's kingdom and gospel proclaim life everlasting and that we must suffer shame, hatred, prison, beating, hardship, and death for Christ and his Word's sake, then no one wants in, and God has plenty of room in heaven, for no one is interested.

12. However, the declaration is that Christ is named Wonderful, Counselor, and so on. He governs his church wonderfully, cloaks her with cross, trial, and suffering. He is also a faithful Counselor, who stands by his church. Though his help may not always be apparent, he, nonetheless, provides his Word by which we can steady ourselves. Therefore, we ought to cling to it and glory in it. If the world elevates its thing—money, goods, glory, and might—we should elevate the Word even higher, for it is at our side in every need. Never, not for ten thousand worlds, should we exchange the single pronouncement in Matthew 5:11: "Blessed are ye, when men shall revile you . . . for my sake." Here is true counsel with which to comfort yourself in suffering, for Christ is calling you blessed and happy because all of this happens to you because of him. The world punishes thieves and murderers; but that the devil maligns me as a heretic and sinner can only happen for Christ's sake as the devil tries to tear me away from him. Were he to succeed, he would then let me alone, of course.

13. For that reason, I say, we must treasure and esteem the Word highly. Let hatred, envy, and persecution come; let sin, death, devil, and the world assail us; we must cling to the Word and repeat the words, "Blessed are ye when men shall revile you for my sake," also "Be of good cheer, I have overcome the world," and, I am greater than a hundred thousand worlds, yes, than heaven and earth. That word will be my faithful counsel and sturdy staff by which to steady myself so that I can endure and overcome. If we don't lean on this staff, we, by ourselves, are much too weak to endure the grim hate and envy of the world, and the crafty assaults and fiery arrows of the devil.

14. I often become so angered and impatient with our peasants, burghers, and noblemen that I think I'll never preach another sermon; they behave so shamefully that a person regrets being alive. The devil, you see, never lets up plaguing me inside and out, so that

I'm almost ready to say, If there's another preacher who can take my place, I'm ready to yield, the way things are going; I have nothing but the world's hatred and ill will and the devil's vexation. Flesh and blood get ticked off, and human nature gets weak and discouraged. Then I have need of the good counsel of God's Word, to take the sturdy staff in hand to steady myself and say, It's bound to be, because peasants, burghers, the rich, and the lords are so wanton, and treat my gospel so shamefully. My Lord Christ said it would be that way: "If ye were of the world, the world would love his own," and, "Blessed are ye when men shall revile you and persecute you for my sake." I cling to these words, for they surpass all of the world's evil, and I think to myself, Carry on as you began.

15. Christians have learned this art; but as for the rest—the godless bishops, rulers, nobility, burghers, and peasants—none have it, because they reject the Word, for they are blocks and stones, against whom we have to preach as against a rock wall. The Holy Spirit, in fact, calls them blocks and stone idols; they have ears but cannot hear (Ps. 115:6). For since they make idols for themselves out of silver and gold, and seek and hope for answers and counsel from them who have mouths that cannot speak, eyes that cannot see, ears that do not hear, they themselves are like them, neither seeing nor hearing, though they have eyes and ears for sure. This sermon, therefore, is meant for us who believe on him and suffer for his sake. His name is Wonderful and Counselor: Wonderful, because of the wonders he has done for us; Counselor, because he comforts and upholds us by his Word.

THE MIGHTY GOD

16. The third name of this King shows that he not only comforts in time of suffering, but has the power to assure its outcome. For were it only good counsel, it could only be words, with no effect, finally availing nothing. But that something will be effected beyond mere counsel is shown by the designation "Mighty One." So, if indeed he lets all manner of misfortune befall us and lets the devil plague us within and without, he strengthens us with his faithful counsel and by his Holy Word, effecting this by his power and might, we may be sure. He will do this because it belongs to his nature as

God and so that we do not despair. Were there to be no end to our suffering, with God never once intervening, he would forfeit his Godhead over the world, and we would despair and lose hope. His Word on which we depended would seem to be false. But he is the Mighty God who has the last word always.

17. Thomas Muentzer created such a storm that we thought we would all be shipwrecked, and that it would continue to get worse. There was nothing left except God's good counsel and comfort. As I clung to the Word, I said, Lord, this man doesn't belong with us, but opposes you, attenuating your holy baptism, your Word, and gospel. And God intervened with his might and set Muentzer to the side. Therefore, he is called Mighty, as he pushes first this one out of the way, then tomorrow another; as in our day, while the gospel stands, he has demonstrated mightily his hand over many different people. For this verse must remain true (Ps. 9:20): "Put them in fear, O Lord, that the nations may know themselves to be but men."

18. That will most certainly happen at the hour when our sufferings are ended and our persecutors' time is up. God knows that time best of all. We must not prescribe or fix the hour for him. He knows the time, hour, and end point best of all. We do not, nor ought we know, and, therefore, we should hold to his Word, leaving time and hour to him to act when he deems best. He will come at the right moment, and we will then witness his might and see with our own eyes how the ungodly will be recompensed. Only let us cling firmly to him with all confidence. Then we will see how the ungodly will be made to pay. Even though we do not now see how all of our enemies have been avenged, yet we see some of them get their due and we perceive the might of God.

19. But God alternates in what he does, one action following upon another, just as he brings an end to night and lets day dawn, and then again night. So he brings an end to suffering, grants a break, and then lets it soon begin again. In the midst of trouble he grants a rest, but he arranges things so that continuously it's up the hill, then down, and then up again; now it's night, then day, and soon night again; but not night all the time, nor day continuously, but one alternates with the other, in regular pattern. So he also governs in his church, as we observe throughout the history of the Old and New Testament. St.

Paul knew and experienced this ebb and flow often as he recounts in the second Epistle to the Corinthians. St. John does this even more so, since he lived longer. The Old Testament is replete with such highs and lows. When the people under suffering held firmly to the Word, they found comfort and help; and yet they were not without the cross thereafter.

20. That's the significance of the Mighty one; the Lord is a Counselor or Comforter not only in word, doing nothing more than that, but he also acts with effectual help. When trouble comes he gives us his good counsel and might through his Word, so that we don't succumb in weakness but are able to endure. However, when the time comes that we lie exhausted he acts with his might and enables us to pull through and triumph. We need both, his counsel, so that we are comforted and endure our trials, and also his might to overcome. All of the Psalms provide Christians with strength under suffering, that is, they comfort under trial and suffering, so that our backs don't break and we continue to persevere in hope. But we also finally petition God to remove the cross from us, so that his good counsel not merely strengthens our backs for suffering patiently, but that he also revives and delights us with his victorious might. In this manner he governs and deals with his Christendom. Whoever doesn't discern this doesn't know what sort of king Christ is.

21. So, up to now, we have three names. The first, "Wonderful," because the Lord deals with his Christian church in a manner different from what flesh and blood can understand or do, in short, quite contrary to the stream. The second name is "Counselor," because in trials he counsels us with his Word and comforts us. His third name is "Mighty God," because he also wants to help us triumph. He is Wonderful, guides us wonderfully, through cross and trials; also a faithful Counselor and Comforter; and Mighty, able to help us endure and gain the victory.

Festival of Christ's Nativity

*Fifth Sermon**

Isaiah 9:1–7

1. We have heard about the first three names by which the child is called: Wonderful, Counselor, and Mighty. There follows now the fourth name by which he is called, "Conqueror," that is, warrior. In German we use the term giant, one strong and mighty in battle, able to slash and beat down troop after troop on all sides. With this name, the prophet portrays this King as "Conquering Hero"** against all his enemies.

2. The first three names serve to tell us how he governs, comforts, sustains, and protects us. First of all, he brings us through various crosses and trials; then he affords us good counsel and comfort by his Word; and third, he is by our side with his might, to bring us through. Now his fourth name designates and teaches how he will extend and increase his kingdom, how he will engage his foes, overcoming them on all sides, so that we, wonderfully sustained by him, cheered by his good counsel, upheld and guarded by his might, will be able to expand our numbers and increase.

3. That's why he bears this name and is called "Conqueror," for he is, in fact, an invincible champion who repels all foes. Here, too, there is power and might, but not in the sense of the third name according to which he helps us, but rather as he defeats and overcomes also those whom he wishes to bring under his governance; however, not by any kind of swordplay. It is like the governing by which he rules his church, wonderful, that his conquering of people who oppose him is not by military armament, with the raw power of sword

---

*Preached on the Day of St. John the Evangelist, December 27, 1532, at the parish church.

**Christ has six names in Luther's translation of the Hebrew text: *Wunderbar, Rath, Kraft, Held, Ewig-Vater, Friede-Fürst*. Thus "The Mighty God" of the English (KJV) text includes also the concept "Conquering Hero" or "Champion," in Luther's translation.

or artillery. He casts only his gospel into the pack, which is the sword by which he vanquishes the world, in keeping with what Isaiah (11:4) prophesied: "He shall smite the earth with the rod of his mouth, and with the breath of his lips shall he slay the wicked." His sword is the rod of his mouth and the breath of his lips. The gospel which he placed into the mouths of the apostles is the sword by which he smites the world like thunder and lightning.

4. The apostles did no more than confidently preach the gospel to the world, staging their assault on people's most vulnerable place, their hearts. They slew no one with the naked sword, robbed no one of anything, coerced no one by force. But with the spiritual sword of the Word of God they struck confidently everywhere—against the world's thinking, wisdom, piety, power, and might—taking people's hearts captive, bringing them into Christ's kingdom, thus thrashing and ravaging the devil's realm in every land. On Pentecost, prompted by the Holy Spirit, St. Peter stood up and struck with the sword of the gospel among the Jews, and in one day, through one sermon, cut away three thousand souls from the devil. And because, under the Circumcision, he was the apostle entrusted with the gospel, he continued his attack among the Jews, until many others responded and were converted as Christians. His opponents, meanwhile, and, finally, all of Judaism that opposed itself against the gospel and rejected the "Conquering Hero," Christ, ended up in a heap. St. Paul, in contrast, soon after his conversion, contended with the high priests, scribes, and Jewish leaders, and, eventually, since he was entrusted with the gospel among those of the Uncircumcision, carried the name of Jesus before the heathen and before kings, teaching that all people, Jews and Gentiles, sinners all, needed to become righteous solely by God's grace, without works, through the redemption which is in Christ Jesus (Rom. 3:23–24). That seemed like an insignificant word, but it was a powerful thunderbolt by which the whole of the Roman Empire was shaken with wisdom, might, and godliness, leaving Minerva and the gods of the Pantheon lying in the dust. All fell before this Conqueror, both Jews and Gentiles, as a result of the apostles' preaching of his mighty Word.

5. And even today, what have I wrought against the pope? I have never drawn a sword, but struck hard only with the mouth and the

gospel, and continue to do so against pope, bishops, monks, and clergy, against idolatry, false teaching, and sects, accomplishing more thereby than the emperor and kings could have done with all their might. Solely with the rod of his mouth have I hammered upon people's hearts, letting God and his Word work, and this caused such an upheaval and rumble within the papacy, so that if the bloodthirsty radical peasants had not stirred things up for us, the papacy would even be in worse shape now.

6. From this we see this Conqueror's might. Such a champion needs no other weapon than the Word. He lets it sound forth before the world that all mankind, with all its wisdom, righteousness, and piety, is sinful and damnable before God. But, also, that whoever wishes to be saved must repent of his sins and believe in the forgiveness of sins in Christ's name. Before such preaching, indulgences, purgatory, private Masses, monkery, and papacy all fall to the ground, without physical force or weapons. A truly wonderful and unique giant he is, to be able to smack the devil's ongoing flea market with such an insignificant (as it seems!) and lightweight instrument.

7. But the Jews and Gentiles object and say that it is not right for the apostles to cause such a rumble in Jewry and the Roman Empire. Who is Peter? and who is Paul? They are anarchists who mislead the people and the country, stirring up insurrection everywhere on this planet. How, indeed, can this be God's might? as the pope today says of our gospel, that it is not God's but the devil's work. Quite so, for no one can understand this name "Conqueror" correctly if he does not have faith. Human reason does not agree that it is right for Masses, pilgrimages, saint worship, indulgences, and the like, to be abolished because of the preaching of the gospel nowadays. It cannot understand who this giant and almighty warrior is, but says rather that he stirs up insurrection like that of his own people, the Jews, who crucified him on these grounds. But we who have identified with the first name, Wonderful, preach and confess him, and as a result are persecuted in the world, knowing that we have comfort in the true Counselor, Christ, upon whose power we wait. And because we do so, we come to know and perceive that he is indeed a real Victor who strips the devil's realm of so many people, so easily, without sword, merely by the breath from his lips.

8. Such is the warfare he daily wages, not only against foes whom he rescues from the devil and brings to his heavenly kingdom, but also in our behalf, so that we, through him, might prevail over the devil, sin, and death in our hearts. For sins are the devil's fiery darts. When they terrify and cause my conscience to doubt, it is time for the devil to be dealt a death blow. How and with what? By the Word, which Christ as true Counselor gives to our hearts. For where Christ is preached and his name earnestly appealed to there the devil flees away.

9. Such is the warfare waged by this Conqueror. When the gospel enters, it hammers away in the world, to win people over and increase Christ's kingdom. It is a blessed campaign and blessed warfare, for by it people are cut away from the devil and brought to Christ in his kingdom. He, indeed, is Conqueror and Champion. Psalm 149:6–9 tells of this, that the saints will have sharp swords in their hands, to execute vengeance among the heathen nations, to bind their kings with chains and their nobles with fetters of iron, so that they deal justly with them, as is right. Such honor, all his saints will have, and it comes about in this manner. The saints will take sharp swords into their hands, that is, not naked swords of this world, but the sword of the Spirit from Christ's mouth. With this sword they will advance against the heathen people and their kings, overpowering them in all their wisdom and religious practices, and taking them captive for Christ. This is the glory that is theirs as soldiers and saints of God.

10. In this manner God punishes and avenges himself with the gospel on people who under the papacy despised him with their Masses. For the word of the gospel infiltrates into people's hearts, also among our detractors, shames them, and takes them captive in a blessed captivity, freeing them from sin, death, and the devil, and saving them with a precious imprisonment. God would dearly love to have all the world to be there, to be safe forever from the devil.

11. The sword is drawn from its scabbard and in action, and will be to the Last Day. It was first drawn and put into action for the sake of the Jews by the apostles, until all of Jewry was deeply affected; thereafter, among the Gentiles throughout the Roman Empire, causing doors to be closed on idolatry. Now it is drawn against the papacy, and it will not cease its activity until the papacy is forever

crushed. The stubble will remain, but the sword of the gospel will continue on, in constant rebuke of the papacy's idolatry. Although for a time there will still be breath left to popedom, nonetheless, the spirit of Christ's mouth will finally extinguish it at the time of his final advent.

EVERLASTING FATHER

12. So, we have now heard concerning four names and how they serve mightily for our sakes against our foes. The fifth is next, and it is "everlasting Father" or "eternal Father." This name has bearing for us in our relationship to Christ; it is a very lovely name and full of comfort, for it declares that those who are Christ's are not slaves, but children and free men, who have come out of slavery to possess the rights of children, no longer under the law but under grace. For the name "Father" stands opposed to the word "Tyrant" and "Judge." Moses and the Law condemn and oppress, causing people to tremble by its demands that put us under God's judgment. But, in the words of David, we pray: "And enter not into judgment with thy servant: for in thy sight shall no man living be justified" (Ps. 143:2).

13. This is a name we must assuredly remember, that Christ is not denominated as tyrant or judge, but as Father, who very plainly shows himself caring for us in a fatherly way, and not only once upon a time, as the sophists taught, but as our everlasting Father. Under popedom, when I desired to go to the Sacrament, I had the idea: If only I could even for just one hour after confession remain free of sin, then I might receive the Sacrament worthily. That was because I did not know or understand the meaning of the forgiveness of sins, or why Christ bears this name, "Everlasting Father." Therefore, we must learn this name well. When you live under Christ in his kingdom, he lifts the servant's yoke and law off your back, not merely for an hour, not only for a day, but on and on till the Last Day, in other words, now and forever. For he is my Father forever, as here named by the prophet, and I need no longer be under the Law. He himself states this (John 3:17–18): "For God sent not his Son into the world to condemn the world; but that the world through him might be saved. He that believeth on him is not condemned." If Christ is not

come to condemn the world, that means the Law has been set to the side, and if the believer is not to be condemned, he must be free of the Law. In short, a Christian is not under the law because Christ is named everlasting Father, and if Christ is our everlasting Father, then a Christian must be his child forever.

14. That's the meaning of the forgiveness of sins. In Christ's realm absolution is declared not for our works' sake but because of what Christ is and effects, true to his name, everlasting Father. When you, therefore, believe on Christ, the Law has no further claim on you. For all eternity Christ does not wish to condemn you, but to be your Father, and you his child. If you have sinned and repented and believe that you have forgiveness in his name, he wants to deal mercifully with you, like a father with his children. This we must learn well, that above all things Christ in his kingdom does not wish to condemn, but to forgive, and to be our everlasting Father. Unbelievers, who do not belong to Christ's kingdom, will end up before the judge and hangman. But if you believe on Christ, you will be his child, and Christ forever and always is your Father. If there's need for the Law, however, then let it be laid against your flesh, to keep it chaste and submissive to God's Ten Commandments. Your faith, however, your heart and conscience, must remain free from the Law and by virtue of this name, "everlasting Father," should crush the Law in your heart, like ice melts before the summer's heat.

15. Accordingly, when the devil seeks to demand that the Christian's heart be under the Law's condemnation, the believer must answer, I know of no judgment, for it is written, "He that believeth on the Son is not condemned." The Law is done with, its burden removed, for I belong to a Lord whose name is Father, not for an hour, not for a day, but forever. I am not, therefore, a slave of the Law, but by and under grace a child and an heir, free, with the rights of a child. Out of fatherly love a father bestows everything upon his children that belongs to them, but a slave must earn everything he wants to receive from his master.

16. Thus Christ is not only Conqueror over his enemies, but also the everlasting Father for those who are his friends, Christians, whom he governs, and whose hearts and consciences are not subject to the Law. It no longer counts in the relationship between my con-

science and Christ, but forgiveness of sin only. As regards my faith and my conscience, judge, tribunal, judicature, rod, whip, accuser, hangman, and the like, are all abolished, and all that matters in my heart is that Christ is Father, everlasting Father. Farthest from my mind should be the thought that Christ stands behind me with a cudgel, for only the judge or hangman does that, not a father. But Christ is called Father, everlasting Father, and because I believe on him, he will not be my judge.

17. Is this not a pleasant realm for a child to be under? Is this not an amazing grace that we poor sinful human beings should be in such a kingdom where there is no wrath, only forgiveness? Let your "old Adam" be weighed down and troubled by the Law, bridled and compelled to be obedient. Your only concern is that your heart has joy and your conscience is clear and at peace before God. For Christ stands by us, taking up our cause, saying he wants to have nothing to do with a judgment seat but be only an everlasting Father. He removes the Law from our hearts and lays it upon our "old Adam," and as a result our heart is at peace. And if the devil approaches to trouble us with the Law, we must declare, Christ is called everlasting Father and will not judge me by the Law. He himself has said (John 12:47): "I came not to judge the world, but to save the world," and (John 3:18): "He that believeth on him is not condemned." That's what Everlasting Father means. The hearts and consciences of those who are Christ's are not under the Law, even though according to the flesh and "old Adam" they must still remain there.

PRINCE OF PEACE

18. This is the sixth name. This King is to be a prince whose reign will bring peace and rejoicing, for "peace" in Hebrew signifies good fortune and happiness, when all goes well. So David said to Nabal (1 Sam. 25:6): "Peace be both to thee, and peace be to thine house, and peace be unto all that thou hast." So Christ is named Prince of Peace because in his kingdom there is to be plenty, and richness will be multiplied beyond our wildest imagination. His kingdom is to overflow with riches and happiness. He is our everlasting Father whose everlasting grace covers us before God against all accusations of sin,

death, and the devil. And, in addition, in his kingdom we will have goodness and riches in abundance.

19. But even as we are unable with the eyes of reason to comprehend that he is our everlasting Father, so also that he is the Prince of Peace. It is entirely faith's bailiwick, if we are to know and perceive it. For this peace has to do with the goodness and wealth which is ours in Christ's kingdom, something no human eye can now see, or reason understand. The fact that we now possess the gospel, baptism, the Sacrament, God, Christ, the Holy Spirit, a proper understanding of Scripture—by means of which treasures we are able to enrich the whole world spiritually—who can really recount the value of this heavenly treasure trove, such goodness and blessing?

20. Christ, therefore, is called Prince of Peace because everything in his kingdom proceeds in goodness. He rules those who are his in a friendly way, gently and kindly, and causes them to be at peace and overflowing in all spiritual gifts. But here faith is of the essence, if we are rightly to perceive and esteem them. If a person could but see and perceive just one of the gospel's promises piled upon that wagon of gold, how great and how valuable it is, he would count all the kingdoms on earth as worthless dust in comparison. Indeed, if one could but perceive what a gem and treasure baptism is, he would value it above all the world's treasure; but because he doesn't see it, he does not esteem it for its worth. These treasures, however, surpass all there is in the world. For whoever possesses God's Word, baptism, the Sacrament, and so forth, with proper understanding, possesses true wisdom and can comfort himself and others over against sin and death, keep himself and others from false doctrines, and rejoice in God now and into eternity. It is a treasure so great that words fail to express it. Such are the blessings that abound in fullest measure under this King, in his realm where he governs with his gospel.

21. What, however, is the situation under the papacy where manmade laws and monks' dreams hold sway? As we ourselves learn, to our own detriment, we did not know the meaning of baptism, who Christ is, what faith is, or really understand a single word of the Lord's Prayer, or really know how to pray, or understand a single one of God's commandments or even one article of the Symbol or Confession of faith, or know how to interpret a simple verse of the whole

Psalter, or how many sacraments there are, or understand the place of father, mother, servant, or maidservant. When good works were preached about, there was no instruction on how before God each person in his station was to be obedient and serve his neighbor. Instead, they were told, if you want to do good works, then run to St. James, to Rome, or to a cloister, and become a monk. Things were truly miserable and shameful then, in contrast to which now under the gospel we have so many benefactions of God in his kingdom.

22. Such is the King this child is, a gentle Father who deals with his own in fatherly manner, and an opulent Lord who can and will enrich and bless us with all manner of spiritual blessings in heavenly places, as St. Paul states (Eph. 1:3). In his kingdom there is an overflowing abundance, but these are spiritual blessings, which are not discernible to the eye, or to human reason, but must be discerned and apprehended by faith, as is true of his other names as well, for they are spiritual.

23. Therefore, we must not be troubled if the world hates, despises, persecutes, and throttles us, as long as this abundance of spiritual blessings in heavenly places remains ours in Christ. With this treasure I am able to defy the pope, emperor, and the whole world, and say, You may be great lords, and I a poor beggar in comparison, but I have a penny in my pocket that you do not have: I understand this verse of Scripture which you neither comprehend nor esteem; I will not exchange it for all of your opulence, yes, for the whole world.

24. In conformity with what these six names teach, this child rules over Christendom. He is named Wonderful, Counselor, Mighty, Conqueror, gentle, Everlasting Father, beneficent Prince of Peace, who makes his children to be kings and exceedingly rich in spiritual and heavenly blessings.

THE DAY OF THE HOLY INNOCENTS

Matthew 2:13–23*

And when they were departed, behold, the angel of the Lord appeareth to Joseph in a dream, saying, Arise, and take the young child and his mother, and flee into Egypt, and be thou there until I bring thee word: for Herod will seek the young child to destroy him. When he arose, he took the young child and his mother by night, and departed into Egypt: And was there until the death of Herod: that it might be fulfilled which was spoken of the Lord by the prophet, saying, Out of Egypt have I called my son. Then Herod, when he saw that he was mocked of the wise men, was exceeding wroth, and sent forth, and slew all the children that were in Bethlehem, and in all the coasts thereof, from two years old and under, according to the time which he had diligently inquired of the wise men. Then was fulfilled that which was spoken by Jeremy the prophet, saying, In Rama was there a voice heard, lamentation, and weeping, and great mourning, Rachel weeping for her children, and would not be comforted, because they are not. But when Herod was dead, behold, an angel of the Lord appeareth in a dream to Joseph in Egypt, saying, Arise, and take the young child and his mother, and go into the land of Israel: for they are dead which sought the young child's life. And he arose, and took the young child and his mother, and came into the land of Israel. But when he heard that Archelaus did reign in Judæa in the room of his father Herod, he was afraid to go thither: notwithstanding, being warned of God in a dream, he turned aside into the parts of Galilee: And he came and dwelt in a city called Nazareth: that it might be fulfilled which was spoken by the prophets, He shall be called a Nazarene.

1. Although it is not our custom to observe the day of the holy innocents, yet we shall read the story and consider it, to understand the events surrounding our dear Lord's lowly birth, which the angels extol so highly, proclaiming it and singing of it for our comfort.

2. First, we shall speak of this historical event as to what actually happened. When the wise men came from the east, they found the

---

*Preached at he parish church, 1541, on the eve of the Day of Circumcision, December 31. (According to the Weimar edition the year was 1540.)

child with Mary, his mother, still at Bethlehem. As I see it, this would have taken place at the end of six weeks. For the law of Moses needed to be kept which required that a woman who had given birth to a son had to stay indoors forty-two days, that is, six weeks, and be considered unclean, meaning that she was to have no social intercourse with anyone, nor could she go out in public; for everything she touched would be unclean. If a woman had given birth to a daughter, then according to the law she had to be sequestered 84 days, that is, twelve weeks, and be unclean. Now, although Mary was not required to do this—the Law of Moses having no claim over her, for she had given birth without pain and her virginity remained unsullied—nevertheless, she kept quiet, and submitted herself to the common law of all women and let herself be accounted unclean.

3. She was, without doubt, a pure, chaste virgin before the birth, in birth, and after the birth, and she was neither sick nor weakened from the birth, and certainly could have gone out of the house after giving birth, not only because of her exemption under the Law, but also because of the uninterrupted soundness of her body. For her son did not detract from her virginity but actually strengthened it; but, in spite of this, not only the mother, but also the son, both allowed themselves to be considered unclean according to the Law. He is, we know, not under obligation, but does it readily and gladly, as St. Paul says in Galatians 4:4: "But when the fulness of the time was come, God sent forth his Son, made of a woman, made under the law, To redeem them that were under the Law." Now, the fact that the Magi visited the child and his mother before the time of purification was over, contrary to the Law, is a remarkable thing, as also the star that brought them. And Joseph, who was perfectly aware that the case of this child and this mother was a completely different one from that of other children and mothers, welcomed them; otherwise, the Magi would have not been allowed in the house to see her.

4. When the Magi, upon departing from Bethlehem, did not return to Herod, but went to their own country by another way, an angel of the Lord appeared to Joseph in a dream, and commanded him to take the child and his mother and flee to Egypt; for Herod was about to have the child sought for, in order to kill him. And Joseph took the child and his mother and departed by

night. Herod ordered that all children in Bethlehem and in all the surrounding country be put to death, all children who were two years of age and younger. Joseph, with the child and his mother, stayed in Egypt for seven years, till after the death of Herod, and then returned again from Egypt, having been so commanded by the angel, and lived at Nazareth. That is the history of the event in a few words.

5. At this point two *disputationes* or questions come up. The first question is: How do St. Luke and St. Matthew harmonize with each other? Luke says in Luke 2:39: "When they had performed all things according to the law of the Lord, they returned into Galilee, to their own city Nazareth." But Matthew writes: "They fled into Egypt," which could not have happened before the period of six weeks was over. For even if Mary had been physically strong enough, the Law, nevertheless, did not allow it; first they had to appear at the temple to present the child to the Lord and offer a sacrifice. If then they returned from there to Nazareth, as Luke writes, how could they have fled from Bethlehem to Egypt, as Matthew writes? And second: Why does Herod have children two years old put to death if it happened soon after the period of six weeks?

6. The historians try to harmonize in the following way. They say that after Herod had bidden the Magi to return to him, he had in the interim been invited to Rome through his sons, and so an entire year passed before he had the children killed. But according to the Gospels it seems that Herod was very much in haste in putting the children to death. The Magi came to Bethlehem during the six weeks. When Herod learned that they first came to Jerusalem in search of the newborn King, but afterwards did not return to him, as he had counted on, no doubt in his thinking the child perhaps was born a year to a year and a half ago. So, I will hunt down the child quickly, he figured, and put a large number to the sword, two years and under, to ensure that I do not miss. This is very wily counsel. For he was sure that the King had to be born at Bethlehem, as it was announced by the prophet Micah; moreover, the tribes of Israel did not intermarry. Now because Herod was certain of the place and the tribe, that the King was to be born at Bethlehem of the tribe of Judah, he concluded that the child would remain at this place and in this tribe.

So, he shall not elude me, he said, I will deal with a large number, to make sure that I get him.

7. He began prudently enough; for he had thirty years' experience of murder to his credit as well; and in this time he had massacred many, many Jews who refused to have him as king because he was a foreigner, and not of the house of David. The Romans, with their authority and power, installed him as king. For this reason the high priests and elders had opposed him stubbornly, and Herod was pleased to exact retribution, until all the high priests and eminent people among the Jews had been put to death. He eliminated the priests, nobles, and councilors in the Sanhedrin. Then he took the office of high priest wholly into his own control, removing the high priestly garments out of the temple, selling the privilege to wear them to those of his own choosing. He was a self-righteous hypocrite, like M.H. and K.V.C.* in our day. He had oppressed them and raged against them like this for thirty years, almost exterminating their nobility and priesthood. In his bloodthirstiness he spared no one, not even his own children; he had two of his own sons put to death with their mother, as well as others, which when Caesar Augustus learned of it, led him to comment that he would rather be Herod's pig than his son. Yet, for all that, the people did not cease their murmuring, but stood staunchly by their conviction that no foreigner but one of David's blood and descent should be king, and fomented two major uprisings against the Roman prefect. For they were constantly insisting: We are God's people; therefore, we shall tolerate no foreign king. This drove Herod into frenzied and senseless passions, and he was only too pleased to tyrannize over them.

8. Now, after having tyrannized over the people for so many years, as we have said, with the Jews constantly murmuring against him and staging occasional rebellions, the rumor now came that a new king of the Jews had been born. For the shepherds, and others who had heard it from them, were not silent about it. And on top of all this, the Magi arrived in Jerusalem shortly afterward asking, Where is the newly-born King of the Jews? So then Herod became even more

---

*M.H. is an apparent reference to Melchior Hoffmann, a lay preacher with an enthusiast, apocalyptic message. K.V.C. is a possible reference to the emperor, Charles V.

crazed, senseless, and irrational. It caused him to feel threatened as he thought about it and so he dealt craftily with the Magi, directing them to Bethlehem. He urged them to leave no stone unturned in seeking the child out, pretending that the matter was of great personal importance. He admonished them to be sure to let him know where the child was if they found him, so that he might go and worship him also—indeed, with a sword thrust through his heart!

9. When this first attempt failed to come to fruition, and the Magi did not return, he began to cast about for another route, thinking: I will find the child yet. I have put so many of them to death already, but I am by no means finished; I am not about to spare them now. And so he ordered all children, two years of age and under, to be put to the sword and murdered, not only in Bethlehem, but also in the whole surrounding region, through a sudden attack without warning which he ordered secretly the night before. And all this would have happened, I think, after the six weeks, after everything they had to do at the temple had been done.

10. Now while Herod was purposing this, and had already issued the command for the children to be killed, there came this other command, as the angel appeared to Joseph in a dream and said that he must flee to Egypt, and that without delay. For there was no time to spare, since the next morning the slaughter would begin. Therefore, the angel did not say go, or make a journey, but flee, get up and flee without delay, get out of here right now; tomorrow morning or the next day disaster will reign. And Joseph did not waste any time, did not wait till morning, but got up that very night and fled from the place, obedient to the angel's command, and that same night traveled beyond the environs of Bethlehem. For I believe that the environs of Bethlehem could have been no more than three miles' journey in any direction. This happened, I think, after the six weeks, after they had fulfilled their obligations at the temple and were intending to return to Nazareth; at this juncture the command of the angel came to escape to Egypt, and Joseph with the child and his mother lost no time in leaving. For at that moment Herod was dispatching soldiers to slay the children.

11. Just consider what a cruel tyrant he is! Rather than restrain such violent acts, he is willing, deliberately and indiscriminately, to

kill right and left no matter that they were harmless. So, they think they will hide the newborn King from me? he muses. Then I will take measures which I will likewise hide from them. They are now rocking their children to sleep, giving them their porridge to eat, but I swear it will be for the last time. He kept this bloody plan of his to himself, and pounced upon them without warning. Otherwise, every mother would have fled beyond the danger zone. It was a cruel, treacherous act which goes beyond human comprehension, beyond all excuse. The mothers, accordingly, felt secure in Bethlehem, asleep with their little children, totally unaware of any danger. In the morning the king's executioners arrived with the frightful order, seized the children, and slaughtered them without mercy. It must have been a horrible sight, for there would have been few houses in all Bethlehem and the surrounding territory, in which two or three children would not have been found, for a mother frequently bears two children in two years. There was sobbing and shrieking about this bloodthirsty tyrant in every house, as the Evangelist also adduces from the prophet Jeremiah. It is as if we had witnessed the Turks tearing the children from the mothers' breasts and slaying them.

12. This is how the life of our Lord Jesus commenced, with the devil appearing soon on the scene to foment suffering and grief. But he must have soon realized what he actually gained by it. For the children were taken out of this world, and his kingdom, into heaven. If Caesar Augustus of Rome, himself, had wanted to present them with his whole empire, he would not have served them so well as Herod did by his butchery. He tore the little children from the mothers' bosoms, and sent them to heaven, making nothing less than martyrs of them, whose blood is precious in the sight of God! For the parents it was a terrible thing, but it happened for the eventual good of the children; they felt no anguish in their souls. So the Lord took them away at the time of his own advent into the world, as a sweet-smelling sacrifice to himself. Thus much good would yet come from Herod's murdering.

13. Joseph and Mary were unaware of this fiend's intention. Mary was pronounced clean with her child in the temple, and intended to set out from Bethlehem back home to Nazareth. But the angel brought other tidings, telling Joseph, If you remain here, that diabol-

ical Herod will find you. Get out of here immediately; this is no place for you to stay. Joseph obeyed the voice of the angel, arose that night, and fled. The angel could have warned him a day or two earlier, but our Lord God allowed it to come at the moment of extreme peril, and did not tell them where they might obtain food and drink, but dispatched the angel at the very last moment, when delay was unthinkable.

14. But now listen to the angel's words. "Take the child," he says, "and his mother." Not, Take *your* child, whose father you are, but simply, "Take the child and his mother," acknowledging the child's mother alone. He spoke in the same manner in an earlier passage, where he had also appeared to Joseph in a dream (Matt. 1:20), and said: "Fear not to take unto thee Mary thy wife: for that which is conceived in her is of the Holy Ghost." From then on he places the child first and the mother second. Now one ought to put father and mother first according to the fourth commandment; but because the angel mentions the child first and the mother second, he means to say that the child is the mother's God and Lord, and yet calls Mary his mother. It follows from this that this child is true God, but also at the same time truly man by nature, yet conceived without sin by the Holy Spirit, and born of a virgin.

15. Furthermore, the angel explains why Joseph was to flee. "For Herod," he says "will seek the young child to destroy him." As if to say, Herod has gotten wind of the word of the shepherds and the Magi that a new King has been born. He cannot bear this and so he intends to commit an unheard of and fiendish crime against innocent blood, to do away with these defenseless children by mass murder. So, get up right this minute with the child and his mother and flee to Egypt!

16. From this you can get an idea of how the poor mother suffered in the way of adversity and misery. She was in confinement in Bethlehem, a strange place, and was obliged to stay there until the time of her purification. She could have waited out this six-week period much better in her hometown of Nazareth, and she would have been better looked after. But she was compelled to go to an unfamiliar place. Yet this is not all, nor the whole of her cross, for now, as she was hopefully anticipating her return home, the persecution really begins: the child is in imminent danger of being murdered. This nat-

urally awakened terror in both Joseph and Mary, but it would have been a particularly heavy burden for the mother. So they come out of one relatively minor misfortune right into a greater one, and were forced not only to flee from their house and hometown, Nazareth, where they had their livelihood and their possessions, but away entirely from the people of Israel, to Egypt, where none of the people of God dwelt and where they had nothing of their own, neither a place to live, nor a way to sustain themselves. It would mean extreme privation for the young couple. Granted, they had what the Magi had given them, yet it was a great misery to have to be refugees in a foreign country, and to live there six long years. You see, their flight to Egypt would have been in the thirtieth or thirty-first year of Herod's reign, at a time when he had brought the Jews virtually into total subjection. The Lord, therefore, was in Egypt for six or seven years, in a foreign country, a stranger and an alien. There he had to savor what it was like to receive assistance from foreigners, whom he did not know, and Joseph may have been able to obtain food and other relief by his skills as a carpenter.

17. This is the story of Christ's flight into Egypt, and of the treatment which the innocent children at Bethlehem received at the hands of Herod. We see how our Lord fared after the six weeks of confinement, what persecution, distress, misery, and bloodshed ensued. Why did he do this? Why did he venture to enter into such squalid conditions, and acquiesce to so many adversities? Why did he not prefer to make use of his divine omnipotence, or the protection and assistance of the angels, who could easily have disposed of Herod? Simply, because in this way the Holy Scriptures would portray for us this Lord as a real, ordinary man who in all things was determined to be like us, except for sin, as St. Paul says in Philippians 2:7: "But made himself of no reputation, and took upon him the form of a servant, and was made in the likeness of men."

18. This is why the book *de Pueritia Jesu,* about how in his childhood he was supposed to have been continually performing miracles, is simply nonsense. For he behaved himself as any other child would; he allowed himself to be treated on the same basis as any other child, and he was protected by the dear angels like other children. For when children at times fall from a table, or bench, or into the fire, it is man-

ifest to an observer that the angels are there, protecting them. Six years ago in Voigtland, not far from Zwickau, a little girl went out to find the flock and bring them back home. She got lost, and was found three days later seated in the woods, in the dead of winter, none the worse for it. Christians are not the only ones benefited by these wonderful angels, but oftentimes the unbelievers also; hence, the proverb: The angels were watching over you today. Sometimes one falls in such a way that it is a miracle that he did not break his neck three times over, and yet is protected from harm. On the other hand, one often hears of someone breaking his leg, or some such thing, though there were no obstacles on the road, for the protecting angel was not there. I must confess myself, when I think back over my life, that I have been protected from harm by angels three times in ways clearly manifest to me. I have also seen people barely out of their house, only to see the house forthwith collapse behind them.

19. And this is how Christ wanted it for himself. He did not want something more extraordinary than others, but because he was determined to be an ordinary human being, he lived and behaved like a human being, allowing himself to be wrapped in swaddling clothes, nursed at his mother's breast, and all the rest; learned to pull himself up on chairs and benches, ate and drank, and, in a word, stood in the same relationship with all other things as other children, with the sole exception that he never committed a single sin—and was so much more wonderfully wise, chaste, and prudent than other children, that his elders surely knew that he would attain to something quite out of the ordinary. For he willed to veil his majesty and deity, until he had accomplished the redemption of mankind. Although upon entering upon his office he did great miracles which no other human being ever did, yet soon thereafter he died, manifesting his divine purpose. For he did not come to destroy the world and to defend himself with the sword. No, he acts as other human beings, is warned of danger by the angels, and flees from it.

20. This was written for us as an example and to instruct us to be more assured and convinced of the article of our Christian faith, that Christ is by nature true man, born of a virgin, who experienced life on earth as any other man. He made no difference between himself and others, but behaved and suffered as other men do, with the ex-

ception of sin. As often as we read in the Gospel that he took refuge from danger, he intended to demonstrate himself to be a true man, keeping his deity under cover, to hide it away from the devil.

21. It's a lesson for us. If we can flee for refuge, we ought not despise this expedient, as certain enthusiasts do, who as a challenge to the devil refuse to flee, though they could. Similarly, there are many today who do not go to church or wish to make use of the stated means of grace which God has ordained, but want something out of the ordinary. But God gave you worldly rulers, princes, lords, and the rest, with pastors, preachers, the Word, baptism, the Sacrament, and many other things, everything that belongs to physical and spiritual life. If you order your life in accord with these things, as other people do, then you will not go wrong. But if you insist on some peculiar innovation, you act contrary to God's will and command. Christ adhered to the common manner of children, willing to be like them, not a changeling—as Manichaeus makes him out to be, who stripped him of his human nature entirely—but instead willed to be in everything exactly as he was and in everything he did, as St. Paul says, that he was found in fashion as a man. And that means he would here have lost his life, if he had not been warned by the angels. So much then in harmonizing the historians' accounts.

22. Now the other question and textual problem concerning the three prophetic texts cited by Matthew still remain. I entrust this question to the scholars. Matthew is faulted because he does not cite the texts properly; for the prophet Hosea in chapter 11 is said to be speaking of the whole people of Israel, which was to be brought out of Egypt. And concerning the quotation, "He shall be called a Nazarene," it is not known where the text comes from. But, rest assured, the Evangelist is not in error, but cited them very properly. But it would take too long to speak of it now.

THE CONVERSION OF ST. PAUL*

Acts 7:57–8:3; 9:1–6; 26:16–18; 9:7–17; 22:14–16; 9:18–25

Then they cried out with a loud voice, and stopped their ears, and ran upon him with one accord, And cast him out of the city, and stoned him: and the witnesses laid down their clothes at a young man's feet, whose name was Saul. And they stoned Stephen, calling upon God, and saying, Lord Jesus, receive my spirit. And he kneeled down, and cried with a loud voice, Lord, lay not this sin to their charge. And when he had said this, he fell asleep. And Saul was consenting unto his death. And at that time there was a great persecution against the church which was at Jerusalem; and they were all scattered abroad throughout the regions of Judæa and Samaria, except the apostles. And devout men carried Stephen to his burial, and made great lamentation over him. As for Saul, he made havoc of the church, entering into every house, and hauling men and women committed them to prison. And Saul, yet breathing out threatenings and slaughter against the disciples of the Lord, went unto the high priest, And desired of him letters to Damascus to the synagogues, that if he found any of this way, whether they were men or women, he might bring them bound unto Jerusalem. And as he journeyed, he came near Damascus: and suddenly there shined round about him a light from heaven: And he fell to the earth, and heard a voice saying unto him, Saul, Saul, why persecutest thou me? And he said, Who art thou, Lord? And the Lord said, I am Jesus whom thou persecutest: it is hard for thee to kick against the pricks. And he trembling and astonished said, Lord, what wilt thou have me to do? And the Lord said unto him, Arise, and go into the city, and it shall be told thee what thou must do. But rise, and stand upon thy feet: for I have appeared unto thee for this purpose, to make thee a minister and a witness both of these things which thou hast seen, and of those things in the which I will appear unto thee; Delivering thee from the people, and from the Gentiles, unto whom now I send thee, To open their eyes, and to turn them from darkness to light, and from the power of Satan unto God, that they may receive forgiveness of sins, and inheritance among them which are sanctified by faith that is in me. And the men which journeyed with him stood speechless, hearing a voice, but seeing no man. And

---

*Preached at home (*Lutherhalle*) on the third Sunday after Epiphany, 1534.

Saul arose from the earth; and when his eyes were opened, he saw no man: but they led him by the hand, and brought him into Damascus. And he was three days without sight, and neither did eat nor drink. And there was a certain disciple at Damascus, named Ananias; and to him said the Lord in a vision, Ananias. And he said, Behold, I am here, Lord. And the Lord said unto him, Arise, and go into the street which is called Straight, and inquire in the house of Judas for one called Saul, of Tarsus: for, behold, he prayeth, And hath seen in a vision a man named Ananias coming in, and putting his hand on him, that he might receive his sight. Then Ananias answered, Lord, I have heard by many of this man, how much evil he hath done to thy saints at Jerusalem: And here he hath authority from the chief priests to bind all that call on thy name. But the Lord said unto him, Go thy way: for he is a chosen vessel unto me, to bear my name before the Gentiles, and kings, and the children of Israel: For I will shew him how great things he must suffer for my name's sake. And Ananias went his way, and entered into the house; and putting his hands on him said, Brother Saul, the Lord, even Jesus, that appeared unto thee in the way as thou camest, hath sent me, that thou mightest receive thy sight, and be filled with the Holy Ghost. And he said, The God of our fathers hath chosen thee, that thou shouldest know his will, and see that Just One, and shouldest hear the voice of his mouth. For thou shalt be his witness unto all men of what thou hast seen and heard. And now why tarriest thou? arise, and be baptized, and wash away thy sins, calling on the name of the Lord. And immediately there fell from his eyes as it had been scales: and he received sight forthwith, and arose, and was baptized. And when he had received meat, he was strengthened. Then was Saul certain days with the disciples which were at Damascus. And straightway he preached Christ in the synagogues, that he is the Son of God. But all that heard him were amazed, and said; Is not this he that destroyed them which called on this name in Jerusalem, and came hither for that intent, that he might bring them bound unto the chief priests? But Saul increased the more in strength, and confounded the Jews which dwelt at Damascus, proving that this is very Christ. And after that many days were fulfilled, the Jews took counsel to kill him: But their laying await was known of Saul. And they watched the gates day and night to kill him. Then the disciples took him by night, and let him down by the wall in a basket.

1. The account of Paul's conversion should be known and preached about in the church, so that we come to understand our Lord God's wondrous work in transforming Saul into a very dedicated and outstanding apostle, and find consolation in it.

2. Paul was present as a consenting accomplice at the time when the blood of Stephen was shed on the ground; he was keeping watch over the garments of those who did the killing. He also helped in apprehending and murdering other saintly Christian believers, fully convinced that he was doing right as regards the killing of Stephen and ferreting out other Christians. The blood of these victims, especially that of Stephen, so absorbed his thinking, that he would have been happy if he could have in one day totally eradicated every last Christian—had not God intercepted him! The same is true with all tyrants: Once they have tasted a Christian's blood the devil does not let them pause to celebrate but incites them to more and more murdering, like a hunting dog that has flushed out the game and now gives furious chase. But now at this point, when Saul raged and panted furiously against the Christians, he is turned around in his tracks and converted to Christ, as St. Luke so excellently and clearly details for us; the story is also replicated for us at many other places in Scripture. It is a truly remarkable account, and there is no other individual in the whole of the New Testament about whom something comparable to this man's story is told. His conversion came about in a truly remarkable manner, as we hear from St. Luke's graphic account telling how Saul becomes a very dedicated apostle for our Lord God.

3. It's a story that deserves to be preached every year, whether the specific day itself is observed or not. Of course, the purpose is not that we want to make a god out of Paul or pray to him, as is done by the papists, but so that we might hear about God's wonderful working and learn to become better people. For here we have in front of us a wondrous miracle above all miracles, as Christ converts and turns around his bitterest enemy. St. Luke very plainly articulates that Paul was a bloodthirsty murderer and betrayer of many Christians, and that he had thereby also blasphemed and offended Christ in highest measure; in short, and in fact, Paul is the kind of man who is ready to wipe out and bury the whole of Christianity in one fell swoop, had he been able. Why? On what grounds? Nothing other than that he had heard Christians proclaiming that no one could be saved by the law of Moses; rather, if a person is to be saved it must come about alone through the crucified Christ; without him there was no forgiveness of sins, let alone eternal life. As he hears that, how

Moses is repudiated as the way to salvation, and how all the prophets had testified to this insufficiency of Moses, Paul had become raving mad with fury.

4. The situation is the same with the pope and his followers when they hear that the canon laws, monkery, orders, prayer, fasting, and saying the Mass, do not avail for salvation before God; they are ready to burst forth with maliciousness and can absolutely not tolerate such preaching. This was the thinking of Paul, except his motivation was on a higher plane than that of the pope and his followers. For his concern was for God's Word and Law; this he wanted to uphold, so that the Law, sacrifices, the temple and all that God had ordained might continue to be kept and not be thrown out; and for this he was prepared to give his life. After all, how could these things be wrong since they were given and ordained by God? The pope does not have God's Word, but his own decrees and human ordinances. Precisely for that reason we stand opposed to their Masses, orders, prayers, and fasting as being wrong and unavailing before God, because they are not ordained by God but conceived out of their own ideas arbitrarily, without regard for what God has ordained. And yet we see how they presume nonetheless to maintain their idolatrous practices.

5. So, when we look into the heart of Paul to see what it was that motivated him to be hostile to the Christians, to obtain incriminating letters against the Christians, and become executioner for the Jews, we perceive that he had much more valid grounds than the papists who persecute the gospel simply for the sake of money, goods, station, and prestige. None of that moves Paul; his only concern is for the Law and for divine service at the temple which God had ordained and commanded, not because of some minor rules or peripheral matter. That is why he is convinced that what he is doing is right. The papists' own conscience, on the other hand, bears witness to them that the reception of both elements in the Sacrament is not wrong, nor to be married, nor to use foods and other things freely; for they cannot belie God's Word, or the teachings of Christ, also not the usages in the early church.

6. Paul, therefore, is more pious than the papists, since he seeks only to uphold God's Word and honor, and is willing to risk his life and suffer any cost; moreover, what he does is done in ignorance, as

he himself states (1 Tim. 1:13): "But I obtained mercy, because I did it ignorantly in unbelief. " That's something the papists of today cannot lay claim to. For the fact is that what they do is simply for their stomach's sake. The Word of God hits them straight between the eyes and lights up their eyes, so that they have to acknowledge that it is true, and yet they refuse to allow or tolerate it. For this reason we have to look elsewhere for the reason why they persecute Christian believers; they do it knowingly, while Paul does it ignorantly.

7. As Paul, now, pursued the matter so earnestly and conceives the idea of suppressing this new sect in other regions beyond Jerusalem, our Lord Jesus has other plans for him and says, Halt! This is a man I want! Whatever he sets his mind to, he does with determination; and this resolve which he now manifests in an evil way, I will turn around with my Spirit and utilize for a good purpose. I will set him in contention against the Jews and cause them to rage and fume, as they rightfully deserve. Similarly, today, the Lord God has used me against the pope and his minions; earlier I was ready to let myself be torn apart because of the pope, but now I must fight against him with might and main. That is bound to make the papists fume and rant with rage. Paul, accordingly, became a very excellent preacher, first of all among the Jews, and then after a while primarily among the Gentiles, whose teacher he boasts of being and whose offspring we must confess we are, for he brought us all, by the gospel, to Christ, as he states (1 Cor. 4:15). This whole incident is so amazing because Christ had gathered all the rest of the apostles and disciples to himself much earlier; but it was Paul whom he sends out immediately to preach to the Gentiles, and as a result Paul is the master who teaches us, for we are Gentiles and not Jews.

8. It was, indeed, a truly great and comforting miracle how our Lord God converts the very man who raged so furiously against and had so determinedly persecuted Christ and his Christendom. The sequence of events went as follows: Paul had obtained letters of incrimination from the high priest to carry with him to the synagogues in Damascus to apprehend those who were Christians and lead them bound to Jerusalem. To himself he thinks: Now I will level charges against them. And so he goes on his way quickly toward Damascus where some of the Jews had become Christians. Undoubtedly, some

of these were his friends, tied to him by blood, and yet he intended to harass them thoroughly.

And as he journeyed, he came near Damascus: and suddenly there shined round about him a light from heaven: And he fell to the earth.

9. The proper time had now come. The Lord caused a brilliant light to envelop him and he fell to the ground. For no heart is strong enough—even though hard as flint or like a diamond—that it could have resisted and not have been smashed. The light totally enveloped him, fells him, and leaves him lying there blinded, unable to see. As he lies there, he thought: I'm about to die! Painters who sketch the scene are in error when they depict it as a lightning stroke that knocks Paul down to the ground. The fact, however, is that here and elsewhere in Scripture, the happening is not described as lightning and thunder, but as a sudden overpowering light that causes him to fear greatly and fall down to the earth. As he now lies there terrified and trembling, he hears a voice speaking to him:

Saul, Saul, why persecutest thou me?

10. With that he became even more terrified, and to himself he thinks, Persecute, who's persecuting? Was I wrong in thinking that I was doing God the greatest possible service? And he replies:

Who art thou, Lord? And the Lord said, I am Jesus whom thou persecutest.

11. In other words, What you do against my Christians you are doing to me. Thus the sin is pressed into his conscience and he is weighed down with all the blood that had been shed, so that it's a wonder Paul didn't succumb and die right there. For when a man is hit right between the eyes, and in his heart, with the charge that he has persecuted God, there is little chance left for consolation. The papists will experience this, too, either at their last moment when they are about to die, or on the Last Day. Their consciences will accuse and fell them, knocking heart and breath from them.

12. The Lord addresses him in the Hebrew tongue, but Paul's companions did not hear what was said, though they saw the light and were terrified. Thus they were unaware of what was happening to him. The Lord proceeds further:

It is hard for thee to kick against the pricks.

13. That is a very pertinent and serious warning which everyone who has in mind to persecute Christ and his teaching should take to heart. But apart from grace, they are unable to believe it, and so they are not converted as Paul was; they continue on in their sin until they finally die and are lost, here in time and hereafter in eternity. Just why is it, Christ is saying to Paul, that you fume so furiously? For, what are you accomplishing thereby? Nothing else than kicking against the spear points! What sort of warrior is he who intentionally kicks his heels against a spear or who treads with his feet upon its sharp point?

14. It is really a consolatory word for poor, persecuted Christians to know that those who persecute Christ will be drawn towards the sharp pike, either hobbling themselves in some way or with other troubles. The fact is that whoever storms against Christ will be drawn towards and run up against the spear. Nowadays Duke George thinks he is strong enough to pull Christ out of the heavens; but he will soon learn what will happen to him. A pike is not intended for anyone to kick against but to equip a person to spear through something. And so whoever thinks he can kick against it will soon learn a lesson. When Paul heard these words, he yielded and tremblingly replied:

Lord, what wilt thou have me to do?

15. He was now ready to be taught. The man, who is called Jesus of Nazareth, is able to speak with such earnestness that it goes deeply to the heart. Paul would have despaired and died, had not Christ again pulled him to his feet and comforted him, as he now says:

Arise, and go into the city, and it shall be told thee what thou must do.

16. Although he speaks with Paul directly from heaven above, God does not intend to put away the pastoral office or establish something extraordinary for him. Indeed, he might have spoken to him directly and revealed what he wanted him to do, but instead he directs him to go to the parish pastor in the city where he would hear and learn what he was supposed to do. Our Lord God does not purpose some special thing for each individual person, but gives to the whole world—one person like the next—his baptism and gospel. Through these means we are to learn how to be saved, and have no need to wait for God to reveal some new thing from heaven, or send

an angel. For it is his will that we should go to hear the gospel preached by the pastor; there we will find him, and in no other way.

17. Those who seek for some special revelation get what they deserve, namely, the devil. The enthusiasts—Carlstadt, Muentzer, and others like them—gather in a corner waiting there for the Lord God and the Holy Spirit. The devil dupes them into thinking that they can importune our Lord God to give them a special direct revelation. Our Lord God, thereupon, purposely sends them a delusion, according to which the devil comes to them in the form of an angel to punish them. Our Lord God did not mandate anything extraordinary for Paul to do, for he, after all, had heard the physical voice of Christ, the Lord, and he was to become a foremost preacher. Instead he is told to go into the city and to hear Ananias. So, get up and go! he says. Nothing special beyond this is done, no further instruction there along the road, no baptism, just the directive to go where his Word and baptism are to be had. And Paul willingly complies with the Lord's directive, although he does not yet know where and by whom this will all happen.

18. At this juncture, then, our Lord God sends Ananias to meet Paul, to preach the Word to him and baptize him; he lays his hands upon him and says:

Brother Saul, the Lord, even Jesus that appeared unto thee in the way as thou camest, hath sent me, that thou mightest receive thy sight, and be filled with the Holy Ghost.

Thus Paul came into the light of the Word, to baptism, to the Holy Spirit, through Ananias who was no more than a finger compared with Paul, like a little candle in comparison with the sun. From him, this little wooden match, Paul was to take his light; from this little doctor the famous Doctor Paul was to hear what he was to do!

19. That is something we must really note well, so that we esteem the preaching office as we ought. Paul receives his sight, his insight, and the Holy Spirit, through the ministry of Ananias, so that he knows who Christ is, understands the power of baptism, and forthwith emerges as, and is, a changed man. However many Christians there were whose blood he had shed, equally as many, yea, many thousand times as many Christians he brought to faith! As a result the disciples themselves were dumbfounded by the number of them,

stating, Think of it, isn't it a wonder, that this man is now preaching, he who destroyed everyone in Jerusalem who called on the name of Christ? and how he enrages the Jews more than the Christians enraged him earlier?

20. This, then, is the account of Paul's conversion, a truly wonderful story! It demonstrates for us the wondrous working of our Lord God as he converts this foremost persecutor of Christ and his church, and out of a wolf makes a gentle little lamb for our salvation's sake and consolation, so that we heathen might acquire a truly great master and teacher. Let us thank God for such grace with all our hearts!

THE DAY OF MARY'S PURIFICATION*

Luke 2:22–32

And when the days of her purification according to the law of Moses were accomplished, they brought him to Jerusalem, to present him to the Lord; (As it is written in the law of the Lord, Every male that openeth the womb shall be called holy to the Lord;) And to offer a sacrifice according to that which is said in the law of the Lord, A pair of turtledoves, or two young pigeons. And, behold, there was a man in Jerusalem, whose name was Simeon; and the same man was just and devout, waiting for the consolation of Israel: and the Holy Ghost was upon him. And it was revealed unto him by the Holy Ghost, that he should not see death, before he had seen the Lord's Christ. And he came by the Spirit into the temple: and when the parents brought in the child Jesus, to do for him after the custom of the law, then took he him up in his arms, and blessed God, and said, Lord, now lettest thou thy servant depart in peace, according to thy word: For mine eyes have seen thy salvation, Which thou hast prepared before the face of all people; A light to lighten the Gentiles, and the glory of thy people Israel.

1. Today we celebrate the feast which under the papacy was called the Candlemas, for on that day the focus was on our beloved women in a special ceremony in which wax candles were consecrated, exorcised, lit, and carried in procession. You have already heard how this originated, namely, that Pope Sergius appropriated this from the Romans, for on this night the heathen sauntered about with torches and lighted candles looking for Proserpine**; and in similar manner, in honor of our women, Christians every year were to process on this day with consecrated, lighted candles. We'll leave that matter in the pope's hands and whoever else keeps the custom. We, however, observe this day in honor of our Lord Jesus Christ, who on this day appeared publicly for the first time as he was brought into the temple at Jerusalem and presented to the Lord.

---

*Preached publicly at the parish church, 1537.
**Goddess of the subterranean world of the dead.

2. St. Luke makes mention of three things: the purification, the presentation, and the offering, adding in each case that it happened in accord with the law of the Lord. What was it he wanted to indicate by speaking at length about each of these things and emphasizing the law of the Lord?

3. First, he wanted to indicate the many laws under which God governed and ruled the Jewish people, and that they were a people requiring such constraint. The law dealing with purification was very severe; for among the Jews, women who gave birth were unclean for six weeks; what they ate, drank, touched, where they stood, walked, sat, that was all unclean, and everyone had to avoid and keep away from such women, as from a person afflicted with leprosy. If she had given birth to a girl, she was to be sequestered twelve weeks and be unclean; but if she had given birth to a boy, she had to remain away from people six weeks.

4. Similarly, the law that dealt with the presentation and offering in behalf of the child was also a rigid and burdensome law. When six weeks had passed, the mother had to bring her first-born son to the temple in Jerusalem, to present and offer him to the Lord with a fourth part of a gulden and a pair of turtledoves, if she was poor, as a redemption offering, and then three times a year present herself in the temple at Jerusalem. This law for the Old Testament Jews was very rigid and demanding. Just think how we would complain if such a hard and oppressive law were imposed on us!

5. We are not bound by such laws in the New Testament. The Jews, however, under Mosaic law had to bear such legal burdens, not merely to the discomfort of the body but also at considerable cost in money. Yearly, too, for each person had to pay the Romans a fourth part of a gulden. In addition, their firstborn sons, cattle, and produce belonged to the temple. They had to give a tithe of all they produced to the Levites, and then almost two-tenths more when you add up what they owed the king, also for offerings, and for the poor. And the pope has, likewise, made a great to-do about giving. Think of how much people had to give on this day just for wax candles! If a man were to possess all the money collected for wax candles on this day, he would be a wealthy man. Now, however, we are free from the heavy burden of the Mosaic law, as well as from the pope's imposition of taxes.

6. Yet, see what thankfulness people have toward God and his gospel, now that they are free—peasants, burghers, noblemen, and whoever! Now no one parts willingly with half a farthing for the gospel and the ministry of the Word; rather, everyone steals and robs the poor church of what has been given in times past! Peasants who live in the villages complain if they have to build a fence for their pastor; yes, they even force him to look after cows and pigs just like other peasants. In the Old Testament under the Mosaic law, Jews were compelled to obey their priests, just as under the papacy no one dared murmur against monks or priests; but now under the gospel everyone does as he pleases, and not only are pastors and preachers despised, they are poorly paid as well. We have to tolerate such tightwads in the same way we have to put up with snot in our nose.

7. Therefore, our Lord God did well to burden the people of Israel with many laws. We have to harness and bridle a horse or mule, otherwise we can't control them, as the psalmist says (Ps. 32:9): "Be ye not as the horse, or as the mule . . . whose mouth must be held in with bit and bridle, lest they come near unto thee." And we read in Sirach 33:26: "The ox is tamed by yoke and harness, the bad servant by racks and tortures." There has to be law, punishment, and coercion in the world; men cannot do without these things, not just because people are so wicked, but because the devil never rests or ceases to incite and stir up people until he has prompted them to adultery, murder, thievery, and all manner of vice. In every way possible we must suppress and curb people whom the devil would drive to sin and vice, if we are to maintain outward decency. People have now been freed, not only from the burden of wax candles, but also from the tangle of oppressive rules under the papacy, free to enjoy the light of the gospel without any interference. For this they ought to thank God, but instead they become insolent and unruly, unwilling to do good. That is one reason why St. Luke so often refers to the Law.

8. His second purpose is to indicate that our dear Lord Christ subjected himself under the Law for our sake, in order that he might redeem us from the Law's curse. He was not conceived or born under the rubrics of what the Law stated concerning the firstborn, for he was conceived by the Holy Spirit and born of a virgin. Nevertheless,

with his mother he submitted to purification in accord with the Law. And it is a very great comfort for us that Scripture sketches and portrays Christ to us as being like us in all things, only without sin. The deeper we plunge Christ into the flesh of mankind, the better for us. For he subjected himself under the meanest purification Law, in order to show that he was an ordinary human being, yet a pure, holy person who places himself under the Law for our sake. As St. Paul says (Gal. 3:13), "Christ hath redeemed us from the curse of the law, being made a curse for us."

9. So it is, also, with the law requiring that the firstborn be presented to the Lord. That law rules that all children are from birth sinners and subject to death. For this reason they were to be promptly brought to the temple and presented for sacrifice, that is, to death. Here now Christ enters in to shoulder not only the law of purification, but also the law requiring the firstborn's presentation for sacrifice, bearing not only the burden of our sins, but allowing himself to be condemned to death for our sake, for the Law required that the payment be death. Thus, to redeem one's firstborn son, offering had to be made to buy him back. Under the old covenant this was the second offering.

10. Thus Christ took upon himself the judgment to be condemned to death just like any other human being. We see from this what we are by nature, with our own reason and free will. The Law subjects us to death and snatches away the primary, the best and noblest treasure of all, indicating thereby that there is nothing good in the individual, even though he was privileged to be the firstborn among his brethren. Because Christ has done this, placed himself under the Law, he thereby has freed us from the Law so that we would not be guilty of death, much less unrighteousness. For he did not break the Law, he is no sinner, and the Law has no right to condemn him to death. Since now the Law has laid hold of him, like other children conceived and born in sin, he nonetheless was set apart from all other children since he was not conceived by human seed but by the Holy Spirit, nor born of an ordinary mother but of a pure virgin; and for this reason the Law has no claim on him, yes, he is the Lord of the Law. Thus he redeemed us from the curse of the Law, so that the Law does not condemn us to death, when we are baptized

in him and believe on his name. This now is the first part of this Gospel relative to the laws of purification and the firstborn.

11. The second part of this lesson is more comforting and reassuring even than the first, as now, under the prompting of the Holy Spirit, aged Simeon enters the temple and takes the child Jesus into his arms and sings a beautiful song with which we may comfort ourselves over against death. It is a song that differs considerably from the requiem of the pope and the priests. St. Luke reports that Simeon had been promised by the Holy Spirit that he was not to see death until he had seen the Lord Christ, that is, the King about whom the prophets prophesied and preached. And in accord therewith, he enters the temple and takes into his arms this child (the parents had brought him into the temple in order to do in his behalf what the Law required), praises God, and says:

Lord, now lettest thou thy servant depart in peace, according to thy word: for mine eyes have seen thy salvation, which thou hast prepared before the face of all people; a light to lighten the Gentiles, and the glory of thy people Israel.

12. Simeon has a very penetrating eye. In this child there is no kingly mien or royal garb to see, merely the form of a poor beggar. The mother is poor, with hardly five pennies in her purse to redeem her child in keeping with the Law. The child is wrapped in very poor swaddling clothes; nevertheless, Simeon comes right up, without anyone's testimonial, and publicly attests: This child is the Saviour of the world and a Light to all the Gentiles. This is a remarkable sermon and wonderful witness on behalf of this child, as Simeon looks upon this little infant wrapped in shabby rags. By reasoned judgment he would have had to say, This is no King, but a beggar-child. But he does not allow his reason to judge by what his eyes behold but denominates this child as a king, greater than all the kings in the world. For he calls him a Saviour, prepared by God for all nations and a Light to lighten the Gentiles all over the world. Indeed, for Simeon, this was to open one's eyes wide and look far beyond oneself! His eyes behold the whole world, from one end of the earth to the other. Wherever in the whole world, he says, there are peoples and Gentiles, there this child is a Saviour and a Light. Thus he comprehends everything that the Holy Scriptures state, and associates it with the child now lying in his arms.

13. First, he calls this child a Saviour of all peoples. By this he indicates that this child redeems from sin and death, and grants righteousness and eternal life. Thus beloved Simeon perceives that this child will achieve these wonderful works of making people righteous and saving them; and he speaks so definitely and consolingly about this, as though sin, death, and misery were no longer to be seen in the whole world, but only righteousness, salvation, and life. "Mine eyes have seen thy salvation!" by which he meant, I am so inspired with hope, that I see nothing but life and salvation in the world, and I shall not die but be in peace. Then, too, he also calls him a Light of the Gentiles, meaning that he is a Light whereby the Gentiles everywhere shall be illumined. He will take away the darkness and, in its stead, pour pure light upon the Gentiles, that is, break up the kingdom of the devil who governs in the world with darkness, error, sin, death, and everything evil, and he will destroy sin and death, as St. Paul writes (2 Tim. 1:10–11): "Who hath abolished death, and hath brought life and immortality to light through the gospel: Whereunto I am appointed a preacher, and an apostle, and a teacher of the Gentiles." These are, indeed, mighty deeds and miracles of God, and Simeon attributes them to this child, as he states that this child will govern the whole world and will kindle the light of his gospel against the devil's error and darkness, and bring people to the knowledge of God.

14. This is not to say, however, that all people will see the light or believe the gospel. The sun, indeed, shines its light into all the world, but many people go on sleeping; they are blind and do not see the light of the sun. It is not the sun's fault that all people do not see the light of the sun, but their own fault, because they are either asleep or blind, or shade their windows and eyes, not wanting to see the sun's light. Our entire city of Wittenberg overflows with the gospel which sheds its light on all, young and old, and yet only a few accept the gospel. This is not the gospel's fault but the people's, because they reject it. Despite the fact that many Gentiles do not see the light, but remain blind, this child, nevertheless, still remains a Light to the Gentiles everywhere.

15. So Christ's kingdom has endured under the pope, Turks, and Tartars; likewise to the present day under the swaggering squires,

bishops, and princes, in fact, also at Rome, where the devil incarnate is ensconced. One can still find baptism there and a few who have the gospel. When, therefore, Simeon says that Christ is a Light to lighten the Gentiles, the meaning is that Christ's kingdom is going into the whole world among all Gentiles, although not all the Gentiles will see and accept it. He has been prepared to be a true King and Saviour for the whole world wherever human beings are, to shed his light everywhere upon the Gentiles. This was aged Simeon's prophecy about Christ, just like the prophet Isaiah foretold concerning him long before, saying (49:6): "I will also give thee for a light to the Gentiles, that thou mayest be my salvation unto the end of the earth."

16. But, as Simeon says, since this child is to be the Saviour of all people and a light to lighten the Gentiles, it follows that all peoples on earth are without salvation and all Gentiles without Light, that is, in darkness; they are blind, lost, and condemned. For if they were not without light and salvation, lost and condemned in darkness, they would not be in need of this Saviour and Light. Simeon now becomes the greatest heretic of all time, for all the world to reject and condemn, as we today see when his song is mightily assailed as being false and heretical. The pope and his cohorts do not want to admit that Simeon's song is true, that is, that this child Jesus is the Saviour of all people and the Light to all the Gentiles. That is why I gladly preach about it, to portray this child like this, so that I who preach it, and you, who listen to it, might grasp it with firm faith, just like Simeon did here. This child, he says, whom I am holding in my arms, is the Saviour of all people and a light to all the Gentiles. Therefore, where this Saviour and this Light, Christ, is not proclaimed, there utter darkness, blindness, sin, death, God's wrath, and eternal damnation prevail.

17. Our opponents, however, cannot tolerate such preaching. When I now preach that everything done and taught by the pope, his monks, nuns, and priests is darkness and error, and so on, they not only will not listen, but call such preaching heresy. Yet they sing this song today in their churches, with candles, lights, banners, and great pomp. They retain the words of this song, sing and confess that Christ is the Saviour of all people and the Light of the Gentiles, but

they deny the fact. For if it is true that this child is the Saviour of the world and the Light of all the Gentiles, it then follows that the Franciscan order, the papal decrees and traditions cannot be this Saviour and this Light. If this text and article are to stand pure and unadulterated, as Simeon composed it, then everything else following from it will of necessity be condemned. So when I preach it and make application from it, then I am called a heretic and liar, and charged with teaching heresy and moral corruption. The papists, therefore, bit themselves in the tongue when they say that Christ is the Saviour and Light of the whole world, and in the same breath also teach that monasticism and good works help save too, as their books attest. This is an atrocious blindness, confessing that Christ is the world's Saviour and Light, and, at the same time, teaching and insisting that good works are the Saviour and the Light. To put it another way, Christ is not the only Saviour and the Light; for if I were to lead a life like that of a monk, fast, and pray, then I also become a savior and a light.

18. These blind people and leaders of the blind we must reject and diligently see to it that we maintain this text pure and unadulterated, namely, that Christ alone is the Saviour and the Light of the World, and that everything else, therefore, outside of Christ is pure sin, death, darkness, hell, and damnation, no matter if they be the best possible rules and ordinances. To be sure, government is certainly ordained by God, something we need and cannot do without, but it cannot bring us to salvation and eternal life with God. Let me give you a crude example. A cow has to have hay and straw; this is a basic rule; it cannot survive without it. However, through this law, it does not become a child, daughter, or heir in the home but stays a cow. The same thing applies here as well. By observing all the laws and ordinances of the emperor, I still am not and do not thereby become God's dear child. Much less am I and do I become God's child through monastic discipline, even though monks were a hundred thousand times holier than they are. This is a crude way of putting it, but I have to speak this way about it because of these crude, lazy chatterboxes. Just as a cow does not become a daughter or heir in the home because it has its law of the stable, so also no one becomes a child and heir of God by the law, be it the emperor's or the pope's, except that the pope's law is still not as good as the emperor's since

the emperor's law is rightly in keeping with an ordinance of God, but the pope's ordinances are merely man-made, presumptuous, wicked traditions that burden and ensnare poor consciences. If a cow were to vaunt itself and say, I am daughter and heir in the home and then lie down in the cradle where the daughter is supposed to lie, we would say, Indeed! Out with the daughter and bring in the butcher, to teach the "daughter" good manners. The selfsame thing applies here: Cast into hell are monks and priests with hoods and tonsures who through their laws and works want to be God's children and heirs in the kingdom of heaven!

19. Simeon, accordingly, sings very clearly: "Mine eyes have seen thy salvation, which thou hast prepared before the face of all people, a light to lighten the Gentiles," and so on. In other words, he is saying, I know of no other Saviour and Light than this one, whom I am now holding in my arms and beholding with my own eyes. From this it follows, as said, that everything that is not Christ is darkness, blindness, death, and the devil before God, even though it be temporal government and the rightful justice of the emperor. For such things carry no weight before God but belong down here in the cow shed, that is, in this perishable, transitory life. But this child, of whom Simeon is singing here, is the world's only Saviour and Light, who sheds light on us and makes us righteous and holy before God.

20. And the dear old father speaks very simply, as he calls the child a Saviour of all people and a Light of the Gentiles. And he does not restrict the little child in the cradle to the Jewish land but allots him to all people, also to those who are not of Abraham's seed and blood. The Jews boast that they alone share in the promise which the fathers received. But Simeon allots this King not only to the Jews, but also to the Gentiles. Therefore, very accurately and in a truly prophetic way he states that Christ is a Light who lightens the Gentiles. Even though I, as a Gentile, am not a kin of the people of Israel according to the flesh, nevertheless, I am a co-heir of this grace and blessing, that Christ is also my Saviour and Light.

21. Much more could be said about this if time permitted. But for the present let's remember that with these words everything except Christ is to be excluded from contributing to righteousness and salvation before God. I want this article to be understood correctly, for I know that the devil is prowling about, trying to stir up factious spirits, for he cannot

remain idle. Whoever has learned and really grasped this article about Christ cannot go wrong, nor will he aid and abet the sectarian spirits. For Christ is the Light and will not allow us to err; he is the only Saviour and does not permit us to founder and come to destruction. We see this in old Simeon; he truly recognized Christ and is so convinced of this knowledge, so that Christ fully and totally occupies his heart. He says nothing about angels or prophets or about the Virgin Mary or John the Baptist; but sings to us only of this child. Nor does he inquire about what the high priests and scribes, the Roman emperor, or other princes think of this child, but publicly confesses and says, This child is not only my Saviour but the Saviour of all people and the Light of the Gentiles.

22. Third, Simeon calls him the glory of his people Israel, that is, the people of Israel will have great honor on account of this child. For Israel was the people that had the promise, that out of them should be born the Saviour of all people and the Light of the Gentiles. It is as Christ states (John 4:22): "Salvation is of the Jews." In him the Jews take precedence over us Gentiles, as St. Paul says (Rom. 9:4), that theirs is the adoption and the glory and the covenant and the Law and the service of God and the promise, and so forth. All the treasures and blessings brought by Christ belong to the people of Israel. We Gentiles do not have the promise, and yet we share in its benefits. Even though we are unable to boast like the Jews that Christ is our cousin, brother, and kinsman according to the flesh, yet the benefit is ours that he is just as much our Saviour and Light as he is the Jews'.

23. This is the song that Simeon has sung to us today. Now, filled with joy he wants to depart in peace; for he has seen so much that there is nothing that now frightens him. Since he has seen the Saviour and the Light which God has prepared, he no longer beholds either sin or death and is prepared and willing to die. "Lord, now lettest thou thy servant depart in peace," he says, and this means: Now I shall depart with my heart filled with joy; I see no death, I cannot even call it a death but a peaceful journey. He does not say, Now I wish to die; but, now I wish to depart in peace. This was a song not just in his mouth, on his tongue, on paper, but in his heart! May our dear God and Father, for the sake of Jesus Christ, his Son, grant us his grace through his Holy Spirit that we may join to sing along with beloved Simeon and also depart in peace. Amen.

THE DAY OF ANNUNCIATION TO MARY

*First Sermon**

Our worship today commemorates the conception of our Lord Jesus Christ. To honor, praise, and give thanks for this event, we want to consider this Gospel, so that this article of faith may always abide in our church. St. Luke describes this event as follows:

Luke 1:26–38

And in the sixth month the angel Gabriel was sent from God unto a city of Galilee, named Nazareth, To a virgin espoused to a man whose name was Joseph, of the house of David; and the virgin's name was Mary. And the angel came in unto her, and said, Hail, thou that art highly favoured, the Lord is with thee: blessed art thou among women. And when she saw him, she was troubled at his saying, and cast in her mind what manner of salutation this should be. And the angel said unto her, Fear not, Mary: for thou hast found favour with God. And, behold, thou shalt conceive in thy womb, and bring forth a son, and shalt call his name JESUS. He shall be great, and shall be called the Son of the Highest: and the Lord God shall give unto him the throne of his father David: And he shall reign over the house of Jacob for ever; and of his kingdom there shall be no end. Then said Mary unto the angel, How shall this be, seeing I know not a man? And the angel answered and said unto her, The Holy Ghost shall come upon thee, and the power of the Highest shall overshadow thee: therefore also that holy thing which shall be born of thee shall be called the Son of God. And, behold, thy cousin Elisabeth, she hath also conceived a son in her old age: and this is the sixth month with her, who was called barren. For with God nothing shall be impossible. And Mary said, Behold the handmaid of the Lord; be it unto me according to thy word. And the angel departed from her.

---

*Preached publicly at the parish church, 1532, on Palm Sunday afternoon, which that year happened to be the eve of Mary's Annunciation Day.

1. The reason for this festival is that it is an article of our faith: "I believe in Jesus Christ, his only Son, our Lord, who was conceived by the Holy Ghost, born of the Virgin Mary." Women call it "becoming pregnant"; the article of faith calls it "conceived." Mary's impregnating or conception was by the agency of the Holy Spirit. This article of faith must forever remain a part of Christian doctrine, a truly excellent, wonderful article of faith, against which, first of all, the devil contends, and then, also, all those who side with the devil. We Christians are called upon to believe and to confess a teaching which by the world is considered to be rank foolishness.

2. From the standpoint of reason, it does indeed appear to be a foolish concept for Christians to believe and confess. Women, no matter how high or low their station, become pregnant in only one way, namely, as is written in Genesis 1:27-28: "So God created man in his own image, in the image of God created he him; male and female created he them. And God blessed them and God said unto them, Be fruitful, and multiply, and replenish the earth." But with Mary, God made an exception, something that had never happened before in the world, or would ever again happen as long as the world endures. She conceived a child and became a mother not by virtue of a man, but by the Holy Spirit. Preposterous to human reason, and to every thinking person! And the more learned and wise they are, the more foolish they find it that Christians believe and confess this, something so totally unacceptable and impossible to human reason!

3. In German we are accustomed to say, If I do as other people do, I won't end up a fool. It's a rule of thumb commonly accepted as making good sense. However, in the matter of confession of the articles of faith we need to shove the proverb into the corner and say, If you're going to be a Christian, you will perforce believe and do things which other people do not believe or do. Yes, I'll have to appear odd and strange to other people who are vexed and offended because of my faith. That's the situation here. I'm to believe that Mary, a virgin, is pregnant, and will become a mother, but no soul on earth knew about it, only she. This sounds foolish and impossible. If something like this had happened before, it would have credence and could be believed. But that God chose this virgin from among all women and makes an exception with this miracle in her case

alone, makes the event unbelievable. Nevertheless, it is true: Mary was pregnant, became a mother, and yet remained a chaste virgin! She is a true to life virgin, not a stone or wooden statue, but a human born virgin. Just as other mortals have flesh and blood and are mortal, so, she too, has flesh and blood and is a mortal person, the same as any other woman. Yet God accomplished something unique with her, that she bore a son and truly became a mother. She carried him, gave birth, and nursed him; yet no one knew the circumstances except she alone.

4. Only we Christians believe this article of faith, and we are considered simpletons and fools by the world for it. For our belief, the Turks and the Jews mock and laugh at us, as do also the wiseacres of the world. But, then, all articles of our faith seem ridiculous and foolish to our reason. The same is true for this article. The angel's announcement seems ridiculous and foolish, that Mary should conceive and bear a son who would be not only a true man, but also true God. The world looks upon us Christians as naive fools for believing that Mary would be this child's true mother and yet remain a chaste virgin. Not only is that contrary to reason, but also to God's order of creation. God said to Adam and Eve, "Be fruitful and multiply." Every woman who conceives a child will say that her pregnancy results from intercourse with a man. When Mary conceived, however, she said, I am with child and give birth, but without a man. Of the essence here, therefore, were the words of the angel's announcement: "And, behold, thou shalt conceive in thy womb, and bring forth a son, and shalt call his name Jesus."

5. But of even greater significance is the angel's further word: "He shall be great, and shall be called the Son of the Highest: and the Lord God shall give unto him the throne of his father David: and he shall reign over the house of Jacob for ever; and of his kingdom there shall be no end." With these words in the picture, the whole world, heaven and earth, become too narrow for this child's domain. This is all above and beyond the laws of nature and the limits of our reasoning power. How is this possible, our reason asks, that this child should be called the Son of the Highest and should at the same time be the natural son of a poor mortal virgin? But the angel announced it and we Christians believe it; Mary was not only a chaste virgin, but

conceived and became a mother of a truly human son. But this child, whom Mary conceived, delivered at birth, cared for, and nurtured, like any mother does her child, is, and is called, the true Son of God. This, above all things, rocks the world's wisdom and particularly riles up the Jews. And who knows what the devil will stir up against this article of the faith by means of the fanatical sects, if the world goes on. They have already launched their attack sowing their poison against it.

6. Therefore, let us comprehend the full significance of this article, firmly resisting reason's objections and listening to what God's Word says. This article is well documented in both the Old and New Testament; so it must certainly be valid. Were it right to do so, I could be as much a smart aleck and deride the article just as sharply as our opponents do, or some other egghead among us who could outstrip them in their sophistries. They figure no one can analyze something as keenly as they do. They take us to be stupid numskulls. Fools though we be, nonetheless, we understand their stupidity which they consider to be great wisdom. Our response to them is: What you consider utter foolishness, we believe, to the praise of our Lord God and our salvation, and in defiance of our wiseacre opponents. I, too, know how to count the fingers on my hand and figure out that no woman, no virgin, according to the fixed order of things in nature, becomes pregnant on her own. It would not only be stupid, but wicked and irrational, for a woman, or virgin to say that she had conceived on her own. But we have a sovereign Lord over us, God in heaven, who attests to this virgin that she conceived and became a mother without the agency of a man.

7. God thus demonstrated that he could create humans in more ways than one. In the beginning he did not create man and woman simultaneously and in the same way. He was not like some fencing master who teaches his students all he knows and then collects his fees when the lessons are over. Rather, God remains Master and Creator forever and ever, and we will never exhaust the limits of his skill, power, and wisdom. He created Adam from a clod of earth and breathed the breath of life into his nostrils, so that he became a living soul. After that he created Eve from a rib of Adam. Now, he could have created man and woman at the same time and, immediately, in

the same manner, but he did not so desire. He could have created Eve first and had other humans born of her, but he did not do that, but created Adam first, then Eve. After that he brought Adam and Eve together and so ordained that from their lineage all mankind should be born. St. Paul states in Acts 17:26: "And hath made of one blood all nations of men for to dwell on all the face of the earth." Here, then, we see three ways in which human beings were created.

8. Now, even as it was our Lord God's will not to limit his creating of mankind to a clod of earth, or the rib of man, or from human seed, so he chose not to be limited by any of the preceding forms of reproduction, but rather instituted a new way, a fourth, namely, to produce a child from a virgin—the one and only time—as the prophet Isaiah states (7:14): "Therefore the Lord himself will give you a sign; Behold, a virgin shall conceive, and bear a son, and shall call his name Immanuel." In other words, God chose here not to follow the usual order of generation, but provide a new way. A virgin would conceive. This would be the sign and wonder. Nevertheless, his arrangement is half of the normal order, in that the child would be born of a young maiden. Accordingly, no husband and wife, but only the one participant, a woman, and she alone, without a man, was to be the mother.

9. True, we Christians might say that according to reason it seems ridiculous that a virgin should conceive, become a mother, and give birth to a son who would not only be her natural son, but also God's true Son. But here I must shove human reason and wisdom under the bench and not listen to what reason has to say, but what God in his Word has to say. For he who is in heaven above, Creator of all wisdom, surely knows a bit more than all of human reason. He who placed the eyes in my head and your head certainly sees more than you and I see, as Psalm 94:9 states: "He that planted the ear, shall he not hear? he that formed the eye, shall he not see?" The Creator must be greater, more discerning, more wise than the creature.

10. That is why we should be held captive by God's Word and not try to speculate beyond it. God announces in his Word that this child is true God and true man, born from eternity by the Father, and born on earth of a true, human lineage, out of the body of a woman, like any other child, from a mother who nurtures him like any other

mother, except that this conception and birth take place in a supernatural way and this son is born of a virgin. We must envelop ourselves in this Word of God, because with our reason we cannot fathom it. Wiseacres literally drown when they try to unravel the miracle with their reasoning.

11. The announcement of the angel as our Creed states is: "I believe in Jesus Christ . . . conceived by the Holy Ghost," in other words, I believe that the Virgin Mary conceived a son, who is also God's only Son. By whom did she become pregnant? There was no one, but herself. She stands alone, without a man and no one has acted in the conception other than the Holy Spirit.

Then said Mary unto the angel, How shall this be, seeing I know not a man? And the angel answered and said unto her, The Holy Ghost shall come upon thee, and the power of the Highest shall overshadow thee: therefore also that holy thing which shall be born of thee shall be called the Son of God.

12. Now, Mary reasoned with the angel as to how this could come to pass. In those days maidenhood was not particularly esteemed. The angel, however, approaches Mary and very gently tells her that she has found favor with God and man. He brings her the tidings that she should conceive and bear a son who shall be called the Son of God. In turmoil, she thinks, I am but a poor Cinderella, and I should become a mother and bear a son when I have had no relationship with a man? Who is going to believe me that I conceived on my own? She also feels that these tidings of the angel place her in danger of death. She wonders, too, when it becomes evident that she is pregnant and people ask about it, how will I then prove that I had no relationship with a man? The truth is, if the Lord God had not placed special protection over Mary, she would have been burned at the stake or stoned. Under the law of Moses, a woman who became pregnant with the child's father unknown was to be burned at the stake or stoned. So, because the normal sequence of events were to be suspended in this conception, Mary was afraid, and she asked what would happen to her.

13. Thereupon, the angel sums it altogether for Mary and says, If you try to analyze it from the standpoint of reason you could never conceive, or if you conceived, the penalty under the Law would be death. But the great difference in your case is that "The Holy Ghost

shall come upon thee." In other words, for you the Holy Spirit is the bridegroom, by whose excellent power and working you will conceive "and the power of the Highest shall overshadow thee." Almighty God will see to it that neither the devil nor the entire world will avail to fault you. You will become a mother and bear a son, but only God on high and the Holy Spirit will really understand how. Therefore, let it be our Lord God's concern in bringing it about. With him in control, who is there that can thwart his action? What power on earth can hinder God Almighty? Indeed, the power of the Most High will overshadow and envelop you, so that the devil will never even know how you became a mother, and this miracle of God will be hidden from the entire world. You will be recognized as the child's mother, but how you became a mother no one will know until it is time for it to be revealed. Do not be afraid, therefore, for nothing will harm you.

Mary said, Behold the handmaid of the Lord; be it unto me according to thy word.

14. That day, that moment when Mary assented to the angel Gabriel's announcement, Christ was conceived. In that hour when she said, "Be it unto me according to thy word," she conceived and became the mother of God; and Christ, therewith, became true God and true man in one person. Even though he is a tiny fetus, at that moment he is both God and man in Mary's womb, an infant, and Mary is the mother of God.

15. The Turks and the Jews make fun of this article of faith and feel that they have excellent reason to deride it. For that matter, we could banter about it as well as they. But as Christians, we must firmly hold onto this article of faith and never waver. From the beginning of time it has been prophesied that God's Son would become man and that his mother would be a virgin. The first prophecy given Adam and Eve soon after the fall (Gen. 3:15) stated: "And I will put enmity between thee and the woman, and between thy seed and her seed; it shall bruise thy head, and thou shall bruise his heel." God does not say the seed of the man, but rather the seed of the woman. Therefore, the mother of this serpent crusher must be a virgin. Later the patriarchs and the prophets also prophesied of this, until finally the beloved apostles proclaimed it to all the world. We have been

baptized into this faith and are called Christians because we believe and confess it to be true. Let us, therefore, persevere unwaveringly in this faith. And if, as time goes on, sectarian spirits deny it, let us take a staunch stand in behalf of it.

16. This article is really the bottom line. Christ wanted his beginning to be like ours, but without sin, because he wanted to sanctify us wholly. We begin life in sin, we are conceived in sin, born in sin, no matter whether we be emperor, king, prince, rich, or poor; every human being is conceived in sin according to Psalm 51:5. Only Christ has the distinction and the honor to have been conceived by the Holy Ghost's power. Since from our conception we are sinful, we are people whose flesh and blood and everything about us are soiled by sin, as indeed we see in ourselves; or when we look at those around us in the world, beset by evil desire, pride, multiple devils, and miserable unbelief. Thus we are conceived and born. For all of mankind is conceived and born in accord with creation's decree, as recorded (Gen. 1:28): "Be fruitful, and multiply, and replenish the earth." Christ could not be subject to such impure sinful conception and birth. He, indeed, was a genuinely true, natural human being, but not conceived or born in sin as all other descendants of Adam. That is why his mother had to be a virgin whom no man had touched, so that he would not be born under the curse, but rather conceived and born without sin, so that the devil had no right or power over him. Only the Holy Spirit was present to bring about the conception in her virgin body. Mother Mary, like us, was born in sin of sinful parents, but the Holy Spirit covered her, sanctified and purified her so that this child was born of flesh and blood, but not with sinful flesh and blood. The Holy Spirit permitted the Virgin Mary to remain a true, natural human being of flesh and blood, just as we. However, he warded off sin from her flesh and blood so that she became the mother of a pure child, not poisoned by sin as we are.

17. Thus what the angel spake came true: "He shall be great, and shall be called the Son of the Highest." For in that moment when she conceived, she was a holy mother filled with the Holy Spirit and her fruit is a holy, pure fruit, at once true God and truly man, in one person. In time, then, this godly mother gave birth to God's Son, a genuine man, but without any sin. Undoubtedly, his blood was red, his

flesh, white; he suckled at his mother's breasts, ate porridge, cried, and slumbered like any other child; but his flesh and blood were holy and pure. He is a holy person, the son of a pure virgin and God's Son, true God and man in one person.

18. On this day we preach about this article of faith, that our Lord Jesus Christ is true God and true man in one person conceived by the Holy Spirit and born of a virgin. It is an article of faith that provides unique comfort against the devil, yes, even over against all angels, as is stated in Hebrews 2:16: "He took not on him the nature of angels; but he took on him the seed of Abraham." He did not become God and an angel, but God and man. He does not assume the nature of angels, but that of Abraham's seed, a human being, flesh and blood. That is why he is called Immanuel, God with us; not just because he is around and with us, living among us and helping us. That would be well and good, but he became like us, of our nature. He assumed flesh and blood and bone like us, yet without sin, which is our lot. The devil hates to hear this joyful tiding, that our flesh and blood is God's Son, yes, God himself, who reigns in heaven over everything. Formerly, each Sunday, we used to sing Nicea's confession of faith, formulated at the Council of Nicea, in the words: *Et homo factus est,* "And he became man," and everyone fell to his knees. That was an excellent, commendable custom and it might well still be practiced, so that we might thank God from the heart that Christ assumed human nature and bestowed such great and high honor upon us, allowing his Son to become man.

19. It almost seems as though God is at enmity with the world. Present conditions are so shameful all around us in the world, as God allows murderous mobs and rabble, so much violence and so much misfortune to prevail, so that we might think God is only Lord and God of the angels and that he has forgotten about mankind. But here in our text we see that he befriends us humans like no other creatures, in the very closest relationship, and, in turn, we humans have a closer relationship with God than with any creature. Sun and moon are not as close to us as is God, for he comes to us in our own flesh and blood. God not only rules over us, not only lives in us, but personally became a human being.

20. This is the grace which we celebrate today, thanking God that he has cleansed our sinful conception and birth through his holy conception and birth, and removed the curse from us and blessed us. By nature our conception and birth are flawed and laden with sin. In contrast, Christ's conception and birth were holy and pure. Through his holy conception and birth our sinful nature, flesh, and blood are blessed and made holy. It is on this basis that we are baptized, so that by means of God's Word, the sacraments, and the Holy Spirit we might have the fruit of his holy conception and birth. May we always thank him for his grace and never become weary or surfeited in hearing and learning this. Unfortunately, most people in the world think they know it all, after they have heard it once.

THE DAY OF ANNUNCIATION TO MARY

Second Sermon—1534

Luke 1:26–38

1. We observe this festival in order to recognize God's inestimable grace and to thank him for the same. We should rejoice in this great miracle whereby God has graciously visited us poor mortals not merely by sending an angel who might redeem us, but by sending his only Son who not only speaks with us to bring us such a message, but clothes himself in flesh and blood and himself becomes a human. If a prince came to a group of beggars, desiring not only to give them money, but himself to become a beggar, then the beggars could hardly rejoice enough because of his kindly goodness. Such a deed, however, cannot compare with the grace God has shown us by his Son becoming a human being. This, therefore, ought to make us happy and awaken in us heartfelt thanks toward our dear Lord God.

2. Cursed and damnable is the man who hears this, but does not believe or accept it with joy. Indeed, the Jews, the Turks, the Tartars, and the pope do not believe it but regard God's sending of his Son to be little more than sending one's servant for a beer. We Christians, however, should learn how greatly God has honored us by allowing his Son to become a human being. How could he have come closer to us? When I take my child up into my arms and kiss him, people consider that to be very loving, God, however, does not do that, but, instead, takes on the nature which I and all other humans have, becomes a human being, eats and drinks as you and I do. He is born of a young maiden, as you and I are born of our mothers. The only difference is that the Holy Spirit engineered this conception and birth, while in contrast we mortals are conceived and born in sin. For this, we Christians should rejoice, that we have been so blessed. Our plight to be stained by sin and to be subject to death, brought on by

Adam's fall into sin, stands in contrast to what has been done for us by Christ who himself became man to redeem us from sin and death. The devil drew close to us, but not so close that he took on our nature. Even though he fell through arrogance and became separated from God, succeeding also to bring mortals to the same plight, yet he did not become a human, or draw as close to us as God's Son, who became our flesh and blood.

3. This, then, should be for our comfort, and we should thank our Lord God from the heart that he has bestowed this honor upon us in that he permitted his Son to become man, so that now our flesh and blood sits in heaven at the right hand of God; God and man in one person, reigning over heaven and earth. Blessed is the individual who believes and takes this to heart, that we humans are of a higher nature than the angels who are the sublimest of creatures. The Epistle to the Hebrews highly extols this (2:5): "For unto the angels hath he not put in subjection the world to come, whereof we speak." Also (vv. 16–17): "For verily he took not on him the nature of angels; but he took on him the seed of Abraham. Wherefore in all things it behooved him to be made like unto his brethren."

4. The angelic nature is far more sublime and glorious than the human nature; because of its great glory the angelic nature cannot live on earth. Now, Christ could have become an angel to be an individual who combined both godly and angelic nature, as divine and human nature are combined in Christ. But he did not wish to do that. God had prophesied to Abraham that of his lineage, Christ, God's Son, would be born. He who would bring a blessing unto all the Gentiles would be born of a virgin, a daughter of Abraham and David. In this, Abraham's lineage has been highly honored. But it pertains to us, too, even though we are Gentiles and not Abraham's descendants according to the flesh, because the promise is that from Abraham's seed all the Gentiles would be blessed. With this, we Gentiles, who are descendants of Adam and Noah, have the same promise which in time was repeated to Abraham. For that reason the promise and its fulfillment pertain to all people on earth. We certainly must find great joy in Christ's coming and in his becoming man, wholeheartedly accepting this fact, that God's Son became man. He did not come to us as a messenger with bad news, but united himself with us in be-

coming true man, never again to be separated from us, now that he has assumed our human nature. He came to us in such a way that he can never again be separated from us. Even though now we do not see him, it matters not. For he has said we should wait for the Day of Judgment; then we will see him, that he is clothed in our flesh and blood, and that we have the same body as he has.

5. Over this we should rejoice and thank God. Whoever does not is an unfortunate human being. For this is such great grace and glory that the angels might well be jealous that our Lord God ignored and passed them by not to assume their nature, but chose instead to accept our human nature though we belonged to the devil. Whoever cleaves and holds to Christ has as much as he, because Christ, indeed, has shared his inheritance with us if we believe that we are now united with him in joint estate. Even if the devil moves in on us, he cannot devour us because Christ became man in all things, like us except for sin. This selfsame Christ speaks to us in his Word: Remain in me, I will not leave you. Just as the devil, death, and hell could not hold me, so also they cannot hold you.

6. Today marks the day our salvation began, as God's Son became man and the divine and human nature were united in one person. Those are unfortunate individuals who dispute and doubt that two natures, divine and human, coexist simultaneously in Christ. That is why we must avoid arguments and sophistry here, for disputing will not avail us. In other matters one may argue and be erudite, but in an article of faith one should let the arguing be. Here the bottom line is that he who clings to God's mercy in simple faith and believes that God's Son became man for us has the benefit of this, namely, eternal salvation. Whoever does not believe has just the opposite.

7. Today we celebrate this miracle, namely, the bonding of God with man, as the two natures, divine and human, are united, never again to be separated, as we confess in the Creed: "I believe in Jesus Christ, his only Son, our Lord, who was conceived by the Holy Ghost, born of the Virgin Mary." That ensued on this day. At Christmas we hear how Christ was born, but today's significance is that the divine and human nature have come to be united in one person. This tiding the angel Gabriel announces as he tells the Virgin Mary that she shall

conceive and bear a son who shall be called the Son of the Highest. He shall sit on the throne of David eternally and be a King above all Kings. These are mighty and very extraordinary words, and it is a great miracle that a young woman could believe such words. If today these words were told to a virgin, she would surely laugh because human nature is difficult and loath to believe God's wondrous works. But Mary believed implicitly, not poking around for proof from reason.

8. It is true that she asked the angel how this could take place, but she did not question whether, according to reason, it would be possible. She merely asked whether for it to take place she was to marry a man. Then the angel answered, "No, the Holy Ghost will come upon you." It was not wrong for her to ask, therefore, because she was betrothed to Joseph. She did not wish to defy convention and become an adulteress, to be reviled by the Jews, but wished to keep an honorable reputation. But when she heard that the Holy Ghost would come upon her, she was satisfied and asked no more, but gave the angel her consent. In that moment she became the mother of God.

9. These are the details of today's celebration, as the articles of the Creed give it, in which we confess that our Lord God sent his only Son to us. We cannot send a messenger to him, but he has come to us himself, personally. We, as monks, sent messengers to our Lord God trying to appease him by our works. That was not right; rather, we are to believe that God's Son came to us, became man, was conceived by the Holy Ghost and born of the Virgin Mary. Therefore, we should not conduct our worship as though we first approach our Lord God, instead of him first coming to us; no, for he first came to us.

10. This is so because, first of all, we are created by him and through him. Then, next, when we were lost and damned because of sin, we were saved through his coming, if we believe that he has become like us and that our human nature has been united with God. Now if I wish to approach God, I must go to the Virgin's lap on which Christ lies, that is, I must listen to what the Christian faith teaches me, that Christ for my sake was conceived by the Holy Ghost and born of the Virgin Mary. When I embrace that and cleave to Christ, who was conceived and born for me, then I am on the right way to heaven, and Christ draws me to himself. Even if the devil wants to devour me, I still remain safely where Christ is. The devil cannot

hold me because Christ has come to me in flesh and blood as I have, but without sin. And, therefore, because he came to me and took to himself my flesh and blood, I must hold tightly to him.

11. That is the fundamental teaching which shows us the way to heaven. We should not succumb to foolish works with which to reconcile God as we did under the papacy. Christ, first of all, came to us and that we must hold fast in firm faith. When I do come to faith in him, then good works should follow—rightful fasting, rightful praying, and rightful giving of alms. Yet always I must remain firmly in Christ who alone gives me salvation, without my works or the merit of my deeds. That is what the Nicean Creed states: *Qui propter nos homines et propter nostram salutem descendit de coelo,* "Who for us men and for our salvation came down from heaven." It does not state: *Nos propter ipsum ascendimus in coelum.* We did not come into heaven for his sake; rather, Christ came from heaven for our sake. The devil forever and a day would very much like to have us stray from the right way. He knows very well that whoever believes in Christ will be saved. That is why he tries with might and main and all manner of tricks to mislead us. If he tears us from this article of faith, he has won. Whoever remains firm in this article of faith, cleaving firmly to Christ, tramples the devil under foot. Whoever falls away from Christ, him will the devil trample under foot. May our dear God grant us his grace, so that we remain steadfast in this article of faith and through Christ are finally saved. Amen.

HOLY TRINITY SUNDAY*

Luke 9:28–36

And it came to pass about an eight days after these sayings, he took Peter and John and James, and went up into a mountain to pray. And as he prayed, the fashion of his countenance was altered, and his raiment was white and glistering. And, behold, there talked with him two men, which were Moses and Elias: Who appeared in glory and spake of his decease which he should accomplish at Jerusalem. But Peter and they that were with him were heavy with sleep: and when they were awake, they saw his glory, and the two men that stood with him. And it came to pass, as they departed from him, Peter said unto Jesus, Master, it is good for us to be here: and let us make three tabernacles; one for thee, and one for Moses, and one for Elias: not knowing what he said. While he thus spake, there came a cloud, and overshadowed them: and they feared as they entered into the cloud. And there came a voice out of the cloud, saying, This is my beloved Son: hear him. And when the voice was past, Jesus was found alone. And they kept it close, and told no man in those days any of those things which they had seen.

1. We celebrate this feast today on the basis of the article which we believe and confess in our Christian faith, three persons of divine majesty, coequal in omnipotence, power, and eternal existence, God the Father, God the Son, and God the Holy Spirit. The bishopric at Mainz reflects today on the gospel about Nicodemus; the bishop at Brandenburg reflects on this gospel about Christ's transfiguration on Mt. Tabor; however, we are not compelled to use either. We might well use the gospel in Matthew 3 relative to the manifestation which occurred at Christ's baptism at the Jordan, the Gospel best suited for this festival, when we ought to preach about the article that there is one eternal God, and yet, three distinct persons in the one eternal, divine essence.

*Preached at the parish church, 1538.

2. At the Jordan each of the persons is distinctly revealed. For the forms in which the persons show themselves are very distinct from one another. The Father reveals himself in the voice that speaks from on high about his Son. The Son appears in the human form and is baptized by John in the Jordan. The Holy Spirit appears in the form of a dove and hovers above Christ. Here each person has his own particular form and image, discretely differentiated. And thus, clearly and plainly, three distinct persons of the divine essence are identified: the Father is a person distinct from the Son and the Holy Spirit; the Son, a person distinct from Father and Holy Spirit; and the Holy Spirit, a person distinct from Father and Son. And, yet, the Father is not without the Son and Holy Spirit. Also, neither the Father nor the Holy Spirit became man but the Son.

3. On Mt. Tabor the forms in which the persons manifest themselves are not too distinct from one another; however, the distinction in the three persons is clearly indicated. The Father manifests himself in the voice and speaks from out of the cloud, saying, "This is my beloved Son: hear him." The Son manifests himself in glorious form and brilliant countenance, and shines like the sun. The Holy Spirit manifests himself in a bright cloud, overshadowing the disciples, and instills faith in them. Here, too, there are three forms or manifestations that clearly indicate the three persons, even though the forms are not as far apart from one another as here. The Father speaks from out of the cloud not about himself but about the Son; hence the Father is a person distinct from the Son. And the Son, of whom the Father speaks, shows himself, here in glorified form; self-evidently the Son is a person distinct from the Father. And the Holy Spirit comes in a bright cloud and overshadows the disciples, thus also a person distinct from the Father and the Son. And yet all three persons are one eternal, all-powerful God.

4. This is what we confess in our Christian faith and should confess in accord with what the Gospels reveal. Before Christ's coming and birth this article was not as clear and evident in the Old Testament, as it is in the New Testament after the coming of Christ. For God suffered and bore with the Jewish people like a mother bears her child at her bosom. The patriarchs and prophets understood this article well; however, the common people clung in elementary belief

to faith in one God. Just so the untaught, simple people among us have persevered in the belief that there is one eternal, all-powerful God and they cannot grasp the distinction of the three persons like the more learned.

5. But the true faith in the New Testament is that we Christians publicly preach and confess that the three persons, Father, Son, and Holy Spirit, are one eternal God; also, that the Son became man, suffered and died for our sins, and rose again for our righteousness; and finally, that the Holy Spirit is sent by the Father and the Son, and by Word and Sacrament sustains, comforts, and strengthens us, forgives sins, raises the dead, and brings us to eternal life. This is the true Christian faith, and outside this faith there is no other valid faith on earth.

6. And this faith has incontestable testimony that evidences outwardly to its being the only true faith. The first is that no faith on earth, call it what you will, has subsisted as long as this faith. Adam and all the fathers from the beginning of the world have had this faith; and all saints to the end of the world will have this faith.

7. The second external proof is that no faith on earth has produced such miracles as has this faith. Reading the narratives of the Old and New Testament, a person will discover what great and excellent miraculous signs and wonders were performed by the saints as a result of this faith. In the Old Testament the holy fathers and prophets performed miracle upon miracle by this faith, yes, even raised the dead, as we read of Elijah and Elisha. Abraham had only 318 members belonging to his household, and yet with their help he slew and overthrew four powerful, mighty kings. Thus at all times, also in the Old Testament, this faith has rumbled and created a stir in the world, doing heroic things as the Epistle to the Hebrews (ch. 11) attests. What miracles Christ and the apostles performed in the New Testament! How easy it was for them to give sight to the blind, to give hearing to the deaf, to cleanse the lepers, to make the lame walk, and to raise the dead! And what deeds the believers performed after Christ and after the apostles! As Christ predicted (Mark 16:17–18): "These signs shall follow them that believe; In my name shall they cast out devils; they shall speak with new tongues; They shall take up serpents; and if they drink any deadly thing, it shall not hurt

them; they shall lay hands on the sick, and they shall recover." No faith on earth has ever performed such deeds. Therefore, it is outwardly sure evidence and proof that this faith is true. Other faiths in the world have not been able to perform such miracles, though they have attempted them; just as the magicians in Egypt could not imitate all the miracles which Moses performed.

8. Likewise, no faith on earth has so gallantly fought and contended against all attacks and persecution as has the Christian faith. The Turk, the pope, the Roman, Greek, and Persian empires have pitted themselves against this faith with all their power and might, but they could not prevail. To be sure, they killed many Christians and were intent on eradicating and exterminating them all; however, this faith persevered against them all, even though it stood all alone while all others assailed it. The Turk does not bother the faith of the Jews; but he is determined to root out the faith of the Christians. And when it is expedient to attack the Christian faith, Turks and Jews join forces, just as Pilate and Herod became one against Christ. Other faiths succumb even when not assailed, while the Christian faith survives even though assailed by enemies joined together. The pope especially, along with countless sects, has attacked the Christian faith, just as we see today still. Because the Christian faith is spreading into all directions during these latter days, the papists are mustering all their forces to fight against the Christian faith. But what is happening? The Christian faith bobs to the top and is gaining the victory, while the pope with his factions and the sects are going under. All such enthusiasts and sects ultimately join forces and become as one in contending against the Christian faith; however, the only thing they accomplish is to weaken themselves and strengthen the Christian faith. The Turk is mighty and powerful, possessing great wealth and property; but all this helps nothing, as the Christian faith abides.

9. The third external proof is that from the beginning of the world there has been no faith which has proclaimed and prophesied the future with such accuracy as has the Christian faith. The Christian faith has foretold with certainty how it and other faiths would fare in the world, up to the time when all faith will cease. Other faiths will perish but the Christian faith will endure until Judgment Day, when all teaching, preaching, and believing will become seeing, face to face.

The Turk cannot determine from his Koran how long his faith will endure, or what will finally happen to the Turks. But the Christian faith and Holy Scripture prophesy about Mohammed's beginning and end, as can be seen in the prophets Ezekiel and Daniel. And St. Paul prophesies about the pope's beginning and end, stating in 2 Thessalonians 2 that Antichrist would rear himself up as God, in the church of God, but Christ will destroy him with the breath of his mouth and by the radiance of his coming. He will annihilate him, he says, not with the fist, but with his mouth and Word, by the radiance of his coming.

10. Therefore, no faith can be the true faith but the one which has come down to us through the patriarchs, prophets, apostles, bishops, and teachers who followed in the footsteps of the apostles. This singular faith has prevailed and endured, and will prevail and remain until Judgment Day. Even though the devil and his likes have opposed it with all power, might, wisdom, and craftiness, and though today still there is no end to the factions and sects that take aim at this faith, nevertheless, it has survived and will survive until the end of the world. To some extent, we have silenced the Sacramentarians and Anabaptists; however, there is no denying it, the devil will stir up other strong tempests, but he will not prevail. He may persecute us, but our faith moves undaunted through it like a fine, well-built wagon through deep water. Dirt, of course, clings to the wagon, and mud, to the wheels; but the wagon lumbers through and does not allow its progress to be impeded. That's the way it is also with the Christian faith. The devil's filth and stench adhere to it, just as Christ and the apostles foretold that there would be many a provocation, but the Christian faith moves on through and endures.

11. This the Turk cannot say about his Mohammedan faith. He even acknowledges the Mohammedan faith will endure only until a new prophet, who establishes a new faith comes along. Yet he fumes and rages against the Christian faith and believes he will exterminate it. He thinks like this: Mohammed is master of the whole world; what can that poor little band that adheres to Christ accomplish? The Christian faith, however, is not overcome, but conquers and is victorious even though the Turk is responsible for many martyrs. Were the Christian faith a human, false thing, it would have perished long

ago, as other faiths in the world have perished. The faiths of the pope and Mohammed have been in existence now for a long time, but in the end have no permanence and will not endure. The Christian faith, however, will abide to the end of the world. Were it not the true faith, it, too, would come to an end, just as the faith of the heathen, along with their idols—Jupiter, Diana, and so on—have all fallen. Should the Turk fall or be converted, no new faith will appear, but the old faith, which has been from the beginning, and is still, and will be unto the end, will still be there.

12. These, now, are the outward evidences and proofs that our faith is the true faith: first, the long duration; that this faith has existed from the beginning of the world and will abide to the end of the world; second, the power, the fact that this faith overcomes all attacks, and that divine might and power are shown in this faith even against the gates of hell; third, the prophecy, that this faith foretells what is yet to come; and the prophecies tally well with history and will assuredly come true. These three properties no other faith has but the Christian faith alone! Therefore, and without question, it is the only true faith.

13. We should, therefore, abide by the old true faith, that in the eternal Godhead there are three distinct persons, Father, Son and Holy Spirit. This is the first and foremost article of the Christian faith, on which all the rest of the articles are dependent. We call it the article of the Holy Divine Trinity. *Dreifaltigkeit*, "threeness" is a very poor German word; for in the Godhead there is the greatest unity. Some call it *Dreiheit* (a group of three), but that really sounds almost like making fun of it. Augustine also bewails the fact that he has no suitable word for it. For I cannot say that just as there are three men or three angels so there are also three Gods, but I must perforce say that there is but one eternal God. True, in the Godhead there is a triad, but that very same triad constitutes the persons of the one Godhead; not three Gods, not three Lords, not three Creators, but one God, one Lord, one Creator, or as we say, there is but one divine essence, and yet there are three distinct persons, Father, Son, and Holy Spirit. I call it a *Gedrittes*, "trigon." However, the term *Dreifaltigkeit* sounds equally perplexing, and I am unable to give it a fitting designation.

14. Today's sermon should be about how our Christian faith requires us to profess that God, who has created heaven and earth, is one eternal God and yet three distinct persons, Father, Son, and Holy Spirit; and that the Son, and not the Father or the Holy Spirit, became man; and that the Holy Spirit writes this in man's heart through faith; also, that the Godhead of the Son and Holy Spirit is of the same eternal Godhead with the Father. The one who worships the Son does not worship a strange God, and the one who calls upon the Holy Spirit does, likewise, not call upon a strange God. In short, whichever person of the Godhead is addressed is addressing the true God.

15. Reference was made also in the Old Testament to this article, as Scripture testifies that Moses and the Prophets understood this article well. However, it is not as clearly presented as in the New Testament. For God led and nourished the Jewish people like a mother suckles her child. But in the New Testament, where the gospel is revealed, this article is not obscure or hidden, but made known in pictures and words; just as Christ taught that one should baptize in the name of the Father, and of the Son, and of the Holy Spirit. We continue to teach this article in Christendom, so that it remains firm that there is one eternal God, and yet that there are three distinct persons in the one, eternal, divine essence; also, that the Son became man, and that the Holy Spirit instills faith in man's heart. Whoever believes this is a Christian and a child of God; he lets Jews, Turks, sects, yes, also his own heart and reason be offended at this, but he adheres firmly to the Word which teaches us so to believe.

16. This is what this Gospel lesson teaches us. The Father speaks from out of the cloud about his Son; the Son stands there with glorified countenance, in dazzling white garments and is praying; the Holy Spirit appears in the form of a bright cloud. Three very distinct persons are present. For the one who speaks from out of the cloud is a person other than the one about whom he is speaking; and the one who appears in the bright cloud is a person other than the one who is speaking, and distinct from the one about whom something is being said. The one who is speaking is the Father and the one about whom he is speaking is the Son; he stands there and is praying; and the one who appears in the bright cloud is the Holy Spirit. Therefore,

according to the person, the Father distinguishes himself from the Son; the Son, from the Father and the Holy Spirit; and the Holy Spirit, from the Father and the Son. Yet the Father is not a God different from the Son, and the Son is not a God different from the Father, and the Holy Spirit is not a God different from the Father and the Son; but Father, Son, and Holy Spirit are one eternal God.

17. But now come the heretics to oppose this article with all their aggressiveness and cleverness. Some, like Arius, zero in on the Son and do not allow the Son to be God, saying, The Son is called God according to name, but not according to the divine nature and essence; that is, he is called a god through whom all other creatures were created, but is not true, natural, eternal God with the Father. Some focus upon the Holy Spirit and will not let him be God. But opposed to this is Holy Scripture, which powerfully testifies that the Son and the Holy Spirit are, in their essence, eternal God, coequal in omnipotence, power, and glory.

18. John 5:20–23 states: "The Father loveth the Son, and sheweth him all things that himself doeth: and he will shew him greater works than these, that ye may marvel. For as the Father raiseth up the dead, and quickeneth them; even so the Son quickeneth whom he will. For the Father judgeth no man, but hath committed all judgment unto the Son: That all men should honour the Son, even as they honour the Father. He that honoureth not the Son honoureth not the Father which hath sent him." What is to be made of this? Here the text says that the Son has the same power that the Father has; that the Son raises the dead and gives them life just as the Father does; and just like the Father is honored, so also should the Son be honored. Now, to raise and give life to the dead is a divine power, and a divine prerogative whereby the Father is glorified. Therefore, the Son must be eternal God with the Father. For if he were not true, eternal God, as Arius asserts, then the divine power and glory which the Father has could not be attributed to him.

19. Similarly, Holy Scripture testifies, and on the basis of Holy Scripture, the Nicene Creed confesses and teaches that it is the Holy Spirit who gives life and who with the Father and the Son is, at the same time, worshiped and glorified. Therefore, the Holy Spirit must also be true, eternal God, and of the same substance with the Father

and the Son. For were he not true, eternal God, then divine power and honor could not be attributed to him, that he gives life, and with the Father and the Son is likewise worshiped and glorified. For this the holy Fathers contended valiantly, upholding it against the heretics on the basis of Holy Scripture.

20. True it is, the persons of the Father, the Son, and the Holy Spirit are very distinct, so that Arius might argue on the basis of reason: The Son (Christ) is not God, but only man; and the heretics might argue, the Holy Spirit is not God, but a creature. But as widely as the persons are distinct, they yet converge here in divine power and glory, so that, as the Father raises the dead and gives them life, so also the Son raises the dead and gives them life, and the Holy Spirit raises the dead and gives them life. And as the Father is worshiped and honored, so also the Son is worshiped and honored; and, at the same time, the Holy Spirit is worshiped and honored with the Father and the Son. St. Paul makes a triad and distinguishes the persons of the divine essence from one another, and yet brings all three persons together again when he says in Romans 11:36: "Of him, and through him, and to him, are all things: to whom be glory for ever. Amen."

21. Accordingly, also, this Gospel very clearly distinguishes the persons. The Father speaks from out of the cloud, the Son stands there and prays, the Holy Spirit overshadows the disciples; yet in accord with the Christian faith, I must bring all three persons together again and say that the three persons, Father, Son, and Holy Spirit, are one, undivided, divine essence. The distinction in the persons is enormous. The Father speaks about the Son. The Son listens to the Father speak. The Holy Spirit hovers not over the voice, but over Christ and over the disciples. Voice, Son, cloud, these three are vastly distinct from one another. However, in accord with the Christian faith, I say that these three persons, Father, Son, and Holy Spirit, are one God, coequal in power, glory, and majesty.

22. For Holy Scripture teaches that all things are created by the Son and the Holy Spirit (Col. 1:16): "By him were all things created, that are in heaven, and that are in earth," and (Ps. 33:6): "By the word of the LORD were the heavens made; and all the host of them by the breath of his mouth." Similarly, Scripture teaches that the Son and

Holy Spirit raise and give life to the dead just like the Father does. These works, creating all things, and raising and giving life to the dead, powerfully compel and close in on the fact that these three distinct persons, Father, Son, and Holy Spirit, are one true God. For Holy Scripture says that there is but one Creator, one Restorer to life. These works, creating all things, and raising the dead, appertain to the one and only God. However, since they are attributed in Holy Scripture also to the Son and to the Holy Spirit, it follows that, even though the Son is a person distinct from the Father, and the Holy Spirit is a person distinct from the Father and from the Son, the Son and Holy Spirit with the Father constitute the one eternal God. This we cannot deny, because, if we did, we would then deny the whole of Holy Scripture. Therefore, Holy Scripture and the Christian faith compel us to distinguish the three persons in the one Godhead, and yet not to divide or separate the one Godhead or make three Gods, but confess and honor one God in three persons and three persons in one Godhead.

23. As Christians, it is not enough to know that we have but one God, like the Turks, who haughtily and flippantly advance the argument that there cannot be three family heads in the home; there must be only one. They think that they cinched the argument by so saying and look on us Christians as stupid geese and ducks, because they think we don't understand that we are worshiping three Gods. But woe to all those who thus have forced the Mohammedan belief on people with that sort of argument. Woe also to all those who write such things about us Christians in foreign lands and lie so brazenly about us.

24. We Christians are not the likes of stupid geese and ducks, or blocks of wood so thick that we don't understand that it is not only folly but idolatry to worship more than one God. We, therefore, also assert that there is only one God and Creator of all creatures, and do not make for ourselves three Gods, but believe and confess that there is only one God; and yet we affirm that this one God wants to be discerned and worshiped in three persons, Father, Son, and Holy Spirit, the Triune God. For God has revealed himself thus, that we should believe and confess that in his divine essence there are three distinct persons, Father, Son, and Holy Spirit. Nor in his creation are

there three distinct Creators; for there is but one; but in his inward divine essence there are three distinct persons. In his creation, viewing it externally from the side of the creatures, God is one, the one and only God and Creator of all creatures. But in his Godhead, reckoning inwardly within himself, there is not one person only but three distinct persons, Father, Son, and Holy Spirit.

25. In the creation and in his works, reckoning from the outside, the side of the creatures, we Christians are at one with the Turks, for we also say that there is no more than one God. But we say that it is not enough merely to believe that there is one God only. For that same one God, whom the Turks extol as being the only Creator of heaven and earth, has revealed himself also as being Father, Son, and Holy Spirit, three distinct persons and one eternal God. Therefore, Jews and Turks do us an injustice when they accuse us of being idolatrous, of worshiping three Gods; for we do not worship three Gods but one God only, with this difference, however, that we discern and worship the one true God, the Triune God, as he has revealed himself.

26. May God the Father through his Holy Spirit and for the sake of his dear Son, our Redeemer Jesus Christ, uphold us steadfastly in this faith against everything to the contrary that might assail us. Amen.

THE DAY OF ST. JOHN THE BAPTIST

First Sermon—1532

Luke 1:5–80

There was in the days of Herod, the king of Judæa, a certain priest named Zacharias, of the course of Abia: and his wife was of the daughters of Aaron, and her name was Elisabeth. And they were both righteous before God, walking in all the commandments and ordinances of the Lord blameless. And they had no child, because that Elisabeth was barren, and they both were now well stricken in years. And it came to pass, that while he executed the priest's office before God in the order of his course, According to the custom of the priest's office, his lot was to burn incense when he went into the temple of the Lord. And the whole multitude of the people were praying without at the time of incense. And there appeared unto him an angel of the Lord standing on the right side of the altar of incense. And when Zacharias saw him, he was troubled, and fear fell upon him. But the angel said unto him, Fear not, Zacharias: for thy prayer is heard; and thy wife Elisabeth shall bear thee a son, and thou shalt call his name John. And thou shalt have joy and gladness; and many shall rejoice at his birth. For he shall be great in the sight of the Lord, and shall drink neither wine nor strong drink; and he shall be filled with the Holy Ghost, even from his mother's womb. And many of the children of Israel shall he turn to the Lord their God. And he shall go before him in the spirit and power of Elias, to turn the hearts of the fathers to the children, and the disobedient to the wisdom of the just; to make ready a people prepared for the Lord. And Zacharias said unto the angel, Whereby shall I know this? for I am an old man, and my wife well stricken in years. And the angel answering said unto him, I am Gabriel, that stand in the presence of God; and am sent to speak unto thee, and to shew thee these glad tidings. And, behold, thou shalt be dumb, and not able to speak, until the day that these things shall be performed, because thou believest not my words, which shall be fulfilled in their season. And the people waited for Zacharias, and marvelled that he tarried so long in the temple. And when he came out, he could not speak to them: and they perceived that he had seen a vision in the temple: for he beckoned unto them, and remained speechless. And it came to pass, that, as soon as the days of his ministrations were accomplished, he departed to his own house. And after those days his wife Elisabeth conceived, and hid herself five months, saying, Thus hath the Lord dealt with me in the days wherein he looked on me, to take away my reproach among men. And in the sixth month the angel Gabriel was sent from God unto a city of Galilee, named Nazareth, To a virgin espoused to a man whose name was Joseph, of the house of David; and the virgin's name was Mary. And the angel came in unto her, and said, Hail, thou that art highly favoured, the Lord is with thee: blessed art thou among women. And when she saw him, she was troubled at his saying, and cast in her mind what manner of salutation this should be. And the angel said unto her, Fear not, Mary: for thou hast found favor with God. And, behold, thou shalt conceive in thy womb, and bring forth a son, and thou shalt call his name JESUS. He shall be great, and shall be called the Son of the Highest: and the Lord shall give unto him the throne of his father David: And he shall reign over the house of Jacob for ever; and of his kingdom there shall be no end. Then said Mary unto the angel, How shall this be, seeing I know not a man? And the angel answered and said unto her, The Holy Ghost shall come upon thee, and the power of the Highest shall overshadow thee: therefore also that holy thing which shall be born of thee shall be called the Son of God. And, behold, thy cousin Elisabeth, she hath also conceived a son in her old age: and this is the sixth month with her, who was called barren. For with God nothing shall be impossible. And Mary said, Behold the handmaid of the Lord; be it unto me according to thy word. And the angel departed from her. And Mary arose in those days, and went into the hill country with haste, into a city of Judah; And entered into the house of Zacharias, and saluted Elisabeth. And it came to pass, that, when Elisabeth heard the salutation of Mary, the babe leaped in her womb; and Elisabeth was filled with the Holy Ghost: And she spake out with a loud voice, and said, Blessed art thou among women, and blessed is the fruit of thy womb. And whence is this to me, that the mother of my Lord should come to me? For, lo, as soon as the voice of thy salutation sounded in mine ears, the babe leaped in my womb for joy. And blessed is she that believed: for there shall be a performance of those things which were told her from the Lord. And Mary said, My soul doth magnify the Lord, And my spirit hath rejoiced in God my Saviour. For he hath regarded the low estate of his handmaiden: for, behold, from henceforth all generations shall call me blessed. For he that is mighty hath done to me great things; and holy is his name. And his mercy is on them that fear him from generation to generation. He hath showed strength with his arm; he hath scattered the proud in the imagination of their hearts. He hath put down the mighty from their seats, and exalted them of low degree. He hath filled the hungry with good things; and the rich he hath sent empty away. He hath holpen his servant Israel, in remembrance of his mercy; As he spake to our fathers, to Abraham, and to his seed for ever. And Mary abode with her about three months, and returned to her own house. Now Elisabeth's full time came that she should be delivered; and she brought forth a son. And her neighbours and her cousins heard how the Lord had shewed great mercy upon her; and they rejoiced with her. And it came to pass that on the eighth day they came to circumcise the child; and they called him Zacharias, after the name of his father. And his mother answered and said, Not so; but he shall be called John. And they said unto her, There is none of thy kindred that is called by this name. And they made signs to his father, how he would have him called. And he asked for a writing table, and wrote, saying, His name is John. And they marvelled all. And his mouth was opened immediately, and his tongue loosed, and he spake, and praised God. And fear came on all that dwelt round about them: and all these sayings were noised abroad throughout all the hill country of Judæa. And all they that heard them laid them up in their hearts, saying, What manner of child shall this be! And the hand of the Lord was with him. And his father Zacharias was filled with the Holy Ghost, and prophesied, saying, Blessed be the Lord God of Israel; for he hath visited and redeemed his people, And hath raised up an horn of salvation for us in the house of his servant David; As he spake by the mouth of his holy prophets, which have been since the world began: That we should be saved from our enemies, and from the hand of all that hate us; To perform the mercy promised to our fathers, and to remember his holy covenant; the oath which he sware to our father Abraham, That he would grant unto us, that we being delivered out of the hand of our enemies might serve him without fear. In holiness and righteousness before him, all the days of our life. And thou, child, shalt be called the prophet of the Highest: for thou shalt go before the face of the Lord to prepare his ways; to give knowledge of salvation unto his people by the remission of their sins, Through the tender mercies of our God; whereby the dayspring from on high hath visited us, To give light to them that sit in darkness and in the shadow of death, to guide our feet into the way of peace. And the child grew, and waxed strong in spirit, and was in the deserts till the day of his shewing unto Israel.

About the Conception, Birth, and Preaching of John the Baptist.

1. Every Christian should know the real reason this day is celebrated so that his joy is not as shallow as that of the world, as though our Lord God allowed John to be born just for the sake of eating, drinking, dancing, and other such ordinary things.

2. We, after all, want to study this text not merely so that our bodies are fed, rejoice, dance, and frolic, but also that our spirits have something about which to rejoice.

3. The very first thing stated in this account is that God performs an extraordinary miracle in this conception and birth. For we hear that the father and mother had been married a long time without having begotten a child, and now, because of old age, they hold no hope of still getting a child. Moreover, the mother not only had grown old, but she was being subjected to reproach because by nature she was barren. Under these circumstances God performs a great miracle and enables them to have a son, and also sends the angel Gabriel from heaven to announce the good news to them. The father, Zacharias, is dumbfounded and loses his power of speech up until the child is eight days old. The mother gives the child his name, stating, He is to be called John, a name she had not heard from any human being. Thereupon, the father regains his speech and confirms what the mother had said, he himself saying, His name is John. The neighbors were all astonished. And upon the prompting of the Holy Spirit he preaches a beautiful sermon about this child.

4. Great are all these miracles whereby God indicates that this son would become an extremely important man. All who heard this are astonished and say, "What manner of child shall this be?" And Christ himself says that never has there been a mother's son greater than this John the Baptist.

5. The reason why he is commended so highly and above all the children of Adam is indicated by the angel in his first announcement, and the father also indicates this in his song of praise. The angel gives the reason as follows: "He shall be great in the sight of the Lord, and shall drink neither wine nor strong drink; and he shall be filled with the Holy Ghost, even from his mother's womb. And many of the children of Israel shall he turn to the Lord their God." The basic reason for his greatness, the angel explains, is that not only will there be extraordinary happenings at his conception and birth, but also that he will hold such a vital and signal office, in fact, the greatest and highest office among all of Adam's offspring. God will elevate John, Zacharias's son, to a higher trust and an office more weighty than any ever given to a human being. He will be the greatest of all, with the

exception of the Lord himself, who, even though he is least in the kingdom of heaven, is nonetheless greater than John. This was the very thing said by the angel to Zacharias shortly beforehand, "Thy wife Elisabeth shall bear thee a son, and thou shalt call his name John. And thou shalt have joy and gladness, and many shall rejoice at his birth."

6. The angel announces two kinds of joy. The first is that of the father Zacharias and the mother Elisabeth; for them to have a son in their old age was undoubtedly a matter of joy. Especially, however, was this true for Elisabeth, who had been a reproach for so long because of her infertility. For in the Old Testament it was a curse and malediction for a woman to be barren. Because Elisabeth for so long had to bear the shame of being barren, compelled to avoid other women, like an owl amongst birds, not being welcome in their midst, it was a joy for her to conceive a child in her old age. She herself acknowledges this by singing, "Thus hath the Lord dealt with me in the days wherein he looked on me, to take away my reproach among men." It was naturally a very happy joy, which both the father and the mother had over this child; and it was in no way a wrongful joy, for also the angel extols and proclaims it.

7. However, the second joy, which brings rejoicing not only to father and mother but also to others because of this child, is even greater, not simply because he was born as the result of such wondrous action; but on account of his office, because the office he would hold would afford great comfort and joy. That's what the angel wants to say with these words, "Many shall rejoice at his birth. For he shall be great in the sight of the Lord." And his father Zacharias explains this precisely in the words, "Thou, child, shalt be called the prophet of the Highest: for thou shalt go before the face of the Lord to prepare his ways; To give knowledge of salvation unto his people by the remission of their sins." In other words: You, child, will be the great, excellent teacher who will instruct the people on how they are to be saved. Up to now we had Moses, but he left us terribly entangled in sins and an evil conscience; we have been unable to escape death; there has been no help, no good counsel. It was just like things under the papacy, as some traipsed to St. James, or to Rome, and others tortured or fasted themselves to death; and yet, after trying lit-

erally everything, their consciences still had not been assuaged. Poor, miserable, distressed people, they did not know where to turn; they could find no comfort or rest in the face of sin and death. That was the way it went for them under Moses. But now, says Zacharias, things will be different. For here God has given us a child who will be the man to show people the way to find remission of sins.

8. "Thou, child, shalt be called the prophet of the Highest . . . To give knowledge of salvation unto his people." You will be the kind of preacher in whom all the world will rejoice. All who see and listen to you will rejoice, thank, and praise God for sending a preacher who would bring such comfort; with his finger he is pointing to the Son of God through whom remission of sins is promised to all who receive and believe in him. O how blessed are these fingers that point to Christ! O how blessed the ears that will hear the voice, "Behold the Lamb of God, which taketh away the sin of the world!" O how blessed the eyes that will see that blessed finger which is pointing to the offering which is to be made for the sins of the world! With these words, beloved John has indeed warmed the cockles of the hearts of people everywhere, who now know from his preaching how they may rid themselves of sin and be saved eternally.

9. For he says, "Behold the Lamb of God, which taketh away the sin of the world." Each human being must, of course, acknowledge that he, too, is part of the world. That is why this preaching of John causes rejoicing for people everywhere, if they will but accept it, for it manifests for them the true comfort over against sin. The sins of the whole world—yours, mine, and everybody's, excluding no one—he says, lie on this Lamb of God. Sins should no longer burden the world, terrify, condemn, or kill us, since they will be taken away from us and be made to lie upon the Lamb of God. That is true joy, that the beloved John brings such tidings into the world for the first time and points to Christ; he admonishes and urges everyone to cling to him and to expect such grace from him. Never since the world began has there been such preaching.

10. Other prophets have prophesied about Christ, how he would come and rid the world of sin; but neither Isaiah nor Jeremiah would have been able to say, Here now is the one whom you should receive, the one who must effect and accomplish it. Only John had the dis-

tinction of being able to cry out and point his finger at the person in whom remission of sins was actually to be found.

11. The real reason, therefore, for observing this festival, the day of St. John, is not because of his austere life, not because of his phenomenal birth, but because of his beloved finger, because of his message and his office. For such office and preaching had up till then not been heard in the world. No other man ever had such fingers as John's, with which he points to the Lamb of God and declares that he is the true Saviour who would redeem the world from sin. Everyone whom sin oppresses, who is marked for death, whom the devil and death terrify, needs only to look to the mouth and finger of this preacher who will teach and show him aright how he may receive remission of sins and peace with God. And this is the joy which all the world, not just Zacharias and Elisabeth, should have in John.

12. And about joy, the father, Zacharias, filled with the Holy Spirit, also speaks when in his hymn of praise he prophesies:

Blessed be the Lord God of Israel; for he hath visited and redeemed his people, And hath raised up an horn of salvation for us in the house of his servant David; As he spake by the mouth of his holy prophets, which have been since the world began: That we should be saved from our enemies, and from the hand of all that hate us; to perform the mercy promised to our fathers, and to remember his holy covenant; The oath which he sware to our father Abraham, That he would grant unto us, that we being delivered out of the hand of our enemies might serve him without fear, In holiness and righteousness before him, all the days of our life.

13. Dear old Zacharias is filled with joy over the birth of his son, not simply on account of his person, but that what is now occurring is what God has promised for so long through his prophets, how he would give David a son who would bring deliverance from all enemies, that is, from devil, sin, death, and hell, which are resolved to devour and condemn us. What is now happening, he says, is what all the prophets have written about and foretold that it would happen one day. Now it has happened! God be praised now and forever! It was promised, and all the prophets have offered consolation with the prospect of it, but they were unable to express or preach about it with the immediacy of my son John, who with his finger will point to this salvation and show it to men. Now the precious word will resound publicly, proclaiming the remission of sins.

And thou, child, shalt be called the prophet of the Highest: for thou shalt go before the face of the Lord to prepare his ways.

14. The father is very happy and yet does not talk boastfully about the holy, strenuous life which his son would lead, but extols only his word and preaching. Moreover, he does not in so many words call him a prophet like other prophets have been, but the kind of a prophet who would immediately precede the Lord. For he himself, the Lord, will now come and will himself preach. But before he does, this child, John, will appear on the scene, announcing, Look! This is the man through whom all the world will be saved; whoever has him has a gracious God. He will be undaunted and fearless all his life solely because of this man. No prophet had ever pointed to the man with his own fingers as John would.

15. John will prepare the way for the Lord, as when a prince travels, his most trusted servant precedes; the prince does not take the lead, but when people see the servant, then everything and everybody gives way. That's the way it will be with my son. He will go before and cry out, Make way! The Lord is coming, he is right on my heels; he will make his appearance and preach soon after I have finished preaching; he will suffer and submit to crucifixion, rise again from the dead, send the Holy Spirit, and will mandate that what I am preaching now be proclaimed openly in all the world.

16. That is the joy, then, that we should be filled with today; rejoice on account of John's mouth and finger, that whoever is terrified on account of his sins, whoever is seized with fear of death should look at this blessed finger and listen to this joyful, comforting voice, "Behold the Lamb of God, which taketh away the sin of the world." This finger we ought to praise mightily today and give thanks to God for the office of beloved John and his comforting words. For he is the ultimate of all prophets and preachers; no more comforting word and finger will ever appear than John's word and pointer.

17. Think back now and tell me, have we not been great fools under the papacy? Then all tributes from the pulpit and all exulting had to do with the austere life John led, drinking neither wine nor strong drink, eating locusts and wild honey, clothing himself in a coat of camel's hair. Of what help is that to you and me? or of what benefit? Is it not true that if a person merely focuses on John's person he will

never be able to draw any comfort from that? For even though it was God who imposed this harsh life on John so that people should all the more take note of his preaching and all the sooner believe, since he was not some wretched individual, but a man who lived a singular life like no others in order to glorify and promote the gospel, such things do not help us today; they produce no special joy for us. However, John's word and his preaching comfort and gladden the whole world, whoever will simply accept that John's mission is to point his finger toward him who is the pinnacle of joy and comfort, namely, to the Lamb of God who takes away the sin of the world. With his finger he points out this Lamb, not for the sake of geese, cows, stone, and wood, but for us humans, to us who are poor, distressed sinners, that we should receive him and take comfort and rejoice in what he has to offer. And Zacharias expounds further as regards John's preaching, in what way it would be the preaching of a new message for the world, saying:

To give knowledge of salvation unto his people by the remission of their sins.

18. Such preaching brought comfort and taught people correctly how they are to be saved. The Jews had the Law, that part of doctrine which is preached so that we learn what we are to do and not do. Indeed, this knowledge is wonderful and great, but it bodes evil for us because we are unable to follow it. For, since we know that God has imposed the Ten Commandments on us and wants us to keep them (yet we must confess that we do not and cannot keep them), it follows that such knowledge of the Law has no other effect than to cause a person to fear God and expect his wrath and punishment. For this reason St. Paul says that the Law works wrath, the Law kills and damns and is like a writ of judgment against us (Rom. 4, 2 Cor. 3, Col. 2).

19. On the other hand, John was now to come and give God's people another knowledge, which was not a recognition of sin, wrath and death, but a knowledge of salvation, that is, a preaching whereby people might learn how they might be rescued from death and sin. Of this art, the world knows nothing. Under the papacy as a monk, I, too, knew nothing about this skill. I knew that I was in need of one who would save me from sin and death; but where I should find such a saviour, I did not know. I called to St. Anna, who was to be my help-

er in time of need. But John was to be a master of this art and give people the knowledge of salvation, that is, bring into the world the kind of preaching through which people might truly learn how to be saved, how to overcome sin and death.

20. But how was all this to come about? What was the doctrine that he would expound? This Zacharias explains when he states, Which is for the remission of their sins. Whoever wishes to know how to be saved must understand that it occurs by grace alone and through nothing else. And that's what John preached: "Behold the Lamb of God, which taketh away the sin of the world"; also: "Of this fulness have all we received, and grace for grace. For the law was given by Moses, but grace and truth came by Jesus Christ" (John 1:16–17). There are many such assertions in his sermons. From them we see how earnestly he advocates Christ and his grace. In other words John wanted us to understand that good works help nothing to salvation; I, too, have fasted and lived an austere life, so that if good works contributed toward salvation, then certainly my works should have helped.

21. Certainly, John, by outward standards, lived a holy life, just as Christ himself did in his life among people, reclining at meals, drinking wine, eating meat, dressing in garments of linen and wool. John, however, lived in the wilderness, drank water, ate wild honey and locusts, wore a cloak of camel's hair. Nevertheless, he says, such an austere life helps nothing towards attaining heaven; to achieve that, only remission of sins will avail. This is what we need to learn and learn well. True, we should be upright and live a godly life. But to be saved will happen only through the remission of sins; each person must come to know God, know that he is gracious and wants to forgive sins, and say, Lord, I cannot measure up to your commands; I know not how to stand before you with my works; for John was much holier than I, and yet he did not base salvation on his holiness. I want so much to guard against sin, to be righteous, to live chastely and virtuously; but that does nothing to save me. The only thing that saves is what you, O God, have preached to me through John, that I must be saved through the remission of sins.

22. Now, then, it follows from this that the whole world is stuck fast in sins, yes, is itself sin. For where there is no sin, there one does

not need remission of sins. On the other hand, where one has need of remission of sins, there, indeed, sin must be. Since now the world must be saved through the remission of sins, it follows that the world is nothing but sin. And, moreover, all people without exception are sinners, and in turn, each one is damned. So, if they are to be saved, the only way for them is to have their sins forgiven. However, as John teaches, this occurs alone through the Son of God; he is the Lamb who must save us, because all our sins lie on him. For were sins to lie on us, for us to bear, we would be damned and lost forever, and it would be impossible for anyone to come into heaven. So, the ground and final cause for the remission of sins is that the Son of God has borne our sins for us.

23. Rightly understanding John's preaching is to know how man is saved, namely, solely through the remission of sins. If we are saved through the remission of sins, all other ways of eradicating sin are thus excluded. This is something the pope and his crowd will not tolerate; daily they sing the Benedictus in the matins but do not understand it; rather, they contravene it; and when we teach that one must be saved through the remission of sins and not through good works, they condemn it as the greatest heresy.

24. From whence, indeed, does remission of sins emanate? Who is responsible for it? Zacharias answers this very precisely, saying:

Through the tender mercy of our God; whereby the dayspring from on high hath visited us.

This means certainly, as I understand it, that all merits and good works are excluded from remission of sins so that no one could say he merits it. The Virgin Mary was holy, John the Baptist led an austere life; but was it for this reason that they received remission of sins? No, says Zacharias, remission of sins results solely from this, that God is merciful and out of his mercy he sent and gave his Son to make payment for us, and, thereby, through him we are saved. That is why the teaching is that remission of sins does not result from our own merits or from our good works, but through God's precious mercy whereby he was prompted within his own heart to love us. By our sins we had merited the fires of hell, but God looked on us in his boundless mercy. This is the reason he sent his Son, and for the sake of his Son he now remits our sins.

25. John, moreover, preaches an especially great sermon about our dear Lord Jesus Christ. He gives him a special name and calls him "The dayspring from on high," that is, above all creatures in heaven. Just as the sun sheds light when it rises, so the Son goes forth from the Father in eternity. Christ himself speaks in those very terms (John 3:13): "No man hath ascended up to heaven, but he that came down from heaven, even the Son of man which is in heaven." For his existence does not begin when first he is conceived and born on earth; he issues forth from the heights of heaven here to the earth. He has visited us, has come to us on earth, he says, and has given remission of sins to us poor sinners who, otherwise, would have to be damned eternally. That is pure grace and mercy.

26. Therefore, we cannot boast that in word or deed we contributed to it; for no one knew about such things. But John is the first to point with his finger and direct us to him, when otherwise we, just like the Jews, might pass on by. The Jews saw him playing in the streets just like any other child, saw him build things, drill into wood, and so forth. In such menial form who would then have thought of him as being the dayspring from on high and the Lamb of God, were John not to have pointed to him and made him known to us? Apart from that the Jews are still annoyed at him and say, O, this is the carpenter, Mary's son, the poor widow's child; his brothers and sisters are all here with us (Mark 6:3). Accordingly, there is no one here who can boast that he has merited it, since he knew nothing about it, and would not have known about it, were John not to have proclaimed it and pointed him out with his fingers.

To give light to them that sit in darkness and in the shadow of death, to guide our feet into the way of peace.

27. At this point, Zacharias concludes his thanksgiving song of joy, and he includes not only his own people, the Jews, but also the Gentiles, by saying that the whole world sits in death and darkness. Regardless how long we live, the final moment never fails to make its appearance; someone will finally close our eyes; everything is subject to death and has to die, since no person is free or exempt from it. Of them who are to be buried in the earth and rest in darkness, Zacharias says, God has shined a light, which should shed light upon the dead buried in the earth. If they have believed in the Lamb and have

been baptized, they will have a light, and a light of life that will illumine them even in death and sustain them so that the devil cannot harm them.

28. This, now, is the joy, not a wildly exciting, worldly joy with dancing and leaping, with eating and drinking, or the likes of what is prompted by wealth and riches, or a worldly kingdom. It has to do with something greater and better, namely, how we remain alive after we are dead and have decomposed in the earth, how we become righteous when we are in him, how we escape out of hell into heaven, out of damnation into salvation. For, ultimately, we must still go down there and see and listen to the devil. This generally happens at the final moment as one is grappling with death; every Christian must reach the point when he truly is conscious of sin and death. Then there is no other help or consolation than to look where John's finger is pointing and see the Lamb, who bears the sin of the world and comforts us with his word: "He that believeth in me, though he were dead, yet shall he live." With such great matters, sin and eternal death, righteousness and eternal life, comes the joy which fills our hearts on this holy day of St. John, and we ought to thank God for giving us such a prophet, for letting us see his finger and hear his preaching.

29. The devil and the pope have other fingers, which point to tonsures and hoods and commandments of men; but that is hellish fire. For if good works were destined to save, they would have saved John also, and he would have taken comfort in them. However, he says nothing about his good works and austere life; and he says to Christ (Matt. 3:14): "I have need to be baptized of thee." He seeks and desires nothing else but that God would be gracious to him through Christ, saying also (John 1:16): "Of his fulness have we all received, and grace for grace." Accordingly, the Virgin Mary and all the saints have, likewise, been saved by grace, through Christ's righteousness and merits.

30. This is St. John's sermon concerning the knowledge of salvation through the remission of sins. A treasure and wisdom which every Christian should have, that the remission of sins is the only way to salvation. John brought this sort of preaching into the world for the first time, pointing to the Lord Christ with his finger; therefore, he well deserves to be loved and to have us rejoice because of him.

For "John" means one who stands in grace, a blessed, wonderful, loveable man, whom everyone gladly looks up to. He is a true John; his preaching is pure joy. It is a name he should have because of his office, not because of his life or his person, else he would be called "eccentric" for his life is of little use to us and brings us no joy, but his preaching brings comfort and joy.

31. Your youngsters and strapping youth should note well that this day we celebrate not for the sake of dancing, eating, and drinking, but because John teaches us how one is to be saved. Everyone, therefore, ought to praise and thank God for having given us beloved John, because through him we have received the joyful word and the blessed finger to know where salvation and eternal life are to be found. Therefore, the purpose of this festival service is to extol God and his mercy, not the person of St. John, so that God might receive thanks from us for giving us his Son and such comforting preaching, because now we need fear neither sin nor death, but may take comfort in God's goodness and grace. God grant this to us all. Amen.

THE DAY OF ST. JOHN THE BAPTIST

Second Sermon—1533

Luke 1:5–80

Concerning the festival, office, and preaching of John

1. Luke, the Evangelist, records that the angel of the Lord appeared to Zacharias in the temple beside the altar of incense. He announced to him that his wife Elisabeth would bear him a son, that he was to call his name John, that he would be a source of joy and gladness, and that many would rejoice at his birth. He also records the miraculous circumstances surrounding John's birth, namely, that he was conceived of aged parents, of a mother who had been barren, and that he was filled with the Holy Spirit while still in the womb, that John's birth, in fact, was particularly notable, much different than that of other human beings.

2. It was not for John's sake that all this was written, but for the sake of his office, in that he, as his father Zacharias stated in his Benedictus, would be teaching the way to obtain forgiveness of sins and entrance into heaven, not by one's own works and merit, as the Pharisees had hitherto taught, but by grace alone, through the tender mercy of God, who gave his beloved Son for the sin of the whole world.

3. Now, in spite of the fact that all papists used to sing this Benedictus of Zacharias in their churches every day, and even now continue to do so in their morning matins, they have never understood it, nor do they understand it now. They have always kept this festival, and observe it still, but only for the sake of St. John himself and his ascetic life. But we do not observe this day for St. John's sake, but for God's sake. We praise and glorify him because he brought the beloved John into the world and made him the preacher he was, one

whose word of proclamation was that the world cannot be saved in any other way than by the forgiveness of sins.

4. This was the nature of John's preaching, as Zacharias foretold, and his sermons themselves testify. He rebuked and scolded the Pharisees and Jews for teaching that men must obtain salvation by personal piety and holiness. He called them a generation of vipers, and admonished them to exhibit the fruits indicative of a genuine repentance. In other words, as if by a clap of thunder, he hurled everything into one lump, calling all to repent, those whose repentance was not genuine and who supposed that they had already repented, and the counterfeit "holy men" who fancied themselves as not in need of repentance. And his preaching focused solely on the Lamb, who would bear the sins of the world, that is, of all mankind born into the world.

5. So we ought to thank our dear Lord God on this day of remembrance, for giving us the man John the Baptist, who was the first to preach the gospel for us, and to direct us to the Lamb of God. To be sure, the prophets preached Christ and pointed to him, but from afar, as to one who was to come in a future time. But John not only preached Christ by saying that no one can be saved except through the forgiveness of sins and the Lamb of God, who bears the sin of the world, but also pointed with his own finger to the Lamb declaring, Behold the Lamb of God.

6. Formerly, before John came pointing with his finger, no Jew dreamed that this Lamb would bear the sin of the world, and that this Jesus, the son of Mary, would be the Lamb of God. They could not have come to the conclusion by themselves, that he would be the one, although he had already come into their midst, and was standing, walking, and living in their midst. But when John came, he declared, This is he, the one who shall do it. Zacharias says the very same thing in his Benedictus: John would be a prophet of the Most High, who would walk before the Lord to prepare his way, and teach the people the way of salvation, that is, the forgiveness of their sins; in other words, God in heaven would entrust to this preacher the task of pointing out the Lamb of God, through whom the people would obtain pardon for their sins and be saved.

7. So let us observe this day of John the Baptist with joy, not because we adore John himself, a thing which he would not expect of

us or even want, but rather because we acknowledge his office and are glad that he pointed to the Lamb of God, so that we might learn to follow him to whom he pointed. For John took no honor upon himself, but gave it to him who deserved it. "Whose shoe's latchet," he said, "I am not worthy to unloose" (John 1:27); and "I am not the Christ, but I am sent before him. He that hath the bride is the bridegroom: but the friend of the bridegroom, which standeth and heareth him, rejoiceth greatly because of the bridegroom's voice" (John 3:28–29). The pope has given honor and worship to John, and ignored the Lamb of God. He has done the same with respect to the other saints. He has honored and worshiped the virgin mother of God, and ignored the infant Jesus in her lap. John would not tolerate that; instead, he turned all away from himself and pointed to the Lamb alone. "I indeed baptize you with water unto repentance: but he that cometh after me is mightier than I, whose shoes I am not worthy to bear: he shall baptize you with the Holy Ghost, and with fire" (Matt. 3:11). In other words, I am only a tool of God's; I preach and baptize in order to bring you to the Lamb of God. I am not the Lamb; but he is the Lamb of God, who bears the sin of the world. Therefore, do not look to me, but to the Lamb.

8. We must understand this before we rightly perceive and know the Lamb. Then, if we know the love and grace which God has shown in him, giving us the Lamb, through whom we have forgiveness of sins and eternal life, it will follow that we will also demonstrate this love to our neighbor, doing good to him, being gracious to him, and forgiving his sins if we suffer injury or hurt at his hands, just as God has forgiven our sins. If we do this, we shall be true Christians and pleasing to God. Let these few words about the beloved John, whose birth and preaching we rejoice in, suffice for the present and let us thank God for them.

THE DAY OF ST. JOHN THE BAPTIST

Third Sermon[*]

Mark 6:17–29

On the Beheading of John

For Herod himself had sent forth and laid hold upon John, and bound him in prison for Herodias' sake, his brother Philip's wife: for he had married her. For John had said unto Herod, It is not lawful for thee to have thy brother's wife. Therefore Herodias had a quarrel against him, and would have killed him; but she could not: For Herod feared John, knowing that he was a just man and an holy, and observed him; and when he heard him, he did many things, and heard him gladly. And when a convenient day was come, that Herod on his birthday made a supper to his lords, high captains, and chief estates of Galilee; And when the daughter of the said Herodias came in, and danced, and pleased Herod and them that sat with him, the king said unto the damsel, Ask of me whatsoever thou wilt, and I will give it thee. And he sware unto her, Whatsoever thou shalt ask of me, I will give it thee, unto the half of my kingdom. And she went forth, and said unto her mother, What shall I ask? And she said, The head of John the Baptist. And she came in straightway with haste unto the king, and asked, saying, I will that thou give me by and by in a charger the head of John the Baptist. And the king was exceeding sorry; yet for his oath's sake, and for their sakes which sat with him, he would not reject her. And immediately the king sent an executioner, and commanded his head to be brought: and he went and beheaded him in the prison. And brought his head in a charger, and gave it to the damsel: and the damsel gave it to her mother. And when his disciples heard of it, they came and took up his corpse, and laid it in a tomb.

1. We learned in the previous sermon about our beloved John the Baptist, how his conception and birth were announced by the angel of the Lord, how he came to be conceived and born, and how his fa-

[*]Preached publicly at the parish church, 1534.

ther Zacharias foretold what his office would be. It was a particularly glorious episode, everything proceeding beautifully: Angels, mankind, heaven and earth rejoicing, with great things being said about him. His conception and birth are one great marvel. Now we want to learn about the circumstances surrounding his death so that we might encompass the whole of his life and deeds. That is, we will bring together the observances of his conception and birth, and of his death.

2. The details of his life, the things that he did as he was growing up and prior to the time that he entered into his office, are passed over in silence, except that Luke 1:80 states: "The child grew and waxed strong in spirit, and was in the deserts till the day of his shewing unto Israel." He was raised by his godly parents, going into the wilderness, perhaps, at the age of eight years. He was in the wilderness until the age of thirty. Then he came out of seclusion and preached. Now then, the forerunner John, and his Lord, the Christ, were both nearly the same age. For because he was conceived six months before Jesus, he naturally was also born six months before him. And in the year that John came forth and preached, Christ was just about to come forth himself to preach. So John commenced this public ministry a short time before Christ. According to Luke, chapter 3, John began preaching and baptizing at the Jordan in the fifteenth year of the emperor Tiberius. Now it is certain that Christ was crucified in the eighteenth year of Tiberius. So, according to our calculation, John and Christ preached at about the same time, except that John began a little earlier, and Christ preached a little longer than John. John did not preach much over two years, Christ not much over three years. It was but a short time for both the messenger and his Lord. In the fifteenth year of the emperor Tiberius they began to preach and by the eighteenth year of Tiberius they both were gone. Still, the messenger came into his reward earlier than his Lord; for he occupied the preacher's office for barely two years or perhaps slightly longer.

3. John, as we learn from Luke 3:3, "preached the baptism of repentance for the remission of sins." He went along the Jordan, traversing that entire region. He did not preach in one locality only, but covered the whole area surrounding the Jordan, and for these two

years he preached and proclaimed: "Repent, for the kingdom of heaven is at hand." He drank neither wine nor strong drink, but water, ate locusts and wild honey, and led an ascetic existence. He kept it before the people that the kingdom of heaven was at hand, he baptized, and he pointed out Christ with his finger. While John was preaching in this way, Christ soon appeared and also began to preach. These events followed in quick succession. As soon as John began to preach, within half a year, or at the most a whole year, Christ began likewise to preach. And in three years both were dead.

4. There is no denying that this is a very short period of time, and does not agree well at all with the lofty testimony of John given by the angel, by his father Zacharias, and by Christ himself. When the angel brought the tidings of his birth, he prophesied glorious things about his office, adducing Scriptures from Isaiah and Malachi: "He shall be great before the Lord," and "He shall walk before the Lord in the Spirit and power of Elijah." Zacharias said, "And thou, child, shalt be called the prophet of the Highest, for thou shalt go before the face of the Lord, to prepare his ways." Christ said, "Among them that are born of women there hath not risen a greater than John the Baptist." With such an exalted chorus still ringing in the ears, there then follows his activity of such modest proportions. John preached barely two years, without performing any miracles; he did nothing more than baptize and preach repentance for the remission of sins. His testimonies in the Old Testament were from the prophets Isaiah and Malachi; in the New Testament from the angel of the Lord, and from Christ himself. His father Zacharias exalted his office above that of any other prophet. And from all this glorious testimony came nothing more than John's periodic preaching of repentance and his baptisms up and down the Jordan, and this for only two years, after which he was beheaded. For he preached not only in the land of Judæa, but came also into Galilee to King Herod; for he would have liked to convert him. And because Herod liked to hear him, he must have been a frequent visitor at court, hoping to win Herod. But Herod expressed his gratitude by ordering off with his head. He threw him into prison and had him treacherously beheaded for the sake of that whore Herodias.

5. And that is the end of it; so died the great man without equal, so extolled by men and angels, indeed, by the Lord himself, who had to endure such a shameful death on account of a wicked and desperate adulteress and, if that were not all, secretly beheaded in the prison, and his head brought on a platter to that woman in her chamber, so she could savor the fulfillment of her wicked desire. It would have been no surprise if the fires of hell had engulfed the whole scene. This man was acclaimed in the most glorious way by the prophets, by the angel, and by Christ, yet was not to preach for more than two years. And his preaching was to cost him his head, which the daughter of that whore brought to the dance, exhibiting it before the guests and afterwards bringing it to her mother. Such a miserable death for so outstanding a man.

6. When Christ heard of it, he acted as if it meant nothing to him, and as if he were totally untouched by the unjust death of his dearest and most trusted friend. He did not become angry, did not curse, made no threats; in a word, he did nothing. He ought reasonably to have sent down lightning and thunder on the dance; but he did nothing more than withdraw into the wilderness. Who wants to serve a master who allowed his dearest friend and greatest saint, his own messenger, to be so shamefully condemned to death, without doing anything about it? They say, moreover, that the pagans and barbarians descended upon the country and scattered John's remains after his death, and, what is even worse, that they burned them completely to ashes. The nuns at Rome boast that they possess John's head. Others boast that they possess the finger with which he pointed to Christ. But, according to the histories, John's body was taken from his grave, along with the remains of other saints, and burned. Is this what it means to honor the great and holy man, so highly extolled in the Scriptures, the likes of whom, after Christ, the world has never seen, who was to preach for such a brief period of time, barely two years, without performing a single miracle, then die such a disgraceful death, and after his death allow his remains to be scattered and his body burned to ashes?

7. Now if anyone wants to be a Christian, and a preacher in particular, let him learn God's way of dealing with his children and his beloved saints. What are we with our afflictions and persecutions, in

comparison with that holy and incomparable man, John, who endured such deplorable things both during his lifetime and after his death? And indeed Christ, the Son of God himself fared no better. He did not preach much longer than three years either, before he was nailed to the cross. Those must have been particularly infamous days under Annas, Caiaphas, Herod, Pilate, and Tiberius, if, for the sake of his office, John, by the dance, and for the sake of his good works, and Christ on the cross, had to suffer such ignominious deaths. These two illustrious men, the likes of which the world had never seen, and never will see again until the end, were condemned to death within a year and half of each other.

8. But this is the nature of God's wrath against the land, which could not endure these two eminent preachers to occupy their offices for longer than three years. For this people was forever putting its prophets to death. No sooner did one appear, but he was swiftly put to death, as Christ laments in Matthew 23:37–38: "O Jerusalem, Jerusalem, thou that killest the prophets, and stonest them which are sent unto thee, how often would I have gathered thy children together, even as a hen gathereth her chickens under her wings, and ye would not!" Mark it well: The end will come! "Behold, your house is left unto you desolate." Since they had carried this to such an extreme and had delighted to bring the blood of the prophets upon themselves, to fill up the measure of their fathers, God snatched up John the Baptist and Christ his Son quickly, so that John might be the sooner gathered unto the prophets, and Christ into his kingdom, and that the bloodthirsty Jews, Pilate, and Herod might receive what they deserved. For, about forty years after the deaths of Christ and John, the end came for the Jews: the city of Jerusalem was razed, the temple torn down and burned, the kingdom, the priesthood, the temple service, the land, the people, everything was eradicated. After that, Christ sent the gospel into all the world, and brought down all the mighty, all the learned, and all the wise into confusion.

9. So the two most exalted men the world has ever known fulfilled their offices in the shortest amount of time. Other prophets, bishops, and martyrs occupied their offices for longer periods. These two, John and Christ, were the greatest and most exalted preachers ever to come into the world, and ran their race in the shortest amount of

time. But this occasioned no loss to them, but was a sign of the fearful wrath about to come against the Jewish people. Because God snatched up these two preeminent preachers so quickly, I would not have wanted to be left if I had lived in those days.

10. Whenever God takes the godly away, it is always a sign of his wrath; as the prophet Isaiah testifies (Isa. 57:1–2): "The righteous perisheth and no one layeth it to heart: and merciful men are taken away, none considering that the righteous is taken away from the evil to come. He shall enter into peace: they shall rest in their beds, each one walking in his uprightness." Here both things are seen: Whenever God takes the righteous away and separates the wheat from the chaff, it is a sign that he will punish the remainder, and kindle the chaff so as to burn it with fire. But this occasions no harm to them, for they come out of tribulation into rest. Our Lord God does not want them to see the calamity which is about to ensue. God comforts the godly king Josiah with this very thing in 2 Kings 22:20 saying: "I will gather thee unto thy fathers, and thou shalt be gathered into thy grave in peace; and thine eyes shall not see all the evil which I will bring upon this place." So the godly suffer no harm when God recalls them from this evil world through death, but the world ought to be afraid; for it is a sign that calamity is not far off, and things are going to get ugly.

11. So John was taken away, Christ was crucified, and the apostles put to death. And the world rejoices. These good men, John, Christ, and the apostles, departed from the world, and no one said, Let us voice our complaint to God, that the holy men are dying such miserable deaths! Alas, what is in store for us? Instead, all laughed, mocked, and were in high spirits. But as we said, our Lord God willed the premature deaths of his saints so that he might pour out his fury on the Jewish nation so much the sooner.

12. At the present time we see the same phenomenon. The gospel is persecuted more viciously than ever, and the godly are taken away in order that God's present wrath may be unloosed the sooner. For this is what you will experience: As soon as those are gone whose presence still restrains it, hellfire shall rain down on the world and there shall be nothing but lamentation and misery. So God allows the righteous to perish, lest they see the impending calamity. Instead,

they enter into their chambers and repose in peace. When we enter into our rest, we will say, Ah, dear world, you never asked for my preaching, or my consolation, or my rebukes; instead, you laughed, mocked my words, and killed the godly. Now we lie down in our graves to sleep and quietly rest. When adversity and anguish overtake you, we shall neither see nor hear it, as you refused to hear us. Instead, we will be sleeping peacefully and taking our rest, and leaving you to cry out to no avail.

13. I do not like being a prophet and prophesying such things, but the Lord rarely allows his prophets to witness the calamity which they prophesy, and of which they warn the people. Jeremiah is virtually the only prophet to see for himself the fulfillment of his prophecy in having to live through the captivity and the destruction of Jerusalem; as for the rest, generally speaking, God took them away to spare them the sight of the coming catastrophe. Therefore, we ought not to be angry with God for dealing with his saints in this way, as if he did not know them, or did not care about them, letting the world go on in its perversity, as if they were right, after all. But it does not matter to the righteous in the least, for they are promoted to their eternal rest; but the world is hastening its own ruin and storing up the wrath of God, and on that account it must ultimately be destroyed.

14. So John preached barely two years, and then departed from this world. Christ accomplished all his preaching, teaching, and miracle-working in three, or at the most, in three and a half years, and then he was gone. He must have preached and performed miracles almost every day, in order to finish his course. What a gross and horrible termination; what blatant, what outrageous ingratitude of the world! The two most illustrious preachers are put to death in no time at all. The devil lost no time in attacking them viciously. John and Christ dealt him no mere glancing blow; they went for the throat. Thus the devil's response: Destroy them! And if the devil could have kept Christ in the grave, like John, he would have done it. But the Holy Spirit had prophesied of him (Ps. 16:10): "For thou wilt not leave my soul in hell; neither wilt thou suffer thine Holy One to see corruption." "Because it was not possible that he should be holden of it," as St. Peter says (Acts 2:24).

15. The devil thought: If I can only get rid of these two preachers, then I have won. Just as he would now like to get rid of the gospel, baptism, and the Sacrament. But Christ had this in mind: Just you wait, Satan; you want your chance, I will not be around for long; I will be quick about it, and finish my course very soon, so that you can crucify me. But then I will let loose a proclamation which shall force its way into all the world and abide until the Last Day, and you won't be able to do a thing about it. If the devil and the world did not want to hear John and Christ while they were alive on earth, now after they are dead they have no choice but to hear them, whether they want to or not. Just as they have to hear us against their will. It is certainly not due to their benevolence that we have escaped being put to the sword.

16. That is the life of our beloved John, who, together with his Lord, lived only a short while on the earth, but now lives in eternity. And not only this, for, although his body was killed, his spirit lives; it preaches in our midst even now, and forever, because we possess his word and his proclamation, which is the true relic. Even if we do not have John's skull or his actual finger, or Christ the Lord's clothes and linen wrappings, which give rise to so much foolishness at Trier, yet we have the finger and head of John in a very real way—in his word which he preached! Truly, we have all of John and all of Christ; not a piece of their body, but their doctrine and preaching, so that we might hear the wisdom and Spirit which they possessed. That is more precious to us than all the carcasses of the saints. What good does it do us to see their bodies, skulls, and fingers? Nothing, really. But for me to have the finger of John, "Behold the Lamb of God, which taketh away the sin of the world," that is useful and good. I do not see it with my eyes, but with the heart and with faith.

17. Therefore, John is even now and forever alive, and he shall never die. His finger, that is, his words which he speaks and with which he points out the Lamb of God, we are able to possess, to hear, and to follow. That is a finger to be highly esteemed and head truly worthy of John the Baptist. The lifeless finger of John was burned to ashes by the pagans, and we shall witness the same again at the Last Day; but his true living finger, that is, his word and spirit we have. The same finger goes before us and directs us to the man of God,

who redeems us from sin, death, the devil, and hell. Now let us examine the account word for word, and learn what sort of circumstances led to it.

Herod himself had sent forth and laid hold upon John, and bound him in prison for Herodias' sake, his brother Philip's wife: For he had married her. For John had said unto Herod, It is not lawful for thee to have thy brother's wife. Therefore Herodias had a quarrel against him, and would have killed him; but she could not: for Herod feared John, knowing that he was a just man and an holy, and observed him; and when he heard him, he did many things, and heard him gladly.

18. St. Matthew and St. Luke designate this Herod the tetrarch, because he ruled over Galilee and Peraea. For the Romans had divided Judæa into four parcels or jurisdictions, and placed a ruler over each, the better to cope with the Jews. This Herod had a brother, Philip; this same Philip had a wife named Herodias, by whom he fathered the young courtesan who danced here. Now Herod once made a journey to Rome, and while lodging with his brother on the way, he had a conversation with Herodias in which they agreed that he would abscond with her on the return trip from Rome; and her mild-mannered daughter, the dancer, went with them.

19. By the time Herod returned to Galilee with Herodias as his wife, John was also in the country, preaching repentance and baptizing. And Herod liked to listen to John, so John often found himself at court. Herod was his gracious lord and king, and the pious John intended to bring him to repentance. But when he became aware of his gross immorality, that he had taken his brother Philip's wife and daughter and was living in open adultery to the outrage of all, he confronted him with it and said, "It is not lawful for thee to have thy brother's wife." Herod was not likely to stand for John constantly rubbing his nose in his transgression. Although the text says that Herod was able to tolerate John, Herodias was not. Yet it was painful for Herod to be continually censured for this, and admonished to put away his brother's wife. Therefore, his thoughts must have been something like this: There is no way they are going to tolerate each other, John and Herodias. If I am going to lose one—which is bound to happen—then I would rather lose the good and godly preacher, John, than Herodias.

20. Still he continues to feign an interest in John's preaching, readily admitting: This man really preaches well. For he was afraid

of John, knowing that he was a godly man and that the whole country stood in awe of him and considered him to be a holy man. But beware, lords are lords, and always seek their own interests above those of other people. As they say, It is not good to eat cherries with lords; they eat the cherries and shower you with the pits; and, the favor of lords is as capricious as the weather in April. No lord takes kindly to rebukes, except those of an extraordinarily pious nature who could take it. David, Josiah, and Jehoshaphat did suffer the reprimands of the prophets; but the other kings refused it, and had such prophets and preachers beheaded.

21. In our time there are very many of this sort to be found among the princes, the nobility, the townspeople, and the peasants. They like to hear preachers, yet in such a way that they remain uninvolved with the proclamation; if they are, then the cordiality is at an end. They have no problem with other people being on the receiving end; but when they are singled out, as John does here to Herod, this they will not stand for. As our squires always say, You are not to preach about the wise and venerable councilors or the ruling magistrates, but only about the common folk. Yes sir, your honor, as you wish! So Herod heard John gladly, as long as he was directing his rebukes to the common people. But when John turned to Herod and said, "It is not lawful for thee to have thy brother's wife," then Herod said within himself: Wait a minute, if you're going to start harping on that, it will cost you your head.

22. But if, when the pastor rebukes others, you say, What a preacher he is, what a telling message, he really gets across! But when he finds fault with you, you say, These clerics, don't they ever talk about anyone else but me? Then you have not heard it in the proper spirit. Even the devil and the malicious gossips love to hear other people put on the butcher's block; but when their own lying and wickedness are rebuked, they can't stand it. But if I want to hear the truth, even where it touches my person and I must accept rebuke and amend myself, as David, Josiah, and Jehoshaphat did, that is the right way to hear. But those who are willing to hear the truth, even when it is against themselves, are rare birds upon the earth. At least sparrows and ravens are not so common as the sort who love to have themselves patted on the back and praised.

23. When we preach to the townspeople and peasants that they ought not to steal, or practice usury, or inflate prices, the gentry can put up with that; they like to hear it. Herod's hearing was like that. But if I say, You lords ought to do your job, they are indignant. But, your grace, Herod did the same! If our princes and the nobility hear that the people ought to repent, be converted, and believe the gospel, they say, That's right, we like to hear that. But if it is preached to them, You, O Prince, O nobleman, must also repent, your wild and dissolute life is good for nothing—and you are ready to hear this—rest assured that you are greatly beloved of God and such forbearance is no ordinary gift from him. Without a doubt, there are great things in store for you, and God will not forsake you, as Solomon says (Prov. 1:5): "A wise man will hear, and will increase learning; and a man of understanding shall attain unto wise counsels"; and Sirach 1:31: "The fear of the Lord is the true wisdom and discipline, and with faith and patience God is well-pleased." But if you are angry, and murmur, and cannot bear it, then you are like Herod, no child of truth, but a child of lies.

24. This is the first part of the story, in which the Evangelist in the person of King Herod puts his finger on a common vice which is so prevalent in the world, namely, every man, and particularly the great lords, want the reputation of hearing the Word of God gladly, and yet cannot suffer to be rebuked by it. What is this? says Herod. John rebukes me because of Herodias? I will have none of it. Still, I can't just kill him; he is a good, saintly man. If I kill him, there would be an outcry against me for killing this upright and holy man. Herodias would not have been the least bit concerned about such an outcry, but Herod is. Therefore, before men he pretends that he likes to hear John; but not before God, who sees his heart. Yet, so that John can no more censure him publicly, he takes him into custody.

And when a convenient day was come, that Herod on his birthday made a supper to his lords, high captains, and chief estates of Galilee; and when the daughter of the said Herodias came in, and danced, and pleased Herod and them that sat with him, the king said unto the damsel, Ask of me whatsoever thou wilt and I will give it thee. And he sware unto her, Whatsoever thou shalt ask of me, I will give it thee, unto the half of my kingdom. And she went forth, and said unto her mother, What shall I ask? And she said, The head of John the Baptist. And she came in straightway with haste unto the king, and asked, saying, I will that thou give me by and by in a charger the head of John the Baptist. And the king was exceeding sorry; yet for his oath's sake, and for their sakes which sat with him, he would not reject her. And immediately the king sent an executioner, and commanded his head to be brought: and he went and beheaded him in the prison, And brought his head in a charger, and gave it to the damsel: and the damsel gave it to her mother.

25. This is the second part of the story. While John was put away in prison, Herod and Herodias hit upon a plan: Herod would celebrate his birthday, host a banquet, and put on a dance act. So, let his little girl come in and dance; and when the good humor of the guests is at its peak, Herod would swear to give her whatever she wanted, up to the half of his kingdom, and this to exhibit his fatherly heart toward his daughter. He says half of the kingdom; he means John's head. This is the clincher: Who would ever think that they had conspired such a thing against the holy man in the dungeon? Herod, Herodias, and the daughter understood perfectly. The half of the kingdom meant John's head. But the guests did not even suspect. Herodias had instructed the girl beforehand that as soon as the king made mention of the half of his kingdom she would know what to ask for: John the Baptist's head.

26. Therefore, she says, "I will that thou give me by and by in a charger the head of John the Baptist." The head of John, she says, is what I want, and she adds, John the Baptist's, to avoid any misunderstanding or mistake, and, on a charger, to ensure that she actually receives it. She has got some nerve, this daughter of an adulteress, who does not even tremble at the words, to say nothing of the deed, in bearing about his severed head in full view of everyone. For womenfolk have ever been by nature imprudent, especially in serious matters, where thinking is required. Now what is the pious Herod going to do about the young maiden's demand for John's head? He enjoys listening to him, and is afraid of him, as the guests well know. But what can he do? He swore an oath, he would give the girl whatever she asked for, even the half of his kingdom. So he's got to go through with it, the oath compels him; his hands are tied.

27. What a fair assembly of saints are these! Herod swore an oath and intends to keep it. God forbid he should provoke the Almighty by breaking his oath. The guests at the table must have been grati-

fied. And the king is so dejected. My, my, how did such an idea come into her head? He does it with a heavy heart. Just like the farmer (sidling up to a pig) with a lance behind his back!

28. This is how the venomous hypocrites are depicted, covering the murder of innocent and godly men with a veneer of virtue! Herod and Herodias had arranged everything in advance: John must die, yet the murder must be hid from the world. And Herod pretends to be grieved, saying, Alas, alas, how it pains me to do this; I was foolish to promise, and she was foolish to ask it. How some people can thumb their noses at our Lord and God! And he had to just let it melt in his mouth, and act as if he were unconcerned about Herod's wickedness.

29. The hypocrites do the same thing in our day as well; they murder the innocent, and yet put up a facade of reluctant compulsion: It's because these people refuse to remain in the Christian church! Yes, indeed, you go right ahead and persecute the Word of God, blaspheme his holy name, slaughter the innocent, then wash your hands and say that you do these things for the sake of the Word of God and his holy name. Would you like to know what you really are? You are a child of Herod; he is your father. But, my dear lords, princes, and bishops, make sure that you deceive the Lord too, the doddering, old seer. We have to put up with such despicable hypocrites, murderers of Christ and the apostles; but to the world they pretend to do it with a heavy heart, because they must fulfill the oath which they swore. Yes, they say, we cannot pass it by, the Christian church will have it so, God will have it so, and so on. So John is beheaded, Herod maintains his saintly image, and Herodias, her piety.

And when his disciples heard of it, they came and took up his corpse, and laid it in a tomb.

30. This is the third part of the story. The worthy man was buried by his disciples, and Christ says nothing about it; he just lets Herod do it. It is a very exasperating thing for God to just sit there and let him murder this righteous man, and cover himself the way he does with an oath. But you had better get used to it; that is the way of this wicked world. We also have our fair share of such clandestine enemies, who behave themselves just like Herod; they listen to us eagerly, and then bite us like vipers. But Herod was repaid in full; he was eradicated, root and branch, together with the Jews. Our Herods will

likewise meet their end; they will not exculpate themselves forever by their exalted station and the appellation of Christian which they are now making use of. When we suffer adversity, let us not be surprised; Christ and John suffered the same things. Although our enemies, who are now persecuting the gospel, profess themselves to be godly persons, and pose as Herod did, yet they shall receive their just due at the proper time.

THE DAY OF MARY'S VISITATION

First Sermon—1532

Luke 1:39–56

> And Mary arose in those days, and went into the hill country with haste, into a city of Juda; And entered into the house of Zacharias, and saluted Elisabeth. And it came to pass, that, when Elisabeth heard the salutation of Mary, the babe leaped in her womb; and Elisabeth was filled with the Holy Ghost: And she spake out with a loud voice, and said, Blessed art thou among women, and blessed is the fruit of thy womb. And whence is this to me, that the mother of my Lord should come to me? For, lo, as the voice of thy salutation sounded in mine ears, the babe leaped in my womb for joy. And blessed is she that believed; for there shall be a performance of those things which were told her from the Lord. And Mary said, My soul doth magnify the Lord. And my spirit hath rejoiced in God my Saviour. For he hath regarded the low estate of his handmaiden: for, behold, from henceforth all generations shall call me blessed. For he that is mighty hath done to me great things, and holy is his name. And his mercy is on them that fear him from generation to generation. He hath shewed great strength with his arm; he hath scattered the proud in the imagination of their hearts. He hath put down the mighty from their seats, and exalted them of low degree. He hath filled the hungry with good things; and the rich he hath sent empty away. He hath holpen his servant Israel, in remembrance of his mercy. As he spake to our fathers, to Abraham, and to his seed for ever. And Mary abode with her about three months, and returned to her own house.

1. This feast is called also the Feast of Our Ladies. The pope first instituted this festival some time ago against the Turkish threat, in keeping with the lection sung during the Mass, namely, that just as the Virgin Mary went into the hill country and over the mountains, so we are to call upon her to trample down the Turks with the same feet. But the longer people celebrated this feast and called upon the Virgin Mary, the more the Turk trampled on us. Therefore, this cannot be the reason why we would want to observe this feast.

2. For us, indeed, it is an occasion to thank God for the glorious revelation which occurred on this day, that Elisabeth is filled with the Holy Spirit; and although till now she knows nothing about Christ and his conception, she here declares and openly confesses that Mary is in truth the mother of her Lord and God. And John leaps in his mother's womb in witness to his Lord, while Mary sings her beautiful song of praise, the Magnificat, showing most excellently the profundity of her understanding. We still repeat it after her. It expresses the reason for us to celebrate, to learn it, and thank God for it. The purpose of the pope's celebration is to invoke Mary; but our purpose is to praise and thank God, in accordance with the example of the beloved Virgin, so that we celebrate just as she did.

3. On this occasion, then, we wish to discuss two things drawn from this Gospel: first, the example of the Virgin Mary as regards works and outward customs; and, second, praise and thanksgiving. She thanks God and sings a beautiful song of praise for us, so that we might learn to live godly lives, both inwardly and outwardly in this world, with joyfulness, thanksgiving, and faith before our God, which is our reasonable service.

4. The first thing deals with outward decency and morals, as laid before us there are excellent, beautiful virtues. The first of these is humility. The young Virgin Mary, although she is highly honored (for she is the mother of God, and Elisabeth ought really be serving her!), nevertheless, heeds God's teaching to honor older people. Although already exalted, she humbly lowers herself and with gladsome heart travels a very great distance, in order to serve her kinswoman during the six weeks. And for her part, Elisabeth, though older than Mary, nonetheless, humbles herself before the young Virgin, stating, "Whence is this to me, that the mother of my Lord should come to me?"

5. The beloved Virgin adorns herself beautifully by not becoming proud of the honor she has of being the mother of God, to give birth to the Son of God. No one would have been surprised, had she succumbed to haughty arrogance and become more puffed up than Lucifer and his allies. For look how we act, bag of worms that we are! Give us a penny or a gulden, and people can't bear with us blown-up peacocks! A dairymaid with beautiful hair puffs herself up and be-

comes vain; so, too, a young fellow with a splendid coat. Everybody becomes proud and insolent when they possess something special, be it beauty, skill, money, rank, or whatever; their arrogance knows no limit or bounds. Yet everything is like the dust of the street compared to the great grace which the Virgin has here.

6. This is not a matter of silver and gold for her. If all the money in the world were to lie in one big pile, it would be nothing but a smelly pile compared with this great honor. Never has a human being on earth been so privileged, so that even the heavenly angels themselves—as also Elisabeth, the noble woman who gave birth to the next greatest of sons—called her the mother of God and blessed above all women. And yet this greatest, noblest, holiest mother does not dwell on her privileged station, but in good grace demurs and says to the angel, "Behold, I am the Lord's handmaiden!" and travels a great distance in order to be of assistance to Elisabeth.

7. The angel greeted her with glorious words and said that she was blessed above all women; and Elisabeth approvingly says to her, You are the mother of my Lord; I am not worthy of your coming to me. To be honored in such fashion would cause a fleshly heart to swell up and burst with pride, for how could a human heart not become boastful and prideful from that? Ten gulden, or a new coat, cause us to become arrogant. But she does not let the great honor affect her; she remains humble and serves not only her friend, Elisabeth, but us all as well, and brings into the world the Son, who is the Saviour of us all.

8. Ah, how great is the humility of this noble person. It will rebuff our arrogance on Judgment Day to see the beloved Virgin, whose response to us proud wretches will be, I didn't let it go to my head nor did I boast, and yet I have been more privileged than you ever were, proud empress and queen! What, indeed, was the basis for your boast, your arrogance? A gold necklace, a beautiful coat, or a beautiful body, was that your boast? How could that even compare to the fact that I was the mother of God, of whom the angels and all saints have spoken far and wide as the most blessed among women! Yet I did not become overweening with pride because of this.

9. Therefore, you crazy "holies," you heretics, you factious spirits, you have represented yourselves to be so learned that your belly is

about to burst because of your knowledge. What do you really know that gives you such airs, to be so cocky and arrogant? Do you want to compete with me to see whether with all your cleverness you can compose even one verse of the Magnificat? I, too, was able to speak about our Lord God, and yet I didn't become arrogant; I disregarded all personal honor, went on foot over the mountains, assisted the aging Elisabeth for six weeks, cooked, washed diapers, and did all manner of housework willingly and with all my heart, just like a maidservant, and received nothing in return. In this manner, humbly, Mary will cut the ground from under all arrogant people.

10. For shame! For such vile arrogance you deserved to be shamed, every one of you, before this maiden's great humility, as shown here! She is the mother of God and the greatest of women in heaven and on earth. She forgets all else, every good thing, and with truly humble heart sets out on her way, not ashamed to wash diapers, gently care for and bathe the infant John, and so on. Such humility is truly something to behold. It would have been fitting had someone provided her with a gold carriage to ride in, drawn by four thousand horses, with trumpets heralding the carriage's coming, proclaiming that the greatest of all women was approaching, the princess of the whole human race! But there was nothing like this, only silence. The poor maiden travels by foot a great distance, more than twenty miles, and she herself is with child, the mother of God. It would not at all have been astonishing if all the mountains had leaped and danced for joy. Possibly she did not travel alone, but in company with Joseph and another maiden. But Luke speaks only of her, for the focus is concentrated on her, and she alone it is who evinces such humility.

11. That is the first virtue, great humility. Men and women everywhere ought to form a picture of this in their hearts and be horrified because of their proud and obstinate minds. Nowadays we see and experience how rude, haughty, and insolent people are everywhere in the world, workers and domestics especially. Masters and mistresses must wait on their help, their servants and maids. So arrogant have they become, even though they are but poor, miserable beggars. I shall say nothing about what the lofty squires and ladies are doing, who possess station, power, possessions, knowledge, and oth-

er things. They won't always have these things. Eventually thunder and lightning will strike and put an end to their arrogance.

12. But if we are Christians, we would be thinking: Dear friend, if this mother was able thus to humble herself, should a miserable human such as I give the lie to myself as I strut about in such a pompous, useless, and arrogant way? So what that I have golden hair, a red coat, and gold necklace, that I am learned, successful, rich, and powerful? What good is this? Against such arrogance, as the saying goes, the devil wipes his backside; for in truth it is nothing but the shallow vaunting of a poor, miserable, loathsome beggar. For this reason I, a poor bag of worms, do not wish to be arrogant, but be willing rather to learn from and emulate this example of the beloved Virgin. She, who is the mother of God, for honor's sake, might well have stayed at home; but she travels by foot and devotes herself to menial service in a foreign countryside, bathes baby John the Baptist, lifts him up and cradles him, washes his diapers; in short, she does what the lowliest governess is accustomed to do in the home.

13. So the purpose of this example is to teach everyone, especially the youth of our day, to serve willingly and humbly, irrespective of whether one thinks himself more deserving and important than the person whom he serves. Mary does this, and the infant John has a wonderful nursemaid in her. It was a signal blessing from our Lord God, for John was especially dear to him, and for this reason he arranged for the Virgin Mary to tend, wash, sponge, and cradle him in her arms. Truly a high honor bestowed by God on his beloved John! Moreover, it is recorded as an example for us, that we might learn humbly to serve one another, and say, If the holy, highly favored mother of Christ has done it, why shouldn't I want to do it as well? And were I to do ten times more, it still would be nothing; for this person is so great; she is queen and empress among all women and for that reason outstrips me by far when she humbles herself, just the width of a stalk of straw compared with my humility stretched a thousand miles wide! To our scorn and shame, therefore, her example stands as a rebuke of our arrogance, pride, and disobedience.

14. The second virtue is, as Luke reports, that she trudges over the mountainous terrain resolutely, like a faithful servant, not impertinently as on a lark or skipping off to a dance or some religious pag-

eant, chattering along the way from house to house, eyes flitting here and everywhere. Such girls are often not chaste virgins but questionable flirts. Virtuous maidens and women abide at home and, if they must go outside onto the streets, they do so with haste, for no more than a couple hours, not lingering to count all the tiles on the roof or all the sparrows under the eaves, nor dillydallying along the way and clacking like geese. This is not the way the Virgin Mary conducted herself. She straightaway headed to her destination, without counting the trees, nor lingering along the way, for her heart is set on helping. She has one thought in mind: I want to visit (the new) mother Elisabeth, and assist her in caring for her baby, John. Occupied with these thoughts, there was nothing that could divert her mind from what she planned to do. Whomever she met along the way she greeted briefly, and then hurried on her way again to the dear mother, Elisabeth, and her precious baby, John.

15. St. Luke used the words "with haste" intentionally so that maidens and women might not say, Why must I always stay at home, like a nun in a convent, and not even go for a stroll? Mother Mary did it! If it was all right for her, it certainly is no sin for me. Yes, but do it in virtuous manner, as she did, with chaste, and modest behavior. For she did not go as a busybody, but with the thought of serving her elderly female relative to whom the angel announced that she would bear a son in her old age; Mary was to be of greater help outside her home than within. This is also a paradigm for our conduct, that as young women and housewives we behave chastely. Then we, too, will avoid sinning.

16. But just as women do not conform to the beloved Virgin in humility but are arrogant and proud, they also do not opt for chastity, as unfortunately is evident. Few are the women and maidens today that even think they can be happy and chaste at the same time. Their tongues are sharp and coarse, their behavior is worldly and unchaste. This is the lifestyle that's "in" today. Yet chastity and happiness should and could stand side by side, if they would but behold this example. But the situation today is especially bad. Young women are so very loose in their talk and behavior, they swear like troopers, to say nothing of the shameful words and offensively foul talk that passes from one to the next. This happens because of the examples their

mothers set in the home, not diligently concerned about decent behavior in their young. This all is a specially sure sign of an impending judgment, when the womenfolk do not uphold decent behavior. For children take after their mothers, and servant girls after their mistresses, until finally there is neither decency nor honor in any station, as is so evident, unfortunately, in our day. We must expect a well-deserved punishment for this.

17. But here in the person of Mary we have an example of proper behavior and morality, especially of uncommon humility. She shames us for our disgusting, detestable arrogance by humbling herself so deeply that among all maidens and women there is none like her. It is an example to emulate, to drum into our very being, and say, Ah! See how the dear Virgin Mary has behaved, she who was not obligated to do it (for she might well have allowed herself to be extolled, but refrains from it); how could I ever parade around and give myself airs when I ought rather defer and be unpretending? Mary's example, therefore, should set a beautiful pattern for us to follow, though indeed we may be equally beautiful, learned, capable, wealthy, young, and strong. We must certainly not exalt ourselves, but be humble, willingly and diligently serving others.

18. Elisabeth certainly humbles herself, even though she is an elderly matron. She, nevertheless, abases herself before Mary, saying, How did I come by this honor, that the mother of my Lord comes to me? How deep is her humility! But the Virgin Mary's humility is even deeper, because of the greatness of her person. For that reason she should certainly be a pattern for us to emulate, especially all young maidens and women.

19. The second thing in this Gospel is the Magnificat which Mary sings. By this she manifests the prowess of a doctor or master of theology and teaches us how we should comport ourselves toward God. In the previous point she showed us how we ought to comport ourselves properly and decently with others. Here now she teaches us how to comport ourselves before God, with praise and thanksgiving. Before God she does not deny what she is, even though she has already humbled herself. For it is a false humility when we disavow what God has given us, as monks in the monasteries did when they called the people who were extolling them liars. If someone said to

them, You have a fine memory, a good understanding, they would reply, Not so! even though it might actually be true.

20. Young girls act that way. If they are beautiful, they say, No, I'm not really, I'm not fair of complexion; and yet their hearts are not saying that. So with rich folks, when one calls them rich. They cannot leave it uncontested, but they bemoan that they are poorer than the really poor. This is not humility, but double-dyed arrogance, and an obvious lie. It redounds also to God's dishonor.

21. What God has given and bestowed, we should acknowledge and not disclaim. One ought to say, Praise be to God, who has given it! I have a good livelihood; I am not exactly an ugly duckling; I'm intelligent; I have an education; I am no adulterer; I am a princess, a countess. For whatever God has given, be it money or possessions, all is a gift from God. We ought not deny these things but acknowledge and thank God for them, and determine how best to make use of them. For the sun does not say that it is black, but acknowledges and demonstrates that it is the light of the world by beaming its light continuously. Likewise, a tree does not deny its nature, does not say, I bear no apples, no pears, no cherries, no nuts; but whatever God has given to it is manifest for all to see. For that reason it is not humility when you deny what you possess and say you don't have it. For, if God has endowed you with something, admit it, and say that it is true, but that I do not have it of myself, for God has given it to me; and, therefore, I shall not look down upon or disdain others who do not have what I have. It is like the beautiful sun; it is more beautiful than all other heavenly bodies, yet it does not, therefore, disdain the rest of creation, but says, Though you, moon, star, tree, and so forth, do not provide light as beautifully as do I, you, too, are a beautiful creature of God; therefore, I will not look down on you but help you to retain your light, your green foliage, and also serve and provide light for people. It is a lesson for us to follow.

22. This is exactly what the Virgin Mary does. She doesn't say "nay" to this, that she is blessed over other women and is the mother of God. It's all true, she acknowledges; I have experienced the greatest grace and honor from God. But from whence and for what purpose do I have it? I do not magnify myself because of it, but "my soul doth magnify the Lord, and my spirit hath rejoiced in God my Sav-

iour"; for it is from his power that I have it, and not from myself nor any human agency. I have not created it, nor do I have it because of my maternal capacity; all is a gift from our Lord God. Therefore, dear Elisabeth, it is not a case of my wanting to boast of myself, over against you or any other human being. So, even though I possess this treasure, I can still be your maid and serve you and baby John. "He that is mighty hath done to me great things, and holy is his name." May God therefore, keep me from shaming or despising his name, and from exalting my name and saying, I got this on my own. His name is holy, he has done it, him we must praise for it. And even though people will commend me because of such grace and call me blessed, I still want to trace it back to God. For his name is holy, and he is mighty; therefore, he alone should have the praise.

23. It is an especially beautiful song, and it is sung by the papists, monks, nuns, and priests everywhere, in all churches. However, it is sinful and shameful for them to sing it without proper understanding and reverence. They say the words, and they bellow like big jackasses, but the organ pipes it much better than they sing it. They treat it lightly, with no intent to understand it, but simply plod through it, babbling like geese that clack over oat straw.

My soul doth magnify the Lord, And my spirit hath rejoiced in God my Saviour.

24. Mary says that her spirit is magnifying something, that is, extolling and highly praising something, that she is rejoicing with all her heart, and that, therefore, her heart is completely full of joy and delight. What is it? Whom is she thus magnifying? Herself? No! I, she says, have nothing, nor do I want to attach any importance to myself that would cause you to praise me, dear Elisabeth. It is the Lord God, whom all the world should extol and praise, whom I am extolling and praising with all my thoughts, acknowledging that everything I have belongs to him, our Lord God.

25. Thus the word "magnify" has a very pointed meaning. For "to magnify" means to praise highly, just as the opposite, "arrogance," means to puff up oneself. The one who magnifies someone else downplays and humbles himself. By Mary's saying, "My soul doth magnify the Lord," she declares that she is debasing herself and elevating another, namely, our dear Lord God. Moreover, by this she

completely sets us poor beggars down and gives us all a lesson, no matter who we are, whether servants or maids, peasants or townspeople, whether nobles, scholars, intellectuals, or religious leaders. But what are the facts? The common saying among our burghers and peasants is, What? All I've got are a couple of pennies of which to boast compared with their money and possessions, their gulden and dollars! Ah, you jammering fat guts, is that what you are prizing? Shouldn't you be saying, It is property that belongs to another; God has given it, he can also take it away! Why, then, should I be presumptuous about it? A factious spirit, you see, revels in self-praise, regards himself as learned and makes a show of his prowess, like Zwingli, who boasts about his learning. Now, then, be as learned as you wish; whose learning is it? From where did you get it? From yourself? The deuce you say! You got it from above; therefore, you should not boast; the one who gave it to you can take it from you at any moment.

26. It is not just a nasty, shameful thing, but a stupid and ludicrous thing to boast of another's property, as great lords are usually in the habit of doing, like saying, By God's grace, I am king of Jerusalem, and so on, and yet have nothing really but the title. That's what you call boasting about an empty purse. It's the same as boasting: My neighbor has a lot of money, and so do I, but I have it much more precariously. We have life and limb, members, reason, ability, and honor from God, and yet we boast of these things as if they are ours, though they are not ours but God's. "What hast thou that thou didst not receive? now if thou didst receive it, why dost thou glory, as if thou hadst not received it?" St. Paul says in 1 Corinthians 4:7. But it makes no difference to the average person. The devil lives in people; he teaches them to oppose God (from whom they have received everything), to be ungrateful and to swagger and to jab at him with his own gift. Now then, the person who will not let up thinking that way God can again strip, as completely as he stripped Judas. He, too, was arrogant and misused his office by betraying Christ; however, as things turned out, he hanged himself because of it.

27. This is not the way the beloved Virgin does things here. "My soul," says she, "doth magnify the Lord," that is, I praise and extol God, not just with my mouth but with my heart and my life, with all

my strength and members; and with all my soul I want to sing and praise God. For "soul" means nothing else than our whole being, which speaks, hears, sees, eats, drinks, and thinks. In short, everything that pertains to my life; with my hair, my blood, with my whole being, I want to sing the Magnificat and thus praise and extol a gracious God. We miserable wretches, when we commend something, we do it with the mouth only; the body and the soul feel nothing of it; the Magnificat cleaves to us merely like phlegm to our tongue. Were it dollars, gulden, or beautiful houses, beautiful clothes, then we, too, would wax eloquent with a Magnificat; but when it's for God, the fervor is small.

28. "My spirit," she says further, "hath rejoiced in God my Saviour." My "spirit," that is, my innermost being, all the faculties with which I perceive God rejoice not in the temporal things but in God. It is, moreover, true joy when one's rejoicing is in God. However, we are not happy until we have money in the pocket and, to our sin and shame, ten gulden give us more joy than God himself. Now, tell me, isn't that a fact? I have had life and limb upwards of fifty years, sound eyes, ears, hands, and feet; the sun has served me all that time during the day, and the night has given me sleep; but when have I ever been as happy about all this as when a man by chance finds ten gulden? Shame on us for not being able to rejoice in God! So, tell me, who rejoices over the fact that Jesus Christ has been born? Yes, and some are even bent on trampling the gospel. If we were not so stone blind, we would continuously leap for joy because God has given us not only body and soul, but his only begotten Son, and through him, eternal life.

29. Therefore, let all the learned on earth come together and try their hand at composing even a single verse equal to this verse, and then they will see the extent of their skill. Mary sets high her focus, and yet is humble, so humble, that she, a great doctor and prophetess, who is more learned than all apostles and prophets, becomes governess and handmaiden for Elisabeth. And we scoundrels, as soon as we can speak one Greek word, don't know where we belong, because of our arrogance. We ought to be thrown out, one after the other, with hue and cry, because of our shameful arrogance in chasing after trivial things, while failing completely to remember the ex-

ample here of this beloved Virgin who does not exalt herself above the great, sublime blessings, but rejoices in God, extolling and praising him as follows:

For he hath regarded the low estate of his handmaiden: for, behold, from henceforth all generations shall call me blessed.

30. "Me," she says, "all generations shall call blessed," that is, the whole world will sing about me and say that God has so highly exalted and blessed me. Now, dear Virgin, would it then not be time, just once, to show some pride, since the whole world is supposed to extol and praise you? No, she says, for that reason I will not become proud. What causes me to rejoice, however, is that I am a lowly, despised maiden, and yet God, my Lord, has not despised me but looked on me in grace. For she was, after all, just a young maiden and yet poor, to whom no one paid any particular attention; nor did she seek notoriety or notice. I well know, she says, that I am absolutely nothing. But God, who created heaven and earth, turned his eyes graciously toward me, singling me out for this great work. He could certainly have found others, some high and lofty virgins, but he gave them no consideration; but had regard for me, a poor maiden, in my tattered skirt. That is why I rejoice and thank God. In short, she says, I am less than nothing, but what I am and have, that I owe to God's benevolence, goodness, and grace. That is to truly praise God and his grace.

For he that is mighty hath done to me great things; and holy is his name.

31. She does not want to touch upon the name of our Lord God, that is, she does not want to vaunt herself because of her gifts, ever acknowledging that what she has is God's, not hers. And for this reason her desire is that we all might acknowledge him to be mighty, but ourselves as weak, powerless humans; that his name alone is holy, that is, his name alone should be extolled and glorified, while our name is not holy and, therefore, should not be extolled. But look around you in the world. Do you see any who do it? People seek for a great reputation and high esteem with others, especially to be thought highly of for holiness and righteousness. But Mary teaches us to esteem God only as mighty and his name as holy, that is, boast alone of God and his grace and about nothing else.

And his mercy is on them that fear him from generation to generation.

32. Here she breaks off talking about her person and fans out into the whole world and praises God, not just for her own sake, but for the sake of all mankind, because he is gracious and merciful to everyone who fears him and humbles himself before him. Just like we are accustomed to do in our praying, when we thank God not only for the gifts we have but also for those which other Christians share along with us. This, also, Mary does, as she acknowledges, God has done much good not only to me but also to others. And this, especially, is a master stroke as she so precisely ties together God's mercy and the fear of God, that where a person fears God, he will be merciful; on the other hand, where one does not fear God, there no mercy or grace will be shown but punishment and wrath.

He hath shewed strength with his arm; he hath scattered the proud in the imagination of their hearts.

33. Mary, beloved doctor, deals with a lot at one time. There are three sorts of people who cannot let up on arrogance and pride. Some are wise and astute, and they think a lot of themselves and are boastful; others are powerful and wealthy, and they do likewise. They all become arrogant, feeling no need of our Lord God. But here we hear how such arrogance leads to their fall.

34. He is mighty, Mary says, and opposes all that is wise and proud; he can make great things small, and small things great, like a potter at his wheel. He has already divested a great king and emperor of his throne, and advanced a lowly servant in his stead. Now he has taken K. F. by the collar, then H.G., and nearly also M.J.* For they vaunt themselves proudly, become presumptuous, as if they had achieved everything on their own. I am a prince over Saxony, one says, and should I not then lord it over the parish clergy? That's the way they speak about us. All right, says our Lord God, be evil and clever if you want; you still will have to regard me and my station. I also have an arm; if I raise it, look out, it is very strong and will so disconcert you, that you won't know what hit you. That's the way great kingdoms and principalities have been uprooted. The Virgin Mary knows precisely how to sing about this here; she is a learned virgin and a great doctor.

---

*K. F. is a reference to Emperor Ferdinand; H. G. to Duke George of Saxony; and M. J. an apparent reference to Margrave Joachim of Brandenburg.

35. But why does she use such words as, "He hath scattered the proud in the imagination of their hearts"? Because it is God's nature, that when he wants to shame people on account of their arrogance, he first makes fools of them and blinds them, and after they are blinded, they are soon shamed because in their wisdom they make fools of themselves. This is what confounding the wise in the imagination of their heart means. When he wants to shame them, he leads them with their wisdom into ruination. Even at their best, as they decide that this or that is the best way to attack the problem, our Lord God mocks at them and says: Good, good, dear lords, you are very wise; only do so without delay! In their arrogance he leads them on; one blow, and they lie flat in a heap. Thus he crushes and fells them in their high-mindedness. So much for one sort of people who do not fear God but are arrogant, trusting in their cleverness and intelligence. Now we come to the second group which relies on its power and might. The song goes on to tell how:

He hath put down the mighty from their seats, and exalted them of low degree.

36. In short, our Lord God wants humble people; to them he wants to give every good thing. Whatever is arrogant, however, he will punish. If, therefore, the humble whom he has elevated become unmindful of this and proud, they must be brought low. Saul was a herdsman of donkeys, stemming from the lowliest roots in Israel. God said to him, Come, I shall make you a king. But as soon as he became puffed up over this and refused to humble himself before God and his Word, God destroyed him and his entire family so that not one remained. It was the same for David. From a shepherd God made him into a king, and this sovereignty remained with his family until they grew arrogant; then the house had to be brought down again. We see the same thing throughout history; whatever is arrogant is impaled by our Lord God and brought down; on the other hand, what is humble and God-fearing is elevated in the world. Poor students, who are upright and faithful in their studies, often become doctors, bishops, and great lords.

37. This is the nature of God's judgments. The humble he raises up; the proud he brings low. Whoever doesn't believe it, let him try God out. Many have been critical of this song and attempted to dis-

prove it, but to their dismay they found it to be true. For the Virgin Mary cannot lie. Inspired by the Holy Spirit, she speaks from personal experience. She was humble and God-fearing, and because of this God singles her out and bestows great honor upon her. On the other hand, the daughters of Herod, Caiaphas, and other great lords were haughty, and now no one even knows whatever became of them. Let everyone, therefore, learn to fear God and humble himself, and he'll have no need to worry, even if things go badly for a time.

38. Poets also have learned it from experience, as they say, *Magnisque negatum stare diu*, or, "Greatness will not long endure." For the facts are that when greatness is perceived, arrogance follows. Then our Lord must come to bring down and humble what is high. Rome became very great in the world, to the point that, at the mere mention of the name Rome, the whole world had to take off its hat and bow down before her. But finally how did it all end? Snip! and it lay in one heap, three times in ruins and laid waste. It is just as the Virgin Mary says here, No one should vaunt himself too high before God; he will bring low all who venture to swagger.

He hath filled the hungry with good things; and the rich he hath sent empty away.

39. This is the third group, people who are proud and arrogant because they are rich, possessing a lot of money and goods. Here, too, our Lord God must do his handiwork by allowing this great wealth shamefully to dwindle away and not reach the third generation. On the other hand, he favors the poor so generously that they come to possess much. Were everyone now intelligent enough to master this virtue and keep himself humble, God would allow them all to live on and, what is more, would from day to day give them even more. Then even great kings and princes, as also clever and intelligent folks, would continue on, for God could and would very well tolerate them; for he is the one who makes them kings and great lords, if they could just keep from being arrogant. But none is so inclined; everybody still wants to defy our Lord God with his gifts, and God cannot and will not tolerate this, saying, Stop, friend, if that's what you want, let me give you some advice! Since I have made you fat, I am well able to make you thin and scrawny again.

These are the three groups to which God does not show his grace, but his anger, not wishing to endure those who do not fear him, or humble themselves, but boast of their wisdom, power, and wealth.

He hath holpen his servant Israel, in remembrance of his mercy; As he spake to our fathers, to Abraham, and to his seed for ever.

40. This is the final part of the song in which Mary sings about God's highest and greatest grace, that he has visited and redeemed Israel through his only Son. The first part concerns her in particular, that she praises and thanks God for the grace and blessing which he has shown to her person. The second part, in which she sings about the great miracles which God continues to perform upon all mankind, concerns the world, that in time of need he is the helper of the humble and poor, but sends the proud away empty. The third part concerns Christendom and is God's greatest and highest work, that he remembers his promise and gives to us not only body and soul, but also his Son. This is the greatest, the spiritual blessing which he promised to Abraham and the rest of the fathers and now fulfills through this Virgin, that she should bear into the world the Son of God, who by his suffering and resurrection from the dead should save us from sin and eternal death unto eternal life. With that she concludes her song.

41. Now, this song is a model from which we ought to learn how to thank and praise God for all his spiritual and temporal gifts, recognize that they are from him and not exalt ourselves on account of them, but in all humility say, Lord, they are your gifts, and I thank you for them because I know that they are your treasures and not mine. This is the instruction the beloved Virgin provides for us by her example.

42. So, from this Gospel let us learn two things: first, modesty and humility, not to be proud. You gay blades, who do you think you are? Why do you vaunt yourselves? Think of the mother of God; she went and served her cousin Elisabeth and washed baby John the Baptist's diapers. If the holy Virgin could do this, why should I not be willing to do it too? From youth on a young girl and boy, therefore, ought to learn not to be proud, but willingly serve those who are older. Second, praise and thanksgiving; that we thank our Lord God with all our hearts for all his blessings, temporal and spiritual, and, especially, for sending us his dear Son, our Lord Jesus Christ, who has redeemed us from sin and death. To that end may God grant us his grace. Amen.

THE DAY OF MARY'S VISITATION

Second Sermon—1533

Luke 1:39–56

1. The meaning of this festival has not been understood even though it has been celebrated under the papacy for several hundred years, along with the singing of the Magnificat in all the churches. That is why we must preach about the reason for the observance, so that we have a correct understanding of this special day and how to observe it.

2. The events in this story took place soon after the angel left Mary. As Mary received the message, and as she gave her assent, she therewith became the mother of God, and shortly thereafter went to the hill country to visit her cousin Elisabeth. The angel told her that Elisabeth had conceived and would bear a son in her old age and that she was now in her sixth month. These are, indeed, wonderful miracles of God: The Virgin Mary becomes a mother, pregnant now with God's Son, and aged, barren Elisabeth also conceived and would give birth to John the Baptist in her old age. We want to address these two miracles today. Mary travels through the hill country with haste, going from Nazareth in Galilee via a difficult road to Jerusalem in Judaea to visit Elisabeth. This was no stunt on her part, or show-off, but a demonstration of her firm faith in the words of the angel who had said to her that she would conceive and give birth to God's Son. That was truly an extraordinary miracle, that the dear Virgin believes the word of the angel and through the Holy Spirit, because of her faith, conceived God's Son, to become the mother of God. Prompted by this faith she arose to go to her cousin, Elisabeth, about whom she had heard that she was now six months pregnant with her son.

3. On top of this miracle is added another, also very great, namely, that Elisabeth recognizes the Virgin Mary as the mother of God and that the infant John leaped for joy in his mother's womb when she

heard the Virgin Mary's greeting. Imbued with the Holy Spirit, the infant John leaped for joy in his mother's womb when Elisabeth heard Mary's greeting. The Holy Spirit indwelling John goes to the heart of the mother and causes her to speak out with a loud voice, that Mary had conceived and was the mother of the Son of God. Truly a great miracle, that Elisabeth should be so perceptive to say to Mary, Behold, the mother of my Lord! She blesses, praises, and addresses the mother and the child, saying, "Blessed art thou among women, and blessed is the fruit of thy womb . . . and blessed is she that believed," and so on. As though she wished to say that no woman on earth is like unto you, for you are the mother of my Lord; the fruit of your womb surpasses all others.

4. Mary, moreover, is filled with joy and raises a salutation to heaven, as she says, I rejoice from the bottom of my heart that I am the mother of God and that the fruit of my womb is so great a blessing. But this is not because of my own person, for I am not worthy; I have not earned it. However, I rejoice that God has regarded my low estate, not my station, not my golden hair, but rather, that I am a despised nobody whom God chose to elevate to be the mother of his Son. For that may he be praised in all eternity. She gives God the honor as she sings the beautiful Magnificat about our dear Lord God. She praises him in that he has not only shown great favor to her person, but also great mercy to all mankind that fears him. First and foremost, though, he has lifted up his servant Israel. That is his manner and nature, she says, to show mercy to the lowly and downtrodden, for which reason he also calls himself father, ruler, and helper of widows and orphans. That is what he has manifested towards me and continues to prove as he helps the wretched, uplifts those of low estate, and makes the poor rich. Conversely, he opposes and abases those who are mighty, arrogant, and proud.

5. Everyday experience proves that God still rules the world today, as Mary's song portrays. Rich men's sons seldom turn out well, for they are overly secure, arrogant, and proud. They feel they do not need to learn because they are well fixed financially and assured of all their material needs. That is why God brings them down, causing their material possessions to dissipate, and reduces them to beggars. In contrast, the sons of the poor have to pick themselves out of the

dust, and must suffer much. Because they have nothing about which to boast and brag, they learn to trust God, resign themselves, and remain quiet. But our Lord God elevates them so that they achieve honors, the likes of which the wealthy never achieve, in spite of their power, influence, and riches. The poor fear God and God gives them good heads so that they study hard and learn, advancing in knowledge and understanding so that they are able to counsel princes, kings, and emperors wisely, like Joseph and David. With daughters it is the same. The daughters of the poor serve, are modest, and chaste awaiting God's help. When they do that, our Lord God is there to help, so that they get ahead, marry godly husbands, own houses and grounds, becoming well-to-do. In contrast, the proud, haughty maidens end up lacking. The Virgin Mary was poor, miserable, and lonely, but feared God and trusted him. So our Lord God acted and chose her to be the mother of his Son. Here is an example that ought to put fear into all the haughty and proud, but at the same time, encouragement for the humble and God-fearing, assuring them that God wishes to be a God of the humble who fear him. He particularly takes pleasure in uplifting the poor, as Psalm 113:5–8 states: "Who is like unto the LORD our God who dwelleth on high, Who humbleth himself to behold the things that are in heaven, and in the earth! He raiseth up the poor out of the dust, and lifteth the needy out of the dunghill; That he may set him with princes, even with the princes of his people." Who are the great doctors of the law, the chancellors of the princes and kings, counselors of the emperor? Usually they are the children of poor people. These are the doers who rule the country and the people. The rest are merely tankards of the princes.

6. These are the events we are considering and commemorating today, not because of Mary, but because of the great miracle which took place on this day. It is not for the sake of her honor, so that we should pray to Mary, but we should give thanks to our dear Lord God that he gave us these two boys, Christ and John, who communicated with each other in their mothers' wombs and are filled with joy. John is the older, midway to birth; Christ is the younger, not yet the size of a little bee. It is a great and mighty miracle that John, who is six months older than Christ, leaped for joy in his mother's womb as

Christ, through Mary, greeted him. Christ is happy that he has a forerunner; John is happy that his Lord follows in his footsteps. We want to touch upon this today and thank our dear Lord God that he has given us these two boys who here begin the preaching of the gospel.

7. Therefore, we do not commemorate this festival because of the mothers, but because of their offspring, on account of whom we should thank God. Mary and Elisabeth did not preach the gospel to us, but John and Christ did. So the Holy Spirit expresses joy for the Holy Gospel, which everywhere in the world today is despised. John and Christ are wonderful individuals and extraordinary preachers who ought to gladden our hearts with their preaching, but we disdain both, the forerunner and the Lord with their messages. As a result we will receive our due reward and punishment. If we wish to be Christians and avoid punishment, we need to thank our Lord God for his precious gospel, of which John the Baptist was the first minister and preacher. Also, let us thank God for his Son, our dear Lord Jesus Christ, whom he revealed to us on this day through the two mothers, Elisabeth and Mary. The two boys leap for joy and exchange greetings and herald each other in their mothers' wombs. Christ greets John, and John acknowledges the greeting by leaping.

8. This episode also portrays three exceptional virtues of the Virgin Mary which we should diligently emulate. The first is her faith; the second, her chaste behavior in relation to people; the third, a genuinely great humility.

9. Moved by her faith Elisabeth testifies of Mary's faith, as she says, "And blessed is she that believed: for there shall be a performance of those things which were told her from the Lord." Mary is praised not because of her personal faith (which all Christians who are saved must have), but because she believed that she has found favor with God because of the blessed fruit of her womb, by means of which we all have received grace upon grace. She received a special promise which pertained solely to her person, that she should give birth to Christ, the Son of God. This promise she believed, and did not let herself be diverted from it, even though she could not understand how it was to take place.

10. Because she trusted, she arose and went to the hill country to visit her dear kinswoman, Elisabeth. As soon as she heard from the

THE DAY OF MARY'S VISITATION 361

angel that she was to be with child and bear a son, who would be great and would be called the Son of the Highest, and that Elisabeth in her old age was also pregnant, she got ready and went immediately to Elisabeth. She did not hesitate or waver, but firmly believed and was assured in her mind that what God had announced to her through the angel would be fulfilled. It, therefore, was no joke to her, but absolute reality. For she believed that she was to be the mother of God and that Elisabeth was also with child. Perhaps she didn't travel alone, but maybe Joseph went with her. For it is a long trip from Nazareth to Jerusalem, and yet she let nothing hinder her, but undertook the long, hard journey. Thus her faith prompted her to go.

11. We need to follow her example. Even though we do not have such a special promise as Mary had, nor are able to match her, nevertheless, we have a general promise in both temporal and spiritual things. We should cleave to God's Word and never doubt it, but firmly believe that what God has promised he will do for us. For the two are to be correlative, word and faith. Faith cannot exist without the word, and on the other hand, where the word is, there faith must be.

12. The Evangelist points out a second example for us at the beginning of this Gospel as he states that Mary went "in haste" to the hill country. He wishes, thereby, to say she is chaste and went hurriedly, not dawdling along like the country girls like to do, for that matter also the town women, young and old, who rest and visit along the way, never get anywhere or finally accomplish anything. This is a common failing with our workers and menfolks, who, when they go out are like the country folk, ending up at the taverns to guzzle themselves full. Maids and women, too, when they go out on a errand, begin to gossip right and left with nary a thought about home. Lazy employees cause an employer to grind his teeth, just like vinegar when poured on the teeth, as Solomon says (Prov. 10:26): "As vinegar to the teeth, and as smoke to the eyes, so is the sluggard to them that send him."

13. Did St. Luke purposely add the words "in haste" to counteract the objections of impertinent women and maidservants who here raise their voices in protest: Yes, why didn't the Virgin stay home? Was she becoming haughty and proud? Moreover, why shouldn't I go out gallivanting, look about, and enjoy myself? After all, Mary

went out and traveled over the countryside! No, says St. Luke, the purpose of this example is not to invite impertinence. What the Virgin did was not to vaunt herself, but was prompted by faith, because she believed the words of the angel who had told her that Elisabeth was pregnant with a son. She wanted to help her aged cousin; that is why she hurriedly left Nazareth. She didn't gawk about, and her thoughts were not helter-skelter, but only how she might be of help to her cousin. This is the lesson you should learn from this, that with faith in God's Word you go about your calling, faithfully, diligently, to carry it to completion.

14. Since Mary stayed with Elisabeth for three months it would appear that she was a poor, forgotten orphan who no longer had father or mother, or other close friends in Nazareth whom she might have been serving. Since she had no responsibility for a father or mother, nor was she reneging from obligatory service, she needed to make excuses to no one. Mary, at this time, was her own person, since she no longer had father or mother. Even though she stayed three months with Elisabeth, she was not neglecting anyone or shirking any obligations; nor was she idle these three months as she waited upon her aged cousin and her dear little nephew, the precious infant, John the Baptist.

15. The third example is her humility. Mary is God's mother; she knows this and believes that she is God's mother. Elisabeth, too, knows this and praises her publicly. No doubt, the Virgin Mary is the greatest and most excellent of all women, above queens and empresses. This eminence has not made her one hair's breadth more proud. She remains humble, lowers herself to become a maid, places herself in the service of her aged cousin, Elisabeth, remaining with her until John the Baptist is born.

16. Such sincere humility ought to jar our senses and take down our pride. But this miserable pride is dear to people; a poor maidservant elevates herself by donning satin or velvet trappings, and as a result no longer knows herself, nor can anyone get along with her. A peasant who has ten dollars swaggers about not knowing whether he is standing on his feet or his head. It is a bloody shame that we vaunt ourselves and strut as though we were the only ones. We should, therefore, forever bear in mind the example of the mother of God

who had been elevated to such great heights, yet, was as humble as though she were not the mother of God. She thinks no more of herself now, when she is the mother of God, than before when she was a poor, wretched maiden. Women, by nature, are prone to vanity. They incline naturally towards this weakness. It could easily happen, therefore, that she would find cause for being proud. Mary knows very well that she is the mother of the Son of God. Nevertheless, she humbles herself and serves the aged matron Elisabeth, who is heavy with child. That is a noble example, which should shame our pride and prompt us to be of service gladly, as Mary here was for Elisabeth.

17. Now then, it's up to us whether or not we want to follow her example. It stands out and illumines our way; the promise and the warning are side by side. If we are willing to be humble, God will lift us up. If we choose to be proud and arrogant, God can and will humble us. There is many a rich wife who appears proud, yet is not proud. On the other hand, wives of peasants and burghers are more arrogant these days than a countess or princess. We simply have to live with this. That's the way it is. But Mary proves, by her example, and sings about it in the Magnificat, that if you are going to be proud, remember, you have someone, God in heaven, who cannot abide it and will overthrow you. Why wouldn't you, rather, want to be humble in the way that Mary, the noble, godly mother was humble?

18. Young people should particularly learn to humble themselves and to be forebearing. Such forbearance is not harmful to them. It is more harmful if one is rapidly advanced than if one must bear hardship. As Solomon states in Proverbs 16:18: "Pride goeth before destruction, and an haughty spirit before a fall." It is better from cradle days on to be spanked with switches and to be put down than to grow up without punishment and discipline like a young tree and wild brush. Those who humble themselves and endure become worthy people; but those who are proud and are unwilling to bear vexation will be shamed. As Solomon says in Proverbs 13:18: "Poverty and shame shall be to him that refuseth instruction: but he that regardeth reproof shall be honoured."

19. In this gospel lesson we have three characteristics of faith: chastity, industry, and humility, alongside the obligation to thank

God for giving us his Son, our dear Lord Jesus Christ, and, also, for beloved John. John is the first messenger of the gospel in the New Testament. He began the preaching of the gospel. Christ, however, is the one of whom the gospel preaches. It is he who gives what the gospel proclaims, namely, forgiveness of sins and eternal life. Amen.

THE DAY OF ST. MARY MAGDALENE*

Luke 7:36–50

And one of the Pharisees desired him that he would eat with him. And he went into the Pharisee's house, and sat down to meat. And, behold, a woman in the city, which was a sinner, when she knew that Jesus sat at meat in the Pharisee's house, brought an alabaster box of ointment, And stood at his feet behind him weeping, and began to wash his feet with tears, and did wipe them with the hairs of her head, and kissed his feet, and anointed them with the ointment. Now when the Pharisee which had bidden him saw it, he spake within himself, saying, This man, if he were a prophet, would have known who and what manner of woman this is that toucheth him: for she is a sinner. And Jesus answering said unto him, Simon, I have somewhat to say unto thee. And he saith, Master, say on. There was a certain creditor which had two debtors: the one owed five hundred pence, and the other fifty. And when they had nothing to pay, he frankly forgave them both. Tell me therefore, which of them will love him most? Simon answered and said, I suppose that he, to whom he forgave most. And he said unto him, Thou hast rightly judged. And he turned to the woman, and said unto Simon, Seest thou this woman? I entered into thine house, thou gavest me no water for my feet: but she hath washed my feet with tears, and wiped them with the hairs of her head. Thou gavest me no kiss: but this woman since the time I came in hath not ceased to kiss my feet. My head with oil thou didst not anoint: but this woman hath anointed my feet with ointment. Wherefore I say unto thee, Her sins, which are many, are forgiven; for she loved much: but to whom little is forgiven, the same loveth little. And he said unto her, Thy sins are forgiven. And they that sat at meat with him began to say within themselves, Who is this that forgiveth sins also? And he said to the woman, Thy faith hath saved thee; go in peace.

*Preached at the parish church, 1536, on the 7th Sunday after Trinity. The substitution of this text in place of Mark 8:1–9 occurred frequently in the church, since the story of a miraculous feeding of a multitude was treated earlier, on Laetare Sunday (4th Lent) according to John 6:1–15.

1. This is a beautiful Gospel text, well worth an in-depth treatment. But even though there is not enough time to do this in a single session, we do want to speak a few words about it. Our beloved Lord Jesus Christ models the office he has entrusted to his apostles and preachers. In other places he decrees and testifies verbally; but here he confirms it with deed. Moreover, the office and the command is to do as he does, not in order to please mankind. For his office is to rebuke sin and to forgive sin. If he rebukes sin, the world won't stand for it, saying that he ought to preach only gospel and grace. If he forgives sin, then the Pharisees and the holier-than-thou turn up their noses, and say that he prohibits good works and preaches only grace without reproving sin.

2. In this office we preachers are to help our Lord God, also rebuking and forgiving sin for his sake. Those preachers who do not rebuke sin open the gates of hell and close heaven. On their part, those who refuse to forgive sins, likewise, open the gates of hell and close heaven. Therefore, both must be proclaimed, reproof and pardon of sin.

3. But, as we said above, the world wants no part of this. To reprove and punish sin is wrong; to offer comfort and pardon is also wrong. Whatever you do, it makes no difference. What Christ experienced here is exactly what we experience today. He was wrong to forgive Mary Magdalene, and the Pharisees said he was shutting up hell, he was giving people the opportunity and the desire to sin without restraint, and he was blaspheming God. But when he opened to Simon a festering wound and revealed to him the sin of which he had been unaware, who had been flattering himself that he was righteous, it did no good. So the Lord is not complaining in vain or without cause about this sort of evil in the world when he says (Matt. 11:16–19): "But whereunto shall I liken this generation? It is like unto children sitting in the markets, and calling unto their fellows, And saying, We have piped unto you, and ye have not danced; we have mourned unto you, and ye have not lamented. For John came neither eating nor drinking, and they say, He hath a devil. The Son of man came eating and drinking, and they say, Behold a man gluttonous, and a winebibber, a friend of publicans and sinners!" John preached repentance, rebuked sins, lived a disciplined life, and they

said, He keeps himself from the people; he is a devil; who would want to listen to what he says? Christ preached forgiveness of sins, accepted sinners, and they said, He keeps company with harlots and miscreants, makes them insolent and secure; how can he be a true prophet?

4. This is without doubt a very good rule, from the point of view of reason, which Christ has enjoined upon us, to have to endure reproach as blasphemers and heretics before God, like John was, or be labeled an associate of harlots and ne'er-do-wells, as Christ was. But what can we do? If Christ experienced this, we will fare no better. So we may as well accept it, and get used to the fact that people do not like it, especially from us who hold the office. If we did not do this, neither rebuking nor forgiving sin, who would be saved?

5. The Pharisee Simon does not realize that he lacks the essential thing. He imagines that he is doing a good work and considers it a great favor to invite Christ, the prophet, to be his guest, to give him a seat among the Pharisees as a distinguished rabbi. But something needs to be done; he continues to be oblivious of his own sin, and does not desire to have his sins forgiven. So our Lord must rebuke him, and makes this magnanimous work of his, of which he is proud, a sin and a shame to him. You invited me, he says, but in so doing you have only your own pride and benefit in mind. You did not give me water for my feet, and even if you had, it would have been a meager service in comparison with that which this woman has just shown me. For this sinner provided not water, but the tears from her own eyes, and sprinkled neither my hands, nor my head, nor my face, but the lowliest of my members, my feet, which are soiled by the dust of the earth; and she did it from behind. What do you think of this work which the sinner did to me, in comparison with your work of which you are so proud, and yet you gave me no water to wash either my face, my hands, or my feet?

6. You gave me no wipe or towel to dry my face, hands, or feet. But she gave me not a silk kerchief, but her hair, her tresses, the most glorious ornament she possesses (for her hair is a woman's greatest glory, 1 Cor. 11:15). With this she dried not my face, not my neck, but my feet. You gave me no kiss, neither on my hand, nor my cheek, nor my mouth. For in the land of Israel this was the common custom

for one to kiss another, as is still the custom in the Netherlands and elsewhere. Therefore, Christ says, You might have given me a kiss, in keeping with the customs of this people and country; but you did not do this, you proud, haughty ass. But this woman accounted herself unworthy to kiss my hand, or cheek, or mouth; so she fell to her knees, and has not ceased from kissing my feet, however disreputable this might seem to you.

7. You did not anoint my head with oil, or as we might say, with perfume, as we customarily honor guests with oil of spikenard or rose water. You dispensed with this and did not do it. But she poured a costly perfume: balsam, oil of spikenard, which is of exquisite quality and expensive, on my dusty feet. You did not perceive at all what this woman graciously did for me. And as for you, you have not perceived this sin in yourself, which is a very great burden of sin indeed, and a great and deadly corruption, if you must come before God for judgment still encumbered with it. And so the Lord rebukes the Pharisee for his sin, and, in contradistinction, forgives the woman her sins, saying, "Thy sins are forgiven."

8. So this is the office of our Lord which he introduces into the world, namely, that of rebuking sin and forgiving sin. He rebukes the sins of those who do not recognize their sin, and in particular, those who claim not to be sinners but presume to be righteous, as this Pharisee did. He forgives the sins of those who perceive their sin and desire forgiveness; the woman was this type of sinner. For rebukes he receives small gratitude; for pardoning sins he elicits accusations of heresy and blasphemy against his doctrine. We must suffer this to happen. If the Lord himself could not be exempt from this, but voices his complaint, as it is written in Matthew 11, then we shall not fare any better. If we wish to be Christians, and especially preachers, then we must have patience, and consider the saying of Paul (2 Cor. 6:4, 7–8): "But in all things approving ourselves as the ministers of God, in much patience, in afflictions, in necessities, in distresses . . . By the word of truth, by the power of God, by the armour of righteousness on the right hand and on the left, by honour and dishonour, by evil report and good report: as deceivers, and yet true." When the Lord reproves the Pharisees, they become resentful and do not want to hear it. Although the text at this place is silent on this

point, it is clearly evident at other places how they received his reproofs. When he says to the woman, "Thy sins are forgiven," they reply, Did the devil send this prophet? Who is this that claims to forgive sins? This is the kind of thing the Lord had to put up with. So he says not a word until the proud asses have spoken condemnation and judgment upon him, and when they have said their piece and quieted down, he turns to the woman and says, "Thy faith hath saved thee; go in peace."

9. We do the very same thing: we rebuke sin and forgive sin, and have our opponents, the papists, maligning us as heretics. They accuse us of forbidding good works and offering them a pretext to sin, although we rebuke sin more severely than they do. For though they rebuke sins till the end of the age, they stick to the second table, rebuking only the gross, open sins, as does this Pharisee. He thinks: I am a holy man; I am not a sinner as this woman is. He is fairly well acquainted with the second table. He sees, as well as understands that prostitution is wrong and a sin. But he understands, the first table not a whit; he has no idea that he lacks faith in God's goodness and mercy, nor does he recognize that he is worse than a pagan, having no love for God or for his neighbor, but instead is full of pride, arrogance, and presumption. And, yet, for all that he goes along blindly and obstinately, unaware of these sins. So Christ must lance his festering boil, expose the sin, and point out the source of the trouble. True, you did invite me here to eat with you, he says, but what do you mean by being so puffed up and heady about this work of yours? You are, no doubt, a reasonable and intelligent man, and judged correctly that he who receives much loves much. You are also a pious man in the eyes of the world, not an adulterer, not a thief, not a lawbreaker; but you are an unbelieving, godless man; for you are presumptuous, you have neither God, nor grace, nor his mercy, no forgiveness of sins, and you are arrogant and covetous toward your neighbor. Yes, indeed, I mean proud, Simon, vain and self-canonized.

10. This is what needs to be done; that is our office. Sins are not to be pardoned without first being rebuked and brought to the sinner's attention, particularly sins of the first table, such as unbelief, idolatry, no fear of God, presumption, no knowledge of God or respect for him and others. But on the other side, forgiveness is not to

be excluded either. They are operative together, as a pendulum swings from one side to the other: to rebuke sin and to forgive sin, the exhortation to repentance and the declaration of pardon. If sins are not rebuked, the soul is not humbled, and the preaching of grace remains unfruitful. But the soul which is smitten by a rebuke or the preaching of the Law, as this poor harlot, needs a proclamation of grace and forgiveness, or it must be overcome with despondency and despair. The poor woman is not so self-assured as the proud Pharisee, Simon; he is presumptuous and proud, flattering himself to be quite pure, not only outwardly, but also his heart and everything about him. Therefore, he must be reproved and his sins exposed. But this poor woman has recognized and felt her sinfulness; she is sorrowful and humble, so she needs forgiveness.

11. Neither of these can be neglected. The call to repentance and the rebuke are both necessary to bring people face to face with their sins and humble them. The proclamation of grace and forgiveness are necessary too, lest the people lose all hope. Therefore, the office of preaching must walk the middle way between presumption and despair, to preach so that the people become neither proud nor despairing. Both of these sins are proscribed by God in the first commandment: "I am the Lord, thy God," as if to say, You are not to be proud; if you are, I am not the Lord your God; likewise, you are not to despair; if you do I am not the Lord your God. Reprove the sin of the presumptuous and comfortable people who are not aware of their sin; not merely blatant sins of the flesh, but also, and foremost, the subtle, underlying, spiritual sins. As for the others who know their sins and fear death, comfort them and say, Dear brother, you have had enough terrors, I may not frighten you any more. Before you had no God because of your presumption, but now the devil wants to lure you away from God on the other side by despair. God has forbidden both of these, and he has ordained the office of preaching to restrain both: presumption, by the call to repentance and the rebuke; despair, by the preaching of grace and forgiveness of sins.

12. That is the sum total of this Gospel, which teaches of Christ's office—reprove sins and forgive sins—in which office he is either reproached as a devil or a blasphemer in the world. If he preaches repentance, rebuking the people's sins as John the Baptist did, then he

is a devil; if he preaches grace and pardons sins, then he is a glutton and winebibber, a friend of harlots and outcasts. Whatever he does, it's wrong. If he takes a hard line against the obstinate and the haughty, that's not right; if he is gentle, mild, and kindly towards the poor sinners, that's not right either. If he plays the pipe, it's no good; if he sings a dirge, it's no good either.

13. Now this office and twofold preaching are vital to Christianity if anyone is to be saved at all. As Christ commanded, preach in his name repentance and forgiveness of sins, come what may. Moreover, each part is to be rightly distinguished and administered. Therefore, also, St. Paul commands Timothy his disciple (2 Tim 2:15): "Study to shew thyself approved unto God, a workman that needeth not to be ashamed, rightly dividing the word of truth"; as if to say, hold firmly to the word of truth, but take care that you divide one part from the other, and administer it properly. It is a sharp two-edged sword. Keep the word of reproof, so that all sins, both the inward and the outward, the fleshly and the spiritual, which people commit against us may be reproved. Keep the word of grace, so that we and others may have a true and certain consolation against sin. Both are necessary, the preaching of reproof and the preaching of grace, to keep people on the middle way, falling neither to the right into presumption and complacency, nor to the left into despair. Where there is despair, a man is swept over the brink into hell; and where there is presumption, a man rushes into hell full speed ahead.

14. So take careful note of this Gospel; and would to God that everyone would take to heart this example of our Lord Jesus Christ, how he behaved toward the proud Pharisee and toward the poor sinner. To Simon, the Pharisee, he is a strict judge and preaches a severe word, making it especially disagreeable and unpalatable. On the other hand, he is a gracious confessor and a consoling preacher. He pronounces over the woman a merciful remission of sins and makes her a saint; but he commits Simon, the Pharisee, to the devil. That is preaching reproof and grace. The miserable harlot he frees from sin and clothes her with heavenly grace. He shows the proud Pharisee his sin, and burdens his conscience; yet he means him no evil, but seeks his salvation, revealing his sin to him so that he would recog-

nize it, seek counsel, and escape damnation with the other presumptuous hypocrites, if he would only obey.

15. You hear such things preached by us all the time. And this is how we should preach, so that we always find ourselves there with those sinners who know their sinfulness and are fearful because of it, as Magdalene acknowledges her sins and is frightened by them. Let us not be found in the number of those who are without sin and imagine themselves holy, or justify their sins and refuse to be corrected. God grant that we not be found among sinners who refuse to be sinners. If he permits us to fall, let us fall into sins which we acknowledge and that he will pardon; let us not fall into sin which he cannot pardon because it claims to be not sin, but righteousness.

16. A Christian is in this state as long as he is on earth, even if he is no adulterer, or murderer, or thief; even if he does not have the sins which war against the soul, as St. Peter calls them (1 Peter 2:11), that is, against faith and a good conscience; nevertheless he is and remains a sinner in the eyes of God, with a heart full of sins, not just in violation of the first commandment, but against all the commandments of both tables. He does not love God with his whole heart, he does not delight in God's Word and work as he should, and he does not have a fervent love for his neighbor. In sum, he experiences a whole range of evil inclinations, lusts, and desires contrary to God's commandments, although he resists them through the Spirit of God in faith, and does not yield to them. This defilement is with us until we die. St. Paul mortifies his body and keeps it tightly reined up (1 Cor. 9:27). Yet for all that, he grieves that he has still not gotten a firm grip on it, neither shall he completely (Phil. 3:12); and in Romans 7, he says that he longs to be godly, he would only too gladly be ablaze with love toward God and his neighbor; but he has a demon in his heart, drawing him back, that is, his sinful nature. "For I delight in the law of God after the inward man: But I see another law in my members, warring against the law of my mind, and bringing me into captivity to the law of sin which is in my members. O wretched man that I am! who shall deliver me from the body of this death? I thank God through Jesus Christ our Lord" (v. 22–25).

17. This is the case with all Christians: they both possess and feel the sinful nature. But they do not let it rule over them, or even hold

the upper hand; they do not allow the sinful nature to rage against the hope which they have or drive them to despair; neither do they allow it to rage against fear and humility, or drive them to presumption, pride, and arrogance against God and their neighbor. They are, therefore, in a continual struggle, battling against their sins, and praying to God to redeem them from the accursed, sinful body. Everyone who so proceeds is on the right path to salvation. Although he be a sinner, still feeling his sins, they shall not destroy him. He who confesses his sin, submits to discipline, and bestirs himself to resist, can be confident that his sins are forgiven. But if he does not confess his sins, but, on the contrary, defends them, refusing correction, he has no such hope.

18. This is enough for now about the office of our Lord Jesus Christ, which we execute in his name, both to rebuke sins, and forgive them, as he commanded us. This is an indispensable office for us, for all time, until the Last Day. For we will never achieve in this life absolute purity and sinless perfection. The old leaven has spread too far beyond all reasonable bounds, that we will never be free from it until we die to it, bodily as well as spiritually. So we will always be in need of reproof and forgiveness, in order to resist and harness the sinful nature. May God grant us his grace to remain godly sinners rather than holy blasphemers, that is, that we would let God be just and his words be right, so that he might justify us. Amen.

THE DAY OF ST. MICHAEL AND ALL ANGELS

First Sermon—1532

You know that we are here today in order to listen to God's Holy Word. We shall, therefore, let our Lord God be the preacher, and we, his pupils, will listen to his Holy Word. St. Matthew writes as follows:

Matthew 18:1–10

> *At the same time came the disciples unto Jesus, saying, Who is the greatest in the kingdom of heaven? And Jesus called a little child unto him, and set him in the midst of them, And said, Verily I say unto you, Except ye be converted and become as little children, ye shall not enter into the kingdom of heaven. Whosoever therefore shall humble himself as this little child, the same is greatest in the kingdom of heaven. And whoso shall receive one such little child in my name receiveth me. But whoso shall offend one of these little ones which believe in me, it were better for him that a millstone were hanged about his neck, and that he were drowned in the depth of the sea. Woe unto the world because of offenses! for it must needs be that offenses come; but woe to that man by whom the offense cometh! Wherefore if thy hand or thy foot offend thee, cut them off, and cast them from thee: it is better for thee to enter into life halt or maimed, rather than having two hands or two feet to be cast into everlasting fire. And if thine eye offend thee, pluck it out, and cast it from thee: it is better for thee to enter into life with one eye, rather than having two eyes to be cast into hell fire. Take heed that ye despise not one of these little ones; for I say unto you, That in heaven their angels do always behold the face of my Father which is in heaven.*

About the Angels

1. This feast commemorating the angels has been placed in the church's calendar for the sake of our young people, or more correctly, for the sake of all Christians, so that they might train themselves to think about the beloved angels and thank God for appointing

these mighty lords to be his servants for us. It is for this reason that the Epistle to the Hebrews calls them ministering spirits, sent to serve those who are to inherit salvation.

2. It is true, indeed, that God could sustain and preserve us for himself over against the devil and all misery without the ministration of the angels, just as he was able by himself to create us humans, as he did Adam and Eve, without father and mother; also to give us light without the sun and stars, and without plows, soil, and tilling to give us food. But he does not want to do it in this way; instead he has given father and mother in order to establish a household and to beget and rear children; has given us rulers and magistrates to govern; has created sun and moon to give light; in short, has so arranged it that one creature is to serve another. And so, for this reason we are to thank God for giving us father and mother, temporal government, sun, moon, stars, grain, and all sorts of creatures to serve and sustain us in this life. By the same token, we should also learn that God protects and aids us through his angels, for which we should surely thank God as well.

3. Now, you have often heard that the devil is around people everywhere, in palaces, in houses, in the field, on the streets, in the water, in the forest, in fire; devils are everywhere. All they ever do is seek man's destruction. . . . and it is certainly true, were God not continually to put restraints on the evil foe, he would not leave one little kernel of grain in the field or on the ground, no fish in the water, no piece of meat in the pot, no drop of water, beer, or wine in the cellar uncontaminated, nor would he leave a sound member in our bodies.

4. When one, therefore, loses an eye or hand, when someone is killed or contracts a deadly disease, or comes down with another illness, these are nothing but blows and thrusts of the devil. Now he aims at one person, then at another; if he makes a hit, he has achieved what he went after; if he does not, it is a sure indication that God hindered him through the beloved angels. Therefore, when mishaps occur, when one falls into a fire, another into water, these clearly are blows and strokes of the devil who is constantly aiming and pitching at us, hoping to inflict all manner of hurt upon us.

5. Against such a malicious, spiteful, cunning enemy, who is continually hounding us, God has appointed the beloved angels, to keep

watch so that where the devil suddenly comes and strikes with pestilence, with fire, with hail, and the like, an angel is there to counter it, for the struggle between angels and devils is constantly ongoing. The devil would gladly trigger all manner of trouble, as we see and experience daily, when many a bone is fractured on level ground, many a person falls down a staircase or steps, not knowing how such a thing could have happened. This and similar things the devil would constantly be causing, were God not preventing it through the beloved angels. However, he does at times permit us to experience such things, that we might learn, if God were not there all the time preventing their occurrence, they would happen continuously; and for this reason we ought to pray all the more diligently and thank God for such protection.

6. When he wants to chastise, he withdraws his hand, takes away the protection and aid of his beloved angels, and gives the devil free reign and power over us. The devil fells one here, another there, so that in one day hundreds often die in a pestilence. Plagues of the devil, his venomous darts, his lead bullets, are pestilence, glandular disorders, pocks, and other adversities. God permits such things to happen to serve as warnings for us and to draw us to himself, so that we cling to him and obey him.

7. For he is a God of life, who wants to lend a hand and assist wherever it is needed, if we but fear and call upon him. But if we are going to be wicked and show no concern for his Word, nor give him thanks for his fatherly protection and care, he then becomes angry and holds back his angels in heaven, giving the devil free rein to employ his evil scoundrels in causing pestilence and other misfortune, for they simply do not want to do good. To illustrate, it is just as if you withdraw your support from and refuse to give your children food, clothing, or anything else; they then become poor and emaciated. God punishes ungrateful, evil scoundrels in this way by not restraining the devil and keeping his angels in heaven. When he says to Michael, Gabriel, and other angels, Hold on, let the devil be in control, for the scoundrels simply do not want to do what is right; so, leave off, and let pestilence kill them. That's exactly how it goes.

8. We see that this is precisely what happened in Job's case. For the account concerning him states that our Lord God asks of the dev-

il, Where have you been? and the devil answers, "I have been going to and fro in the earth." Undoubtedly, this would not have been without incident, without inflicting harm, for the vagabond prowls around, says Peter, like a lion looking for someone to devour. Then the Lord says further, "Have you considered my servant Job? for there is none like him in the earth, a perfect and upright man, one that fears God, and eschews evil." And Satan replies, Yes, dear God! Job has reason to be upright, for you have put a guard around his house and all that he possesses, even pouring a wall around it all, that is, surrounding Job, his wife, children, fields, and cattle with protecting angels. In other words, the devil is saying, I would have struck, had you not afforded protection.

9. But then our Lord God allows the devil to do anything he wants with Job's possessions. And he sets to work at once, incites some evil scoundrels to carry off a thousand oxen and asses and kill the herdsmen. Next, he causes fire to fall down from heaven, burning up the seven thousand sheep along with the shepherds and everything else. Third, he incites three bands of Chaldeans to make a raid and carry off Job's three thousand camels after killing the drivers. All this happened in one day, and that still was not the end of it. For Job had three daughters and four sons. As they were all together, happy and in good spirits, behold! The devil stirs up such a great wind that the house collapsed in one heap and killed all who were inside. All this the devil was well capable of doing, but not until God had given him permission. The same thing can happen with us. Should our Lord recall the angels, not one of us would survive, but all would be dead in a moment.

10. When in all humility now, Job fell prostrate on the ground and said, "The Lord gave, and the Lord hath taken away; blessed be the name of the Lord!" God said to Satan, "There is none like him in the earth, a perfect and an upright man." Satan replies, That is not at all astounding! There is still much misfortune to be overcome because none has yet affected the body. But let me set upon his body, upon his flesh and bone, let that happen and then there will be no more good words; he will sing a different tune from the one he is singing now, since someone else's skin, not his, has been affected.

11. Then the Lord allows Satan this also and says, "Behold, he is in your hand; set upon his body and torment him all you want; just

spare his life and do not kill him." It is an especially comforting thing that our Lord still has such restraints on the devil that he is unable to do any more harm than what God permits and allows him. For he could not lay hands on Job's body until God allowed it. But when the Lord allowed it, the devil took off and smote poor Job with so many inflamed pustules that there was not a spot on his body, from head to foot, not covered with them, causing him to scratch himself with a piece of broken pot as he sat in ashes.

12. The heathen do not understand from where such misfortune suddenly comes; we Christians, however, know that it is the work of the devil who possesses such an arsenal of halberds and missiles, of spears and swords to hurl, thrust and mount against us, if God allows him. Therefore, let there be no misgivings. If there is a fire and a town or a house burns down, a devil is certainly hovering nearby, blowing upon the fire to make it flare up. So, too, if someone dies as a result of pestilence, drowns, or falls to his death, the devil is involved, with God's allowance, otherwise, we would become far too wicked. As is evident, despite such chastisements, the world does not change, nor by that means is God able to make us righteous.

13. We need to learn this and realize that it is the devil who harms us in body, possessions, and honor; he does this by himself, in the same way he lays hold on Job's possessions and stirs up the Chaldeans and others against him. For our Lord God, as indicated above, is a God of life and it is his nature to do only good. For this he uses the service of the angels, even though he has such power within himself, without the angels, just as through the evil angels he allows punishment and harm to come, even though he could punish by himself.

14. Because of his kindness we ought to thank our loving Lord God for giving us the beloved angels who, like a wall, guard and protect us against the devil; we must not become impudent and secure, as if we were alone on earth and the devil a thousand miles away. No, you are not alone, devils are all around you; as Paul says, They fly in the air like jackdaws and crows, swoop down and dart at us without letup, and if they can knock us down on the first try, they will do so.

15. To oppose these evil spirits and devils, God created the holy angels; they are kind, merciful, benevolent spirits who prevent the devils from doing all they would like to do. If, therefore, the beloved

angels were not at the courts of the emperor, kings, and princes, the devil would be in control; it is evident that no harmony can be created there, for the devil whispers things into their ears and causes all manner of dissension. And were the dear angels not there to prevent these things from happening, they would tear into one another all the time and not a day would pass without war and bloodshed. Our Lord God allows noble lords to be at loggerheads; at times he allows the devil to light a fire, but then you will find the beloved angels extinguishing the fire and making peace. However, where God pulls back his angels because of our sins, there people flare up, murder, kill, and violate women, to the great delight of the devil.

16. It's the same story in running a household; there would be no peace, only endless dissension, scolding, quarreling, stealing, unfaithfulness, neglect, and the like. Nothing would go right but all would be full of misery and heartache if the devil had his way. But God puts the brakes on him through his beloved angels, even though now and then he has lit a fire and caused some sort of trouble, till he had to yield and back off.

17. Accordingly, no one really is safe; the world is filled with devils. They are all too eager to cause harm to body, to possessions, to the soul, through malevolence, hatred, anger, arrogance, and the like, in order to bring us down to themselves in hell. But we have our God to thank that this does not happen because he wards off the devil through his angels, so that always more good than harm results, more peace than war, more grain at harvest than lost by frost, hail, and whatever else, more houses preserved than burned down, more good health than sickly and infirm bodies. Should the devil strike at an eye, a foot, or an arm, the rest of the body remains sound. So, at all times more people grow old and die than die by plague.

18. But that things just do not happen in orderly manner, as the devil causes harm here and there, indicates that God by this visitation wants to get our attention, to get us to open our eyes, to see that aside from the hurt, we have much grace and blessing for which to thank God. When war, pestilence, or other misfortune occurs, the world has not entirely gone to pieces but, by and large, most things have escaped. So the prophet Jeremiah exhorts God's people to be thankful that they have not been exterminated, stating in Lamenta-

tions 3:22: "It is of the Lord's mercies that we are not consumed." In other words, Be still, and do not lament the fact that you have been punished and led into captivity; by God's grace and mercy you are not completely done in. For that is what the devil would gladly have seen done. He is not content when you merely break a leg; he would much rather have seen your head torn off. He is not content when one or two in a house die; he would rather clean out the entire house and pile it all up in one big heap. Therefore, we should fear God and pray that through his angels he would protect us from the devil. And if during pestilence someone dies, or in war another is killed, we ought then say with pious Jeremiah: God be praised that some are still alive and not all have perished! For with this, God wants to teach us concerning the devil's potential evil activity, were he not restrained by the beloved angels.

19. Let us learn, therefore, that we are in grave danger every day and night as targets of the devil. He always has a crossbow stretched tight and a gun loaded, taking aim to strike us with pestilence, syphilis, war, fire, and violent weather. But through his precious angels our beloved Lord God sees to it that the crossbow hits the devil and the gun blows up or misfires. On the other hand, he at times allows him to hit the mark, so that we learn that we are not high and mighty, or in charge of everything, and so should pray all the more fervently that God would not let the devil have free rein, but through his angels graciously restrains him.

20. What we should learn today is that our Lord God has so ordained that each Christian should have not only one but many angels protecting him, just as each also has his own particular devils who slink after him and, if unable to do more, trouble a person with bad dreams, saddle you with scandalmongers who slander, thwart, and defame you. Be aware that these are all wicked henchmen of the devil and be careful that you do not live as do the heathen; they, too, see and experience such misfortune, but in their thinking it just happens accidentally, for they know nothing about the devil. But let us learn to recognize that this is the accursed devil's doing. On the other hand, when you see that something has turned out well, be ready to say that a good angel prompted it, otherwise things would have gone worse for a person. To illustrate, when a person is saved from a flood

or is unharmed when a stone falls on him, this is not luck but the work of a beloved angel.

21. But there are distinctions among angels, as well as among the devils. Princes and lords have great and special angels, as we see in Daniel 10. Children and common folks have ordinary angels. For there will always be a given angel who is greater, mightier, and wiser than the rest. The same is true, also, of the devils. That explains why, as Christ says, that they belong to a kingdom (Luke 11). For just as many persons and different offices constitute a kingdom, so also among the devils there are different ranks. There are the lesser devils who tempt with adultery, greed, vain arrogance, and other similar sins. But then there are higher spirits who tempt with unbelief, with despair, with heresies, and have misled the factious spirits and the pope. It is extremely important, therefore, that we accustom ourselves to prayer, and in time of grave danger conscientiously petition God not to take from us the protection of the beloved angels, lest we come to nought, for we are too weak for the devil.

22. This, then, is what the Lord means in this Gospel where he informs us concerning the beloved angels. It is, however, a shame that we have to preach this Gospel to people who do not take it to heart seriously to reflect on it. For what the Lord says here relative to children is so important: "Take heed that ye despise not one of these little ones; for I say unto you, that in heaven their angels do always behold the face of my Father which is in heaven."

23. It probably would have been enough to say, These little ones have their own angels. However, by saying, "Their angels do always behold the face of my Father which is in heaven," he especially emphasizes the matter. It is tantamount to his saying, I commend little children to you, do not provoke them but rear them well; for God is much concerned about them. And if you look down on them and are unwilling to treat them with consideration, then at least respect their angels and stand in awe of them; and learn from these very great spirits who very lovingly care for them and do for them what is best. They continually stand before the face of God, listen to and behold him, assist and serve him. You who are far, far inferior, should do likewise, and not provoke the little children, but gladly minister to them. The angels are superior servants, who, as at court, surround the prince,

stand before the table, listen to, and observe the prince himself. It is these very same servants whom children also have to watch over them. Therefore, I beseech and warn you not to offend the children, but tend and nurture them.

24. If now this were the only passage we had where Jesus states how greatly his heavenly Father is concerned about little children, we would have to conclude that among all good works, none are greater or better than to properly rear young people. For who would not regard it important to serve those whom angels, who are continually before God's face, serve? For this reason father and mother, servants and maidservants, teachers and preachers, all who have anything to do with the young, should be sincerely happy, willing, and ready to perform such service, letting nothing deter them, since even these great princes of heaven are not ashamed to serve and look after the young. This is the first thing, next to the doctrine concerning the angels, that we ought to learn from today's Gospel.

25. The second thing is that we not only willingly nurture the young—offending them neither in word or deed, so that they are not misled but reared in the best possible way—and also teach them to pray, to be chaste, modest, obedient, faithful, good-natured, serene, and truthful, not profane or lewd in word or conduct, in short, that they do not become carnal, vulgar, rude, wild, dissolute people. This happens soon enough if it is not warded off through diligent training.

26. Everyday experience teaches us that youth is like tinder which is easily ignited, easily affected by what is evil and offensive. Therefore, it takes especial diligence to be attentive to both, children and their angels: to angels, so as not to grieve them; to children, however, so as not to provoke them. For listen how the Lord regards children:

27. "Whoso shall receive one such little child in my name receiveth me." In other words, Whoever is responsible for a child, physically and spiritually, trains him properly so that he learns to know God, learns not to curse, swear, or steal; to him I say that he is receiving me personally, is loving me as if he were carrying me, Mary's child, in his arms and taking care of me just as my mother Mary has taken care of me. That is preaching ever so sweetly and tugging at us ever so winsomely.

28. But why does the Lord do it? Solely for the reason that he understands very well how eager young people are to listen to obscene things and how easily they are misled. Moreover, evil mouths are only too happy to lend assistance here and—may plaintive cries rise to God in heaven!—we now find boys and girls, ten and twelve years old, who can curse and swear a blue streak about hurts, physical disorders, pustules, and the like, and are otherwise devoid of shame and are vulgar in speech. From whom do they learn this? From no one else but from those who should be restraining them, from father and mother, and from shameful, wicked servants. Young people come to know such things more quickly and pay more heed to them than to the Lord's Prayer. This has its roots in that old, evil firebrand, our sinful nature, that sticks within us. That is why Christ preaches here so compellingly and admonishes so tenderly to take care of young people, saying, When you train one of these little ones, when they are brought up in the fear and knowledge of God, in godliness and modesty, you then have done me the greatest service. I have assigned my noble servants, the beloved angels, to serve and attend them. Remember this and do likewise, do not offend them, let them hear no evil, and minister to them willingly.

29. With young people, therefore, one must be circumspect and cautious, careful not to say and do all the things one otherwise says and does. The heathen have said it well: *Maxima reverentia debetur juventuti*, "Young people are owed the highest regard and respect." But Christ preaches much differently here, namely, that when one receives young children and nurtures them, this is as dear to him as if one were to carry him, as the Virgin Mary carried him. But how many are there that do this? Very few. Therefore, the Lord issues a harsh judgment when he says:

Whoso shall offend one of these little ones which believe in me, it were better for him that a millstone were hanged about his neck, and that he were drowned in the depth of the sea.

30. The Lord is very angry, and it grieves him deeply when young people are not carefully trained. "Whoso shall offend one of these little ones," he says, whoever teaches young people to curse, swear, lie, slander, to be unchaste, and so on, it would be better if he were dead. By this he indicates that such sin will be punished not merely with

temporal death, but with eternal damnation. The world regards this punishment as wrong, and that is why all kinds of offenses flourish. It is the accursed devil's doing that the world's young people are now so depraved, wild, and undisciplined. They become the devil's children and are capable of nothing but cursing and swearing, slandering and lying; they live immorally, are disobedient, and guilty of all manner of malevolence. Woe to those who foster this in them. For the sentence has already been pronounced upon such people, as Christ says, "It were better for him that a millstone were hanged about his neck and that he were drowned in the depth of the sea." But the world does not listen until it has to experience firsthand and deal with the havoc wrought.

31. So, our dear Lord Jesus Christ exhorts that we should willingly serve the youth and not mislead them, saying, If you have no qualms as regards the children, then tremble before their angels; and if you are so devoid of shame before the children, then remember that their angels are standing there, horrified at what is going on and finding it incredible. So if the angels are displeased, the very same angels who are always in the Lord God's presence, whom he knows and whose repulsion he observes—although he is already aware of this since nothing escapes him—and how they become angered and grieved, then it is plain that both God himself and his angels are greatly angered when a person offends the children. Therefore, one should see to it that youth are carefully reared, not only that nothing is done to offend them, but that they are kept from all evil and diligently guided to be disciplined in conduct. So, if a child curses or lets go with profanity, we must admonish him earnestly and say to him, You ought to be deeply ashamed of yourself; never do it again; for there stands your angel, who sees and hears and is startled at such cursing and is very depressed by it! When your angel, who stands before the face of God, is startled and depressed, do you not believe that God will see this and be pained and angry? Therefore, take care and never do this again! With such and other words your youth can be properly reared, when otherwise they would grow up as troubled young people, learning and engaging in all manner of foul behavior. Moreover, if words and conscientious admonition are not given or fail to help, there the an-

gels have the command to scourge at once with the rod and not allow children to go their headstrong way.

32. Someone, however, is bound to ask, Should one then not swear at all? Christ and the apostles, after all, swore! True it is, Christ and the apostles did swear and denounce; however, they did so out of love, not to offend someone, but for the sake of castigation and correction. But if a person swears after the fashion of the world, so that neither punishment nor reformation results, but rather offense, particularly with young people, this ought not to be. That is what the Lord means: Every person should lend a hand here and guard against misleading our young people. Whoever does this is thereby doing as great a service as if he were carrying Christ himself in his arms. As Christ here says, safeguarding our young people is doing them a service.

33. Accordingly, both things are stated here: that it is a great service, as if done to Christ himself, when one serves young people, and, on the other hand, that it is a great sin when one offends the young people. If angels watch over and willingly serve young children, then we are to bear in mind that we, too, are to assist in training them well and serving them gladly. But the world does not believe it. For that reason what Christ wants here does not happen, but just the opposite, as is evident everywhere. I would rather be dead than live for ten, yes, even but three years, and see how my rascals are living. For that reason I, too, want to serve our Lord God and not have a millstone hung around my neck on their account.

34. Thus our message and sermon today is that the beloved angels govern in all the world and serve young people, and that Christ wants us to do likewise. Therefore, let us learn that father, mother, and teachers do God the greatest possible service when they properly train and teach young people. Let this suffice, then, concerning this Gospel and about the beloved angels.

THE DAY OF ST. MICHAEL AND ALL ANGELS

Second Sermon—1534

Matthew 18:1–10

1. From this Gospel we are to learn how our Lord God becomes extremely angry with and will severely punish those who offend little ones or teach or allow anything to happen to them that is improper, hurtful, and offensive, be it by word or deed. He warns earnestly against giving offense, saying, If your eye, hand, or foot offends you, pluck it out, cut it off, and so on. Here he does not mean the eye that is located in the head, or the hand or the foot on the body; he means our neighbor, our brother, our sister with whom we associate daily. And he wants us to understand that when we see that our close associates, or even our brothers and sisters, are inclined to teach us what is evil and induce us to engage in wicked and unconscionable activities, we are to flee from them and avoid them; and when we do something wicked, we are not to excuse ourselves by saying that we heard, saw, or learned it from this or that person.

2. And further, he utters dreadful threats against those who offend, that is, cause others to sin, and he warns that God will severely punish those who in this way give offense. In particular, however, he warns and admonishes that we must not offend the children. If a person has no compelling reason to desist from offending the young ones by words or deeds, he should at least do so for the sake of the beloved angels who stand guard over these young folk. We are to take such warning and exhortation to heart and be ever mindful of this: If we curse or otherwise use foul language where a child's angel may be present, to witness and hear this, God will certainly not let it go unpunished.

3. Moreover, as we diligently contemplate this Gospel we should be mindful of the great benefaction which God daily bestows on us

through the service of the beloved angels and thank him most sincerely for it. It is for this reason, also, that we observe and celebrate this festival today, so that we might learn to honor and cherish the beloved angels, yet not for their own sake but for God's sake, that we might love, honor, and thank our God for having commissioned them to guard and protect us from all the power, wiles, and temptations of the devil and the world, and from all that is evil.

4. Also, we are to know for a certainty that every human being has his own appointed angel who looks after and watches over him. We are familiar with the common proverb that expresses people's customary comment when someone is shielded from harm, You had a good angel! or, Your holy angel was with you and protected you. That is well said and, in fact, nicely reminds us of the benefaction God bestows on us through his beloved angels.

5. Further, we are to know that there are distinctions among the angels. Just as among men one person is tall, another short, one is strong and another weak, so also among the angels, one is of higher rank, stronger, and wiser than another. Hence it happens that a prince has a special and more potent angel, also more astute and wise than a count's; and a count has a greater and keener angel than a mere commoner; and so on. The higher the station and the more important the calling, the greater and more powerful, also, the angel that a person has, an angel who protects him, assists him, and safeguards against the devil.

6. It is no doubt true, therefore, that a little child, as soon as it is born, has its own angel who is much greater and stronger than the king of France or the Roman emperor. These same angels guard and protect us so that the devil is unable to harm us. For it is certainly a fact that wherever we are, a great host of devils lies in wait to try to terrify and harm us, to ambush us as with swords and spears. Against these the beloved angels contend, and they ward off many thrusts, and lash out against the devils to keep them from harming us as they are purposing to do. In addition, they also help us at times to escape traps and other perils of body into which the devil has led us, as we read in Holy Scripture that St. Peter and other apostles and saints were led out of imprisonment.

7. Therefore, we should diligently thank our Lord God for the beloved angels through whom he delivers us from such peril and

from the power of the devil, who has but one design and that is to mislead us in matters affecting body and life, as Christ says in John 8:44: The devil is a murderer and a liar from the beginning. And experience also attests that he has zealously pursued this role from the beginning of the world, forever and always at variance with, and hostile to, the human race. Soon after Adam and Eve were created, the devil injected his venom into them and carried matters to the point that they had to die; and as a result every one of us, like them, must die too some day. That is the devil's essential character; that is still his mode of operation. For him it is not enough that, because of the venom we have inherited from Adam and Eve, we must all die; but day and night he seeks for ways by which he might plunge us head over heels into very grievous pestilence and torment, break arm and leg, and even wrench off our necks. Yes, it is very much his modus operandi not only to kill or disable a baby that has just been born, along with the mother, but, where possible to cause it to die in the mother's womb and thrust it into the abyss of hell, along with the rest of mankind. This would be the devil's greatest joy and delight. But that it does not happen we owe solely to our Lord God and his beloved angels.

8. The fact is that my eyes which I have now enjoyed for over forty years, eyes which I well could have lost in the cradle or in my first bath, I must confess that I owe thankfully to no one else but our Lord God and his angels. For this reason we should also strive not to grieve the beloved angels by how we conduct ourselves, and by what we do and do not do, but comport ourselves in such a way that they see or hear nothing bad or unseemly about us. For they are holy and pure spirits, who for that reason cannot bear to see a person leading an ungodly life, living in fornication, or other vices, as Psalm 34:7 states: "The angel of the Lord encampeth round about them that fear him, and delivereth them." The person who does not fear God and, in the meantime, experiences danger and trouble, him the beloved angels will leave and not come to his aid. For their protection is to be provided in such a way that God's Word and order are not thrown into confusion, and the ungodly will not remain unpunished because of their sins.

9. Now then, if by shameless words and behavior we give offense, we should remember that an angel is standing guard there and look-

ing on. When the angel sees that we have no awe or fear of him, he may for a time allow the devil's lash or blow to strike us. That is then why it may happen that many a person breaks an arm or a leg, many even their necks, another drowns, or another is stabbed to death. And though day and night the devil attempts to take our life, we see, nevertheless, that, by and large, mankind remains intact, healthy, and alive. Even though occasionally a woman or two dies in childbirth, the majority still recover. Although some are murdered, drown, break legs and neck, nevertheless, the majority survive, alive and well. For the sake of such service on the part of the beloved angels we should diligently, with all our hearts, give thanks to our dear Lord God. For if the beloved angels were not always there standing guard over and protecting us, we could well succumb to death ten times over in just one hour.

10. Let this suffice for the present concerning these two matters that we should take with us out of this Gospel: first, that we guard against ever giving offense to anyone; second, that we thank God for his beloved angels, who protect and keep watch over us in such a way that the devil can do us no harm. May God, the everlasting Father, through his Holy Spirit, and for Christ's sake, graciously keep us safe from all offense and preserve us graciously in true faith in his Word without faltering and save us eternally. Amen.

Praise and glory be to God the Father, God the Son, and God the Holy Spirit, the one eternal God, for this salutary doctrine and for all his blessings.

CONCLUSION TO THE HAUSPOSTILLE

The following exhortation is appended by the editor, Georg Roerer, for the reader of Luther's *Hauspostille*.

General Guidelines for Leading Worshipers in Prayer at the Conclusion of the Sermon (Drawn and condensed from Luther's many sermons)

My dear friends:

Since we have gathered together in the name of our dear Lord Christ, in order to hear his Holy Word and to pray for the needs of all Christendom, as we are bidden to do and promised that our prayers will be heard, as our Lord Christ himself says (Matt. 18:19–20): "That if two of you shall agree on earth as touching any thing that they shall ask, it shall be done for them of my Father which is in heaven. For where two or three are gathered together in my name, there am I in the midst of them." So let us now pray, first of all, for the spiritual government and the beloved office of the holy ministry, that God would give us devout and faithful pastors, whose desire it is to expound to us in all its purity and without adulteration the treasure of his Holy Word; that he would graciously protect us from fanatical spirits and heresies and not look at our great ingratitude whereby long ago we have well deserved his taking his holy, precious Word from us; that he would not punish us so fearsomely, but allow pestilence and other chastisements rather to befall us than to rob us of his precious Word; that he would give us a grateful heart so that we might love his Holy Word, have great regard for it, and by hearing it bear fruit and amend our lives, so that we not only understand it correctly, but also live in accordance with it and do good works and daily grow in faith and good works, so that thus his name may be hallowed, his kingdom come, and his will be done in us. Furthermore, let us pray also for civil government and for all pastors and ministers within Christendom, that God would enlighten their hearts through his Spirit and word, so that God's Word and honor may be furthered through them and not be hindered, and we may lead a quiet and peaceable life among them in all godliness and honesty; that God would grant our most exalted majesty, the emperor, success against the Turks, and by his grace and mercy prevent us from falling under the rule of the cruel tyrant; also that he would protect the beloved emperor from the devil, the pope. Especially, however, we pray for our prince, under whose oversight God has placed us, that God would be with him in his reign and grant him success and well-being so that God's word, good order, glory, and honor may be furthered, all offense be avoided, of which there still is much, and the common weal governed well and peaceably, and that we may be obedient and upright. In particular, a common intercession is desired from us for our ruler. And may each pray for himself, for his wife and children and for whatever is entrusted to him, also for all who are distressed in body and soul, and so on. For these and all other needs and for ourselves, let us join together in praying the holy Lord's Prayer.

Index of Sermon Texts

Isaiah

9:1–7 3:209, 221, 229, 237, 246
52:13–53:12 1:440

Micah

5:2 1:208

Matthew

1:18–25 1:132
2:1–12 1:196
2:13–23 3:255
3:13–17 1:216
4:1–11 1:312
5:20–26 2:311, 320
6:24–34 3:7, 16
7:15–23 2:335, 342
8:1–13 1:242
8:23–27 1:253
9:1–8 3:79
11:2–10 1:59, 69
13:24–30 1:264
15:21–28 1:321
18:1–10 3:374, 386
18:21–35 3:130
20:1–16 1:278
21:1–9 1:17, 25, 31
22:1–14 3:91, 100, 107
22:15–22 3:146, 157, 169
22:34–46 3:51, 61, 70
24:15–28 3:192
25:31–46 3:207
26 1:372, 387
27 1:404
27:62–66 1:436

Mark

5:21–43 3:176, 184
6:17–29 3:327
7:31–37 2:395
8:1–9 2:327
14 1:372, 387
15 1:404
16:1–8 2:7
16:14–20 2:126

Luke

1:5–80 3:310, 324
1:26–38 3:284, 294
1:39–56 3:341, 357
2:1–14 1:99, 133
2:10–12 1:109
2:15–20 1:144
2:21 1:177, 188
2:22–32 1:294, 3:274
2:33–40 1:153, 165
2:41–52 1:224
5:1–11 2:283, 295, 302
6:36–42 2:258, 269, 276
7:11–17 3:24, 30
7:36–50 3:365
8:4–15 1:285
9:28–36 3:299
10:23–37 2:401, 412
11:14–28 1:329
14:1–11 3:36, 44
14:16–24 2:241
15:1–10 2:250
16:1–9 2:350, 358
16:19–31 2:223

17:11–19 2:422
18:9–14 2:380, 387
18:31–43 1:302
19:41–48 2:365, 375
21:25–36 1:37, 44, 52
22 1:372, 387
22:7–20 1:452
23 1:404
23:32–43 1:420
24:13–35 2:18
24:36–47 2:32

John

1:19–28 1:76, 84, 92
2:1–11 1:233
3:1–15 2:206, 217
3:16–21 2:185, 195
4:46–54 3:117, 122
6:1–15 1:344, 351
8:46–59 1:354, 362
10:11–16 2:73, 79
12:12–19 1:366
14:23–31 2:177
15:26–16:4 2:144
16:5–15 2:96
16:16–23 2:85
16:23–30 2:104
18 1:372, 387
18–19 1:404
19:13–30 1:466
19:31–42 1:435
20:19–31 2:54, 60

Acts

1:1–11 2:112
2:1–13 2:151
2:14–36 2:166
7:57–8:3 3:265
9:1–6 3:265
9:7–17 3:265
9:18–25 3:265
22:14–16 3:265
26:16–18 3:265

1 Corinthians

11:23–26 2:41

CEDS LIBRARY
32113543